Ziba Mir-Hosseini and Vanja Hamzić

Control and Sexuality

The Revival of *Zina* Laws in Muslim Contexts

violence is not our culture

خواتينِ زيرِ اسلامی مُسلم قوانينِ
Women Living Under Muslim Laws
النساء في ظل قوانين المسلمين
Femmes sous lois musulmanes

Control and Sexuality
The Revival of *Zina* Laws in Muslim Contexts
Ziba Mir-Hosseini and Vanja Hamzić

First edition
Copyright © Women Living Under Muslim Laws 2010

All rights reserved.
Part of this book may be quoted or used as long as the authors and publisher are acknowledged. No part of this publication may be reproduced or transmitted for commercial purposes without prior written permission from the copyright owner.

Published by:
Women Living Under Muslim Laws
PO Box 28445
London N19 5NZ
UK

wluml@wluml.org
www.wluml.org

Printed by:
The Russell Press, Nottingham UK

Design:
Kika Sroka-Miller

Cover art:
Vanja Hamzić

Page layout/typesetting:
Nandita Dutta
WLUML Publications Officer

ISBN: 978-0-9544943-9-1

Publications of the international solidarity network, Women Living Under Muslim Laws, aim to provide information about the lives, struggles and strategies of women living in diverse Muslim communities and countries. WLUML publications are meant to make accessible to a wide readership the broadest possible strands of opinion within varied movements or initiatives promoting greater autonomy of women living in Muslim contexts. The publications seek to inform and help share different experiences, strategies and interpretations.

The information contained in WLUML publications does not necessarily represent the views and positions of the publishers or of the network Women Living Under Muslim Laws, unless stated.

Contents

v   Acknowledgements

vii   Glossary

1   Foreword

3   Preface

5   Introduction

19   Criminalising Sexuality:
Zina Laws as Violence Against Women in Muslim Contexts

49   Indonesia

81   Iran

117   Nigeria

153   Pakistan

181   Turkey

215   Conclusion

227   About the Authors

229   Index

Acknowledgements

This book has been inspired by the writings and actions of countless individuals and groups who have paved the way for feminist analyses of the factors that perpetuate violence against women, including in the fields of law and culture.

We would like to extend special thanks to those who have directly contributed to this initiative: Homa Hoodfar, who suggested and encouraged this area of research, and the authors of this book. Ziba Mir-Hosseini's chapter 'Criminalising Sexuality', which was previously published as a policy paper by the VNC Campaign, provided the conceptual framework for the book; she also wrote the country chapter on Iran. Vanja Hamzić wrote the Introduction, the chapters on Indonesia, Pakistan, Nigeria and Turkey, and the Conclusion.

We are also grateful for the research input of Zara Saeidzadeh. We express our gratitude to the expert reviewers for the country chapters: Ayesha M Imam, Sohail Akbar Warraich, Vivienne Wee and Seval Yildirim. The contribution to the Indonesia chapter from colleagues in Solidaritas Perempuan, Koalisi NGO Ham in Aceh and Farid Mottaqin has been invaluable. The authors of the book are also deeply grateful to Richard Tapper, Safet Hadžimuhamedović, Muhammad Khalid Masud and Lynn Welchman for their support, incisive comments and editorial help.

We also wish to acknowledge Aisha Lee Shaheed, Deputy Coordinator of the WLUML International Coordination Office, who initiated the project, co-ordinated the publication, and reviewed and commented on the manuscript at various stages; and Edna Aquino, Campaign Manager of the Violence is Not Our Culture (VNC) Campaign, for her insightful comments and advice drawn from her distinctive lens as a feminist and human rights advocate, and for managing the writing and reviewing process until its completion. Thank you also to Shaina Greiff for her style-editing contributions within a short time frame, and to Carolyn Barnett for her invaluable all-round assistance on the final stages of the book's production.

We appreciate the generous support from two anonymous grants, which have supported the research, production and distribution of this publication.

We dedicate this publication to people around the world for their relentless efforts to claim their rights and those of others, and for affirming that upholding and promoting cultures must be founded on fundamental principles of respect, dignity and justice for all.

Glossary

Across Muslim countries and communities, there are multiple spellings and different words for essentially the same thing. For example, a judge or other authority who hears cases concerning Muslims is known variously as a *cadi/kadi/kazi/kathi/khati/qazi/quazi/qadi/qadhi*. In general, the problem arises from the challenge of transliterating and translating Arabic words into local languages. In the text of this book, we have opted for either the version most commonly accepted or that which we believe would be most widely recognised, without implying that there is any one 'correct' spelling.

Acquis communautaire: 'Accumulated' legislation: legal acts and case law.

Ad absurdum: To an absurd extent.

Ad acta: To archives; not actual any more.

Adalet ve Kalkınma Partisi (AKP): Justice and Development Party (Turkey).

Adhan/Ezan: Muslim call to prayer.

Ahadith: See **Hadith.**

Ahmadi/Ahmadiyya: Islamic religious movement established in British-controlled Northern India; a sect of Islam prevalent in South Asia, largely unrecognised by the Pakistani state and marginalised in other contexts.

Ahwal al-syakhshiyyah: Personal matters such as marriage, divorce and inheritance.

Aisyiyah (Nasyiatul Aisyiyah): Women's branch of the major Indonesian Muslim politico-religious organisation Muhammadiyah, representing so-called 'modernist' Muslims.

Al-zaniah wa al-zani: Fornication.

'Alim: 'One who has knowledge'; a scholar. See **Ulama/Ulema.**

Alkali: Judge of a Muslim court (Hausa) (Nigeria).

Analisa gender: Gender analysis (Indonesia).

Anayasa Mahkemesi: Constitutional Court (Turkey).

Aqd al-nikah: 'Contract of coitus'; contract of marriage, religious marriage ceremony.

Askeri: Ottoman Turkish term that refers to a class of imperial administrators in the Ottoman Empire. The term itself literally means 'of the military', it more broadly encompasses all higher levels of imperial administration.

Askeri Yargıtay: Military Court of Cassation (Turkey).

Askeri Yüksek İdare Mahkemesi: Supreme Military Administrative Court (Turkey).

Atatürk: Lit. 'The Father of the Turks', exclusive surname of Mustafa Kemal, first president of Turkish Republic, via a legal act.

'Awra: Shameful; pudenda – for men, the area between knees and navel; for women, all the body apart from hands, feet and face.

Badal-i-sulh: Customary compensation.

Baghi: Rebellion.

Bahá'í: Monotheistic world/global religion that originated in 19th century Persia/Iran.

Barelvi: School of thought, named after seminary established in colonial India – has preferred an esoteric path, which is associated with the subcontinent's numerous Sufi orders.

Basij: Volunteer militia set up by the Islamic Republic of Iran as the vanguard of the Islamic revolution; today they often act as Moral Police in Iran.

Başörtü: Traditional Turkish head cover for women, still worn by elderly women in rural areas.

Bernuansa: Nuances (Indonesia).

Bhinneka tunggal ika: Motto of the Republic of Indonesia: 'fragmented, yet one' (Old Javanese); unity in diversity.

Çağdaşlaşma: Modernisation (Turkey).

Carte blanche: Lit. 'white paper' (French); complete freedom to act on one's wishes.

Chador: In Iran, this is a long semicircle of fabric, which is wrapped to conceal the whole female body from head to toe except the face and worn by women as a loose outer garment. Traditionally of many different colours and patterns, in the Islamic Republic it is usually black. In Pakistan, it is available in all colours and made of a long rectangular cloth, which can be of any material, such as wool in winter, cotton or other fabrics in summer. Traditionally, it is worn loosely wrapped around the upper part of the body and over the head. The length and width of the cloths, and therefore the extent to which it covers the body, varies from community to community.

Chador aur char diwari: Lit. 'veil and four walls' referring to gender segregation, i.e. women veiled and within the confines of the home (South Asia).

Da'awah/da'wa: Preaching and teaching; proselytising.

Daerah istimewa: Special territory (Indonesia).

Danıştay: Council of State (Turkey).

Glossary

Darul Islam: 'Abode of Islam' – also, more common name for *Negara Islam Indonesia*, an insurgent state in West Java.

Deobandi: School of thought, named after a seminary established in colonial India, which tends toward literalist interpretation.

Diyah/Diyat/Diyeh: 'Blood money'.

Diyanet İşleri Başkanlığı: Presidency of Religious Affairs (Turkey).

Diyanet İşleri Başkanlığı Teşkilat Kanunu Yasası: Diyanet Organisation Act (Turkey).

Dokhul: Penetration.

Elm-e qazi: 'Judge's intuition' – a notion used by the Islamic Republic of Iran, referring to personal information that is not presented or examined by the court. In practice, this allows the judge to decide if an offence has been committed.

Ezan /Azan/Azaan: See **Adhan**.

Fahisha: Lewdness; adultery and fornication.

Fatayat NU: Women's branch of the Nahdlatul Ulama (NU) (Indonesia).

Fatwa pl. ***Fatawa***: Religious opinion, often intended as a ruling or decree, usually issued by a body of religious scholars or an individual scholar, or even a mosque imam, with or without sanction by the state.

Fedayin-e Khalq: Marxist group (Iran).

Fez: Traditional male hat worn throughout the Ottoman Empire.

Fiqh: Jurisprudence; generally used to refer to Muslim laws as developed by jurists.

Fitna: Chaos, a threat to the social order.

Fordism: Certain social theories on mass production, standardisation and labour discipline, named after Henry Ford, a prominent American industrialist.

Ghairat: 'Honour'.

Gyale: Headscarf worn by Hausa women (Nigeria).

Hacı: Title predominantly used in the Ottoman Empire for Muslims who made the annual pilgrimage to Mecca (*hajj*) or for Jews and Christians who made a pilgrimage to Jerusalem.

Hadd pl. ***Hudood, Hudud***: lit. 'the limits'. Used mainly with reference to Muslim penal laws, and the evidentiary requirements and maximum punishments as prescribed in the Qur'an. Note the *hudud/hudood* laws operative in Pakistan and certain states of Nigeria.

Hadith pl. ***Ahadith***: Reported sayings of the Prophet Muhammad.

Hafiz: Lit. 'guardian' (Arabic); a person who has completely memorised the Qur'an.

Halal: Lit. 'lawful' (Arabic); an act which is permissible; usually used to refer to food whose consumption is permissible according to the *shari'a* and it is opposite to *haram* (see below).

Halka rağmen halk için: 'Despite the people, for the people' – maxim of the Kemalist regime (Turkey).

Hanafi: A Sunni school of Muslim law; Hanafis are the most widespread Sunni school, predominant in most of the former Ottoman Empire (Turkey, Balkans, Egypt, Levant and Mesopotamia) as well as in Central and South Asia.

Haqq Allah: 'The right of God'.

Haram: Prohibited, illegal.

Haya: Shame.

Hayasızca hareketler: 'Shameless behaviour' (Turkey).

Hijab: Comes from the Arab verb *hajaba* that means 'to veil, hide, conceal'. Probably the most common style of veiling in the Muslim diasporas in the West, the *hijab* is a simple square piece of cloth folded into a triangle and wrapped around the head. It is fastened under the chin or the sides such that the face is visible but the neck and hair are covered. Today, the *hijab* is available in many different fabrics, styles and colours.

Hirabah: Robbery.

Hisbah: Moral supervision and enforcement group, often 'police-like'.

Hoca: A title of wisdom, used throughout the Ottoman Empire.

Hudood/Hudud: See **Hadd.**

Hudud al-Allah: God's limits.

Ibu rumah tangga: 'Mothers of the household' (Indonesia).

Ibu Teladan: Nationwide state-sponsored contest *The Model Mother* (Indonesia).

Ibuisme: 'Motherism' (Indonesia).

Idda/Iddah/Iddat/Eddah: Waiting period which begins from the time a Muslim woman is divorced or widowed. The period varies depending on the type of divorce, whether she is pregnant, whether she is still menstruating or not and whether she is widowed. During this time, she is not free to contract another marriage. In some systems *idda* does not apply after dissolution of an unconsummated marriage.

Iffet/Iffat/Effat: Chastity.

Glossary

Ijab & Qabul: Lit. 'offer and acceptance'; used to refer to the offer and acceptance of the terms and conditions of a marriage contract.

Ijbar: The power to compel an unmarried virgin into marriage, recognised by certain schools. The power usually resides in the father and paternal grandfather (Nigeria).

Ijtihad: Independent reasoning to arrive at a legal principle based on religious understanding.

Ilaj: Penetration.

'Ilm: Knowledge, science (Arabic); in the context of religious jurisprudence it means religious knowledge.

Ilmiye: Institution into which the *ulema* as a whole was organised (Turkey).

Imam: One who leads the prayers (usually male).

In flagrante delicto: Lit. 'in a blazing offence' (Latin) – equivalent of English: 'caught in the act'; a legal term indicating that an offender has been caught in the act of committing an offence.

Inkılapçılık: Reformism (Turkey).

Instruksi Presiden 1/1991 tentang Penyebarluasan Kompilasi Hukum Islam: 1991 Compilation of Islamic Laws, promulgated via presidential instruction (Indonesia).

Instruksi Presiden 9/2000 tentang Pengarusutamaan Gender Dalam Pembangunan Nasional: Presidential instruction on the Mainstreaming of Gender in National Development (Indonesia).

Iqa': Unilateral act.

Irz: Purity, honour (Turkey).

Irza geçmek: Rape described as 'penetrating one's honour', in the 1926 Penal Code (Turkey).

'Iwad: Compensation to the husband in return for the release of his wife, in divorce by mutual consent.

Jinayah: Acts that are considered criminal, such as gambling and consuming alcohol (Indonesia).

Jirga: Council of elders who adjudicate upon local customary laws (Pakistan/Afghanistan).

Jus cogens: Principles which form the norms of international law that cannot be set aside; peremptory norms.

Kabupaten: Regencies (Indonesia).

Kadi: See ***Qadi***.

Kadınlar Saltanatı: The Sultanate of Women (Turkey).

Kallabi: Headscarf worn by Hausa women (Nigeria).

Kanun: See ***Qanun***.

Karahiya: 'Reluctance'; a wife's extreme reluctance to her husband.

Kepala keluarga: 'Heads of the family' (Indonesia).

Ketuhanan: God (Indonesia).

Ketuhanan Yang Maha Esa: Almighty God (Indonesia).

Khalwat: Close proximity between persons of different gender; refers to when a non-related man and woman are left alone together.

Khilaf al-awla: 'Contrary to what is most appropriate'.

Khul'/Khul/Khul'u/Khula: Form of divorce available to a Muslim woman, generally on compensating the husband. Interpretations, laws and practices differ regarding the husband and/or court's role and agency, and whether or not this is an irrevocable divorce (*bain sughra*).

Khutbah: Sermon.

Komiteh: Organised supporters of the Islamic revolution in the 1980s (Iran) who often acted as unofficial moral police force.

Komnas Perempuan: National Commission on Violence against Women (Indonesia).

Kompilasi Hukum Islam ('kompilasi'): 1991 Compilation of Islamic Laws (Indonesia).

Kongres Wanita Indonesia (Kowani): Strong central federation of women's associations, formed in 1946.

Kul: Slaves (Turkey).

Kyai: Male spiritual scholars of unique mystico-legal mastery (Indonesia).

Laicism: The nonclerical, or secular, control of political and social institutions in a society.

Laikliğin bekçileri: Coloquial name for the military forces: 'the guardians of *laiklik*' (Turkey).

Laiklik: Turkey's secular character (laicism).

Laporan Pemantauan tentang Kondisi Pemenuhan Hak-Hak Konstitusional Perempuan: *Monitoring Report on the Fulfilment of Conditions for Women's Constitutional Rights* (Indonesia).

Laskar: Muslim militias (Indonesia).

Lawat/*Liwat*: Penetrative sex between men.

Legislative misbaksel: Dutch: legislative monstrosity.

Ləfaya: Head covering worn by Kanuri women (Nigeria).

Madhab/*Madhhab*/*Mazhab* pl. *Madhahib*: Muslim legal school of thought.

Ma'dhur: An excused person.

Ma'fu: Exempt from liability.

Mahkamah Konstitusi Republik Indonesia: Constitutional Court of the Republic of Indonesia.

Mahkamah Syar'iyah: *Shari'a* court (Indonesia).

Mahr/Mahari/Mehr: Dower; the goods and/or cash to be given by the groom to the bride as a requisite of a valid Muslim marriage. It may be given at the time of the marriage ceremony (prompt), or promised at a later date or to be paid upon divorce or the death of the husband (deferred) or divided into prompt and deferred portions.

Mahram: Arabic word used to refer to members of the opposite sex (who have reached puberty) with whom marriage and sexual intercourse is not permissible. In Islam, a woman's opposite-sex *mahrams* fall into four categories (three categories in the strict-sense definition that does not count one's spouse).

Majelis Mujahidin Indonesia (MMI): Indonesian Holy Warrior Assembly.

Majelis Permusyawaratan Rakyat: People's Consultative Assembly (Indonesia).

Majelis Permusyawaratan Ulama: Consultative Council of *'Ulama'* (Indonesia).

Majelis Ulama Indonesia (MUI): Indonesian *'Ulama'* Council.

Majles/Majlis: Parliament (Iran).

Majles-e khebregan-e rahbari: Assembly of Experts (Iran).

Mala fide: In bad faith.

Maliki: A Sunni school of Muslim law; the dominant Sunni school of law in West and North African countries.

Mandil: Head covering worn by Kanuri women (Nigeria).

Maqasid: Goals and purposes.

Maqasid al-shari'a: Goals and purposes of *shari'a*.

Mayafi: Headscarf worn by Hausa women (Nigeria).

Mecelle: Turkish civil code, promulgated in 1868 and fully completed in 1876.

Medrese: Public school (Turkey).

Meunasah: Religious/social house (Aceh, Indonesia).

Millet/mellat: Nation/ethnic group. Under the Ottoman *millet* system, Muslim, Christian and Jewish communities were organised as 'nations'/'peoples' and enjoyed a semi-autonomous status within the empire.

Mohsen/Muhsan/Muhsin: A man with a permanent wife with whom he has had intercourse and may have intercourse when he so desires.

Mohseneh: A woman in a permanent marriage who has had intercourse with her husband and is able to do so again.

Mojahedin-e Khalq: Islamist-socialist group (Iran).

Muamalat: Trade and commerce (Indonesia).

Müftü/Mufti: Sunni scholar of *fiqh*.

Muhsan: See ***Mohsen***.

Mujaddid: Reformer.

Musahaqa: Sex between women.

Mushalla: Religious/social house.

Nafaqa/Nafaqah: Maintenance of wife and children.

Nahdlatul Ulama (NU): Religious organisation (Indonesia).

Nakşibendi/Naqshbandi/Naqshbandiyya: A Sufi order.

Namus: Sexual honour.

Negara Islam Indonesia: Indonesian Islamic State.

Nikah: Marriage, and regulations concerning it.

Nushuz/Nusyuz/Nashezeh/Nashiz/Nashizah: Disobedient (usually used in reference to wives who do not obey their husband).

Nyai: Female spiritual scholars of unique mystico-legal mastery (Indonesia)

Örf: See *'Urf.*

Pancasila: Sanskrit: 'five principles'; the state ideological concept in Indonesia.

Panduan: Faith-based guidance.

Par excellence: Better or more than all others of the same kind.

Partai Kebangkitan Bangsa (PKB): National Awakening Party (Indonesia).

Pembimbing: Mentor (Indonesia).

Pendapat berbeda: Dissenting opinion (Indonesia).

Peraturan daerah/Perda: regional regulations (Indonesia)

Peraturan Desa 5/2006 tentang Pelaksanaan Hukuman Cambuk: Regulation concerning the Muslim village of Padang in North Sulawesi on the implementation of penalties executed by public whipping.

Piagam Hak-Hak Perempuan di Aceh: Charter of the Rights of Women in Aceh (Indonesia).

Piagam Jakarta: Jakarta Charter.

Pornoaksi: 'Pornoaction', e.g. public acts such as spouses kissing, women's failure to cover their navel or sunbathing in swimwear (Indonesia).

Purdah: Literally a veil or a curtain, has come to mean an entire code of conduct for Muslim women; veiling (Nigeria/Pakistan); a by-word for seclusion in general (South Asia).

Purdah aur char divari: Veiling and cloistering within four walls.

Qabul: See *Ijab*.

Qadhf/Qazf: Unfounded allegation of *zina;* slander.

Qadi/Qadhi/Kadi: Muslim court judge or registrar.

Qadiri/Qadiriyya: A Sufi order.

Qanun/Kanun: Law; canon.

Qanun Jinayat: Muslim Criminal Code.

Qanun-e-Shahadat (Order): Revision of the 1872 Evidence Act, which restricted the evidence of women in financial matters, purely on the basis of their gender (Pakistan).

Qat' al-tariq hiraba: Highway robbery.

Qavadi: Pimping.

Qazf: See *Qadhf*.

Qisas: Retribution; covers bodily harm and homicide, defined as matters of private claim; punishments are fixed but not mandatory, the offender can waive the claim.

Qiwama: Mixture of a husband's dominion and protection over his wife.

Qur'an/Koran: The holy book of Islam, regarded as divine for those who believe it to consist of the exact words of God (Allah) as revealed to the Prophet Muhammad.

Rahbar/Rahbar-e enqelab: 'Leader of the Revolution', the term commonly used, both in the constitution and in everyday political discourse in Iran, for the leading jurist (*faqih*).

Rahbari: Leadership.

Raison d'être: The most important reason or purpose for someone or something's existence.

Rajm/Rejm: Death by stoning.

***Raqqad*/Sleeping foetus**: The principle recognised by some schools of *fiqh* that an embryo may 'sleep' in the mother's womb and be born many months, even years, after the dissolution of her marriage and still be attributed to her former husband; the embryo is believed to remain dormant in the mother's womb until it is awakened, for example by a magical potion or intervention by a saint. This belief is still widespread in North and West Africa.

Reaya: Tax-paying lower class in the Ottoman Empire.

***Reformasi* movement**: Reform movement (Indonesia).

Ridda: Apostasy.

Roko: Traditional Hausa eulogy or praise-singing, typically performed by musical artisans and bards called *maroka* (sing. *maroki*) (Nigeria).

RUU Anti Pornografi dan Pornoaksi: Draft Anti Pornography and 'Pornoaction' Bill (Indonesia).

Salb: Crucifixion.

Sarengat: Law (Indonesia)

Sariqah: Theft.

Satr: 'Covering' – in terms of dress; concealing.

Şeriat: See ***Shari'a***.

Seyhülislam/Shaikh ul-Islam: The highest-ranking religious legal advisor to the Ottoman sultan.

Shari'a/Shariyah/Şeriat: A term commonly but erroneously used to refer to the body of religious 'laws' that are said to be derived from Islam. The debate around divine injunctions and 'law' can be clarified by the following definition of *shari'a* given by Ziba Mir-Hosseini: "*Shari'ah* is the totality of God's will as revealed to the Prophet Muhammad. *Fiqh* is the process of human effort to identify and extract legal rules from the sacred sources of Islam: the Qur'an and the Sunnah. Thus, the *shari'ah* in Muslim belief is sacred, eternal and universal, whereas *fiqh*, consisting of the vast literature produced by Muslim jurists, is like any other system of jurisprudence: human, mundane, not eternal, and local" (source: www.

musawah.org). See ***fiqh***, and the chapter 'Criminalising Sexuality: *Zina* Laws as Violence Against Women in Muslim Contexts' in this book.

Shi'a: A branch of Islam: Shi'a followers are majorities in Iran and Iraq, and substantial minorities in several other countries, though only 10 per cent of all Muslims. See also **Twelver Shi'ism**.

Shubha: Semblance (of marriage); doubt, ambiguity.

Shura-ye negahban: Guardian Council (Iran).

Shurb al-khamr: Drinking alcohol.

Sihaq: Lesbianism.

Siyasa: Governance law.

Sleeping embryo/foetus: See ***Raqqad.***

Sui juris: Lit. 'of one's own laws' (Latin); the capacity to manage one's own (legal) affairs.

Sunna/Sunnah: The practice (acts, deeds/omissions and words) of the Prophet Muhammad.

Sunni: A branch of Islam, traditionally with four main schools of thought/*fiqh*: Hanafi, Maliki, Shafi'i and Hanbali.

Suo motu: On its own motion.

Ta'a: See ***Tamkin***.

Talaq: Islamic term for a divorce. A unilateral and extra-judicial process, *talaq* occurs in three stages: initiation, reconciliation and completion.

Tamkin/Ta'a: The principle that the wife must remain in the marital home, implying 'obedience' and sexual availability.

Tanzimat: 'Reorganisation' period (Turkey).

Taqlid: Literally translates as 'to follow' or 'imitate' in Arabic; refers to the unpremeditated following of the decisions of a religious authority.

Tarekat/Tarikat/Tariqa: Mystical way, Sufi order.

Tasikmalaya Peraturan Daerah 28/2000 tentang Pemberantasan Pelacuran: Regulation of the district of Tasikmalaya in Western Java on eradication of prostitution.

Ta'zir/Ta'zirat: Discipline; punishments that are at the discretion of the judge.

Tecavüz: Violation (Turkey).

Tijaniyya: Name of a Sufi order (Nigeria).

Tim Pengarus-Utamaan Gender Departemen Agama: Gender Mainstreaming Team of the Department of Religion (Indonesia).

Türban: Turkish equivalent for *hijab* and usually worn by female students in higher educational institutions. Also an imam's hat.

Türk Ceza Kanunu: Turkish Penal Code.

Türk Kanunu Medenisi: Turkish Civil Code.

Türkiye Büyük Millet Meclisi: Turkish Grand National Assembly.

Twelver Shi'ism: For Shi'a Muslims, after the death of the Prophet, leadership of the Muslims passed not to elected caliphs but to his descendants, the Imams. The majority of the Shi'a are Twelvers or Imamis, who believe in the line of 12 Imams, starting with 'Ali, the Prophet's cousin and son-in-law and ending with Mohammad Mehdi, the Imam of Time, who went into Occultation; his return will mark the end of time. See also **Shi'a**.

Ujrat al-mithl: Exemplary wages; domestic wages payable to the wife on divorce in certain conditions (Iran).

Ulama/Ulema sing. **'Alim**: Muslim religious scholars or jurists.

Umma: Arabic word meaning 'community' or 'nation', often used to refer to a diaspora or community of Muslims (what many consider to be an imagined community) all over the world.

Umayyad Caliphate: The Umayyad caliphate was the second of the four caliphates established after the death of Muhammad, lasting 661–750. The lands of the Umayyad rulers spanned more than 5 million square miles.

Undang-Undang 1/1974 tentang Perkawinan: 1974 Marriage Law (Indonesia).

Undang-Undang 23/2004 tentang Penghapusan Kekerasan Dalam Rumah Tangga: 2004 Law for the Eradication of Domestic Violence (Indonesia).

Undang-Undang 44/2008 tentang Pornografi: 2008 Law on Pornography (Indonesia).

Undang-Undang *7/1989 tentang* Peradilan Agama: 1989 Law on Religious Judicature (Indonesia).

'Urf/Örf: Customary law.

Uyuşmazlık Mahkemesi: Court of Jurisdictional Conflicts (Turkey).

Valide: Mother of the Ottoman sultan.

Velayat-e faqih: The rule or guardianship of the jurist.

Vilayet: Province (administrative unit) in the Ottoman Empire.

Waaf/Wakaf/Waqf: Religious endowment.

Wahhabism: Reductionist Sunni Muslim doctrine, still a predominant religious force in Saudi Arabia.

Wali: In the context of marriage, a marriage guardian. Usually recognised by some schools as the father or paternal grandfather who has authority to contract the marriage on behalf of the bride.

Wat al-bahimah: Bestiality.

Wilayatul Hisbah: Acehnese Muslim law enforcement forces.

Yan Izala: Right-wing politico-religious movement (Nigeria).

Yargıtay: Court of Cassation (Turkey).

Yüce Divan: Supreme Criminal Court (Turkey).

Zoroastrian: Religion and philosophy founded in 6th century Persia/Iran. Zoroastrians are counted by Muslims as 'Peoples of the Book' (*ahl al-kitab*) alongside Jews and Christians. Today there are Zoroastrian communities in Iran, South Asia (Parsees, Iranis) and elsewhere.

Zina: Sexual intercourse between parties not married to one another.

Zina-bil-jabr: Rape; lit. '*zina* by force'.

Foreword

It is most timely that this publication should emerge when issues of culture and human rights are being debated in many venues in the international arena: within the United Nations; in national and transnational, mainstream and alternative media outlets; and across social and political movements. Laws, like cultures and traditions, change over time. The cultural norms of the majority tend to reinforce the existing structural arrangements of power in a society. Nevertheless, within every tradition and structural limitation, people have a certain relative power to act differently, including by drawing upon different aspects of the same cultural traditions. Moreover, all cultural communities – including those of women, minorities and minority views – must be encouraged to develop their own vocabulary, specific to their contexts, which upholds the universality, indivisibility, interdependence and inter-relatedness of women's human rights.

The collective dimension of cultural rights can be a source of solidarity and progress without, however, implying the denial of individual cultural rights. Individuals have the right to participate, or to not participate, as well as to challenge existing precepts and norms in their communities; to hold multiple identities simultaneously; to access their cultural heritage; and to be recognised as active and legitimate producers of culture(s). The contributions of women and girls to the cultural development of every community they choose to be a part of, including but not only the one they inhabit, especially in the development of new common values, are crucial in the implementation of cultural rights for all.

I note that some cultural practices may be particularly detrimental to the rights of women and girls. All harmful practices, regardless of provenance and justification, must be eliminated. All human rights are universal, indivisible and inter-related. All states, regardless of their political, economic and cultural systems, have an obligation to uphold the principle of non-discrimination and to respect, protect and fulfil the cultural rights of all persons. There is a need to work simultaneously at the level of both society and state; legal measures by themselves are rarely, if ever, sufficient. Due diligence must be exercised to address rights violations by non-state actors, including those undertaken in the name of culture and religion.

It is my hope that by building upon the progressive, equitable and just aspects of culture which are inherent to all, this book can make a substantial contribution towards the promotion of rights, under law and custom.

Farida Shaheed
UN Independent Expert on Cultural Rights *November 2010*

Preface

The Violence is Not Our Culture (VNC) Campaign[1] and the Women Living Under Muslim Laws (WLUML) network are very pleased to present this publication, which offers a comparative study and feminist analysis of *zina* laws, to help activists, policy-makers, researchers and other civil society actors to acquire a better understanding of the challenges facing those initiatives that would ensure that culture and/or religion are not invoked to justify laws that criminalise women's sexuality and subject them to cruel, inhuman and degrading forms of punishment. This is one strategy for attaining gender equality and social justice, and could – and should – be used alongside other rights-based approaches, including the promotion of secular spaces, reinterpretation of religious and cultural traditions, engaging with human rights laws, and awareness-raising through creative mediums. As a contribution to the broader objective of ending violence in the name of 'culture', we hope this book goes some way to unpacking *zina* laws in some Muslim contexts and communities in order to tease out connections between the criminalisation of sexuality, gender-based violence and women's rights activism.

This book has been a long time in the making. It has been recognised that laws and customs that restrict women's rights, and prescribe or enable violent punishments to be meted out for alleged transgressions, must be better understood by civil society and decision-makers. This publication addresses *zina* laws: those that regulate any illicit sexual activity outside of marriage in Muslim contexts, including adultery and fornication. Some Muslim contexts have not historically had laws regulating *zina,* and in others, they have been instated or reinstated in the 20th century. These are one type of laws that can prescribe violent punishments to women and men who violate social norms when they engage in consensual sexual activities, and in some contexts, in cases of rape. Other times, allegations of *zina* can mask other divisions in society such as socio-economic disparity or the treatment of widows and other unmarried women. They are often linked to other laws and customs that limit women's rights, including inequitable marriage and divorce laws, guardianship laws and public order laws. Like all laws, they vary widely from country to country in terms of their development and implementation. And in all contexts, those who defend the rights of women have challenged the criminalisation of sexuality and so-called 'morality', using strategies drawn from religion, human rights and customary traditions.

Most Muslim-majority countries do not legislate *zina* formally, but regardless of its sources of legitimacy, violent punishments continue to be meted out through extra-judicial means, in parallel legal systems and in the private sphere based on customary precedents. This is the intersection in which the VNC Campaign and the WLUML network largely operate: addressing the laws and customs that affect women's lives in diverse contexts and the various strategies that women's rights defenders can employ to reclaim and redefine them.

---

1 This grows out of the Global Campaign to Stop Killing and Stoning Women (SKSW Campaign) that was launched in 2007.

Since 1984, the WLUML international solidarity network has provided information, support and a collective space for women whose lives are shaped, conditioned or governed by laws and customs said to derive from Islam, from a feminist perspective. Created by individuals from eight countries in Africa, Asia and the Middle East, since its inception, the network has responded to the use of religion and culture as an excuse to deny women's human rights through the invocation or reference to laws, practices and customs which are said to be 'Islamic'. Laws are influenced by many factors, including colonialism, religion, culture and patriarchy, and they are created and recreated by human beings within ever-changing contexts. WLUML has linked individuals and organisations to address, assess and demystify the laws and customs that shape women's lives.

Over time, however, it has become increasingly apparent that addressing women's legal equality is only one aspect of ensuring women's full and equal enjoyment of their rights. As many violations of women's rights are committed in extra-judicial arenas and often by non-state actors (including armed groups as well as family and community members), simply having equitable laws in place is not enough to protect women from discrimination and violent punishments. Against this background, the Global Campaign to Stop Killing and Stoning Women was launched in November 2007, bringing together groups from Pakistan, Iran, Nigeria, Indonesia, Turkey and beyond. The campaign was inspired by, and grew out of, local and national initiatives of women's groups to challenge, resist and change what was happening in their societies: as legitimate and authentic contributors to their ever-changing cultural contexts. The campaign has aimed to link local strategies for resistance and reclamation with the international community, by linking groups through 'sister campaigns' and by liaising with international human rights mechanisms that address the universality and indivisibility of women's rights. The campaign maintains that there can be no justice in any justifications for violence based on culture, tradition or religion. The freedom of belief cannot be translated into the freedom to harm others.

The countries chosen for case studies are by no means exhaustive, but are designed to show the diversity and similarities between contexts. In some, adultery and fornication are formally criminalised as crimes against the state, and in others, they are regulated by non-state actors. In all contexts, however, women's rights defenders have challenged, redefined and overturned discriminatory regulations and highlighted violations from a gender-informed and feminist perspective. We hope this publication encourages more research, analysis, debates and collective actions in order to support advocacy initiatives at all levels and raise these issues in the global arena. We take this opportunity to thank those who have contributed to this project and look forward to the next steps we invite you to take with us, on our journey to reclaiming our rights.

Edna Aquino
Violence is Not Our Culture (VNC) Campaign

Aisha Lee Shaheed
WLUML International Coordination Office *November 2010*

Introduction

Introduction

Bariya was only 13 and unmarried when her pregnancy was spotted by her uncles. She was summoned before the court which, under the newly enacted by-laws of the state of Zamfara in northern Nigeria, sentenced her to 100 cane lashes for having pre-marital sexual relations and an additional 80 lashes for slander, as no witness could corroborate her claim that any of the three men she previously identified had fathered her child. The men denied the charges and were quickly acquitted. The reports that Bariya was coerced into the act were not taken into consideration by the court. She remained detained throughout the remainder of her pregnancy. A month after giving birth to her baby, Bariya was given 100 cane lashes and released. Soon after her release, she was married off.[1]

Bariya's case is just one of many. Certain contemporary Muslim-majority states and societies face an unprecedented revival, or in some cases an introduction, of laws, regulations and customs based on the notion of *zina* – an Islamic jurisprudential term denoting illicit sexual relations, particularly adultery and fornication. On the pretext of *zina*, states and societies condone or even encourage the most extreme forms of gender-based violence and discrimination, which affects women especially. Such injustice is ordinarily justified by reference to the classical *fiqh* (Islamic jurisprudence) and some of its interpretative frameworks used to ascertain *shari'a* (God's injunctions) contained in the Qur'an and the Sunna (sayings and practices of the Prophet Muhammad).

This study is an attempt to unearth and analyse the historical and present-day cultural, legal and – above all – political motives and circumstances that *really* have caused the revival of *zina* laws. These catalysts, as apparent throughout this book, do not coincide with the official rhetoric on *zina* as 'God-given' moral stipulations which state or society simply strives to adhere to. Instead, they reveal how *zina* laws, which were obsolete and had rarely ever been applied in Muslim contexts, are now employed by state and non-state actors alike to assert and maintain control over the general populace's sexuality and sociality, for the sake of a variety of political and social ends. Age-old patriarchal motives – those that originate in an assumed 'right' of the man to control and subjugate the woman – prevail over other causes of the introduction or revival of laws that criminalise sexuality and mete out disproportionally severe punishments, which have detrimental consequences to women's human rights and their access to justice. Of course, such laws are not only present in Muslim communities or maintained solely with reference to Muslim religious and cultural norms. As the cases of violence against women throughout the world aptly demonstrate (Ertürk 2009), patriarchies have emerged everywhere and have invariably used cultures and religions to justify their detrimental effects on gender justice. Other catalysts of the (re)introduction of *zina* laws include protracted socio-economic crises; covert ambitions of political, military and religious elites; post-colonial and post-nationalist anxieties; and theopolitics – i.e. politics based on (mis)use of religion.

---

1   For a detailed account of this case, which took place in 2000, and other similar *zina* trials in Nigeria, see BAOBAB 2003.

Another aim of this study is to comprehensively relate and reflect on civil society's resistance to the (re)emergence of *zina* laws and other measures that criminalise consensual sexual relations, in particular those mounted and sustained by national women's movements. The strategies and actions employed by these movements in their struggle for gender justice, seriously challenged by *zina* regulations, represent an invaluable legacy for all societies affected by similar havoc. Despite significantly different circumstances from country to country, this study reveals that certain approaches – such as demystification of the purported 'religious' concerns beyond *zina*-related laws and customs – can work well across various polities and religio-cultural setups. This book itself builds on the scholarly and activist engagements with the discourses of power and domination within and between Muslim communities, which falsely market themselves as the supreme moral agency, risen to restore or, indeed, 'revive' the *umma* (Muslim community), which is perceived to be 'morally challenged', whether in local or international contexts. These discourses are strengthened by reference to a mythical pan-Muslim past, which is portrayed as homogeneous in terms of social, cultural and legal norms, when in reality a vast diversity of these norms existed – and exist – across Muslim contexts. Such currents, as well as other pertinent factors, are analysed and then systematically opposed by the national women's movements, not least because the purported 'revivals' and 'restorations' invariably carry a forceful gender bias. The 'ways forward' this study discusses are fully grounded in these national and transnational narratives of resistance, with a view to revisiting, summarising and making them more accessible to a broader audience.

This book is the product of a multi-country socio-legal research project instigated by the Violence is Not Our Culture (VNC) Campaign[2] and the Women Living Under Muslim Laws (WLUML)[3] international solidarity network. The research experience and subsequent revisions opened up many valuable avenues of analysis, which warranted a cross-disciplinary methodological approach. It was mainly based on literature review (spanning legal, political, historical, sociological, anthropological, cultural, theological and other academic studies, as well as a corpus of national laws and regulations, case law, civil society reports and publications, journalist articles, international human rights treaties and documents of their treaty bodies), with some brief local empirical research conducted for the case study on Indonesia. Organisations highlighted in the study largely reflect the network of the VNC Campaign and WLUML.

Structure of the Book

These introductory remarks are followed by a chapter offering a feminist and rights-based critique of *zina* regulations, which dissects their supposed foundations in classical *fiqh* as well as in later socio-political circumstances. It is a 'critique from within' and a contribution

---

2 Please visit www.stop-stoning.org. The VNC Campaign is waged under the auspices of WLUML's three-year programme Women Reclaiming and Re-defining Culture.

3 Please visit www.wluml.org

to the emerging Islamic feminist scholarship. The subsequent five chapters are country-specific case studies on the revival of *zina* laws in Indonesia, Iran, Nigeria, Pakistan and Turkey. These states were selected to illustrate and substantiate the astonishing diversity of national contexts in which the concepts of *zina* re-emerged, taking various legal and social forms. In Indonesia, *zina* legislation was introduced on the level of provincial/local by-laws and regulations in the 2000s, mainly and most dramatically in the autonomous province of Aceh. In Iran, sentences for *zina*, including *rajm* (stoning to death), were carried out as stipulated by national legislation in the aftermath of the 1979 Revolution that brought Shi'a clerics to power and 'Islamised' the laws and legal system. In Nigeria, the early 2000s were also the turning point, when 12 of its northern Muslim-majority states criminalised the offence of *zina* in accordance with their own understanding of some classical *fiqh* and lumped it together with other criminal offences, including those conceptualised through its colonial (British) legal legacy. In Pakistan, *zina* was introduced as a 'crime against state' in 1979 by the then military dictator Zia-ul-Haq, as an important 'asset' of his politically motivated 'Islamisation' programme. Finally, in Turkey, *zina* is not a crime under national law, but it is preserved in society as a transgression against one's 'family honour'; thereby, punishable extrajudicially by (male) members of the 'transgressor's' familial circle. The Turkish laws have implicitly condoned this horrendous 'custom' until the mid-2000s, by meting out lesser punishments to the perpetrators of 'honour' crimes, which still abound. All studied revivals of *zina* laws – except, arguably, in the Turkish case[4] – were introduced at times of significant political changes, as part of a new elite's opportunistic theopolitics, seizing a particular momentum for greater influence and control. Oftentimes, however, such laws were successful because the societal and legal outlook of the state in question was chronically patriarchal anyway, thus being a fertile ground for such reprehensible ruptures. As a result, mainly, of the women's movements' arduous resistance, *zina* laws, while still present 'on paper', are by and large obsolete in Pakistan and Nigeria. The advocacy of Acehnese civil society representatives succeeded in blocking the passage – via the governor's opposition – of the notorious Qanun Jinayat (Muslim Criminal Code), which would have provided for the offence of *zina* to be punishable by stoning to death or flogging in that province. In Iran, women's activism has so far not succeeded in bringing about legal change, but it has taken the judiciary to task and exposed the injustices that *zina* laws entail, thus inserting human rights concerns into the very heart of the public debate. Those are but some of the significant victories documented and analysed in this book. The country-specific case studies are, finally, followed by a chapter with concluding remarks.

The structure adopted for the five case studies in this book is largely uniform. It is divided into six specific subsections, relating to: (1) introductory remarks; (2) historical background; (3) domestic legal system; (4) state responsibility; (5) existing civil society activism for change; and (6) conclusion. These thematic units are then customised to address state-

---

[4] Even in Turkey, however, the discourses on *zina* were widely used for political purposes. See, e.g., İlkkaracan 2008.

specific circumstances and developments. Thus, notwithstanding the idiosyncrasies of each studied society, they allow for a comparative analysis of each scrutinised sub-theme. The final, concluding remarks of this study are, in particular, based on such comparative insights.

The Emergence and Re-Emergence of Zina *Laws*

The atrocities caused by the revival and reinvention of *zina* laws are discussed in the general media almost on a daily basis.[5] They have also provoked both activist and academic circles to produce studies, reports, articles and other resources for a better understanding of this phenomenon.[6] Parallel to such attempts, however, the public is also continuously fed by simplistic and historically unsubstantiated accounts of *zina* regulations, which are then employed by religious, political and military elites to justify the crimes and human rights violations committed on this pretext. For example, in a popular and widely disseminated book by Sheikh Yusuf al-Qaradawi, one of the most influential scholars at Al-Azhar University in Egypt, we learn that:

> Islam [sic] [...] is very strict in prohibiting zina, for zina leads to confusion of lineage, child abuse, the breaking-up of families, bitterness in relationships, the spread of venerable [sic] diseases, and a general laxity in morals: moreover, it opens the door to a flood of lusts and self gratifications (al-Qaradawi 2001 [1997]: 146).

Even the current Wikipedia entry for *zina* informs us that, "[i]n addition to the punishments [for *zina*] rendered before death, sinners are punished severely after death, unless purged of their sins by a punishment according to shari'a law [sic]" (Wikipedia 2010). As we shall see, those purportedly '*shari'a*-stipulated' punishments for *zina* are, in fact, some injunctions of classical *fiqh*, which are ordinarily taken to prescribe stoning to death for adultery (extra-marital sex, when the offender is married or – according to some scholars – a widow(er) or divorcee) and 100 lashes for fornication (pre-marital sex). Both the Qur'anic verses, e.g. 24:2–3, and various *hadith* – such as those collected by Bukhari, entries 3829, 8804, 8805 and 8824 – are cited in support of these severe sentences. *Zina*, we are told, is punished so drastically because, amongst other things, it "go[es] against the interest of society" (al-Qaradawi 2001 [1997]: 146). This 'interest', however, is not always stated in clear terms. Could it be patriarchal subjugation of women and control of one's sexuality by the 'guardians of faith'? Is it 'only' concerned with public and familial moral standards, or does it also provide for certain 'righteous men' to attain and/or stay in power? What, after all, are the consequences of the legal and social imposition of this 'interest'? These 'conundrums'

---

5 See, for example, a series of articles in *The Guardian* on the case of Sakineh Mohammadi Ashtiani, a 43-year-old Iranian woman detained in Tabriz jail since 2006 and sentenced to death by stoning on charges of *zina* and other offences,
http://www.guardian.co.uk/world/sakineh-mohammadi-ashtiani

6 See, for instance, the bibliographical notes after each country-specific case study chapter for many such examples from the studied states.

are often neglected in favour of a simplistic, 'widely understandable' message, ideologically charged and purposefully devoid of comprehensive historical, sociological or even theological analysis. It is designed to preclude, rather than spark, debate and research.

The history of *zina* is far more complex and telling than formulaic moralist prescriptions are prepared to admit. Classical Islamic jurisprudence is today mainly studied with reference to the surviving schools of thought (*madhahib*, singular: *madhhab*). Jurists of mainline Sunni (Hanafi, Maliki, Shafi'i and Hanbali) and Shi'i (Ja'fari) schools, which were all formed between the 8th and the 9th century, have sought to ascertain *shari'a* (divine 'Law' – God's instructions to humankind) by studying and interpreting the Qur'an and the Sunna. The results of these endeavours, often written and preserved in voluminous treatises, are known as *fiqh*. These works have neither emerged in a 'historical vacuum' nor have they conveyed a uniform and unambiguous body of legal knowledge. Their understanding of *shari'a* has been invariably coloured and compelled by the cultural, social and political circumstances of their time and by their individual capacities and interests in studying this transcendent subject. Hence, many of them, humbly aware of the limitedness of their expertise, have warned against unpremeditated following (*taqlid*) of their deliberations.[7] Some contemporary researchers have particularly warned of the political elements – the aspects of governance law (*siyasa*) – that have informed and directed the classical jurists' *fiqh* (e.g. Shalakany 2008). In sum, "[f]*iqh* is not divine law that Muslims have a duty to implement. *Fiqh* is juristic law, humanly constructed to deal with times and circumstances" (Masud 2009: 89). Yet, where *zina* laws have been implemented, they have been regularly conceptualised – or, at least, strategically justified – upon blind reverence of some elements of classical *fiqh*.

Classical jurists have categorised *zina* as a *hadd* (plural: *hudud*) crime, a transgression against 'the right of God' (*haqq Allah*), liable to either flogging (in reference to their interpretations of the specific Qur'anic verses) or to death by stoning (unmentioned in the Qur'an, yet supposedly derivable from the Sunna). Yet, for these punishments to be executed, the accused person must either have confessed to the offence – just once or repeatedly, depending on a particular school of *fiqh* – or refused to take an oath of denial (Shalakany 2008: 46–47). The only alternative left has been the unlikely testimony of four 'righteous' Muslim male witnesses that they have "personally seen the act of '*ilaj*' or penetration *in flagrante delicto*" (Shalakany 2008: 47). The testimony of less than four appropriate witnesses or any significant difference in their accounts would make them liable for the *hadd* offence of *qadhf* (slander). Under such circumstances, conviction for *zina* has effectively been made next to impossible. The 17th century jurist 'Ali al-Qari' al-Harawi explained this peculiar measure:

---

7 For instance, the 8th century scholar of *fiqh*, Imam Malik, after whom the Maliki *madhhab* was named, famously cautioned: "I am but a human being. I may be wrong and I may be right. So first examine what I say". Less than a century later, Imam Hanbal, who is considered the founder of the Hanbali *madhhab*, also demanded: "do not imitate me, or Malik, or al-Shafi, or al-Thawri and derive directly from where they themselves derived" (BAOBAB 2003: 3).

[I]t is a condition that the witnesses are four [...] because God the Exalted likes [the vices of] his servants to **remain concealed**, and this is realised by demanding four witnesses, since it is very rare for four people to observe this vice (quoted in El-Rouayheb 2005: 123; [emphasis added]).

Because concealing (*satr*) has been an integral value of the overall Muslim respect for privacy, to witness or publicly confess *zina* has been commonly rendered as 'contrary to what is most appropriate' (*khilaf al-awla*).[8] Accordingly, *zina* trials and punishments have occurred extremely rarely.

In the era of 'early modern' Muslim empires – Ottoman (1299–1923), Safavid (1501–1736), Afsharid (1736–96) and Mughal (1526–1858) – the virtue of *satr* in relation to *zina* has been consistently valued and adhered to. The Ottomans even outright abolished the *hadd* punishment of stoning to death for *zina* in 1680 (Koçak 2010: 234; Toprak 2003: 118). Other capital *hudud* punishments were also mostly replaced by the Ottoman sultans with flogging or – in most cases – with monetary fines (Schacht 1964: 91). The stipulations of classical *fiqh* have thus been moderated to meet the exigencies of the then Muslim communities. During colonial struggles and with the emergence of Muslim-majority nation-states, the influence of classical *fiqh* has been further diminished; at the advent of the 20th century, it was applicable *almost exclusively* to the realm of (Muslim) family law. Instead of the injunctions of classical *fiqh*, the emergent states' new criminal codes were modelled after European laws, which – although markedly gender-biased themselves – considered adultery a relatively minor offence.

The last quarter of the 20th century witnessed the great bulk of efforts to (re)introduce *zina* laws, both in the form of '*fiqh*-inspired' national legislation and through the increase of 'honour' crimes committed on the pretext of *zina*. They are, by and large, the result of complex socio-political circumstances, analysed throughout this book. On the one hand, Muslim theopolitical movements employed some injunctions – including those on *zina* – of classical *fiqh* to justify their political and social demands. In so doing, they intentionally misrepresented classical *fiqh* as the final and only understanding of *shari'a*, thereby giving it a 'divine weight'. Whether or not they eventually succeeded in their aspirations to power, their tactics were quickly adopted by other political instances, particularly certain Muslim governments. *Fiqh* rendered '*shari'a*' "is potentially a construct of limitless reach and power, and any institution that can attach itself to that construct becomes similarly empowered" (El Fadl 2009: 135). On the other hand, 20th century Muslim societies and communities – much like their non-Muslim counterparts – preserved a great deal of patriarchal bias, in particular in relation to societal (and legal) subjugation of women. Hence, the criminalisation of women's sexuality – enabled through the revival of *zina* laws – provided the contemporary patriarchs with an efficient and novel means to further assert their control. This is, however, a complex phenomenon, and its origins are to

---

8 In support for this thesis, Khaled El-Rouayheb quotes a number of early Ottoman scholars, including Ibn Nujaym, Ibn 'Abidin, Zurqani, Ibn 'Allan and Ramli. See El-Rouayheb 2005: 123.

be sought both in 'traditional' Muslim patriarchies – that is, in those found within a wide range of historical Muslim communities and their equally diverse customs – as well as in the 'encounters' – in particular those provoked by European imperialism and, later, neo-liberalism – with mostly non-Muslim patriarchal systems and their laws, customs and moral purviews. Other plausible lines of analysis could certainly include the intersections of capitalism and patriarchy (Jackson 1999) and their detrimental consequences for women's access to (gender) justice, which facilitated the spread of *zina* laws despite formal (often constitutional) human rights guarantees in many of the affected states. These and other catalysts provided for an indubitable rupture in historical treatments of *zina* in Muslim contexts, which have escalated into the most severe forms of gender-based violence and discrimination.

Resisting the Revival

The revival of *zina* laws in each society has provoked strong outcries, spearheaded by the national women's movements. Progressive Muslim (and non-Muslim) intelligentsia, religious scholars, trade unions, student movements, and domestic and international human rights organisations have often followed suit by joining in or supporting the activities organised by women's movements. These groups, often coalescing into a kind of resistance movement, have revealed and then resisted a number of strategies that are used by political, military and/or religious elites to enable the revival of *zina* laws. Some approaches the resistance movements have devised to counter these strategies are briefly discussed below.

Not Our Culture; Not Our Religion
Zina laws have often been justified with regards to particular cultural and religious traditions – such as *purdah*.[9] The resistance movements have responded by squarely rejecting those misconceptions on the grounds of carefully collected and analysed historical, theological and cultural evidence. Patriarchal biases within certain interpretations and practices of religion and culture can thus be revealed, in an attempt to demonstrate that it is not *integral* to them; that they *can* be freed from it; that, indeed, "[t]here is another life".[10]

---

9 The literal meaning of *purdah* is a veil or a curtain. In different societies, however, it has come to signify various moral stipulations for women. In Pakistan, for example, it has been framed as a comprehensive code of conduct for Muslim women, expressed through the concept of *purdah aur char divari* (veiling and cloistering within four walls), which patriarchal ideologues, such as Sayyid Abul A'la Maudoodi, have heavily used to promote starkly gender-discriminatory ideas, including women's 'proneness' to *zina*. See, for example, Maudoodi 1967: 193, 199. Among the Nigerian Muslims, *purdah* relates to the seclusion of women, often justified in reference to *zina*. See, for instance, Abdullah-Olukoshi 1990.

10 Reflecting on developments within the Turkish feminist movement in the 1980s, Ayfie Düzkan sums up its crucial impact on society as follows: "since we have begun to talk, a new phrase has been coined in this country: There is another life [...]. Another life is possible" (WLUML 1994).

Zina Laws are Part of a Broader Legal Scheme for Control of Sexuality
An important aspect of resistance to the (re)criminalisation of *zina* is to make it obvious that such a legislative development does not occur in isolation – i.e. that there is a significant incidence of gender-discriminatory laws (whether or not religiously justified) in the respective legal system, all of which are demonstrably used to control women's sexuality. Hence, the revival, often marketed as a 'moral reform' *par excellence*, is exposed as continuation (and an opportunistic 'upgrade') of an established legal mechanism constructed to provide its 'managers' with exceptional power over the general populace and, in particular, over women. Even in societies where *zina* is not explicitly criminalised by law, but instead regulated and 'punished' extrajudicially, an analysis of the domestic legal system discloses that such social malpractice continues to be effectively condoned or even encouraged by certain laws for a considerably long time. This was the case in Turkey until recent criminal justice reforms.

Supporting and Producing Knowledge
Studying the historical, political, cultural and legal circumstances surrounding the (re)emergence of *zina* laws has been an all-important aspect of civil society's resistance. The production and dissemination of knowledge gained through such insights, often in contrast with the dominant narratives put forward in support of the revival, have helped scholars, activists and the wider populace to understand what the *zina* laws were really about. One of the primary goals of this book is to further develop and encourage the struggle towards comprehensive non-patriarchal knowledge on *zina* laws and customs.

Overcoming the Divide between 'Religious' and 'Secular' Approaches and Activisms
In a number of national/local contexts, the stark divide between 'religious' and 'secular' activists against the revival of *zina* laws and other social injustices, supposedly based on the incompatibility of the base values informing the two camps, has markedly hampered the prospects of gender justice. Therefore, initiatives have emerged to 'reconcile' these approaches, insisting on the existence and necessity of common ground between the two movements. Their importance cannot be overstated. Whether arrived at through religious or other ethical frameworks, concepts such as justice or gender and sexual rights need to be negotiated across civil society movements if they are to become more than single-sided ideological catchphrases.

The Universal Applicability of Human Rights
Those who support the criminalisation of *zina* regularly attempt to preclude or derail the legal, political and moral consequences of the violation – which *zina* regulations, simply put, always constitute – of both domestic and international human rights guarantees by resorting to a cultural relativist critique of human rights. They are represented as an alien import, a 'Western' project, encroaching upon domestic 'values' and 'traditions'. Against such well-known tirades, the resistance movements produce a wealth of accounts suggesting the opposite – that human rights are a universally shared moral agency, applicable irrespective of a particular religious or cultural milieu. Notwithstanding

the sizeable attempts of global northern (neo)imperialisms to usurp the discourse of human rights, usually within a broader (neo)liberalist ideology, for their own political ends, the movements often showcase how both national and international human rights obligations of the state are an indispensable instrument for the attainment of gender and social justice. Their violations, clearly dramatically amplified by the revival of *zina* laws, therefore create a serious aberration not only in international but also in domestic justice system(s).

The Politics of *Zina*

Apart from the patriarchal demands, the primary reasons for (re)introducing *zina* laws have been purely political; that is, based on (overt or covert) ambitions to gain or hold political influence and power. Exposing this, however, is not always an easy task, given that '*zina*-related' politics are carefully coated with a highly moralist religious veneer, and are often part of larger projects to regulate the public and private behaviour of the *umma*. Moreover, the political appetites of some *'ulama'* (Muslim religious scholars), populist religious movements or military elites are frequently justified as 'moral necessity', given a supposed failure of politicians to provide good governance. Hence, the dictator General Muhammad Zia-ul-Haq sought to consolidate his power as a political leader in Pakistan by means of an 'Islamisation' programme, which included a forceful legal revival of *zina* legislation, as well as the imposition of dress codes and the repression of religious minorities. The resistance movements use various strategies to counter the politics of *zina*, from street demonstrations to co-operation with national and international human rights institutions (in particular within the mechanisms of the United Nations), from media campaigns to strategic political coalitions.

The Community Impact of the Revival of *Zina* Laws

'Honour' murders, rape, physical and psychological torture, cruel and degrading treatment, domestic violence and an outright denial of a wide range of fundamental rights, as well as impunity for perpetrators of such atrocities, are some of the widespread consequences of the revival of *zina* laws. They are clearly at odds with the goals and purposes (*maqasid*) of Islamic jurisprudence, as well as with the objectives of *any* national legal system. Hence, monitoring, documentation, litigation and other forms of direct support for victims of human rights violations, committed – by state or non-state actors – on the pretext of *zina*, represent essential tools in exposing and countering the true nature of the re-emergence of *zina* regulations. An analysis of these cases reveals that factors such as social and economic status or level of education intersect with sex, gender, sexual orientation or gender identity of the victim to the effect that certain categories of people are much more affected by the revival of *zina* laws than others. Those severely affected are, in particular, poor women and girls from rural areas with limited access to education; female migrant workers; and lesbian, gay, bisexual, trans, intersex and queer (LGBTIQ) individuals. Resistance movements have demonstrated how the markedly uneven community impact of the revival of *zina* laws attests to its inherently patriarchal nature.

The explanatory systems behind resistance strategies are equally diverse. Islamic feminism has proved a valuable analytical approach, since it provides for a comprehensive understanding of two tremendously important aspects of the revival of *zina* laws – the misconception of religious justice and the misconception of gender justice. Political, historical, legal and other discipline-specific analyses are also important, as they reveal the complexities and inconsistencies behind purportedly 'straightforward' moralisms advocating the re-emergence of *zina* laws. Overall, an informed human rights-based critique is also necessary, especially on the aspect of state responsibility to abide by international human rights law.

The abovementioned levels of analysis have also been utilised by the two authors of this book in an attempt to develop a holistic and integrated approach to the phenomenon of contemporary *zina* legislation. The key message this book intends to convey is that current and historical *zina* regulations are not fundamental to Islam and Muslim cultures. They stand in stark and alarming contrast to the Qur'anic obligation (e.g. 3:110, 3:104, 7:157, 9:71) to *enjoin what is good and forbid what is wrong*. This study, therefore, offers some existing and some novel avenues towards their eventual and necessary eradication.

Bibliography

Abdullah-Olukoshi, H. (1990), 'Women in Islamic Societies in the Kano Setting', mimeo. Hull: University of Hull.

Abou El Fadl, Khaled (2009), 'The Human Rights Commitment in Modern Islam' in Zainah Anwar (ed.), *Wanted: Equality and Justice in the Muslim Family*. Kuala Lumpur: Musawah.

BAOBAB for Women's Human Rights (2003), *Sharia Implementation in Nigeria: The Journey So Far*. Lagos: BAOBAB for Women's Human Rights, http://www.baobabwomen.org

Chandrakirana, Kamala (2009), 'Women's Place and Displament in the Muslim Family: Realities from the Twenty-First Century' in Zainah Anwar (ed.), *Wanted: Equality and Justice in the Muslim Family*. Kuala Lumpur: Musawah.

El-Rouayheb, Khaled (2005), *Before Homosexuality in the Arab-Islamic World, 1500–1800*. Chicago: University of Chicago Press.

Ertürk, Yakin (2004), 'Considering the Role of Men in Gender Agenda Setting: Conceptual and Policy Issues', *Feminist Review* 78: 3.

——— (2009), *15 Years of the United Nations Special Rapporteur on Violence against Women, Its Causes and Consequences (1994–2009) – A Critical Review*. Geneva: OHCHR, http://www2.ohchr.org/english/issues/women/rapporteur/docs/-15YearReviewofVAWMandate.pdf

Greiff, Shaina (2010), 'No Justice in Justifications: Violence against Women in the Name of Culture, Religion, and Tradition', Resource Paper, *Global Campaign to Stop Killing and Stoning Women*, March 2010, http://www.stop-stoning.org/node/881

Hefner, Robert W. (ed.) (2005), *Remaking Muslim Politics: Pluralism, Contestation, Democratization*. Princeton, NJ: Princeton University Press.

İlkkaracan, Pınar (2008), 'How Adultery Almost Derailed Turkey's Aspirations to Join the European Union' in Pınar İlkkaracan (ed.), *Deconstructing Sexuality in the Middle East: Challenges and Discourses*, 41–64. Surrey: Ashgate.

International Council on Human Rights Policy (2009), *When Legal Worlds Overlap: Human Rights, State and Non-State Law*. Geneva: International Council on Human Rights Policy.

Jackson, Stevi (1999), 'Marxism and Feminism' in Andrew Gamble, David Marsh and Tony Tant (eds.), *Marxism and Social Science*. London: Macmillan Press.

Kardam, Filiz (2005), *The Dynamics of Honor Killings in Turkey: Prospects for Action*. Ankara: UNDP.

Koçak, Mustafa (2010), 'Islam and National Law in Turkey' in Jan Michiel Otto (ed.), *Sharia Incorporated: A Comparative Overview of the Legal Systems of Twelve Muslim Countries in Past and Present*, 231–272. Leiden: Leiden University Press.

Masud, Muhammad Khalid (2009), '*Ikhtilaf al-Fuqaha*: Diversity in *Fiqh* as a Social Construction' in Zainah Anwar (ed.), *Wanted: Equality and Justice in the Muslim Family*. Kuala Lumpur: Musawah.

Maudoodi, Sayyid Abul A'la (1967), *Purdah and the Status of Women in Islam*. Lahore: Islamic Publications Ltd.

Mir-Hosseini, Ziba (2009), 'Islam and Feminism: Whose Islam? Whose Feminism?', *Contestations: Dialogues on Women's Empowerment* 1, http://www.contestations.net/issues/issue-1/response-to-hania-sholkamy/

—— (2009), 'Towards Gender Equality: Muslim Family Laws and the *Shari'ah*' in Zainah Anwar (ed.), *Wanted: Equality and Justice in the Muslim Family*. Kuala Lumpur: Musawah.

Okkenhaug, Inger Marie and Ingvild Flaskerud (eds.) (2005), *Gender, Religion and Change in the Middle East: Two Hundred Years of History*. Oxford: Berg.

Otto, Jan Michiel (2010), 'Introduction: Investigating the Role of Sharia in National Law' in Jan Michiel Otto (ed.), *Sharia Incorporated: A Comparative Overview of the Legal Systems of Twelve Muslim Countries in Past and Present*, 17–49. Leiden: Leiden University Press.

al-Qaradawi, Sheikh Yusuf (2001) [1997], *The Lawful and the Prohibited in Islam*, translated by K. al-Hilbawi, M. Siddiqi and S. Shukri. Cairo: Al-Falah Foundation.

'Sakineh Mohammadi Ashtiani', *The Guardian*, http://www.guardian.co.uk/world/sakineh-mohammadi-ashtiani.

Schacht, Joseph (1964), *An Introduction to Islamic Law*. Oxford: Clarendon Press.

Shalakany, Amr A. (2008), 'Islamic Legal Histories' *Berkeley Journal of Middle Eastern and Islamic Law* 1: 2.

Sonbol, Amira El-Azhary (2009), 'The Genesis of Family Law: How *Shari'ah*, Custom and Colonial Laws Influenced the Development of Personal Status Codes' in Zainah Anwar (ed.), *Wanted: Equality and Justice in the Muslim Family*. Kuala Lumpur: Musawah.

Toprak, Binnaz (2003), 'Türk Modeli Laikliğin 21. Yüzyılda Geleceği' in *Devlet ve Din İlişkileri: Farklı Modeller, Konseptler ve Tecrübeler*. Ankara: Konrad Adenauer Vakfı Yay.

Wadud, Amina (2009), 'Islam Beyond Patriarchy Through Gender Inclusive Qur'anic Analysis' in Zainah Anwar (ed.), *Wanted: Equality and Justice in the Muslim Family*. Kuala Lumpur: Musawah.

Women Living under Muslim Laws (WLUML) (1994), 'Feminism in Turkey in the 1980s: An Interview with Ayfle Düzkan and Meltem Ahiska', WLUML Occasional Paper No. 6. Grabels: WLUML, http://www.wluml.org/node/351.

'Zina (Arabic)', *Wikipedia: the Free Encyclopaedia*, http://en.wikipedia.org/wiki/Zina_%28Arabic%29

Criminalising Sexuality
Zina Laws as Violence Against Women in Muslim Contexts

Islamic legal tradition treats any sexual contact outside a legal marriage as a crime.[1] The main category of such crimes is *zina*, defined as any act of illicit sexual intercourse between a man and woman.[2] The punishment for *zina* is the same for men and women: 100 lashes for the unmarried and death by stoning for the married; however, instances of these punishments are rarely documented in history.

In the early 20th century, with the emergence of modern legal systems in the Muslim world, the provisions of classical Islamic law were increasingly confined to personal status issues.[3] *Zina* laws, which were rarely applied in practice, became also legally obsolete in almost all Muslim countries and communities. In the late 20th century, the resurgence of Islam as a political and spiritual force reversed the process. In several states and communities, once-obsolete penal laws were selectively revived, codified and grafted onto the criminal justice system, and, in varying forms and degrees, applied through the machinery of the modern state. Most controversial among these have been the revival of *zina* laws and the creation of new offences that criminalise consensual sexual activity and authorise violence against women. Activists have campaigned against these new laws on human rights grounds; campaigns in countries as diverse as Nigeria, Pakistan and Iran have revealed the injustice and violence brought by the 'Islamisation' of criminal justice systems. The issues addressed in these campaigns resonate in many other Muslim contexts where traditional and patriarchal interpretations of Islam's sacred texts are invoked to limit women's rights and freedoms.

There is extensive literature on the issues from a human rights perspective.[4] This chapter offers a feminist and rights-based critique of *zina* laws that engages Islamic legal tradition from within. It aims to broaden the scope of the debate over appropriate concepts and strategies for the campaigns to decriminalise consensual sex. It is intended as a contribution to the emerging feminist scholarship on Islam, by showing how *zina* laws can also be challenged from within. Exploring the intersections between religion, culture and law that legitimate violence in the regulation of sexuality, this chapter aims to contribute to the development of a framework that can bring Islamic and human rights principles together. Such a framework can empower activists, at both theoretical and practical levels, to engage in an internal discourse within communities so as to bring about sustainable legal and cultural reform.

---

1 This chapter is a revised version of a discussion paper published at http://www.stop-stoning.org/node/882

2 Apart from *zina*, other categories of sexual relations criminalised in classical legal tradition are *liwat*, homosexual relations between men, and *musahaqa*, homosexual relations between women, neither of which are a major focus of this chapter.

3 For instance, many Arab states adopted the penalty for adultery and so-called 'crimes of passion' from European penal codes (Abu Odeh 1996, Welchman 2007). The same happened in Iran.

4 See the websites of Women Living Under Muslim Laws (http://www.wluml.org) and the Violence is Not Our Culture (VNC) Campaign (http://www.stop-stoning.org)

Zina laws are part of Islamic legal tradition, and must be situated within that tradition's classifications of human behaviour and, especially, sexual relations and gender roles, and the penalties that it prescribes for different categories of offences. Drawing on anthropological insights and feminist scholarship on Islam, this chapter show how *zina* laws are also embedded in wider institutional structures of inequality that take their legitimacy from patriarchal interpretations of Islam's sacred texts. They are an element in a complex system of norms and laws regulating sexuality, and they are closely linked with two other sets of laws: those concerning marriage (*nikah*) and women's covering (*hijab*). This link is at the root of violence against women, and must be broken from within the tradition.

To do so, this chapter needs to address two blind spots in approaches to the issue. First, scholars who work within an Islamic framework are often gender-blind, being largely unaware of the importance of gender as a category of thought and analysis and often opposed to both feminism, which they understand as arguing for women's dominance over men, and human rights, which they see as alien to Islamic tradition. Secondly, many human rights and women's rights activists and campaigners are not well versed in religious categories of thought and religious-based arguments; they consider it futile and counter-productive to work within a religious framework. These blind spots must be eliminated; approaches from Islamic studies, feminist and human rights perspectives, far from being mutually opposed, can be mutually reinforcing, particularly in mounting an effective campaign against revived *zina* laws.

After outlining the approach and the premises on which it is based, this chapter traces the historical context of shifts in the politics of religion, law and gender that led to the recent revival of *zina* laws and punishments, and the clash between two systems of values and two conceptions of gender rights: those of international human rights law and the Islamic legal tradition. The chapter then examines *zina* laws in the context of classical Islamic legal tradition, exploring the links with the laws of marriage and dress code that regulate women's sexuality, and the theological assumptions and juristic theories that inform them. Finally, the chapter shows how *zina* laws and punishments can be challenged on legal and religious grounds, and how essential elements of Islamic legal tradition are in harmony with human rights law. The conclusion offers suggestions or guidelines for developing a framework that can bring Islamic and human rights principles together. Such a framework can empower activists, at both theoretical and practical levels, to engage in an internal discourse within communities to bring about sustained legal and cultural reforms.

Approach and Premises

This chapter starts from the premise that 'human rights' and 'Islamic law' are 'essentially contested concepts'; that is, they mean different things to different people and in different contexts.[5] However, advocates of both claim universality, that is, they claim that their objective is to ensure justice and proper rights for all humanity.[6] The notion of 'human rights' is used in a relatively limited sense, as a framework that began in 1948 with the Universal Declaration of Human Rights, and has been developed by the United Nations in subsequent documents and instruments. As human rights approaches are relatively well-known, more attention is devoted here to Islamic legal traditions and discourses.

Secondly, a discomfort with the term 'Islamic law(s)' must be noted here. 'Islamic laws', like other laws, are the product of socio-cultural assumptions and juristic reasoning about the nature of relations between men and women. In other words, they are 'man-made' juristic constructs, shaped by the social, cultural and political conditions within which Islam's sacred texts are understood and turned into law. From the perspective of this chapter, it is more analytically fruitful and productive to speak of 'Islamic legal tradition'.

This tradition is approached from a critical feminist perspective and from within the tradition, by invoking one of its main distinctions, which underlies the emergence of the various schools in the tradition and the multiplicity of positions and opinions within them; that is, the distinction between *shari'a* and *fiqh*. *Shari'a* in Arabic literally means 'the path or the road leading to the water', but, in Muslim belief, it is God's will as revealed to the Prophet Muhammad. As Fazlur Rahman notes, "in its religious usage, from the earliest period, it has meant 'the highway of good life', i.e. religious values, expressed functionally and in concrete terms, to direct man's life."[7] *Fiqh*, jurisprudence, literally means 'understanding', and denotes the process of human endeavour to discern and extract legal rulings from the sacred texts of Islam – the Qur'an and the Sunnah (the Prophet's practice, as related in the *hadith*, or traditions).

Thus, the rulings derived from the sacred texts are matters of human interpretation. However, some specialists and politicians today – often with ideological intent – mistakenly equate *shari'a* with *fiqh*, and present *fiqh* rulings as '*shari'a* law', hence as divine and not open to challenge. Too often statements are heard that begin with "Islam says …" or "According to *shari'a* law …"; too rarely do those who speak in the name of Islam admit that theirs is no more than one opinion or interpretation among many. A distinction between *shari'a* and *fiqh* is crucial, from a critical feminist perspective, because it both engages with

---

5 See Gallie (1956: 167–72); an essentially contested concept, in Gallie's terms, has 'disagreement at its core'. Terms and concepts like 'work of art' or 'democracy' or 'religion' inevitably involve endless disputes about their proper use on the part of their users. In other words, contestedness is an essential part of such concepts; there cannot be only one definition on which all agree.

6 For discussions of the tension between universalism and relativism in human rights, see: An-Na'im (1990, 1995a), Dembour (2001), Merry (2003), Sen (1988). For debates on the compatibility between Islam and human rights law, see: Baderin (2001, 2007), Bielefeldt (1995, 2000), Hunter (2005), Jahanpour (2007), Sajoo (1999), Strawson (1997).

7 Rahman (2002: 100); in Kamali's words, "*Shari'a* demarcates the path which the believer has to tread in order to obtain guidance" (2006: 37).

the past and enables action in the present; it enables the separation of the legal from the sacred, and to reclaim the diversity and pluralism that was part of Islamic legal tradition. It also has epistemological and political ramifications, and allows contestation and change of its rulings from within.[8]

Thirdly, this chapter rejects statements beginning "Islam says…" or "Islam allows…" or "Islam forbids…" Islam does not speak, rather it is people who claim to speak in the name (with the authority) of Islam, selecting sacred texts (usually out of context) that appear to justify their claims, and repressing other texts that oppose them. Moreover, those who talk of *shari'a*, or indeed religion and law in relation to Islam, often fail to make another distinction now common when talking of religion in other contexts, namely, between faith (and its values and principles) and organised religion (institutions, laws and practices). The result is the pervasive polemical and rhetorical trick of either glorifying a faith without acknowledging the abuses and injustices that are committed in its name, or condemning it by equating it with those abuses. Of course, faith and organised religion are linked, but they are not the same thing, as implied by conflating them in the labels 'Islamic' or 'religious'.

Fourthly, although this chapter may talk about religion, law and culture as distinct arenas of human behaviour, in practice it is hard to separate them. Social reality is far too complex. Religious beliefs and practices are not only shaped by the cultural contexts in which they originate, function and evolve, but they also influence cultural phenomena. Law, too, not only controls behaviour but is also shaped by religious as well as cultural practices; all these beliefs and practices are, in turn, subject to relations of power – rulers, governments, structures of inequality. The meanings of laws and religious practices also change with shifts in the power relations in which they are embedded, and in interaction with other cultures and value systems. In other words, it must be recognised that laws and religious practices are not fixed, unchanging and uniform, but rather they are the products of particular social and cultural circumstances, and of local and wider power relations.[9]

Finally, issues are created through social movements and political debates and struggles. The systematic and institutionalised regulation of female sexuality and behaviour by man-made and man-enforced laws is not confined to Muslim contexts, nor is it recent. It is ancient and found in most human societies, sanctioned by religious texts and cultural tradition, and often enforced by violence. What is new is that the human rights framework

---

8   For instance, Al-'Ashmawi, the Egyptian reformist and chief judge of the High Court of Appeals, in a book entitled *Usul al-Shari'a* (The Principles of *Shari'a* – not *Usul al-Fiqh*), contends that *shari'a* is not legal rules but ethical principles and values in the Qur'an, in which justice is primary. For a sample translation of his work, see Kurzman (1998: 49–56).

9   See Merry (2003) for an insightful discussion of ways in which culture – and along the way, anthropology as a discipline that studies culture – has been demonised in certain human rights discourses, which do not take into consideration the rethinking of the concept of culture in anthropology in recent decades. This has parallels with the demonisation of religion by those unaware of theoretical developments in religious studies.

and contemporary ideas of gender equality enable the identification of the issue of *zina* laws as a violation of women's human rights.[10]

Why *Zina* Laws and Why Now?

Current *zina* laws reflect centuries-old, human-made interpretations of Islam's sacred texts, which can be criticised from within the framework of Islamic principles, in accordance with the changing realities of time and place and contemporary notions of justice. As in other religious and legal traditions, notions of justice among Muslims have not until recently included gender equality in its current sense. The idea of gender equality became inherent to conceptions of justice only in the 20th century, and has only recently presented Islamic legal tradition with a challenge that it has been trying to meet.[11] Thus, the revival of *zina* laws, and the emergence of a global campaign against them, must be understood in the context of the recent conflict between two systems of values, the one rooted in pre-modern cultural and religious practices that often sanction discrimination among individuals on the basis of faith, status and gender, and the other shaped by contemporary ideals of human rights, equality and personal freedom.

This conflict of values is not confined to Muslim contexts, rather it is ubiquitous, and shades into the animated and ongoing debate between universalism and cultural relativism. But it acquired a sharper political edge in the Muslim world in the second half of the 20th century with the emergence of the question of Palestine, and the rise of Islamist movements that sought to merge religion and politics.[12] In the aftermath of the 11 September 2001 ('9/11') attacks, the politics of the so-called war on terror and the invasions of Afghanistan and Iraq – both partially justified as promoting democracy and women's rights – added a new layer of complexity to the situation. Rightly or wrongly, many Muslims perceived the war to be directed against them. This has not only increased their sense of insecurity and the appeal of traditional values, but it has also, in their eyes, eroded the moral high ground of human rights law and delegitimised the voices of dissent and reform from within.

In many ways, 1979 proved to be a turning point in the politics of religion, culture and gender, both globally and locally. It was the year when the United Nations General Assembly adopted the Convention on the Elimination of all forms of Discrimination against Women (CEDAW), which gave gender equality a clear international legal mandate. But it was also the year when political Islam had its biggest triumph in the popular revolution

---

10 For excellent accounts of anthropological approaches to violence against women, see Merry (2006, 2009).

11 This challenge has been the subject of many research projects and initiatives; see, for instance, New Directions in Islamic Thought and Practice, initiated in 2003 by the Oslo Coalition for Freedom of Religion and Belief (www.oslocoalition.org/nd.php), and Musawah: A Global Movement for Equality and Change in the Muslim Family, launched in 2009 (www.musawah.org).

12 For a definition of Islamists as 'Muslims committed to public action to implement what they regard as an Islamic agenda', see Mir-Hosseini and Tapper (2009: 81–2).

that brought clerics to power in Iran, and when the ambit of *fiqh* was extended in Pakistan to criminal law, with the introduction of the Hudood Ordinances.

The decades that followed saw the concomitant expansion, globally and locally, of two equally powerful but opposed frames of reference. On the one hand, the human rights framework and instruments such as CEDAW gave women's rights activists what they needed most: a point of reference, a language and the tools to resist and challenge patriarchy. The 1980s saw the expansion of the international women's movement and of women's non-governmental organisations (NGOs) all over the world. By the early 1990s, a transnational movement further coalesced around the idea that violence against women was a violation of their human rights, and succeeded in inserting it in the agenda of the international human rights community. In their campaigns, they made visible various forms of gender-based discrimination and violation rooted in cultural traditions and religious practices, and protection from violence became a core demand of women's human rights activists. In 1994, the UN Commission on Human Rights condemned gender-based violence and appointed a special rapporteur on violence against women, its causes and consequences, as requested in the Vienna Declaration at the 1993 UN Conference on Human Rights.[13]

In Muslim contexts, on the other hand, Islamist forces – whether in power or in opposition – started to invoke Islam and *shari'a* as a legitimising device. They presented the 'Islamisation' of law and society as the first step to bring about their vision of a moral and just society, as a remedy for the problems of rising criminality, corruption and 'immorality' that they understood to be the consequence of the mixing of sexes. This spoke to the masses, and played on the popular belief among Muslims that Islam is the essence of justice, thus no law that is 'Islamic' could be unjust.

Tapping into popular demands for social justice, the Islamist rallying cry of 'return to *shari'a*' led to regressive gender policies, with devastating consequences for women: compulsory dress codes, gender segregation, and the revival of outdated patriarchal and tribal models of social relations. The 'Islamisation' of law and society centred on the criminal justice system, an area of public law that had lost ground to codified law, influenced by European models, both under colonial rule and with the modernisation of legal systems.[14] At the same time, the Islamists criminalised – and thus politicised – areas of sexual and moral behaviour that had previously not been the concern of the state, and thus facilitated the enforcement of their authoritarian and patriarchal interpretations of the law.

Fiqh-based penal laws had already been revived in codified form in Libya in 1972.[15] After

---

13 For a good account of these developments, see Merry (2006: 77–84).

14 For a general discussion of the 'Islamisation' of criminal law, see Peters (1994).

15 They were grafted onto existing Italian-based criminal law; but they did not have stoning as punishment for *zina* (Peters 1994*)*. Meanwhile various Gulf states already had *fiqh*-based penal codes: Kuwait (1960, 1970), Oman (1974), Bahrain (1976). Codification came later in the United Arab Emirates (1988) and Qatar (2004).

1979, the same happened in Pakistan (Enforcement of Hudood Ordinances, 1979), Iran (1979), Sudan (Penal Code, 1983, and Criminal Act, 1991), and Yemen (Penal Code, 1994). The same has occurred at a provincial level in Kalantan state in Malaysia (Syariah Criminal Code Act, 1993), several states in Nigeria (1999–2000), and Aceh Territory in Indonesia (2009). In other cases, such as Afghanistan under the Taliban (mid-1990s to 2001), in Algeria since the rise of the Islamic Salvation Front (FIS), and in Somalia for many years, there are reports of the arbitrary application of Islamic penal laws.[16] Actual instances of stoning as a result of judicial sentences remain rare; currently, they only occur in Iran. But wherever classical penal laws have been revived, and in whatever form, nearly all those sentenced under *zina* laws to lashing, imprisonment or death by stoning have been women. In many instances, women have been brought to court on the basis of false accusations by family members or neighbours, or have been punished by non-state actors and communities.[17]

To understand why women have been the main target of the revival of *zina* laws, two prime questions need to be asked: What is the place of *zina*, both as a concept and as a set of legal rulings, in the Islamic legal tradition? How can it be argued – within that tradition – for the decriminalisation of consensual sexual relations? To explore these questions, the links need to be examined, in *fiqh* (Islamic jurisprudence), between three sets of rulings that regulate sexuality, i.e. those concerning *zina*, marriage and *hijab*. And what are the juristic constructs and legal theories on which they are based?

Zina as Defined in Classical *Fiqh* Texts

Classical *fiqh* divides crimes into three categories according to the penalties they incur: *hudud*, *qisas*, and *ta'zir*.[18] *Hudud* (singular *hadd*: limit, restriction, prohibition) are crimes with mandatory and fixed punishments derived from textual sources (Qur'an or Sunnah). *Hudud* crimes comprise five offences. Two are offences against sexual morality: illicit sex (*zina*) and unfounded allegation of *zina* (*qadhf*). The others are offences against private property and public order: theft (*sariqa*), highway robbery (*qat' al-tariq hiraba*), and drinking wine (*shurb al-khamr*); some schools also include rebellion (*baghi*); and some include apostasy (*ridda*). The jurists defined these offences as violations of God's limits (*hudud al-Allah*), i.e. violation of public interest. *Hudud* assume the central place in the call for 'return to *shari'a*' by Islamists, who consider them crimes against religion, though

---

16 For instance, 16 October 2009, Somali hardliners Islamic militia whipped women for wearing bras, as they defined it 'provocative': http://www.alarabiya.net/save_print.php?print=1&cont_id=88238&lang=en

17 There is now a substantial literature on this; for instance, for Pakistan, see Jahangir and Jilani (1988); for Iran, Terman (2007); for Sudan, Sidahmed (2001); for Nigeria, Imam (2005) and Peters (2006).

18 For *fiqh*-based accounts, see Safwat (2008) and Bassiouni (1997); for an analytical view, see Peters (2005); for reformist and critical accounts, see El-Awa (1993), Kamali (1998, 2000, 2006:184–89).

not every such crime or punishment has a textual basis.[19] They are the main focus of international criticism, since they entail forms of punishment, such as lashing and amputation of limbs, which were common in the past but have been abandoned by modern justice systems that consider them cruel and inhumane – and are defined in international human rights law as torture.

The second category, *qisas* (retribution), covers offences against another person, such as bodily harm and homicide. The penalty is defined and implemented by the state, but unlike *hudud*, *qisas* offences are a matter for private claims, in the sense that the penalty is applied only if the individual victim – or, in case of homicide, his or her heir – asks for full *qisas*. Alternatively, the victim or heir may forgive the offender, or ask for the lesser penalty of *diya* (compensation, blood money), or waive any claim. In the case of homicide, whether intentional or not, blood money or compensation given for a female victim is half of that of a male. By making homicide a private matter, the revival of *qisas* laws allows so-called 'honour' crimes, whereby families can kill female members for presumed 'sexual transgressions' and the killer can escape with at most a few years imprisonment.[20]

The third category, *ta'zir* (discipline), covers all offences not covered by the first two. Punishments for these crimes are not established by textual sources, and are not fixed but left to the discretion of the judge. As a general rule, *ta'zir* penalties are less than *hadd* punishments. Under the category of *ta'zir*, Islamic states have introduced new punishments with no precedence in classical *fiqh*, in order to impose their notions of 'Islamic' morality and to limit women's freedom, for example by a dress code. As it sanctions and legitimates the state's power to enforce laws, this is also the area of criminal justice most open to abuse by Islamists.

There are differences between legal schools and among the jurists as to the definition, elements, evidentiary requirements, legal defences, exonerating conditions and penalties applicable to each of these three categories of crime, and to each crime within each category. The boundaries between the sacred and the legal are particularly hazy with respect to *hudud* crimes, which are viewed as having a religious dimension because of their textual basis. This is certainly the case with respect to *zina*, which is treated at times as a sin to be punished in the hereafter, rather than as a crime. There is room for repentance and God's forgiveness. The objective is not punishment but rather self-reformation and the shunning of evil ways.[21]

Yet there is a consensus in *fiqh* on the definition of *zina*, and the rulings are clear. *Zina* is defined as sexual intercourse between a man and women outside a valid marriage (*nikah*),

---

19 The inclusion of drinking alcohol and apostasy has no textual basis. Hanbali jurists do not define apostasy as a *hadd* crime (Peters 2005: 64–5); some jurists do not consider drinking alcohol as a *hadd* crime (El-Awa: 1993: 2).
20 Welchman (2007).
21 Kamali (1998, 2000); Rahman (1965).

the semblance (*shubha*) of marriage, or lawful ownership of a slave woman (*milk yamin*). *Zina* can be established by confession or by the testimony of four eyewitnesses, who must have witnessed the actual act of penetration, and must concur in their accounts. The punishment is the same for men and women, but offenders are divided into two classes: *muhsin*, defined as free men and women, of full age and understanding, who have been in a position to enjoy lawful wedlock; and non-*muhsin*, who do not fulfil these conditions. The penalty for the first class is death by stoning, and for the second, 100 lashes. The lashes have a Qur'anic basis, as will be shown; but stoning does not, being based only on the Sunnah.[22]

The juristic consensus ends here. There are significant differences among the legal schools and among jurists within each school as to the conditions required for a valid confession and for testimonial evidence. These differences, based on arguments supported by reference to sacred texts, have practical and important legal consequences. For instance, while jurists in Hanafi, Hanbali and Shi'a schools require the confession to be uttered four separate times, Maliki and Shafi'i jurists consider one confession sufficient to establish the offence. The majority view among Maliki jurists is unique in allowing an unmarried woman's pregnancy to be used as evidence for *zina*, unless there is evidence of rape or compulsion; in other schools, pregnancy does not automatically constitute proof and *zina* must be established by confession or the testimony of eye-witnesses. Yet again, it is important to stress that, for Maliki jurists, the duration of pregnancy can be as long as seven years, which clearly suggests their humanitarian concern to protect women against the charge of *zina*, and children against the stigma of illegitimacy. That is to say, like their counterparts in other schools, Maliki jurists did their best to make conviction for *zina* impossible.[23]

A closer examination of classical jurists' rulings on *zina* confirms that they did their utmost to prevent conviction, and provided women with protection against accusations by their husbands and the community. In this, they relied on Qur'anic verses and the Prophet's example in condemning the violation of privacy and honour of individuals, in particular those of women, and leaving the door open for repentance. These verses define requirements for valid evidence of *zina* in such a stringent way that, in practice, establishment and conviction of an offence are almost impossible. An uncorroborated accusation (*qadhf*) is itself defined as a *hadd* crime, punishable by 80 lashes (Qur'an, Surah an-Nur, 24: 23). If the wife is pregnant and her husband suspects her of *zina*, but has no proof, all he can do, in order to avoid the *hadd* offence of *qadhf*, is to deny

---

22 For an outline of *zina* rulings in Sunni schools and differences of opinion among the jurists, see Ibn Rushd (1996: 521–30).

23 A belief in the 'sleeping foetus' (*raqqad*) is still widespread in North and West Africa. According to this belief, the embryo for some unknown reason goes to sleep in the mother's womb, and remains there dormant until it is awakened, for example by a magical potion or intervention by a saint. Malik ibn Anas, founder of the Maliki school of jurists, was reputed to have been a sleeping foetus. See Jansen (2000), Mir-Hosseini (1993: 143–46).

paternity and divorce her by the procedure of *li'an*, mutual cursing by swearing oaths; if the wife swears an oath of denial, she is exonerated from the charge of *zina* (Qur'an, Surah an-Nur 24: 6–7). Further, a confession of *zina* can be retracted at any time; and the doctrine of *shubha* (doubt, ambiguity)[24] prevents conviction for *zina* in cases where one party presumes the sexual intercourse to be licit, for example when a man sleeps with a woman he believes to be his wife or a slave, or when a woman has sex with a man she presumes to be her husband.

Scholars suggest that the Qur'anic penalty – 100 lashes for men and women – was intended to reinforce a single form of marriage and to forbid other forms of union and promiscuity. This is evident in the verse that follows: "Let no man guilty of Adultery or fornication marry any but a woman similarly guilty, or an Unbeliever: Nor let any but such a woman or an unbeliever marry such a man. To the Believers such a thing is forbidden" (Surah an-Nur 24: 3). Likewise, the penalty for slaves (both male and female) is half of that of a free person, which means that in no way did the Qur'an envisage death as a penalty for *zina*.

In pre-Islamic Arabia several forms of sexual union existed, including temporary ones: female slaves were prostituted by their masters; women as well as men could have multiple partners; and adultery was not considered a sin, but an injury to the property rights of a fellow tribesman – the male partner paid a fine, while the female was punished by being detained in her house for the rest of her life.[25] The Qur'an clearly disapproves of the prevalent sexual and moral codes among the Arabs, and introduces measures to reform them: it forbids the prostitution of female slaves (Surah an-Nur, 24: 33); speaks of sex outside marriage as a sin to be punished in the Hereafter (Surah al-Isra' 17: 32; Surah al-Furqan, 25: 68–71); and modifies existing practices to promote chastity and a standardised form of marriage. Eight verses (Surah an-Nur 24: 2–9) deal with the law-like issue of illicit sexual relations and form the basis of *fiqh* rulings on *zina*. These verses introduce new sanctions to safeguard a new form of marriage, subject men and women to the same punishment for extra-marital relations, and protect women in the face of accusations against their chastity.

Two verses prescribe punishment for illicit sexual relations. The first reads as follows: "If any of your women are guilty of lewdness, take the evidence of four (reliable) witnesses from amongst you against them; and if they testify, confine them to houses until death do claim them, or Allah ordain for them some (other) way" (Surah an-Nisa 4: 15). The verse does not use the term *zina*; instead, *fahisha* (lewdness) is used, which most commentators understood as implying adultery and fornication. However, Yusuf Ali, one of the notable translators of the Qur'an, in a note states that *fahisha* "refers to unnatural crime between women, analogous to unnatural crime between men,"[26] the subject of the next verse, which

---

24 The doctrine of *shubha* is based on a saying of the Prophet: "God's sanction will not be applied in cases where there is room for doubt." *Hadd* is suspended in cases where there is any ambiguity as to facts and proofs; for discussion, see Fierro (2007).

25 Gibb and Kramers (1961: 658)

26 Ali (1999: 189). For a groundbreaking study, see Kugle (2003, 2010).

states: "no punishment is specified for the man, as would be the case when a man was involved in the crime" (Surah an-Nisa 4: 16). It has also been argued that *fahisha* in Surah an-Nisa 4: 15 denotes a sexual act in public and prostitution, not private consensual sex, whether it is heterosexual or not. The verse endorses the existing punishment for *fahisha* – of which only women, it appears, could be accused. They should be confined to the home for the rest of their lives, or humiliated by having to appear in public covered in animal dung. The verse, however, while not abolishing this penalty, contains it by requiring the evidence of four witnesses and, perhaps more importantly, promises women a way out. In any case, jurists agree that the punishment was superseded by Surah an-Nur 24: 2, which reads: "The woman and the man guilty of adultery or fornication (*al-zaniah wa al-zani*) – flog each of them with a hundred stripes."

It seems clear that not only the Qur'anic verses but also the jurists, with their intricate rules for proof of *zina*, aimed to reform existing practices in the direction of justice, as understood at the time. But both the spirit of the verses and the rules of the jurists lose their force for justice when classical *fiqh* rulings are codified and grafted onto a unified legal system, and implemented by the coercive machinery of a modern nation state.[27] Hence, it is not enough to take the classical *zina* rulings at face value, as some do. Defenders of current *zina* laws often hide behind the reassurance that they are impossible to enforce in practice; they ignore how they are actually used, and that it is women and the poor who are most often the victims.

Marriage (*Nikah*) and Covering (*Hijab*)

What defines *zina* is the absence of a legal marriage (*nikah*); thus, *zina* rulings intersect with and in practice are maintained by other rulings that the classical jurists devised for the regulation of sexuality, namely those concerning marriage and women's covering. These patriarchal rulings sustained the power and sanction of *zina* provisions, and continue to do so today, even if they have been eliminated from modern legal codes. In all Muslim countries – apart from Turkey – the source of family law is classical *fiqh*, which grants men the right to polygyny and unilateral divorce. Thus a closer examination of marriage and *hijab* as defined in classical *fiqh* texts is in order.

Classical jurists defined marriage (*'aqd al-nikah*, 'contract of coitus') as a contract with fixed terms and uniform legal effects. It renders sexual relations between a man and a woman licit; any sexual relation outside this contract is by definition *zina*. The contract is patterned after the contract of sale, and has three essential elements: the offer (*ijab*) by the woman or her guardian (*wali*); the acceptance (*qabul*) by the man; and the payment of dower (*mahr*),

---

27 For instance, the Islamic Republic of Iran uses the notion of *'elm-e qazi* ('judge's knowledge') which refers to personal information that is not presented or examined by the court. In practice, this allows the judge to decide if an offence has been committed; often women are tricked into confession, see Terman (2007).

a sum of money or any valuable that the husband pays or undertakes to pay to the bride before or after consummation.[28]

The contract automatically places a wife under her husband's *qiwama*, which is a mixture of dominion and protection. It also defines a default set of fixed rights and obligations for each party, some supported by legal force, others with moral sanction. Those with legal force revolve around the twin themes of sexual access and compensation, embodied in the two concepts *tamkin* (obedience; also *ta'a*) and *nafaqa* (maintenance). *Tamkin*, defined as sexual submission, is a man's right and thus a woman's duty; whereas *nafaqa*, defined as shelter, food and clothing, is a woman's right and thus a man's duty. In some schools, a woman becomes entitled to *nafaqa* only after consummation of the marriage, in others this comes with the contract itself; but in all schools she loses her claim if she is in a state of *nushuz* (disobedience), which the classical jurists defined only in sexual terms. In other words, all schools share the same logic that links a woman's right to maintenance and protection to her obedience and sexual submission to her husband. Among the default rights of the husband is his power to control his wife's movements and her 'excess piety'. She needs his permission to leave the house, to take up employment, or to engage in fasting or forms of worship other than what is obligatory (for example the fast of Ramadan). Such acts may infringe on the husband's right of 'unhampered sexual access'. There is no matrimonial regime; the husband is the sole owner of the matrimonial resources, and the wife remains the possessor of her dower and whatever she brings to or earns during the marriage.

In discussing the legal structure and effects of the marriage contract, classical jurists had no qualms in using the analogy of sale. They allude to parallels between the status of wives and female slaves, to whose sexual services husbands/owners were entitled, and who were deprived of freedom of movement. This is not to suggest that classical jurists conceptualised marriage as either a sale or as slavery.[29] Certainly, there were significant differences and disagreements about this among the schools, and debates within each, with legal and practical implications.[30] They were keen to distinguish between the right of access to the woman's sexual and reproductive faculties (which her husband acquires) and the right over her person (which he does not). Rather, the intention in this chapter is

---

28 This discussion is concerned with marriage as defined by classical jurists, not marriage in practice; for more detailed treatment of the subject, see Ali (2008, 2010), Mir-Hosseini (2003, 2009). *Mahr* is sometimes inaccurately translated as 'dowry', but this means property or cash that a wife brings her husband on marriage, as occurs in India and used to occur in Europe; the Muslim *mahr*, by contrast, is property that a husband gives his wife, and thus resembles the English 'dower' – a more appropriate translation.

29 For similarities in the juristic conceptions of slavery and marriage, see Marmon (1999) and Willis (1985).

30 For these disagreements, see Ali (2003, 2008) and Maghniyyah (1997); for their impact on rulings related to *mahr* and the ways in which classical jurists discussed them, see Ibn Rushd (1996: 31–33).

to stress that the notion and legal logic of 'ownership' and sale underlie their conception of marriage and define the parameters of laws and practices, where a woman's sexuality, if not her person, becomes a commodity and an object of exchange.

The logic of women's sexuality as property, and its sale on marriage, which informs the classical *fiqh* texts, is at the root of the unequal construction of marriage and divorce, and sanctions the control over a woman's movements. It is also this logic that justifies polygyny and defines the rules for the termination of marriage. A man can enter up to four marriages at a time,[31] and can terminate each contract at will. Legally speaking, *talaq*, repudiation of the wife, is a unilateral act (*iqa'*), which acquires legal effect by the declaration of the husband. A woman cannot be released without her husband's consent, although she can secure her release through offering him inducements, by means of *khul'*, which is often referred to as 'divorce by mutual consent'. As defined by classical jurists, *khul'* is a separation claimed by the wife as a result of her extreme 'reluctance' (*karahiya*) towards her husband. The essential element is the payment of compensation (*'iwad*) to the husband in return for her release. This can be the return of the dower, or any other form of compensation. Unlike *talaq*, *khul'* is not a unilateral but a bilateral act, as it cannot take legal effect without the consent of the husband. If she fails to secure his consent, then her only recourse is the intervention of the court and the judge's power either to compel the husband to pronounce *talaq* or to pronounce it on his behalf if the wife establishes one of the recognised grounds – which again vary from school to school.[32]

Another set of rulings that are invoked, today, to sanction control over women and to limit their freedom of movement are those on *hijab*.[33] They are used to prescribe and justify the punishment of women for non-observance of the dress code, using *ta'zir*, the discretionary power of the judge or Islamic state. But this has no basis in Islamic legal tradition. Unlike rulings on marriage and *zina*, classical *fiqh* texts contain little on women's dress code. The prominence of *hijab* in Islamic discourses is a recent phenomenon, dating to the Muslim encounter with colonial powers in the 19th century, when there emerged a new genre of Islamic literature in which the veil becomes both a marker of Muslim identity and an element of faith.

Classical texts – at least those that set out legal rulings – address the issue of dress for both men and women under 'covering' (*satr*). These rulings are found in the Book of Prayer,

---

31 In Shi'a law a man may contract as many temporary marriages (*mut'a*) as he desires or can afford. For this form of marriage, see Haeri (1989).

32 Classical Maliki law grants women the widest grounds (absence of the husband, his mistreatment, failure to provide and failure to fulfil marital duties), which have been used as the basis for expanding women's grounds for divorce in the process of codification, see Mir-Hosseini (1993, 2003).

33 Many terms commonly used today in different countries for 'the veil', such as *hijab, purdah, chador, burqa*, are not found in classical *fiqh* texts.

among the rules for covering the body during prayers, and in the Book of Marriage, among the rules that govern a man's 'gaze' at a woman prior to marriage.[34]

The rules are minimal, but clear-cut: during prayer, both men and women must cover their 'awra, their pudenda; for men, this is the area between knees and navel, but for women it means all the body apart from hands, feet and face. A man may not look at the uncovered body of an unrelated woman. The ban can be relaxed when a man wants to contract a marriage; then, in order to inspect a prospective bride, he may be allowed the same privileges as one of her male close relatives.

There are also related rules in classical *fiqh* for segregation (banning any kind of interaction between unrelated men and women) and seclusion (restricting women's access to public space). They are based on two juristic constructs: the first defines all of a woman's body as 'awra, pudenda, a zone of shame, which must be covered both during prayers (before God) and in public (before men); the second defines women's presence in public as a source of *fitna*, chaos, a threat to the social order.[35]

A Critique from Within

In their rulings on *zina*, classical jurists sought to safeguard sexual order, personal honour and blood relations, and to ensure legitimate paternity. But these rulings were designed and perceived to protect the sanctity of marriage and to be a deterrent, not to be codified and enforced by the machinery of a modern state. As shown, these rules are, in theory, gender-neutral. They specify the same punishments for men and women, and contain measures to protect women against false accusations, with such strict requirements of evidence that it is almost impossible to prove a case.

The power and sanction of *zina* rulings, it must be stressed, lie not in their implementation, but in how they define the limits of permissible sexual conduct. Their power is exerted and sustained through the other rulings just outlined, those regulating marriage and women's covering. To understand how all these rulings work, it is necessary to examine how classical jurists thought of gender and female sexuality, and identify the underlying legal theories and juristic assumptions. As is evident from the rulings on marriage and *hijab* discussed above, *zina* laws rest on two juristic constructs: woman's sexuality as property acquired by her husband through the marriage contract, and woman's body as a shameful object ('awra) that must be covered at all times. Such constructs, in turn, hinge on a patriarchal reading of Islam's sacred texts and an underlying theory of sexuality that sanctions control over female behaviour. All *fiqh* schools share this patriarchal ethos and conception of sexuality and gender; if they differ, it is in the manner and degree to which they translate them into legal rulings.

---

34 For the evolution of *hijab* in Islamic legal tradition, see Mir-Hosseini (2007, forthcoming).

35 For a critical discussion of these two assumptions, see Abou El Fadl (2001: 239–247). In some extremist circles today, even a woman's voice is defined as 'awra.

Islamists and traditional Muslim scholars claim that the classical *fiqh* rulings are immutable and divinely ordained. It is not the intention here to enter a discussion on the theological validity of such a claim, or whether such a patriarchal reading of the Qur'an is justified. The legal logic of classical *fiqh* rulings must, of course, be understood in their own context. They must not be approached anachronistically. Judgement should be suspended when dealing with past tradition. But this does not mean that this tradition has to be accepted blindly or that it can't be dealt with critically. In this time and context it also needs to be asked: How far does such a conception of sexuality and gender rights reflect the principle of justice that is inherent in the very notion of *shari'a* as a path to follow? Why and how did classical jurists define these rulings so that women are under men's authority, and women's sexuality is men's property? What are the ethical and rational foundations for such notions of gender rights and sexuality? These questions become even more crucial if it is accepted – as it is here – that the classical jurists sincerely believed both that their findings were derived from the sacred sources of Islam and that they reflected the justice that is an indisputable part of the *shari'a*, as they understood it.

There are two sets of related answers. The first set is ideological and political, and has to do with the strong patriarchal ethos that informed the classical jurists' readings of the sacred texts and their exclusion of women from the production of religious knowledge. The further one moves from the era of the Prophet, the more it is found that women are marginalised and lose their political clout: their voice in the production of religious knowledge is silenced; their presence in public space is curtailed; their critical faculties are so far denigrated as to make their concerns irrelevant to law-making processes.[36] Women had been among the main transmitters of the *hadith* traditions, but by the time the *fiqh* schools were consolidated, over a century after the Prophet's death, they had reduced women to sexual beings and placed them under men's authority.[37] This was justified by a certain reading of Islam's sacred texts, and achieved through a set of legal constructs: *zina* as a *hadd* crime, with mandatory and fixed punishments; marriage as a contract by which a man acquires control over a woman's sexuality; and women's bodies as *'awra*, shameful.

The second set of answers is more theoretical, and concerns the ways in which patriarchal social norms, existing marriage practices and gender ideologies were sanctified, and then turned into fixed entities in *fiqh*. In brief, the genesis of gender inequality in Islamic legal

---

36 There is an extensive debate in the literature on this, which will not be entered into here. Some argue that the advent of Islam weakened the patriarchal structures of Arabian society, others that it reinforced them. The latter also maintain that, before the advent of Islam, society was undergoing a transition from matrilineal to patrilineal descent, that Islam facilitated this by giving patriarchy the seal of approval, and that the Qur'anic injunctions on marriage, divorce, inheritance, and whatever relates to women both reflect and affirm such a transition. For concise accounts of the debate, see Smith (1985) and Spellberg (1991).

37 As Abou-Bakr (2003) shows, women remained active in transmitting religious knowledge, but their activities were limited to the informal arena of homes and mosques, and their status as jurists was not officially recognised.

tradition lies in an inner contradiction between the ideals of the *shari'a* and the patriarchal structures in which these ideals unfolded and were translated into legal norms. Islam's call for freedom, justice and equality was submerged in the patriarchal norms and practices of 7th-century Arab society and culture and the formative years of Islamic law.[38]

In short, classical jurists' conceptions of justice and gender relations were shaped in interaction with the social, economic and political realities of the world in which they lived. In this world, patriarchy and slavery were part of the fabric of society; they were seen as the natural order of things, the way to regulate social relations. In their understanding of the sacred texts, these jurists were guided by their outlook, and in discerning the terms of the *shari'a*, they were constrained by a set of gender assumptions and legal theories that reflected the social and political realities of their age. The concepts of gender equality and human rights – as they are meant today – had no place and little relevance to their conceptions of justice.

It is crucial to remember that even if ideas of gender equality belong to the modern world, and were naturally absent in pre-modern legal theories and systems, nevertheless, until the 19th century, Islamic legal tradition granted women better rights than did its Western counterparts. For instance, Muslim women have always been able to retain their legal and economic autonomy in marriage, while in England it was not until 1882, with the passage of the Married Women's Property Act, that women acquired the right to retain ownership of property after marriage.

For Muslims, however, the encounter with modernity coincided with their painful and humiliating encounter with Western colonial powers, in which both women and family law became symbols of cultural authenticity and carriers of religious tradition, the battleground between the forces of traditionalism and modernity in the Muslim world – a situation that has continued ever since. As Leila Ahmed observes, this has confronted many Muslim women with a painful choice, between betrayal and betrayal. They have to choose between their Muslim identity – their faith – and their new gender consciousness (Ahmed 1984: 122).

One of the paradoxical and unintended consequences of political Islam has been to help create an arena within which many women can reconcile their faith and identity with their struggle for gender equality and human dignity. This did not happen because the Islamists offered an egalitarian vision of gender relations – they clearly did not. Rather, their very agenda of 'return to *shari'a*', and their attempt to translate *fiqh* rulings into policy, have provoked Muslim women to increased activism, which some refer to as 'Islamic feminism'.[39] The defence of patriarchal rulings as *shari'a*, as 'God's Law', as the authentic 'Islamic' way of life, brought the classical *fiqh* books out of the closet, and unintentionally exposed them to critical scrutiny and public debate. A growing number of women came to question whether

---

38 Mir-Hosseini (2003, 2007, 2009).

39 There is a growing literature on the politics and development of 'Islamic feminism'; for discussions and references, see Badran (2002, 2006) and Mir-Hosseini (2006 and 2011).

there was an inherent or logical link between Islamic ideals and patriarchy. This opened a space for an internal critique of patriarchal readings of the *shari'a* that was unprecedented in Muslim history. By the early 1990s, there emerged a new consciousness, a new way of thinking, a gender discourse that is arguing for equality for women on all fronts within the framework of Islam. This new discourse is nurtured by feminist scholarship in Islam that is showing how gender is constructed in Islamic legal tradition, uncovering a hidden history and rereading textual sources to unveil an egalitarian interpretation of the sacred texts.[40]

The emerging feminist scholarship on Islam is helping to bridge the wide gap that exists between the conceptions of justice that inform and underpin the dominant interpretations of the *shari'a* on the one hand, and human rights legislation on the other. This scholarship is part of a new trend of reformist religious thought that is consolidating notions of Islam and modernity as compatible, not opposed. Following and building on the work of earlier reformers, the new religious thinkers contend that human understanding of Islam's sacred texts is flexible; the texts can be interpreted as encouraging pluralism, human rights, democracy and gender equality. Revisiting the old theological debates, they aim to revive the rationalist approach that was eclipsed when legalism took over as the dominant mode and gave precedence to the form of the law over its substance and spirit. Where earlier reformers sought an Islamic genealogy for modern concepts, the new thinkers place the emphasis on how religious knowledge is produced and how religion is understood; how interpretations of the *shari'a* and *fiqh* constructs must be evaluated in their historical contexts.[41] This new trend of reformist thought helps to assess how these legal constructs have been reproduced, modified and redefined by those countries and communities that have reintroduced *zina* laws by 'Islamising' penal laws.

More importantly, this new religious thinking and its language can open a new and meaningful dialogue between Islamic law and international human rights law. Such a conversation can help to build an overlapping consensus and give human rights advocates the conceptual tools and the language to engage with Muslim communities. It can enable them to see *zina* laws as neither part of an irredeemably backward and patriarchal religion, nor as divine and immutable, but as an element in the complex web of norms and laws that classical jurists developed for the regulation of sexuality.[42] In other words, this conversation can help human rights advocates to see these laws for what they are: juristic constructions that have their roots in the tribal structures and patriarchal ideology of pre-Islamic Arabic, which continued into the Islamic era, though in a modified form.

For example, it can be shown how death by stoning (*rajm*) takes its textual justification not from the Qur'an but from the Sunnah. Jurists of all schools rely on three *hadith* to build

---

40 Feminist studies in Islam are too numerous to list here, but see especially Ahmed (1992), Al-Hibri (1982, 1997), Ali (2003, 2006, 2010), Barlas (2002), Hassan (1987, 1996) Mernissi (1991), Mir-Hosseini (2003, 2006, 2009, forthcoming), Wadud (1999, 2006).

41 For general introductions and some sample texts, see Kurzman (1998, 2002); Abu Zayd (2006).

42 For a discussion of Muslim feminists' discourse on *zina*, see Serrano (2009)

their legal arguments for stoning. This has been contested both by invoking arguments from classical *fiqh* theory, such as the textual primacy of Qur'an over *hadith*, and the fact that the authenticity of these *hadith* has been questioned,[43] as well as on human rights grounds. It can be stressed how the legal rulings in the Qur'an and the Sunnah must be understood in their historical and social contexts. For example, some have argued that stoning was a common form of execution at the time of the Prophet, and that it came into Islamic legal tradition as punishment for *zina* from Jewish tradition.[44]

Moreover, the Qur'an neither mandates stoning as punishment for adultery, nor speaks of any punishment for consensual sexual relations in private. As Asifa Quraishi rightly argues, *zina* as defined by classical jurists must be seen as a crime of public indecency rather than private sexual conduct. In her words, "(w)hile the Qur'an condemns extramarital sex as evil, it authorizes the Muslim legal system to prosecute someone for committing this crime *only* when the act is performed so openly that four people see them without invading their privacy."[45]

Defining crimes according to punishment is itself a juristic development. The expression *hudud Allah,* limits prescribed by God, appears 14 times in the Qur'an. Nowhere is it used in the sense of punishment, fixed or otherwise, nor is it stated specifically what these limits are.[46] As Fazlur Rahman notes, in two verses (Surah al-Baqarah 2: 229–30) the term appears six times in relation to divorce, demanding that men either retain or release their wives *bil-ma'ruf,* i.e in accordance with 'good custom'; each time, the term carries a slightly different meaning, but neither here nor elsewhere is it used in the sense of punishment. In his words:

> These facts should compel us to pause and think how little concerned the Qur'an is about the purely legal side and how much more and primarily with setting the moral tone of the Community. The legal side has undoubtedly to be done justice to and an adequate law has to be developed. But it is left to the Community to formulate this law in the light and moral spirit of the Qur'an which itself shows little tendency to lay down hard and fast laws. And doubly mistaken are those who claim to take the law of God into their own hands and seek to implement it literally.[47]

Summary and Conclusions

What are the implications of the analysis offered here for the Violence is Not Our Culture Campaign? This chapter has been mindful of two broad questions: What are the main

---

43 For examples, see Burton (1978, 1993), Engineer (2007), Kamali (2000).

44 For a discussion of debates in classical sources, see Burton (1978, 1993) and for new arguments based on human rights, see Baghi (2007), Engineer (2007), Quraishi (2008).

45 Quraishi (1997: 296). See also Karamah (n.d.).

46 See Kamali (1998: 219; 2000: 45–65).

47 Rahman (1965: 240).

challenges faced by women's rights activists in their campaign to abolish the *zina* laws? Can Islamic and human rights frameworks coexist, or in other words, how can an overlapping consensus be built? The chapter located *zina* laws in the context of the intersection between religion, culture and law in the regulation of sexuality in the Islamic legal tradition, and the shifting politics of relations between religion, law and gender in recent times. The premise here has been that a campaign against *zina* laws must be fully informed about the legal, social and political justifications of these laws, and the link between them and other laws and customs that sanction men's control over women's sexuality. *Zina* laws should not be treated in isolation; they are part of complex system for regulating women's behaviour, which is informed by a patriarchal reading of Islam's sacred texts and sustained by a set of outdated assumptions and juristic constructs about female sexuality, which are at the root of violence against women.

The reform and secularisation of penal laws and criminal justice systems in the first half of the 20th century, and their 'Islamisation' in the second half, has made it clear there can be no sustainable improvements in Muslim women's legal and social position while patriarchal interpretations of Islam's sacred texts remain unchallenged. Shifts in the 20th century in the politics of religion, law and gender led to the emergence of two powerful, yet opposing, frames of reference: international human rights law and political Islam. The encounter between them has produced a productive dialogue, and opened a new phase in the politics of gender and the battle between forces of traditionalism and modernism in the Muslim world. The crucial element of this phase has been that women themselves – rather than the abstract notion of 'women's rights in Islam' – are now at the heart of the argument.[48]

International human rights law gives activists a conceptual framework and language in which to criticise these laws as gender-based violence. But such an argument meets powerful opposition in countries and communities where religious discourse is paramount, where religious identity has become politicised, and where the Islamists set the terms of sexual and moral discourses. To be effective in such contexts, human rights norms and values must be articulated in a language that can engage with local cultures, practices, and religious traditions (Dembour 2001). This is a difficult task, a challenge that all human rights advocates must deal with in one way or another. Each context has its own specificities and dynamics, and presents its own challenges. In Muslim contexts, this challenge is given a particular edge by the domination of traditional *fiqh* and the ways in which its rulings have become embedded in customary cultural practices and sexual codes. The very fact that *zina* laws come under *hudud* – seen as 'God's limits' – gives the Islamists and the fundamentalists a real advantage, a ready-made argument for rejecting and denouncing reform as 'contrary to Islam'; hence the power of the Islamist rallying cry of 'return to *shari'a*'.

One of the main strategies adopted by human rights advocates is to name and shame offending governments into respecting and protecting rights. States that invoke religious

---

48 For elaboration on this, see Mir-Hosseini (2010).

misinterpretations to justify discrimination and violence against women have signed up to international human rights conventions; their lack of accountability in enacting the latter must be exposed. But in the eyes of many Muslims, the moral high ground and justice of international human rights law have been undermined by the politics and rhetoric of the so-called war on terror in the aftermath of the 9/11 attacks, as well as the West's unwavering support for Israel despite its escalating violations against the Palestinians and their land.[49] Claiming to be advocates of justice, Islamists thrive on being seen to oppose such outside interventions. In these new 21st century conditions, activists must also be able to engage in an internal discourse within Muslim communities (An-Na'im 2005). As Abdullahi An-Na'im points out, "although the apparent dichotomy between the so-called religious and secular discourses about the rights of women in Islamic societies is somewhat false or grossly exaggerated, its implications are too serious to be ignored in practice" (1995b: 51). A campaign that can bring Islamic and human rights perspectives together can be more persuasive and effective.

To reiterate the main points of the argument in this chapter:

- Strategies should be diverse and multi-levelled, and must be able to engage in an internal discourse within communities. Given the intimate links between Islamic legal tradition and culture, it is essential to frame arguments for reform and change concurrently within both Islamic and human rights frameworks.
- In a campaign against *zina* laws or stoning, for strategies of confrontation such as 'naming and shaming' to be more than political rhetoric and be effective in persuading governments or Islamists to change laws or practices, they must be combined with a process of engagement, dialogue and debate in which all sides have the opportunity to articulate principles and defend practices. This has worked, for example, in Morocco with the reform of Family Law following years of women's activism and engagement with clerics;[50] and in Pakistan, with the amendment of *zina* laws following the intervention of the Council of Islamic Ideology.[51]
- As a general principle, if the aim is to persuade some other group to change their practices or laws, it is more effective to argue that they transgress their own principles; that an alternative law or practice might be more in accordance with both their principles and those of others – including international human rights law.
- The principles and ideals of the Qur'an reflect universal norms that have resonance in contemporary human rights standards, and provide the basis for an ethical critique from within an Islamic framework of penal laws based on classical jurisprudence.

---

49 For an incisive discussion of dilemmas encountered by international NGOs working in Muslim contexts, see Modirzadeh (2006).
50 Buskens (2003); Collectif 95 Maghreb-Egalité (2005).
51 Council of Islamic Ideology (2006); also Lau (2007).

Bibliography

Abou-Bakr, Omaima (2003), 'Teaching the Words of the Prophet: Women Instructors of the Hadith (Fourteenth and Fifteenth Centuries)', *Hawwa: Journal of Women of the Middle East and the Islamic World* 1 (3): 306–328.

Abou El Fadl, Khaled (2001), *Speaking in God's Name: Islamic Law, Authority and Women*. Oxford: Oneworld.

——— (2004–5), 'The Place of Ethical Obligations in Islamic Law', *UCLA Journal of Islamic and Near Eastern Law* 4 (1): 1–40.

Abu-Odeh, Lama (1996), 'Crimes of Honour and the Construction of Gender in Arab Society', in Mai Yamani (ed.), *Feminism and Islam*. Reading: Ithaca Press.

Abu Zayd, Nasr Hamid (2001), 'The Qur'anic Concept of Justice', *Polylog: Forum for International Philosophy* 3, http://them.polylog.org/3/fan-en.htm

——— (2006), *Reformation of Islamic Thought: A Critical Analysis*. Amsterdam: Amsterdam University Press.

Ahmed, Leila (1984), 'Early Feminist Movements in the Middle East: Turkey and Egypt', in Freda Hussain (ed.), *Muslim Women*. London: Croom Helm.

——— (1991), 'Early Islam and the Position of Women: The Problem of Interpretation', in Nikki Keddie and Beth Baron (eds.), *Women in Middle Eastern History,* 58–73. New Haven: Yale University Press.

Al-'Ashmawi, Muhammad Sa'id (2004), *Usul al-Shari'a* (The Principles of Shari'a), 5th Ed. Beirut: Al-hintasar al-Arabi.

Al-Hibri, Aziza (1982), 'A Study of Islamic Herstory: Or How Did We Get Into This Mess', in *Islam and Women*, special issue of *Women's Studies International Forum* 5(2): 207–19.

——— (1997), 'Islam, Law and Custom: Redefining Muslim Women's Rights', *American University Journal of International Law and Policy* 12: 1–44.

Ali, Kecia (2003), 'Progressive Muslims and Islamic Jurisprudence: The Necessity for Critical Engagement with Marriage and Divorce Law', in Omid Safi (ed.), *Progressive Muslims: On Justice, Gender, and Pluralism*, 163–189. Oxford: Oneworld.

——— (2006), *Sexual Ethics and Islam: Feminist Reflections on Quran, Hadith and Jurisprudence*. Oxford: Oneworld.

——— (2010), 'Marriage in Classical Islamic Jurisprudence: A Survey of Doctrines', in Asifa Quraishi and Frank Vogel (eds.), *The Islamic Marriage Contract: Case Studies in Islamic Family Law*, 11–45. Cambridge, MA: Islamic Legal Studies, Harvard Law School.

——— (2010), *Marriage and Slavery in Early Islam*. Cambridge, MA: Harvard University Press.

Amnesty International (2008), 'Iran: End Executions by Stoning', 15 January 2008, http://www.amnesty.org/en/library/info/MDE13/001/2008/en

An-Na'im, Abdullahi Ahmed (1990), 'Problems of Universal Cultural Legitimacy of Human Rights', in Abdullahi An-Na'im and Francis Deng (eds.), *Human Rights in Africa: Cross-Cultural Perspectives*, 331–367. Washington: Brookings Institution Press.

—— (1995a) "What Do We Mean By Universal?", *Index on Censorship* 4 (5): 120–28.

—— (1995b), "The Dichotomy Between Religious and Secular Discourse in Islamic Societies', in Mahnaz Afkhami (ed.) *Faith and Freedom: Women's Human Rights in the Muslim World*, 51–60. London and New York: I B Tauris.

—— (2005), 'The Role of "Community Discourse" in Combating "Crimes of Honour": Preliminary Assessment and Prospects', in Lynn Welchman and Sara Hossain (eds.), *Honour: Crimes, Paradigms, Reproductive Health and Women's Rights*, 64–77. London: Zed Books.

Baderin, Mashood (2001), 'Establishing Areas of Common Ground Between Islamic Law and International Human Rights', *International Journal of Human Rights* 5 (2): 72–113.

—— (2007), 'Islam and the Realization of Human Rights in the Muslim World: A Reflection on Two Essential Approaches and Two Divergent Perspectives', *Muslim World Journal of Human Rights* 4 (1), http://www.bepress.com/mwjhr/

Badran, Margot (2002), 'Islamic Feminism: What's in a Name?', *Al-Ahram Weekly Online* 569 (17–23 Jan), http://weekly.ahram.org.eg/2002/569/cu1.htm

—— (2006), 'Islamic Feminism Revisited', *CounterCurrents.Org*, http://www.countercurrents.org/gen-badran100206.htm

Baghi, Emadeddin (2007), 'The Bloodied Stone: Execution by Stoning', International Campaign for Human Rights in Iran, 2 August 2007, http://www.iranhumanrights.org/2008/08/baghibloodiedstone

Barlas, Asma (2002), *Believing Women in Islam: Unreading Patriarchal Interpretations of the Qur'an*. Austin: University of Texas Press.

Bassiouni, M. Cherif (1997), 'Crimes and the Criminal Process', *Arab Law Quarterly* 12 (3): 269–86.

Bassiouni and G. Badr (2002), 'The Shari'ah: Sources, Interpretation, and Rule-Making', *UCLA Journal of Islamic and Near Eastern Law* 1(2): 135–81.

Bielefeldt, Heiner (1995), 'Muslim Voices in the Human Rights Debate', *Human Rights Quarterly* 14 (4): 587–617.

—— (2000), '"Western" versus "Islamic" Human Rights Conceptions? A Critique of Cultural Essentialism in the Discussion on Human Rights', *Political Theory* 28 (1): 90–121.

Burton, John (1978), 'The Origin of the Islamic Penalty of Adultery', *Transactions of the Glasgow University Oriental Society* 26: 16–26.

—— (1993), 'Law and Exegesis: The Penalty for Adultery in Islam', in G.R. Hawting and Abdul-Kader A. Shareef (eds.), *Approaches to the Qur'an*, 269–284. London: Routledge.

Buskens, Leon (2006), 'Recent Debates on Family Law Reform in Morocco: Islamic Law as Politics in an Emerging Public Sphere', *Islamic Law and Society* 10 (1): 71–131.

Clark, Linda (2003), 'Hijab According to the *Hadith*', in Sajida Alvi, Homa Hoodfar, and Sheila McDonough (eds.) *The Muslim Veil in North America: Issues and Debates,* 214–286. Toronto: Women's Press.

Collectif 95 Maghreb-Egalité (2005), *Guide to Equality in the Family in the Maghreb* (English ed.). Washington DC: Women's Learning Partnership for Rights, Development and Peace (WLP).

Council of Islamic Ideology (2006), *Hudood Ordinance 1979: A Critical Report*. Islamabad: Government of Pakistan.

Dembour, Marie-Bénédicte (2001), 'Following the Movement of a Pendulum: Between Universalism and Relativism', in Jane Cowan, Marie-Bénédicte Dembour and Richard Wilson (eds.), *Culture and Rights: Anthropological Perspectives,* 56–79. Cambridge: Cambridge University Press.

El-Awa, Mohamed S. (1993) [1981], *Punishment in Islamic Law*. Plainfield, IN: American Trust Publications.

Engineer, Asghar Ali. (2007), 'Adultery and Qur'anic Punishment', *Future Islam* (1 May), http://www.futureislam.com/20070501/insight/asgharali/Adultery_and_Quranic_Punishment.asp

Fierro, Maribel (2007), 'Idr'u l-Hudud bi-l-Shubuhat: When Lawful Violence Meets Doubt', *Hawwa: Journal of Women of the Middle East and the Islamic World* 5 (2–3): 208–38.

Gallie, Bernard (1956), 'Essentially Contested Concepts', *Proceedings of the Aristotelian Society* (New Series) 56: 167–198.

Gibb, H.A.R and J.H. Kramers (1961), 'Zina', *Shorter Encyclopedia of Islam*. Leiden: Brill, pp658–59.

Haeri, Shahla (1989), *Law of Desire: Temporary Marriage in Iran*. London: I. B. Tauris.

Hajjaji-Jarrah, Soraya (2003), 'Women in Qur'anic Commentaries', in Sajida Alvi, Homa Hoodfar, and Sheila McDonough (eds.) *The Muslim Veil in North America: Issues and Debates,* 181–213. Toronto: Women's Press.

Hallaq, Wael (1997), *A History of Islamic Legal Theories*. Cambridge: Cambridge University Press.

Hassan, Riffat (1987), 'Equal Before Allah? Woman-Man Equality in the Islamic Tradition', *Harvard Divinity Bulletin* 7 (2) (Jan–May); also in her *Selected Articles*, Women Living Under Muslim Laws, n.d., 26–29.

——— (1996), 'Feminist Theology: Challenges for Muslim Women', *Critique: Journal for Critical Studies of the Middle East* 9: 53–65.

Hunter, Shireen T and Huma Malik (eds.) (2005), *Islam and Human Rights: Advancing a US-Muslim Dialogue*. Washington: Center for Strategic and International Studies.

Ibn Rushd (1996), *The Distinguished Jurist's Primer*, vol. II (*Bidayat al-Mujtahid wa Nihayat al-Muqtasid*), translated by Imran Ahsan Khan Nyazee. Reading: Garnet Publishing.

Imam, Ayesha (2005), 'Women's Reproductive and Sexual Rights and the Offence of Zina in Muslim Laws in Nigeria', in Wendy Chavkin and Ellen Chesler (eds.), *Where Human Rights Begin: Health, Sexuality, and Women in the New Millennium*. New Brunswick, NJ: Rutgers University Press.

Jahangir, Asma and Hinda Jilani (1988), *The Hudood Ordinances: A Divine Sanction?* Lahore: Rhotac Books.

Jahanpour, Farhang (2007), 'Islam and Human Rights', *Journal of Globalization for the Common Good* (spring), http://lass.calumet.purdue.edu/cca/jgcg/2007/sp07/jgcg-sp07-jahanpour.htm; also at http://www.payvand.com/news/07/apr/1173.html.

Jansen, Willy (2000), 'Sleeping in the Womb: Protracted Pregnancies in the Maghreb', *The Muslim World* 90: 218–37.

Kamali, Mohammad Hashim (1998), 'Punishment in Islamic Law: A Critique of the Hudud Bill of Kelantan, Malaysia', *Arab Law Quarterly*: 203–34.

—— (1999), *Freedom, Equality, and Justice in Islam*. Kuala Lumpur: Ilmiah Publishers, and Markfield: The Islamic Foundation UK.

—— (2000) [1995], *Punishment in Islamic Law: An Inquiry into the Hudud Bill of Kelantan*. Kuala Lumpur: Ilmiah Publishers.

—— (2006), *An Introduction to Shari'ah*. Kuala Lumpur: Ilmiah Publishers.

Karamah: Muslim Women Lawyers For Human Rights (n.d.), 'Zina, Rape, and Islamic Law: An Islamic Legal Analysis of the Rape Laws in Pakistan', position paper available at http://www.karamah.org/articles.htm

Kugle, Scott Siraj al-Haqq (2003), 'Sexuality, diversity and ethics in the agenda of progressive Muslims', in Omid Safi (ed.), *Progressive Muslims: On Justice, Gender, and Pluralism*, 190–234. Oxford: Oneworld.

—— (2010), *Homosexuality in Islam: Islamic Reflections on Gay, Lesbian, and Transgender Muslims*. Oxford: Oneworld.

Kurzman, Charles (ed.) (1998), *Liberal Islam: A Sourcebook*. Oxford: Oxford University Press.

—— (ed.) (2002), *Modernist Islam 1840–1940: A Sourcebook*. Oxford: Oxford University Press.

Lau, Martin (2007), 'Twenty-Five Years of Hudood Ordinances: A Review', in *Washington and Lee Law Review* 64: 1291–1314.

Maghniyyah, Muhammad Jawad (1997), *Marriage According to Five Schools of Islamic Law*, vol. V. Tehran: Department of Translation and Publication, Islamic Culture and Relations Organization.

Marmon, Shaun (1999), 'Domestic Slavery in the Mamluk Empire: A Preliminary Sketch', in Shaun Marmon (ed.), *Slavery in the Islamic Middle East*, 1–23. Princeton: Department of Near Eastern Studies.

Masud, Muhammad Khalid (2009), '*Ikhtilaf al-Fuqaha*: Diversity in Fiqh as Social Construction', in Zainah Anwar (ed.), *Wanted: Equality and Justice in the Muslim Family*, 65–93. Kuala Lumpur: Sisters in Islam, also available at www.musawah.org

Mernissi, Fatima (1985), *Beyond the Veil: Male-Female Dynamics in Muslim Society* (Revised ed.). London: Al Saqi.

——— (1991), *Women and Islam: An Historical and Theological Enquiry*, translated by Mary Jo Lakeland. Oxford: Blackwell.

Merry, Sally Engle (2003), 'Human Rights Law and the Demonization of Culture (and Anthropology Along the Way)', *Political and Legal Anthropology Review* 26 (1): 55–76.

——— (2006), *Human Rights and Gender Violence: Translating International Law into Local Justice*. Chicago: Chicago University Press.

——— (2009), *Gender Violence: A Cultural Perspective*. Malden/Oxford: Wiley-Blackwell.

Mir-Hosseini, Ziba (1993), *Marriage on Trial: A Study of Islamic Family Law, Iran and Morocco Compared*. London: I. B. Tauris.

——— (2003), 'The Construction of Gender in Islamic Legal Thought: Strategies for Reform', *Hawwa: Journal of Women of the Middle East and the Islamic World* 1 (1): 1–28.

——— (2004), 'Sexuality, Rights and Islam: Competing Gender Discourses in Post-Revolutionary Iran', in Guity Nashat and Lois Beck (eds.), *Women in Iran from 1800 to the Islamic Republic*, 204–217. Urbana and Chicago: University of Illinois Press.

——— (2006), 'Muslim Women's Quest for Equality: Between Islamic Law and Feminism', *Critical Inquiry* 32 (4): 629–645.

——— (2007), 'The Politics and Hermeneutics of Hijab in Iran: From Confinement to Choice', *Muslim World Journal of Human Rights* 4 (1) (Summer-Fall), http://www.bepress.com/mwjhr/vol4/iss1/art2/

——— (2009), 'Towards Gender Equality: Muslim Family Laws and the *Shari'ah*', in Zainah Anwar (ed.), *Wanted: Equality and Justice in the Muslim Family*, 23–63. Kuala Lumpur: Sisters in Islam, also available at www.musawah.org

——— (2011), 'Beyond "Islam" vs "Feminism"', forthcoming in *IDS Bulletin* 42 (1).

——— (2011 forthcoming), 'Hijab and Choice: Between Politics and Theology', forthcoming in Mehran Kamrava (ed.), *Innovations in Islam: Traditions and Contributions*. Berkeley: University of California Press.

Mir-Hosseini, Ziba and Richard Tapper (2009), 'Islamism: *ism* or *wasm*?', in Richard Martin and Abbas Barzegar (eds.), *Islamism: Contested Perspectives on Political Islam*, 81–86. Palo Alto, CA: Stanford University Press.

Modirzadeh, Naz K. (2006), 'Taking Islamic Law Seriously: INGOs and the Battle for Muslim Hearts and Minds', *Harvard Human Rights Journal* 19: 193–233.

Peters, Rudoph (1994), 'The Islamization of Criminal Law: A Comparative Analysis', *Die Welt des Islams*, New Series 34 (2): 246–274.

―――― (2003), 'From Jurists' Law to Statute Law or What Happens When the Sharia is Codified', in B. A. Roberson (ed.), *Shaping the Current Islamic Reformation*, 82–95. London: Frank Cass.

―――― (2005), *Crime and Punishment in Islamic Law: Theory and Practice from the Sixteenth to the Twenty-First Century*. Cambridge: Cambridge University Press.

―――― (2006), 'The Re-Islamization of Criminal Law in Northern Nigeria and the Judiciary: The Saffiyatu Hussaini Case', in Muhammad Khalid Masud, Rudolph Peters and David Powers (eds.), *Dispensing Justice: Qadis and their Judgements*. Leiden: Brill, pp219–241.

Quraishi, Asifa (1996–1997), 'Her Honor: An Islamic Critique of the Rape Laws of Pakistan From a Woman-Sensitive Perspective', *Michigan Journal of International Law* 18: 287–320.

―――― (2008), 'Who Says Shari'a Demands the Stoning of Women? A Description of Islamic Law and Constitutionalism', *Berkeley Journal of Middle Eastern & Islamic Law* 1: 163–77, http://ssrn.com/abstract=1140204

Rahman, Fazlur (1965), 'The Concept of Hadd in Islamic Law', *Islamic Studies* 4: 237–252.

―――― (1966), 'Shari'a', Chapter 6 of his *Islam*. Chicago: Chicago University Press. 1st Ed., 100–16, http://www.globalwebpost.com/farooqm/study_res/default.html

―――― (1982), 'The Status of Women in Islam: A Modernist Interpretation', in Hanna Papanek & Gail Minault (eds.), *Separate World: Studies of Purdah in South Asia*. Delhi: Chanakya Publications.

Reuters (2009), 'Somali Hardliners Whip Women for Wearing Bras; Men Whipped for Shaving, Women Made to Shake Breasts', *Al Arabiya*, 16 October, http://www.alarabiya.net/save_print.php?print=1&cont_id=88238&lang=en

Safwat, Safia (1982), 'Offences and Penalties in Islamic Law', *Islamic Quarterly* 26 (3): 149–81.

Sajoo, Amyn B. (1999), 'Islam and Human Rights: Congruence or Dichotomy', *Temple International and Comparative Law Journal* 4: 23–34.

Sen, Amartya (1998), 'Universal Truths: Human Rights and the Westernizing Illusion', *Harvard International Review* 20 (3) (Summer): 40–43, http://www.mtholyoke.edu/acad/intrel/asian values/sen.htm

Serrano, Delfina (2007), 'Rape in Maliki Legal Doctrine and Practice (8th–15th Centuries C.E.)', *Hawwa: Journal of Women of the Middle East and the Islamic World* 1 (1): 167–207.

―――― (2009), 'Muslim Feminists' Discourse on *zina*: New Paradigms in Sight?', in Roswitha Badry, Maria Rohrer and Karin Steiner (eds.), *Liebe, Sexualitat, Ehe und Partnerschaft-Paradigmen im Wandel*, Freiburg: Fördergemeinschaft wissenschaftlicher Publikationen von Frauen e.V.

Sidahmed, Abdel Salam (2001), 'Problems in Contemporary Applications of Islamic Criminal Sanctions: the Penalty for Adultery in Relation to Women', *British Journal of Middle Eastern Studies* 28 (2): 187–204.

Smith, Jane (1985), 'Women, Religion and Social Change in Early Islam', in Yvonne Yazbeck Haddad and Ellison Banks Findly (eds.), *Women, Religion, and Social Change,* 19–36. Albany: SUNY Press.

——— (2000), 'Islamic Revival and Reform: Theological Approaches', in *Reason, Freedom, & Democracy in Islam: Essential Writings of 'Abdolkarim Sorush*, translated and edited with a critical introduction by Mahmoud Sadri and Ahmed Sadri. Oxford: Oxford University Press.

——— (2002), 'Islam, Revelation and Prophethood: An Interview with Abdulkarim Soroush about the Expansion of Prophetic Experience', *Aftab* 15, http://www.drsoroush.com/English.htm

——— (2007), 'The Beauty of Justice', *CSD Bulletin* 14 (1–2) (Summer): 8–12, http://www.drsoroush.com/English.htm

Spellberg, Denise (1991), 'Political Action and Public Example: A'isha and the Battle of the Camel', in Beth Baron and Nikki Keddie (eds.), *Women in Middle Eastern History: Shifting Boundaries in Sex and Gender.* New Haven: Yale University Press.

Strawson, John (1997), 'A Western Question to the Middle East: "Is There a Human Rights Discourse in Islam?"', *Arab Studies Quarterly* 19 (1) (Winter): 31–57.

Terman, Rochelle (2007), 'The Stop Stoning Forever Campaign: A Report', Women Living Under Muslim Laws, http://www.meydaan.com/UserFiles/File/Terman_stoning-2.pdf

Wadud, Amina (1999), *Qur'an and Woman: Rereading of the Sacred Text from a Woman's Perspective*, New York: Oxford University Press.

——— (2004), 'Qur'an, Gender and Interpretive Possibilities', *Hawwa: Journal of Women of the Middle East and the Islamic World* 2 (3): 317–336.

——— (2006), *Inside the Gender Jihad: Women's Reform in Islam*. Oxford: Oneworld.

——— (2009), 'Islam Beyond Patriarchy Through Gender Inclusive Qur'anic Analysis', in Zainah Anwar (ed.), *Wanted: Equality and Justice in the Muslim Family*, 95–112. Kuala Lumpur: Sisters in Islam; also available at www.musawah.org

Weiss, Bernard G. (1997–98), 'Interpretation in Islamic Law: The Theory of Ijtihad', *American Journal of Comparative Law* 26: 199–212.

——— (2003), *The Spirit of Islamic Law*. Atlanta: University of Georgia Press.

Welchman, Lynn (2007), 'Honour and Violence Against Women in Modern Shari'a Discourse', *Hawwa: Journal of Women in the Middle East and the Islamic World* 5 (2–3): 165–47.

Willis, John Ralph (1985), 'The Ideology of Enslavement in Islam Introduction', in John Ralph Willis (ed.), *Slaves and Slavery in Muslim Africa*, vol. 1, 1–15. London: Frank Cass.

Zuhur, Sharif (2008), "Criminal Law, Women and Sexuality in the Middle East", in Pinar Ilkkaracan (ed.), *Deconstructing Sexuality in the Middle East*, 17–40. Aldershot: Ashgate.

Yusuf 'Ali, 'Abdullah (1999), *The Meaning of The Holy Qur'an* (10th Ed. with Revised Translation, Commentary and Newly Compiled Comprehensive Index). Maryland: Amana Publications.

Indonesia

COUNTRY PROFILE

The Republic of Indonesia comprises a vast archipelago of at least 17,503 islands in South East Asia, populated by 232 million people from over 300 different ethnic groups. As more than 86 per cent of its citizens are considered Muslim, Indonesia is often referred to as the world's most populous Muslim-majority country. Muslim communities in the country are exceptionally heterogeneous, although the majority are nominally Sunni, following the jurisprudential traditions of the Shafi'i school.

Indonesia today is a democratic presidential republic, subsequent to turbulent political changes and the first direct presidential elections held in 2004. After the declaration of independence by Sukarno, who became the first president of Indonesia, an anti-colonial war was waged against the Dutch (1945–50), followed by parliamentary democracy with the government responsible to the House of Representatives elected directly by the people (1950–56), which was then superseded by 'guided democracy' and martial law (1957–65). The subsequent president, Suharto, imposed an equally, perhaps even more, authoritarian regime called the 'New Order' (1965–98), which was brought down by an uprising of people mobilised by the *reformasi* (reform) movement. The post-Suharto era, from 1998 onwards, is marked by political decentralisation, which created greater regional autonomy and the development of democratic institutions and procedures.

Indonesia has three concurrent legal systems: the inherited system of Dutch colonial laws; the system of Muslim laws derived from selective interpretations of the predominantly Shafi'i *fiqh*; and, the system of local customary 'laws' based on what the Dutch recognised and codified as custom within different indigenous cultures.

While human rights enshrined in the 1945 Constitution, as well as a number of state laws, most notably Law 7/1984 on the Ratification of the 1979 Convention on the Elimination of All Forms of Discrimination against Women (CEDAW), guarantee gender equality and freedom from gender-based discrimination, some Indonesian legal provisions have a markedly adverse effect on access to gender justice. The latter derives from two distinct patriarchies: (1) a largely secular, state-based, gender-discriminatory ideology conceived of during the Suharto era; and (2) a right-wing political manifestation of Muslim 'revivalism' promoted by non-state actors and members of provincial/local governments, in hopes of greater political influence. The first current is mainly responsible for gender-biased national legislation, while the second camp is by and large responsible for discriminatory provincial and local regulations and by-laws. Under Suharto, the gender-biased national laws are exemplified particularly by the Marriage Law 1/1974 (Undang-Undang Perkawinan) and a state-sanctioned version of controversial legal rules of some Shafi'i *fiqh*, in the guise of the 1991 Compilation of Islamic Laws, promulgated via presidential

> instruction (Instruksi Presiden 1/1991 tentang Penyebarluasan Kompilasi Hukum Islam). In the post-Suharto era, there is a worrying confluence of the two forms of patriarchy, epitomised in the oppressive Law 44/2008 on Pornography (Undang-Undang Pornografi). As an example of the right-wing religious and political influence, there were at least 63 regional regulations (*peraturan daerah* or *perda*; in Aceh *qanun*) issued at either the provincial or district level between 1999 and 2009, which directly discriminate against women. Some of them are implicitly related to *zina*; for example, the Acehnese *qanun* (14/2003) – which regards the 'illicit' seclusion of persons of opposite genders (*khalwat*) – is justified as a preventive measure against adultery, or via the regulations of various municipalities, including Tasikmalaya, Tangerang and Bekasi in West Java, which have outlawed prostitution, on the grounds that it is a form of *zina*. The Acehnese Muslim Criminal Code (Qanun Jinayat) was meant to criminalise *zina* as a *hadd* crime and includes lashes and stoning to death as legitimate punishments for this offence. However, its entry into force is indefinitely barred due to opposition from the provincial governor.

The national motto of the Republic of Indonesia is often loosely translated as 'unity in diversity' (Old Javanese: *bhinneka tunggal ika*, 'fragmented, yet one') and it is, as the prime national value, enshrined in the 1945 Constitution (Article 36A). Indeed, it seems only right that this colourful archipelago, ripe with so many natural, historical, cultural and religious differences, is kept together on the promise of its state ideologues that such plurality must be preserved. Along with these pluralities, however, a variety of patriarchies have also developed and established themselves by means of totalising discourses on gender, sexuality and religion. For instance, during the Suharto era (1965–98), the state promoted *ibuisme* ('motherism') as an important part of its nation-building project, which claimed that the 'ideal' Indonesian woman is a mother that forgoes all her personal ambitions for the sake of her children and country. In contrast to this state-sponsored model of the past, oppositional Muslim right-wing political forces have utilised the decentralised political arena of post-Suharto Indonesia to usher in another form of patriarchy, which defines women as almost exclusively confined to the household and subordinate to their husbands, and adhering to strict dress codes and moral rules derived from the 'revivalist' visions[1] of an 'Islamic society'.

Both of these patriarchies have sought to legitimise their *raison d'être* by reference to *shari'a* (Indonesian: *syariah, syari'ah, syariat, syari'at*), particularly by demanding '*shari'a*-inspired' legislative reforms. In so doing, they have aspired to quite specific political gains. Suharto's regime, on the one hand, sought to establish the state as the only 'right' interpreter of religious law, which would destabilise oppositional forces who were also quite keen

---

1 'Revivalism' is an ideological concoction of various 'reformist' Muslim religio-political movements; it purports to 'revive' an 'original' 'Islamic society' through literal interpretations of the Qur'an and the Sunna. See, for example, Perwita 2007: 32.

on employing religion in their political agendas. In other words, it was the strategy of a predominantly secular state elite to instrumentalise religion to ensure societal control. The Muslim right-wing political groups, on the other hand, have played the '*shari'a* card' in the hopes of gaining greater access to state power or retaining positions in local governments, by appealing to and radicalising certain religious sentiments in the general populace. Thus, the Suharto government's 'official' patriarchy manifested itself mainly in the domain of national family law; the 'oppositional' Muslim right-wing politics of the post-Suharto era, unable to take over the central government, have succeeded in enacting certain gender-discriminatory provincial regulations and by-laws, mainly related to family law, dress codes and 'public morality' regulations. The Indonesian special territory (*daerah istimewa*) of Aceh, owing to its exceptional political autonomy, has gone even further by outlawing *khalwat* and trying, albeit (still) unsuccessfully, to criminalise *zina* in accordance with its own reading of the classical Shafi'i *fiqh*.

In this chapter, these developments are scrutinised and contrasted with an analytical portrayal of Indonesian civic resistance against them, organised primarily by the country's vibrant women's movement. Civil society's resistance to legislative oppression is analysed both through the available documentation (reports, case law, policies, academic accounts, etc.) and via a brief empirical research of some prominent local human rights defenders.[2]

This chapter, firstly, delves into the various historical developments upon which the Indonesian political, cultural and religious considerations of gender and sexuality have been predicated and, subsequently, legally determined. Secondly, it assesses the national laws and the provincial by-laws that are intrinsically gender-biased and designed to control women's sexuality and sociality. Thirdly, this chapter analyses the failure of the Indonesian administrative and judicial authorities to fulfil their constitutional and international legal obligations with respect to women's human rights and non-discrimination. Fourthly and finally, in search of best practices for combating gender injustice and the control of sexuality by both the state and non-state actors, this chapter interrogates civil society's resistance to sexual and gender-discriminatory legislation.

Historical Background

Indonesian cultural plurality and its resultant heterogeneous Muslim communities have been famously described by the anthropologist Clifford Geertz as "remarkably malleable, tentative, syncretistic, and, most significantly of all, multivoiced" (Geertz 1971: 12). Although contemporary knowledge of the historical emergence of Muslim communities throughout

---

2 Indonesian human rights activists/experts, working predominantly in Aceh, were asked to complete a questionnaire, wherein their opinions on relevant legislative developments were sought. Acehnese civil society representatives were the main focus of the empirical segment of this study because of the paradigmatic legal changes in this autonomous province leading to a 'step by step' introduction of a number of 'Islamic' by-laws based on gender-discriminatory interpretations of the selected Shafi'i *fiqh*.

the Indonesian archipelago is still being developed, it is certain that this emergence has been distinctly uneven and shaped by various geopolitical and cultural factors (Ricklefs 2001).

The Javanese Muslims, for instance, have developed a distinctly esoteric approach to their faith and lifestyle, concomitantly inspired by Sufism and their pre-Muslim spiritual traditions. The mystical way (Javanese: *tarekat*) and idea of law (Javanese: *sarengat*) have been perceived as inextricable from one another, resulting in the emergence of spiritual scholars of rather unique mystico-legal mastery, called *kyai* (for men) or *nyai* (for women) (Lukens-Bull 2005; Dhofier 1999; Ricklefs 2001). They are known as the so-called 'traditionalist' stream of the Indonesian *umma*, which is publicly represented primarily by the Nahdlatul Ulama (NU), a religious organisation of approximately 60 million members, which has an affiliated political party – Partai Kebangkitan Bangsa (PKB; the National Awakening Party).

In 1948 – in contrast to the *kyai/nyai*-style of adherence to the Muslim faith – militant Muslim guerrillas, spearheaded by the Javanese 'mystic' SM Kartosuwirjo, declared an insurgent state in West Java named Negara Islam Indonesia (Indonesian Islamic State), better known as Darul Islam (from Arabic *dar al-Islam*, 'abode of Islam'), which was founded upon his own 'revivalist' interpretations of *shari'a*. Muslim rebels in South Sulawesi and Aceh joined Kartosuwirjo, acknowledging him as their leader. The central government waged a bloody war against Darul Islam until Kartosuwirjo was captured and executed in 1962 (Ricklefs 2001: 279). Despite its relatively short existence, Darul Islam is significant as a paradigm of the 'revivalist' political aspirations in Indonesia, which regained strength during the post-Suharto *reformasi* era, particularly in Aceh. This province's distinct history – a sultanate with seemingly strict adherence to a more legalistic, classical *fiqh*-inspired, Muslim praxis – and complex and mostly antagonistic relationship with the central state's administration have paved the way for such a radical, right-wing political vision of Islam to thrive.

'Revivalist' political Islam, with its distinct version of patriarchy and generally right-wing orientation, is a century-old phenomenon in Indonesia (Feener 2007; Hooker 2003; Bowen 2003; Ricklefs 2001). Following the 1998 upheavals, which resulted in the demise of the 'New Order' regime, this phenomenon became even more pronounced with the emergence of Muslim militias (*laskar*), militant delinquents (specialising in 'mob justice' and 'moral-imposing' raids) and radical student organisations (Abuza 2007).[3] The *reformasi*

---

3 Notable militias include: Laskar Jihad, Laskar Mujahidin and Laskar Jundullah. Front Pembela Islam (the Defenders of Islam) are often associated with the oppressive public raids and 'sweeps', resulting in open violence against those who, in their view, transgress Muslim moral norms. Radical (non-violent) student groups include: the Komite Indonesia Untuk Solidaritas Dunia Islam (Indonesian Committee for Solidarity of the Islamic World), Himpunan Mahasiswa Muslim Antar Kampus (Association of Inter-Campus Muslim Student Action) and the Kesetuan Aksi Mahasiswa Muslim Indonesia (Indonesian Muslim Students Action Front). At the extreme end, there are also semi-underground movements linked with international terrorist networks, such as Jemaah Islamiyah; and overt branches of transnational right-wing religio-political movements, such as Hizb ut-Tahrir. See Abuza 2007.

movement, however, unified Indonesian Muslim humanists and human rights activists with allies among top state officials. Such allies included *kyai* Abdurrahman Wahid, the president of Indonesia in 1999–2001 and, before that, the long-time reformist leader of the NU; and Indonesia's first woman president (2001–04), Megawati Sukarnoputri, whose presidential candidacy was jointly defended (against the 'revivalist' assertions that a woman cannot be the leader of a state) by the women's branches of both the NU and another major Indonesian Muslim politico-religious organisation representing the so-called 'modernist' Muslims (the respective branches are called Fatayat NU and Aisyiyah) (Machrusah 2010: 79).

One of the paradigmatic features of the Indonesian right-wing in both political and religious domains has been its consistent and pervasive focus on the regulation of gender roles. These roles have been modelled on stark patriarchal systems, purporting to reflect '*the* Muslim' division between women's and men's social rights and responsibilities. The state version of patriarchy, as promoted by the Suharto regime, endeavoured to regulate women's bodies and behaviour in order to use them as the 'living tokens' of the (permanently endangered) national unity and its ideological foundations (Martyn 2005: 23). Thus, the constitutional promise of the status of "Indonesian women as equal citizens [has been] undercut by the government's recognition that their membership of subordinate groups in society actually overrides their 'equal' membership of the polity" (Blackburn 1999: 192). In one of the governmental family welfare educational programmes, women's role in society has been reduced to the following five duties: (1) wife and faithful companion to her husband; (2) manager of the household; (3) producer of the nation's future generations; (4) mother and educator of her children; and (5) citizen (Hull 1976; Sullivan 1994; Bennett 2005: 26). In a similar vein, since the early 1970s, the nationwide, state-sponsored contest *The Model Mother* (*Ibu Teladan*) has outlined the following criteria for its prospective winner: she "was expected to have been married for at least 15 years (increased in 1976 to 25 years, and by 1992 to 30 years), to have children, be able to cook, sew, decorate the house, make herself beautiful for her husband, and assist in her husband's career advancement while preventing him from engaging in corruption" (O'Shaughnessy 2009: 69–70).

An additional Religious Ministerial Instruction of 1992 further specified that *ibu teladan* should never have been divorced, recognise her husband as the household's head, keep the house tidy and have a sound knowledge of state and Muslim marriage law (O'Shaughnessy 2009: 70). These and similar positions, regularly justified with the reference to both Muslim and national values, have been further reiterated by a variety of media, including the national laws.

The 'revivalist' takes on gender roles have insisted on asserting male dominance over both the public and private spheres, whereby the former has only been open to women to a very limited extent. Primarily, women have been imagined as weak and prone to (moral) transgressions; hence, their attire, sociality and sexuality have warranted the utmost scrutiny and control by male leaders. Such views have been widely disseminated in various ways, including through religious rulings (Arabic: *fatawa,* sing. *fatwa*), faith-based guidance (*panduan*) literature for women, Friday sermons (Arabic: *khutab,* sing. *khutbah*) and, of course, the regulations and the by-laws of the state's provinces whose local governments have had a sufficient number of 'revivalists' and their political partners (Hooker 2003: 122–156).

Domestic Legal System

Even prior to Indonesia's independence, there were tensions between those who wanted Indonesia to be an 'Islamic state' and those who wanted a 'secular state'. The two factions supposedly arrived at a compromise in the form of the 'Jakarta Charter' (*Piagam Jakarta*), which contained five points. The first point declared the state as founded on the belief in God (Ketuhanan), with all Muslims obliged to follow *shari'a*. When some non-Muslims threatened to secede from Indonesia if it were to become a state founded on 'Muslim' principles, and under the effect of the politically dominant secularism, the first point of the Jakarta Charter was altered to include a reference to Almighty God (Ketuhanan Yang Maha Esa), but not to Muslims, Islam or *shari'a*. The remaining points of the Jakarta Charter became the basis of the so-called Pancasila (Sanskrit: 'five principles') as the foundation of the state's ideology. These Pancasila principles are: (1) belief in Almighty God; (2) just and civilised humanitarianism; (3) national unity; (4) democracy through consultation and consensus; and (5) social justice for all the people of Indonesia.

The independence of the Indonesian judiciary is guaranteed in Article 24 of the Constitution. The same article was much less precise in the original 1945 Constitution. It merely stated that "judicial power shall be exercised by the Supreme Court and other courts of justice in accordance with the law". Yet, the 2001 amendments to the article emphasised that "the judicial power shall be independent and shall possess the power to organise the judicature in order to enforce law and justice". In practice, however, the independence of the judiciary is open to question.

Since the time of Dutch colonial rule (1800–1942), three parallel legal systems have coexisted in Indonesia: the legal system inherited from Dutch colonial laws; the system of Muslim laws, derived from certain interpretations of the predominantly Shafi'i *fiqh*; and the system of local customary 'laws', based not necessarily on actual practices in different cultures, but on what the Dutch recognised and codified as *adat* (custom).

The status of the legal system based on interpretations of Shafi'i *fiqh* was disputed even prior to Indonesia's independence. By deleting seven words from the Jakarta Charter in 1945, which had required all Muslims in Indonesia to be governed in accordance to the *shari'a*, the secularist founders of the Republic, Sukarno and Mohammad Hatta, limited the scope of the religious courts to Muslim family courts. From 1945 to 1989, these religious courts were concerned only with matters of marriage and divorce. However, in 1989, the Religious Judicature Act expanded the jurisdiction of religious courts to inheritance. "The

Act also strengthened the standing of the Islamic courts in relation to the civil courts by eliminating a rule dating from the nineteenth century which had required that decisions of Islamic courts must be ratified by a civil court to be enforceable" (Cammack 1997: 143).

The increasing tendency to adopt certain interpretations of Islam as the law of the land is the context in which to analyse recently introduced laws and by-laws related to *zina*. The most drastic law passed at the national level is Law 44/2008 on Pornography (Undang-Undang Pornografi), which was pushed through Parliament on 30 October 2008 by right-wing Muslim political parties. This law greatly expanded the use of certain interpretations of Islam beyond just the religious courts; these interpretations were now spread to the entire legal system, including the District Courts and the Constitutional Court, and to society in general. For example, on 10 March 2010, the Bandung District Court used this law to sentence four female dancers, their dance co-ordinator and the manager of the café where they were dancing to two and a half months imprisonment and a significant monetary fine. Furthermore, the law invites members of the public to assist in enforcement – an invitation that human rights activists fear would give *carte blanche* to the vigilante groups who already commit human rights violations in the name of religion. Nevertheless, on 25 March 2010, the Constitutional Court rejected an appeal against the law, which was launched by some secular parties, ethnic minorities and artists who were concerned about what this law portends. Instead, the Constitutional Court upheld the Pornography Law as part of the law of the land, to be enforced by the entire legal system.

Prior to the passing of the Pornography Law as a national law, a number of by-laws were enacted by various local governments based on reductionist and politically motivated interpretations of Islam. The National Commission on Violence against Women (Komnas Perempuan) reported: since 2001, 254 local by-laws have been passed; 154 of these laws are based on such interpretations and 63 discriminate against women explicitly. For example, a number of regencies (*kabupaten*) and municipalities, including Tasikmalaya, Tangerang and Bekasi in West Java, have outlawed prostitution on the grounds that it is a form of *zina*. This has allowed the police in these districts to arrest any woman on the streets on suspicion of prostitution, especially if she is out at night. Such cases have already occurred. Most recently, the Pamekasan regency administration is planning to propose a by-law that would impose a curfew on all women after 11pm (The Jakarta Post: 2010).

The proliferation of 'reductionist' interpretations in the legal system is most advanced in the Aceh Province, which – supposedly to decrease the threat of secession from Indonesia – has been granted special autonomy by the Indonesian government. As such, religious courts in the province have acquired a much wider jurisdiction than religious courts elsewhere in the country. The approach adopted in Aceh was to achieve an eventual convergence of state law and religious law. The Arabic term *qanun* (law, regulation) is used to refer to the local by-laws passed there. Thus, Qanun 10/2002 on Islamic Shari'a Justice (Article 49) provides that the jurisdiction of the religious court (Mahkamah Syar'iyah) is to include *ahwal al-syakhshiyyah* (personal matters such as marriage, divorce and inheritance), but also *muamalat* (trade and commerce) and *jinayah* (acts that are considered criminal, such as gambling and consuming alcohol) (Salim 2007). In 2003, the Qanun Jinayah (Muslim Criminal Code) was expanded through by-law 14/2003 on *khalwat*, which outlawed any proximity between a man and woman who are not married to each other or not blood-related as a form of *zina*. In September 2009, Aceh's regional legislature proposed that the Qanun Jinayah should be expanded to include the following punishments for *zina* offences: 100 cane lashes for those who are not yet married and stoning to death for those who are married. As of December 2010, this proposal is yet to become law, as it was rejected by the Governor of Aceh. However, the earlier by-law on *khalwat* still stands. Civil society groups in Aceh and elsewhere continue to advocate against the implementation of the Qanun Jinayah and raise awareness about its implications.

All these laws and by-laws based on certain interpretations are 'legitimised' by reference to the *shari'a*, and are presented as its 'nuances' (*bernuansa syariat Islam*) even though, as mentioned above, these are derived from the Shafi'i school of jurisprudence. In recent years, the sources include some distinctly 'revivalist' interpretations of the classical *fiqh*, such as those linked with Wahhabism.[4]

National Level

While religious courts deal with issues of family law in Indonesia, including marriage, divorce and inheritance, recurrent attempts to impose certain interpretations of the Shafi'i *fiqh* as the comprehensive law of the land have been unsuccessful. It all began in the early days of the country's independence (June–August 1945), when some right-wing Muslim political leaders tried without success to introduce the Jakarta Charter into the Constitution (Salim 2008: 1). Subsequent attempts to reintroduce references to *shari'a* – which occurred three times (1957–59; 1966–68; 2000–02) in the country's top legislative body (Salim 2008: 85), currently known as the People's Consultative Assembly (Majelis Permusyawaratan Rakyat) – were also unsuccessful. The Indonesian Constitution, therefore, does not privilege any specific religious legal tradition; although monotheism is pronounced both in the preamble and in Article 29(1) as the prime national value. Instead, the Constitution enshrines a number of fundamental human rights and principles, such as equality before the law and in government "without any exception" (Article 27(1)), which is often cited in gender justice claims.

Despite the constitutional limits to the applicability of *shari'a* in the national legal system, several far-reaching legislative interventions were introduced over the past four decades: the 1974 Marriage Law (Undang-Undang 1/1974 tentang Perkawinan); the 1989 Law on

---

4 Wahhabism is a reductionist Sunni Muslim doctrine based on the teachings of Muhammad ibn Abd-al-Wahhab, an 18th century scholar from the area that is modern-day Saudi Arabia, who advocated to 'purge Islam' of what he considered harmful and forbidden innovations. It is politically linked with the present regime of Saudi Arabia.

CASES OF HUMAN RIGHTS VIOLATIONS

A Widow's Fate

In December 2008, around 8pm in Aceh, N – a widow with three children – was talking to a male friend that she was visiting with one of her children at his home. N was approached by two young men from the village, who forcefully abducted her together with her friend's brother. N demanded an explanation, but to no avail. Instead, she was separated from her friend's brother. She later discovered that her male friend was beaten by those two young men, because of allegations that he had committed *khalwat* with her.

The next morning, N was summoned to the office of the village head. There she was accused of *khalwat* with her male friend. N rejected such allegations, but her defence was not accepted. N was reported to the Wilayatul Hisbah and expelled from her village.

At the office of the Wilayatul Hisbah, N was unlawfully detained for two nights. Since there were no beds, N was left to sleep on the desk. N was also ordered to buy her own food. During the detention, N was continuously forced to 'confess' that she had committed *khalwat*, which N repeatedly refused to do because of the following facts, in her own words:

> Although I did not read the *qanun* I knew that my actions were not illegal. We were not in a dark place, [although] we were in the house. Inside, there were lights. There was also my child with me. That wasn't the time to be alone [...] and it was still within the limit of the [ordinary] visiting time. Can't a widow be or receive a guest?

During the interrogation, the Wilayatul Hisbah tried to trick N to 'admit' that she had sex with her male friend and his brother, by telling her that his brother has signed a letter of confession stating that they had twice had sexual intercourse. N, however, again refused to 'confess' to *khalwat*.

After two days of arrest and interrogation, N was finally released after agreeing to sign a statement in which she promised not to make any similar mistakes. However, N could not return to her village, as she had been expelled. Recalling these events, N says:

> Before [in Aceh], there was a war fought amongst men. Women might someday also be fighting for justice. Look at my case! I was denied justice. [...] Just because of an ordinary time visit to a friend, I was wrongly accused and expelled from my village. [...] If there is a chance, I'll come [to the Legal Aid Institute] for consultations. I want to know more. [...] If, for example, today we manage to help ourselves, perhaps someday we will be able to help other people as well.

[Source: 'Atas Nama Otonomi Daerah: Pelembagaan Diskriminasi Dalam Tatanan Negara-Bangsa Indonesia', *Laporan Pemantauan tentang Kondisi Pemenuhan Hak-Hak Konstitusional Perempuan*, Komnas Perempuan, 2009 (available only in Indonesian).]

Religious Judicature (Undang-Undang 7/1989 tentang Peradilan Agama) in combination with the 1991 Compilation of Islamic Laws, enacted by presidential instruction (Instruksi Presiden 1/1991 tentang Penyebarluasan Kompilasi Hukum Islam); and the much-disputed 2008 Law on Pornography (Undang-Undang 44/2008 tentang Pornografi). All of these laws are, chronologically, briefly analysed below.

1974 Marriage Law
Although the 1974 Marriage Law was the first unified state regulation on marriage, which in itself meant the culmination of five decades of campaigning by Indonesian women's groups, this law was predicated on a stark patriarchal vision of gender order (O'Shaughnessy 2009). It stipulated that all marriages include a religious ceremony and state registration, and all divorces be ratified by a court. Although formally accorded equal rights, husbands were defined by this law as 'heads of the family' (*kepala keluarga*) and wives as the 'mothers of the household' (*ibu rumah tangga*) (O'Shaughnessy 2009: 1). Given the requirement of a religious marriage, women's access to divorce – although officially on equal footing to men's – was restricted (O'Shaughnessy 2009: 35). In the 2007 Concluding Comments on Indonesia, the United Nations Committee on the Elimination of Discrimination against Women expresses its concern "about the discriminatory provisions" in this law, "which perpetuate stereotypes by providing that men are the heads of households and women are relegated to domestic roles, allow polygamy and set a legal minimum age of marriage of 16 for girls" (para 18).

1989 Law on Religious Judicature and 1991 Compilation of Islamic Laws
With the enactment of the 1989 Law on Religious Judicature, the so-called *shari'a* courts were formally granted independent powers; however, marital disputes, including, for example, divorce proceedings based on infidelity charges, had to first be decided in civil courts and, even if subsequently adjudicated on in a religious court, remain compliant with the Marriage Law (Hooker 2003:22). Once the religious courts were granted a formal quasi-independence, the Indonesian state endeavoured to further regulate their operations via the 1991 Compilation of Islamic Laws, colloquially known as *kompilasi*: a non-binding set of guiding principles intended for use in the deliberations of *shari'a* courts. In so doing, the state effectively endorsed a number of overly simplified *fiqh* rules on marriage, inheritance and religious endowment (Arabic: *waqf*; Indonesian: *wakaf*) (Hooker 2003:23). In Cammack's view, the 1991 Compilation Laws enabled the secular state to be the official interpreter of 'Islamic laws', thereby strengthening its power over the Muslim citizenry (Cammack 1997). In the footsteps of the classical *fiqh*, the *kompilasi* reiterated the patriarchal roles of husband and wife in the household, already contained in the Marriage Law. In addition, a husband was defined as a 'mentor' (*pembimbing*) to his wife, whose paramount obligation, in contrast, was "to loyally serve her husband in all matters, physical and spiritual, within the limits allowed by Islamic law" (Kompilasi Hukum Islam, Article 83(1), quoted in O'Shaughnessy 2009:36). The *kompilasi* determines *zina* as the primary reason for divorce (Article 116(a)), which is also irreconcilable (Article 163(2)).

2008 Law on Pornography

Since 1999, the central government – encouraged by the 'quasi-official' (Abuza 2007:86) yet politically powerful Indonesian 'Ulama' Council (Majelis Ulama Indonesia) (MUI) – has consistently tried to devise a law against pornography, despite widespread public outrage. In 2005, the drafting committee, dominated by conservative religio-political members, proposed a draft bill containing 11 chapters and 93 articles, which was given the name RUU Anti Pornografi dan Pornoaksi (Draft Anti Pornography and 'Pornoaction' Bill). While defining 'pornography' in very loose terms, thus allowing for gender-discriminatory and intrusive interpretations, this proposal infamously attempted to criminalise what it called 'pornoaction' (*pornoaksi*), which may have included public acts such as spouses kissing, women's failure to cover their navel or sunbathing in swimwear. The Indonesian general public may not have been fully aware of the implications of this far-reaching law, instead viewing it as a positive move to limit, for example, sexist portrayals of women in pornography. However, many sectors of the Indonesian public – including feminist, human rights and artistic organisations – highlighted these implications and strongly rejected the legal encroachment on public freedoms. In response, 'pornoaction' was deleted from subsequent drafts and the number of articles was decreased to 45; but, even this 'lighter'

CASES OF HUMAN RIGHTS VIOLATIONS

Public Whipping of a 13-Year-Old Girl

A 13-year-old girl called Fatma was punished under the so-called 'whipping law' (*hukum cambuk*) in the Muslim village of Padang in Bulukumba, North Sulawesi. Fatma frequently went to her neighbour's house to watch television in the evenings. One night, as usual, she visited her neighbour's house. When she went to the toilet, which was outside the house, the neighbour's nephew followed her and tried to hold her hand. She was so frightened that she ran away from the outhouse and the man ran after her. The chase disturbed some of the village officials.

Eventually, Fatma and her assailant were caught by the village officials and were brought to the village office for questioning. Without a formal trial, and even though she was a minor, Fatma was punished with a number of lashes, while the man was merely fined for the alleged *zina*.

The psychological stress suffered by Fatma resulted in a prolonged trauma. Her family was excluded and isolated from the village and Fatma herself did not dare to join any public activity as she would always be bullied by her neighbours.

[Source: *Report on Successful Campaign to Halt Sharia Laws in South Sulawesi*, Women's Empowerment in Muslim Contexts & Solidaritas Perempuan Anging Mammiri, www.wemc.com.hk/web/e-bulletin/09-2009/files/campaign_against_discriminatory_regulations_bulukumba.pdf]

version of the draft bill retained a number of problematic definitions and provisions. Despite numerous civil and political protests – including outright rejection of the proposal by Abdurrahman Wahid, the NU religious leader and former president of Indonesia, who called it "a politicisation of religion"[5] – and a clear message from the Balinese provincial government that it would never implement such a law,[6] the draft bill, now simply termed the Law on Pornography, was eventually passed in 2008. A year later, a number of feminist, human rights, cultural and artistic organisations, as well as individual experts in these fields, filed three petitions with the Constitutional Court of the Republic of Indonesia (Mahkamah Konstitusi Republik Indonesia) requesting a constitutional review of the bill. On 25 March 2010, the Constitutional Court issued its Decision, declaring the petitioners' reasonings ungrounded and affirming that the Law on Pornography does not violate the 1945 Constitution.[7] The only female member of the Court, Maria Farida Idrati, issued a dissenting opinion (*pendapat berbeda*) in which she criticised, among other points, the bill's loose definition of pornography,[8] the overall lack of legal clarity, the bill's attempts to usher in a singular, culturally insensitive vision of public morality, and its discriminatory provisions against women and sexual and gender minorities.[9] Indeed, the bill is not concerned with the protection of those groups it deems vulnerable to pornographic exploitation – i.e. women and children. Instead, its main purpose is to strictly regulate public morality. Although the fight against pornography is specifically stipulated in several other national laws, this bill insists that further provisions are required. However, the new provisions fail to demonstrate their applicability, thereby rendering the entire act a political sham. Particularly worrying is, of course, the Constitutional Court's reluctance to perform its legal function; the 2008 Law on Pornography indeed violates Indonesia's Constitution, as well as several key international human rights treaties ratified by the state. By stipulating

---

5 For the former president Abdurrahman Wahid's public repudiation of the draft bill, see Patung, 'Gus Dur Rejects Anti Porn Bill', *Indonesia Matters*, 12 March 2006, http://www.indonesiamatters.com/167/gus-dur-rejects-anti-porn-bill/

6 See G Suardana, 'DPRD Bali Bakal ke Senayan Tolak RUU Pornografi', *detikNews*, 17 September 2008, http://us.detiknews.com/read/2008/09/17/124034/1007774/10/dprd-bali-bakal-ke-senayan-tolak-ruu-pornografi (in Indonesian).

7 See *Decision of the Indonesian Constitutional Court on the Petitions 10, 17 and 23 Testing the Applicability of the Law 44/2008 on Pornography in Relation to the 1945 Constitution*; No 10-17-23/PUU-VII/2009; promulgated on 25 March 2010 (available only in Indonesian).

8 The first clause of the 2008 Law on Pornography defines pornography as "pictures, sketches, illustrations, photographs, articles, sounds, voices, moving pictures, animations, cartoons, conversations, body movements, or other forms of messages through various communication media and/or public displays that contain obscenity or sexual exploitation that violates community norms". See UU 44/2008 tentang Pornografi (available only in Indonesian).

9 For example, the Elucidation of the Article 4(1)(a) explains that what is meant by the term 'deviant behaviour' includes lesbianism and (male) homosexuality. Maria Farida Idrati further explains that the definition of pornography in the bill allows for the criminalisation of women's attire and even 'body movements' deemed inappropriate, thus curtailing their constitutionally guaranteed freedom of expression.

that "community [moral] norms" (Article 1(1)) take precedence over individual rights and freedoms, this bill has implicitly signalled state-sanctioned impunity for 'mob justice' incidents, which are so often associated with the allegations of *zina*, particularly in rural areas.

Marriage, family and public morality are continually featured as the quintessential sites of state power in Indonesia (O'Shaughnessy 2009:1).[10] Their regulation, however, increasingly reflects a religious overtone, modelled against a politicised and reduced *ad absurdum* interpretation of the selected classical *fiqh*.[11] This tendency has given the social discourses on *zina*, invariably tainted with patriarchal bias (Bennett 2005: 18), a dangerous legal legitimacy.

Provincial and Local Levels

Following the downfall of the President Suharto's autocratic regime (1967–98), known as the 'New Order', the emerging leaders of the *reformasi* movement committed to decentralise and democratise state governance. While these attempts have yielded moderate success, they have been instrumental to the subsequent usurpation of provincial autonomy by the previously marginalised local *'ulama'* (Salim 2008), radical political leaders and right-wing religious parties, at the expense of gender justice and religious freedoms. The political parties and their 'reductionist' ideologues have laboured to mobilise religio-political constituencies by creating radical programmes on 'societal moral renaissance' and similar propagandist concepts, all referencing *shari'a* as their primary 'inspiration'. These developments have been meticulously researched and brilliantly analysed in the *Monitoring Report on the Fulfilment of Conditions for Women's Constitutional Rights* (*Laporan Pemantauan tentang Kondisi Pemenuhan Hak-Hak Konstitusional Perempuan*), concerning 16 districts/cities within seven Indonesian provinces, prepared and published in 2009 by the Indonesian National Commission on Violence against Women (Komnas Perempuan). The report was entitled: *In the Name of Regional Autonomy: Institutionalisation of Discrimination in the Indonesian National System* (*Atas Nama Otonomi Daerah: Pelembagaan Diskriminasi*

---

10 The newest example of this governmental strategic orientation is the draft bill on the religious courts' legal material (Rancangan Undang-Undang Hukum Materiil Peradilan Agama), proposed by the Indonesian Ministry of Religious Affairs, which is currently (May 2010) in parliamentary procedure. The bill is expected to criminalise 'informal' Muslim marriages (*nikah siri*), as well as contractual marriages, which are said to be "a cover for prostitution". If adopted, the bill will effectively assert state control over all forms of marriage, while, at the same time, leaving no alternative option for Muslims in (search of) intimate relationships but to marry. See Patung, 'Nikah Siri Marriages', *Indonesia Matters*, 17 April 2009, http://www.indonesiamatters.com/3758/nikah-siri/

11 One should, however, as Vivienne Wee has noted (personal communication), be careful to recognise these models as no more than political claims of ideologues to be pure custodians of the past.

Dalam Tatanan Negara-Bangsa Indonesia). This chapter proceeds with a brief summary of the findings of this report, followed by an analysis of the two Acehnese *qanun* that bring the provincial criminalisation of *zina* to an unprecedented level.

154 Provincial/Local Discriminatory Regulations

The Report by the National Commission on Violence against Women (*Komnas Perempuan*) significantly reveals that, since the beginning of the *reformasi* era in 1989 until 2009, as many as 154 local regulations (*peraturan daerah* or *perda*; in Aceh *qanun*) were enacted which stand in clear violation of the 1945 Constitution. Interestingly enough, all of them – save one, which invokes the New Testament – refer to *shari'a* as the source of legitimacy. According to the report, 19 of these regulations were issued at the provincial level; 134 were district by-laws; and one was issued by a village authority. Out of the 154 regulations, 63 were found to be discriminatory against women, by limiting their (1) constitutionally guaranteed freedom of expression (21 regulations on 'Muslim' dress code); (2) the right to legal certainty and protection from arbitrary discrimination (37 regulations on the eradication of prostitution and one by-law on the prohibition of 'illicit' seclusion); and (3) the elementary right to legal protection (four regulations concerning the migrant workers).

A further 82 discriminatory by-laws violate the right of every citizen of Indonesia to practise their religion in accordance with their own beliefs and lead to the systemic exclusion of the minority religious groups. Finally, the remaining nine regulations impose unlawful restrictions on the freedom of religion for members of the Ahmadiyya community. Among the local regulations which hinder women's rights, the concept of *zina* is often invoked to either mask a given provision as a form of legal prevention or, indeed, to legalise outright punishments for the 'offences' that are indirectly or directly associated with adultery. Thus, the enactment of the notorious Acehnese *qanun* (14/2003) on the 'illicit' seclusion of persons of different genders (*khalwat*), which is analysed below in some detail, has been

---

CASES OF HUMAN RIGHTS VIOLATIONS

Public Humiliation of a Couple

In May 2010, in a village close to the town of Lhokseumawe, Aceh, at approximately 5pm, a group of young men raided a boarding house and forcefully snatched a woman and a man that they found inside. They accused the couple of committing *zina* without any supporting evidence. The couple was then paraded through the village and brought before its religious/social house (*mushalla*, in Aceh: *meunasah*). There they were publicly humiliated and doused with the dirty water from a sewer. The couple was never asked to either confirm or reject the accusation of *zina*.

[Source: Several Acehnese human rights activists in a written correspondence with the author, from 16 to 20 May 2010, on file with the author.]

justified as a pre-emptive measure against *zina*. In contrast, the regulation of the district of Tasikmalaya in Western Java on the eradication of prostitution (Tasikmalaya Peraturan Daerah 28/2000 tentang Pemberantasan Pelacuran) simply defines prostitution as a form of adultery. Finally, the regulation concerning the Muslim village of Padang, in North Sulawesi, on the implementation of public whipping (Peraturan Desa 5/2006 tentang Pelaksanaan Hukuman Cambuk) was enacted as a form of punishment for *women* who commit *zina*.[12] A 13-year-old girl was whipped in that village, as a 'perpetrator' of *zina*, simply because she tried to run away from a neighbour's nephew, who had followed her to the outhouse.[13] As a result of a large-scale women's movement's campaign, it seems that the Padang 'whipping law' was silently repealed by the provincial governor.[14] All other discriminatory regulations in the state, however, still await the central Parliament's or the provincial government's review.

Developments in Aceh

In the Indonesian special territory of Aceh, which at the dawn of the *reformasi* era was given wide autonomy (via Law 44/1999 and Law 18/2001), the local regulations (*qanun*) have been increasingly concerned with criminalising the 'offences' that are deemed contrary to certain interpretations of the selected Shafi'i *fiqh*. The preparation and enactment of such by-laws is greatly influenced by the local (mostly rural) *'ulama'* (Salim 2008: 156–159) and – in particular – by right-wing religious political parties and 'reductionist' ideologues (Baswedan 2004; Riddell 2002). Thus far, alcohol (Qanun 12/2003), gambling (Qanun 13/2003) and *khalwat* (Qanun 14/2003) have been explicitly prohibited, with penalties of up to 40 public cane lashes. In addition, Qanun 11/2002 prescribes public flogging for the following 'offences': the propagation of 'deviant sects or cults'; failure to observe Friday prayers three weeks consecutively without a religiously legitimate reason; provision of amenities that 'encourage' Muslims to break fasting during the month of Ramadan; and eating or drinking in public during the daylight hours in the month of Ramadan (Salim 2008: 158). The introduction and wide-ranging application of flogging as a legitimate form of punishment has no precedent in the legal history of the Indonesian Republic. Their legitimacy is defended with reference to the corporal punishments developed by the scholars of *fiqh* in early Muslim communities, many of which were already reformed or repealed by the Ottoman Empire (in the 15th century), to which Aceh acceded in 1565. This trend, therefore, has a very little (if any) historical or theological salience. Rather, it seems to be primarily rooted in the political ambitions of the province's *'ulama'* (Salim 2008), the Acehnese right-wing political leaders and their religio-political parties.

---

12 For further information on this village regulation, see *Report on Successful Campaign to Halt Sharia Laws in South Sulawesi*, Women's Empowerment in Muslim Contexts & Solidaritas Perempuan Anging Mammiri, www.wemc.com.hk/web/e-bulletin/09-2009/files/campaign_against_discriminatory_regulations_bulukumba.pdf

13 *Ibid.*

14 *Ibid.*

Disconcerting as they may be, these legislative developments are specific to the province of Aceh and its distinct historical and political make-up. They are unlikely to simply 'spill over' and spread to other provinces,[15] as they are guided by different socio-political, religious and cultural conditions. The Acehnese 'exceptionality' provides for more radical (ab)use of religious tenets for political purposes due to its provincial identity being directly linked to legalistic, 'straightforward' expressions of adherence to one's Muslim faith, born in a protracted political and social crisis caused both by provincial political (and religious) leadership and the central government's history of mistakes in building relationships with this special territory.

While the majority of the enacted Acehnese religious *qanun*, in comparison with the categories of classical *fiqh*, deal with so-called *ta'zir* offences,[16] they have clearly paved the way for a gradual introduction of *hudud* penalties, including stoning to death for the offence of *zina*. Hence, several years after the introduction of Qanun 14/2003 on *khalwat*, the Acehnese Parliament has attempted to enact the draconian Qanun Jinayat – a *zina* (and generally *hudud*) law *par excellence*. Both of these *qanun* are analysed below.

Aceh: Qanun 14/2003 tentang Khalwat (Mesum) (Bylaw on *Khalwat*)

The 'offence' of *khalwat* is defined as 'close proximity' between persons of different gender – at least one being Muslim – who have no marriage or familial relationship in a 'secluded' place where intimate contact is possible (Salim 2008: 158). This 'seclusion' is understood as "a wrong in itself", even if *zina* has not been committed (Hooker 2003: 191). The introduction of this oppressive *qanun* has led to a number of violent attacks by local vigilantes, predominantly in the rural areas of Aceh, on those perceived as perpetrators of *khalwat*. The majority of the victims are either women or young couples.[17] For example, in April 2010, a couple was paraded naked through the village close to the town of Meulaboh; a month later, in another village nearby the town of Lhokseumawe, a couple was publicly humiliated and then doused with water from the sewer.[18] While the perpetrators of such 'mob justice' remain unpunished, their victims are often beaten or imprisoned by the infamous law enforcement forces known as Wilayatul Hisbah – founded by Decree 01/2004 of the governor of Aceh. Only a handful of cases have ended up before a *shari'a* court, which, in one such instance, punished the female victim with a 3 million rupiah (GBP £225) fine.[19] Furthermore, due to an unbearable social stigma, victims are usually forced

---

15 The author is grateful to Vivienne Wee for raising this point in her commentary on this chapter.

16 From the perspective of the classical *fiqh*, it is debatable whether the consumption of alcohol (Arabic: *shrub al-khamr*), criminalised by the Acehnese Qanun 12/2003, constitutes a *hadd* or a *ta'zir* offence, since the medieval jurists had disagreed on the matter. However, since the *qanun* in question prescribes the punishment of 40 lashes, it seems that the Acehnese lawmakers have followed the Shafi'i school of *fiqh*, as the majority of Shafi'i jurists render *shrub al-khamr* a *hadd* offence. See, for example, Hallaq 2009: 315–316.

17 Information received by the Acehnese civil society members, through the empirical segment of this research.

18 *Ibid.*

19 *Ibid.*

to leave their village and/or to marry.[20] Needless to say, these methods of 'investigation' and punishment contravene guarantees of human rights in the Indonesian Constitution.

Aceh: Qanun Jinayat (Muslim Criminal Code; unenforced)

On 14 September 2009, the Acehnese provincial assembly, at the time dominated by the right-wing Muslim parties[21], adopted the Qanun Jinayat. This was followed by a strong public outcry, led by the various civil society organisations. Also, despite the political pressure, the (non-partisan) governor of Aceh firmly refused to sign the bill, thereby leaving it in a legal limbo where it still dwells, until it is either fully repealed or passed. For the first time in Indonesian legal history, the offence of *zina* in the Qanun Jinayat incurs 100 cane lashes for the unmarried and stoning to death for those who are married. In addition, understood as a form of *zina* – yet judged upon alleged 'homosexual behaviour' based on attire and mannerisms, not the 'usual' eye-witness testimonies of four righteous male Muslims – same-sex sexual intercourse warrants 100 cane lashes and a maximum fine of one kilogram of fine gold. This *qanun* is also problematic in the context of rape, as its application might criminalise the very victims of rape (if they were to report the rape, but were unable to provide four male witnesses) and pardon the perpetrators who rape at the command of an authoritative superior. The *qanun* stipulates that a confession of *zina* without any additional evidence is, in itself, sufficient proof that the said offence was committed. Given the situation with the *khalwat* cases in Aceh, in which confessions of *zina* are regularly obtained under psycho-physical duress, this provision would surely lead to fast-track convictions. The *khalwat* cases further showcase that the majority of the convicted 'perpetrators' of *zina* would be women.

The motivation behind the *'shari'a*-oriented' Acehnese by-laws, as well as other discriminatory local regulations throughout the country, is clearly of a political, rather than religio-spiritual, nature. The legislators of these regulations are very aware of the detrimental consequences to social justice, 'humanitarianism' or national unity in diversity – all of which are enshrined in Indonesia's ideological concept Pancasila – of such regulations. The human rights violations these provisions incur are, therefore, expected rather than incidental consequences of their implementation. As explained by Muslim Ibrahim, the chairman of the Majelis Permusyawaratan Ulama (Consultative Council of 'Ulama'), which is extensively involved in the *qanun*-making process in Aceh, "the issue of human rights [...] must not be extensively taken into account. Otherwise, most *qanun* will be non-starters" (Salim 2008: 161).

How does the Indonesian state, at its various levels of governance, respond to such clear-cut legislative manipulations, in light of its constitutional obligations and international human rights responsibilities? The ensuing analysis is centred on this question.

---

20 *Ibid.*

21 Who were heavily defeated by the centrist Aceh Party in local elections only two weeks later.

State Responsibility

Responsibility to protect and promote human rights is deeply entrenched in the Indonesian legal system. Below is the list of only those elementary rights, contained in national legislation, that have been seriously violated by the enactment of the previously analysed '*fiqh*-inspired' laws and by-laws.

The 1945 Constitution guarantees a wide range of individual rights and freedoms, including:

(1) the right to life (Article 28A);
(2) protection and freedom from violence and discrimination based upon any grounds whatsoever (Article 28B(2) and Article 28I(2));
(3) the right to personal development through the fulfilment of one's basic needs (Article 28C(1));
(4) the right to legal protection and certainty before a just law, and of equal treatment before the law (Article 28D(1));
(5) the right to work (Article 28D(2));
(6) freedom to choose and practise the religion of one's choice (Article 28E(1)) and in accordance with one's own conscience (Article 28E(2)), free from coercion;
(7) the right to freedom of expression (Article 28E(3));
(8) the right to freedom from torture or inhumane and degrading treatment (Article 28G(2));
(9) the right to live in physical and spiritual prosperity (Article 28H(1));
(10) the right to social security and dignity (Article 28H(3)).

The Constitution, in Article 28I(1), also defines, amongst others, the rights to life, freedom from torture, freedom of thought and conscience, and freedom of religion as peremptory norms (*jus cogens*) from which no derogation is allowed. It further states that "[t]he protection, advancement, upholding and fulfilment of human rights are the responsibility of the state, especially the government" (Article 28I(4)).

The preamble of Law 39/1999 on Human Rights stipulates that,

> as a member of the United Nations, the nation of Indonesia has a moral and legal responsibility to respect, execute and uphold the Universal Declaration on Human Rights promulgated by the United Nations, and several other international instruments concerning human rights ratified by the Republic of Indonesia.

This law also explains that limitations, affronts or ostracism based on one's sex constitute discrimination (Article 1(3)). It reiterates the peremptory norms and numerous other human rights proclaimed by the Constitution, and enshrines some of the following individual rights and freedoms:

(1) the right to an objective, impartial judiciary (Article 5(2));
(2) the right to peace, happiness and wellbeing (Article 9(2));
(3) the right to marry with the free and full consent, absent of any coercion (Article 10(2));
(4) the right to (legal) justice (Article 17);
(5) the right not to be "charged or held guilty of a penal offence for any act or omission which did not constitute a penal offence under **prevailing law**" (Article 18(2); [emphasis added]);
(6) the right to freedom of movement (Article 27(1));
(7) the right not to be subject to arbitrary interference with one's home (Article 31);
(8) the right not to be subject to arbitrary arrest, detention, torture or exile (Article 34);
(9) the right to just conditions of work (Article 38).

Significantly, Section Nine of the 1999 Law on Human Rights is entitled 'Women's Rights', which guarantees that "women's rights are human rights" (Article 45) and that women and men have equal rights in matters related to marriage and divorce (Article 51). The Law also firmly establishes, in Article 74, that "[n]o provisions set forth in this Act shall be interpreted to mean that the government, or any political parties, factions, or any party whosoever is permitted to degrade, impair or eradicate the basic rights and freedoms governed by this Act".

In terms of international human rights law, the Republic of Indonesia has acceded to a number of key international human rights instruments, including:

(1) the 1948 Universal Declaration of Human Rights (via the Preamble of the Law 39/1999);
(2) the 1966 International Covenant on Economic, Social and Cultural Rights (ratified by Law 11/2005);
(3) the 1966 International Covenant on Civil and Political Rights (ratified by Law 12/2005);
(4) the 1979 Convention on the Elimination of all Forms of Discrimination against Women (CEDAW) (ratified by Law 7/1984);
(5) the 1984 Convention against Torture and Other Cruel, Inhuman or Degrading Treatment or Punishment (ratified by Law 5/1998).

All of the above cited human rights, guaranteed by the 1945 Constitution and the 1999 Law on Human Rights, as well as numerous other personal freedoms and fundamental rights enshrined in international human rights instruments that are now a part and parcel of the Indonesian national legal system, have been clearly violated by the 1974 Marriage Law, the 1989 Law on Religious Judicature, the 1991 Compilation of Islamic Laws, the 2008 Law on Pornography, and at least 155 discriminatory local regulations, most notably the Acehnese Qanun on Khalwat. Thus, in the 2007 Concluding Comments on Indonesia, the UN Committee on the Elimination of Discrimination against Women, which oversees the implementation of CEDAW by the states that have ratified it (including Indonesia), "urges the State party [Indonesia] to give high priority to its law reform process and to amend, without delay and within a clear time frame, discriminatory laws and regulations and bring them in line with the [CEDAW]" (para 11). It also compels the Indonesian government "to review, monitor and evaluate the implementation of local and regional laws to ensure that they fully comply with national human rights laws and the obligations of the State party under [CEDAW], so that women's rights are fully protected throughout the country" (para 13). The incongruence of gender-discriminatory laws and by-laws with the state's Constitution and international human rights obligations is one of the greatest destabilising factors of the Indonesian democratic polity and of a sensitive cultural, inter- and intra-religious diversity.

Not only do the political manipulations of religion and the resultant gender injustice run contrary to the state's elementary values, pronounced in the Pancasila, they are also in violation of Law 32/2004 on Regional Administration. This law is one of the prime achievements of the *reformasi* era; it renders the usurpation of provincial/local autonomy unlawful, as such leads to discrimination against a particular group of citizens, who, in this case, are primarily women. Thus, those Indonesian laws and by-laws – such as several Acehnese *qanun* – that promote systemic discrimination against or even criminalisation of women (and some men) on the pretext of *zina* warrant the state's revision or revocation of these laws and by-laws on a number of grounds, as a matter of utmost urgency.

The reluctance of both executive and judicial branches of the Indonesian state to strike down gender discriminatory legislation reveals an acute patriarchal condition, hidden behind false moral and religious concerns. It is a 'joint venture' between otherwise incompatible secular state ideologues and Muslim 'reductionists', through which they perpetuate the ideas of male dominance, of whichever ideological background. Thus, the two generally exclusivist ideologies – that of Suharto-style secularism, which construes religion as but an auxiliary toolkit of its politics, and that of the religious right, which considers secular elements of the Indonesian state as a temporary necessity, soon to be dismantled – have become intriguingly receptive to one another's patriarchal discourses; as if those discourses stem from some ancient and naturalised 'alliance of men', overarching any particular ideological conviction.

Yet a number of developments, spearheaded, in the first place, by the country's vivid civil society, challenge the present politico-juridical stalemate on multiple grounds. This chapter now turns to an analysis of those strategies and activities, with a view to arrive at some potentially salient recommendations for their further enhancements.

Existing Activism for Change

A great number of the Indonesian civil society movements are, in fact, considerably older than the state of Indonesia itself; at least if we assume that its nascence coincides with the proclamation of its independence, from Dutch colonial administration, in 1945. The women's movement has been socially and politically active since the beginning of the 20th century, alongside, and as an important segment of, the nationalist movement (Martyn 2005:30). Its relationship with the male-dominated nation-building project, however, has been difficult; Indonesian women activists have continuously had to balance their contribution to public affairs with their necessary resistance to the hegemonic patriarchal discourse of the time, which had sought to 'de-individuate' their specific roles and convert them into general 'symbols' of national development, thus keeping them a safe distance from the real power centres (Blackburn 1999). Nevertheless, the first large-scale congress of women's associations was held in 1928, and by 1946 a strong central federation, known as Kongres Wanita Indonesia or Kowani, was formed (Kartowijono 1976:8). Indonesian independence, which was finally won by 1950, fulfilled two crucial demands of the women's movement: a nation-state had been formed and its 1945 Constitution guaranteed women equal and full citizenship rights (Martyn 2005:55). Yet, with the patriarchal normative and cultural systems still largely in place, women soon realised that "our fight is not over yet" (Persit 1954:2). That slogan, coined in the early 1950s, will remain the movement's rallying cry and a simple fact for many coming years. Its newly risen challenge, embodied in a form of a unitary state hijacked by next to absolute presidential powers, made every effort to uphold and further entrench the pervading gender stereotypes in the Indonesian legal, political and social reality. It is, therefore, not until the end of the 'New Order' regime, in 1998, that the women's movement, as well as many other social justice civic projects, was able to assume a more influential role in Indonesian society.

The *reformasi* era brought about many long fought-for changes. In 2000, the then president of the Republic, Abdurrahman Wahid, released a presidential instruction on the Mainstreaming of Gender in National Development (Instruksi Presiden 9/2000 tentang Pengarusutamaan Gender Dalam Pembangunan Nasional). In this policy document, gender is explicitly defined "as a concept relating to roles and responsibilities of men and women which could be changed by social conditions and culture", which is why it is important to use 'gender analysis' (*analisa gender*) to ascertain the impact of one's gender on their access to development resources, including human rights (O'Shaughnessy 2009:37). This instruction marked the beginning of a series of positive developments, including at least 11 new national laws promulgated with a view of addressing – whether directly or indirectly – gender injustice; Law 39/1999 on Human Rights and the 2004 Law for the Eradication of Domestic Violence (UU 23/2004 tentang Penghapusan Kekerasan Dalam Rumah Tangga) are of particular importance. These changes were invariably conceptualised and advocated by the country's burgeoning human rights and feminist organisations, and made possible by the new, less powerful and politically unstable central government, which was now in need of wider social recognition and support.

While instrumental to the rise of civil society social justice movements, the new distribution of power has also compelled some politically hopeful and morally complacent *'ulama'* to seek novel ways of self-organisation. This is epitomised in the leadership crisis that befell all major Muslim politico-religious organisations and, perhaps most dramatically, their state-financed yet largely independent 'umbrella' forum, the Indonesian 'Ulama' Council (Majelis Ulama Indonesia) (MUI). While some of these organisations – most notably the NU

(Nahdlatul Ulama) under the charismatic leadership of the late *kyai* Abdurrahman Wahid – have managed to resist the challenge of neo-conservative wave, the MUI eventually became its primary stronghold. Hence, the prominent members of Majelis Mujahidin Indonesia (Indonesian Holy Warrior Assembly) (MMI), an ultra-right-wing organisation, are now quite vocal and active members of the MUI as well (Hasan 2002).

In October 2004, in the spirit of *reformasi*, the Gender Mainstreaming Team of the Department of Religion (Tim Pengarus-Utamaan Gender Departemen Agama) sought to reform the state's existing gender discriminatory legislation. It released an alternative draft compilation of Muslim laws for public discussion (the so-called Counter-Legal Draf Kompilasi Hukum Islam). Overseen by departmental gender expert, Siti Musdah Mulia, this compilation essentially aimed at eradicating all discriminatory gender differentiations contained in the existing 1991 Compilation of Islamic Laws. Along with other provisions, it proposed to allow women to marry without a guardian (*wali*), equal inheritance rights between the genders, equal access to inter-faith marriage, and equal divorce rights and maintenance duties (O'Shaughnessy 2009: 38). The draft, however, met with fierce opposition, spearheaded by the MUI. For instance, the MUI's head at the time, KH Ali Mustafa Yaqub, "expressed a fear that Indonesian Muslims who obeyed this law risked apostasy" (O'Shaughnessy 2009: 38). As a result, the minister of religion, who had initially openly supported the draft, withdrew it for revision just a day after receiving the MUI's complaint (O'Shaughnessy 2009: 38). The draft was eventually cancelled.

The rekindled 'Islamic' political opposition to the human rights and social justice struggles led by civil society resulted, in recent years, in a number of disconcerting setbacks. These include: the passing of the oppressive 2008 Law on Pornography and the decision of the Constitutional Court to uphold it; another of the same court's controversial decisions to uphold the national discriminatory laws on 'defamation of religions';[22] and a series of violent incidents, in 2010, threatening the constitutional rights to freedom of association and freedom of expression of the Indonesian lesbian, gay, bisexual, transgender, intersex and queer (LGBTIQ) communities, most notably in Surabaya, East Java, in relation to an international human rights conference.[23]

Responses of Indonesian civil society to these setbacks, as well as to the state's general reluctance to fulfil its constitutional human rights obligations, are manifold. They include increased cross-movement strategising and co-operation, resulting in joint public campaigns or programmes and moderately successful attempts to reach out to law- and policy-making governmental bodies. The proceeding analysis focuses on recent civil society responses,

---

22 For more information, see 'Court Decision Upholding "Defamation of Religions" Laws is Major Setback', Article 19/CIHRS/IFEX, 28 April 2010, *International Freedom of Expression eXchange: The Global Network for Free Expression*, http://www.ifex.org/indonesia/2010/04/28/defamation_of_religions/

23 See Grace Poore, 'LGBT Activism under Attack in Surabaya, Indonesia', 2 April 2010, *International Gay and Lesbian Human Rights Commission*, http://iglhrc.wordpress.com/2010/04/02/lgbt-activism-under-attack-in-surabaya-indonesia/

particularly those of the women's movement, to the politically motivated 'Islamisation' of the provincial legal system in Aceh and its detrimental social consequences.

The Lessons from Aceh

Although doubly burdened by a particularly harsh economic and political situation in this northernmost Indonesian province, Acehnese civil society has come up with a number of salient strategies to combat both the societal and legislative roots of widespread gender injustice. The results of their activities range from the inclusion, in the relevant provincial by-laws, of a mandatory 30 per cent quota for women in the provincial election commissions and in the candidates' lists of the political parties, to the creation and promotion of the draft *qanun* on women's empowerment and protection of women's human rights.[24] On 11 November 2008, thanks to the sustained efforts of women's human rights organisations, the province of Aceh adopted the Charter of the Rights of Women in Aceh (Piagam Hak-Hak Perempuan di Aceh), which guarantees, amongst other things, that "[w]omen in Aceh shall have the right to freedom from discrimination, intimidation and violence" (Article 3).[25] In a similar vein, the local human rights defenders, briefly surveyed for the purposes of the present study, all agree that the governor's decision not to sign the Qanun Jinayat counts among their chief successes. When it became evident that the conservative provincial assembly was going to pass this draconian *qanun*, local human rights defenders made a concise study outlining the most problematic matters its implementation might incur and sent it to the governor, Irwandi Yusuf.

The empirical evidence collected from written correspondence with Acehnese human rights activists, whose names are not published here for their own security, reveals a number of important patterns that are briefly considered below.

Types of Activities

Acehnese civil society, in particular women's rights organisations, is predominantly oriented towards human rights campaigns; strategic – advocacy and information sharing – meetings with the representatives of the provincial government, *'ulama'* and local (village) leaders; providing policy- and law-making assistance to the provincial government; specialised religious and legal (non-formal) studies; and, to a lesser degree, monitoring human rights violations.

What Works the Best

The activities considered most effective are those which result in direct dialogue and co-operation with either the provincial government or local *'ulama'* – i.e. activities that persuade these influential persons to change the oppressive regulations and policies. This

---

24 For more information, see 'Women's Legal Rights and Access to Justice', UNIFEM East and Southeast Asia Region, http://unifem-eseasia.org/Governance/Women_Legal_Rights.html
25 The Aceh Charter on Women's Rights is available at http://piagamhakperempuanaceh.org

is best achieved via joint non-governmental human rights advocacy that brings various organisations and social justice movements together, as it demonstrates that the society, as a whole, demands certain actions be taken.

Ways of Improvement
One of the recurrent issues highlighted by Acehnese human rights defenders is the need for in-depth, gender and human rights-sensitive interpretations of legal traditions pertinent to historical and contemporary Muslim communities. This would enable grassroots activists to engage in a comprehensive dialogue with local religious and political authorities. The need for improved networking amongst themselves and the involvement of all relevant stakeholders in the law-making processes is also mentioned. Once progress is made along these three key avenues of development, local activists are convinced that they will be able to make the provincial government and *'ulama'* realise that the current religious legislation runs contrary to both national human rights legal standards and, perhaps even more importantly, the goals and purposes of *shari'a* (Arabic: *maqasid al-shari'a*).

Acehnese activists are deeply aware that the introduction of the concept of *zina* to the provincial legal system "is part of the politic[s] of morality used by certain people with political power for their [own] political interests".[26] Hence, they are aware that the strategies of sensitisation and dialogue are dependent upon their counterparts' good will and political interests. Nonetheless, they are confident that a learned and methodological use of a Muslim framework in addressing the issues of gender and social justice can melt the political ice.

While the monitoring of human rights violations has already become an integral part of the provincial social justice movements' activities – resulting in, for example, documenting 49 cases of (communal and state-sanctioned) discrimination and violence across Aceh in 2009, associated with the emergence of the infamous Qanun on Khalwat – there is still considerable room for improvement. It has to do with the methods used in the monitoring process as well as with the follow-up activities, which Acehnese civil society has not had a chance to improve. The development of this important segment of their advocacy efforts should, therefore, be given greater priority in their strategic considerations.

Finally (and this invariably applies to other regions of Indonesia as well), in a situation whereby the Constitutional Court, let alone the lower levels of the juridical sector, clearly does not perform its legal duties, civil society movements should consider filing complaints with international human rights instruments – such as the relevant United Nations treaty bodies and special procedures. While such applications may not always trigger immediate results, they have proven effective in the longer-run in a number of similar contexts.

---

26 A written response from an anonymous Acehnese human rights and religious expert, provided on 12 May 2010, on file with the author.

Indonesian civil society, in particular the experienced and well-developed women's movement, remains the cornerstone of the state's constitutional promise of social and gender justice. Its capacity to influence the ambiguous and often inconsiderate state policies is steadily increasing, but warrants some strategic improvements given the complexity of the religio-political situation. The recent emergence of a number of gender discriminatory religious by-laws, coupled with some disconcerting legislative tendencies on the national level and the overall ineffectiveness of the Constitutional Court (which in itself is a recent development, too), signals that some non-governmental efforts should perhaps be revisited in order to increase their much-needed socio-political impact. A brief look at Acehnese society suggests a number of salient avenues for change, and applicable to a broader context. In fact, those avenues seem plausible for the country as a whole, because, invariably throughout Indonesia, the relationship between religion and the political power remains so multifaceted and deep-rooted.

Conclusion

This chapter has offered a brief analysis of the historical and contemporary socio-political conditions allowing for the development of the Indonesian national and provincial/local legislation that purports to exert control over women's (and, to a lesser degree, men's) sexuality and sociality. It has found that such legislative monstrosity (from Dutch: *legislative misbaksel*) (cf. Sahetapy 2009) is primarily owed to two distinct, albeit mutually supportive, patriarchal systems – that of the largely secular 'New Order' regime and that of the right-wing Muslim political opposition. The second task of this chapter has been to establish how state and civil society responded to the constitutional and human rights challenge posed by the introduction of gender-discriminatory legislation. It was found that, despite the fact that these laws clearly violate at least 25 elementary human rights enshrined in the 1945 Constitution and the 1999 Law on Human Rights (some of which are defined in the strongest possible terms – as the peremptory norms), not to mention a number of strictly binding international human rights treaties that Indonesia has ratified, the state remains reluctant to review the laws in question. In contrast, social justice organisations in Indonesian civil society, particularly its century-old women's movement, are devising a number of strategies to combat both the problematic legislation and the state's indolence. This chapter, therefore, presented some of the strategies employed by human rights defenders in the state's autonomous province of Aceh, which has enacted the largest number of discriminatory by-laws (*qanun*).

Indonesian pluralism and democratic tradition, as well as values enshrined in the Pancasila and Constitution, oblige the state to take the steps necessary to combat the gender-discriminatory, political misuse of religion (and its pertinent legal traditions). Social, religious and gender justice can be successfully met within a single legislative framework only if it is free of patriarchies, whether 'religious' or 'secular'.

Bibliography

Abuza, Zachary (2007), *Political Islam and Violence in Indonesia*. New York: Routledge.

Allen, Pam (2007), 'Challenging Diversity?: Indonesia's Anti-Pornography Bill', *Asian Studies Review* 31: 101.

Asmawaty, Andi Cipta (2009), 'Tubuh Perempuan: Pertaruhan Makna Di Balik Undang-Undang'. Presentation, Jakarta, June, on file with the author.

Baswedan, Anies Rasyid (2004), 'Political Islam in Indonesia' *Asian Survey* 44 (5): 669.

Bennett, Linda Rae (2005), *Women, Islam and Modernity: Single Women, Sexuality and Reproductive Health in Contemporary Indonesia*. New York: Routledge.

Blackburn, S. (1999), 'Women and Citizenship in Indonesia', *Australian Journal of Political Science* 34 (2): 189.

Blackburn, S. (2004), *Women and the State in Modern Indonesia*. Cambridge: Cambridge University Press.

Bowen, John R. (2003), *Islam, Law, and Equality in Indonesia: An Anthropology of Public Reasoning* Cambridge: Cambridge University Press.

Cammack, Mark (1997), 'Indonesia's 1989 Religious Judicature Act: Islamization of Indonesia or Indonesianization of Islam?' *Indonesia* 63: 143.

Colombo, Valentina, 'Women and Islam: Religion, Tradition, or Simply Human Rights?' Resource paper, *Global Campaign to Stop Killing and Stoning Women*, http://www.stop-killing.org/node/895

Davies, Matthew N. (2006), *Indonesia's War over Aceh: Last Stand on Mecca's Porch*. New York: Routledge.

Derichs, Claudia and Andrea Fleschenberg (eds.) (2010), *Religious Fundamentalisms and Their Gendered Impacts in Asia*. Berlin: Friedrich-Ebert-Stiftung.

Dhofier, Zamakhsyari (1999), *The Pesantren Tradition: A Study of the Role of the Kyai in the Maintenance of the Traditional Ideology of Islam in Java Tempe*. Tucson: Arizona State University Program for Southeast Asian Studies Monograph Series.

Eddyono, Sri Wiyanti (2007), 'Politicizing Islam: New Challenges for Indonesian Women'. Resource paper, *Global Campaign to Stop Killing and Stoning Women*, November, http://www.stop-killing.org/node/886

Federspiel, Howard M. (2001), *Islam and Ideology in the Emerging Indonesian State: The Persatuan Islam (PERSIS), 1923 to 1957*. Leiden: Brill.

Feener, R. Michael (2007), *Muslim Legal Thought in Modern Indonesia*. Cambridge: Cambridge University Press.

Ford, Michele and Lyn Parker (eds.) (2008), *Women and Work in Indonesia*. London: Routledge.

Geertz, Clifford (1971) [1968], *Islam Observed: Religious Development in Morocco and Indonesia*. Chicago: University of Chicago Press, Chicago.

Hallaq, Wael B. (2009), *Sharī'a: Theory, Practice, Transformations*. Cambridge: Cambridge University Press.

Hasan, Noorhaidi (2002), 'Faith and Politics: The Rise of the Laskar Jihad in the Era of Transition in Indonesia', *Indonesia* 73: 145.

Hooker, M.B. (2008), *Indonesia Syariah: Defining a National School of Law.* Singapore: Institute of Southeast Asian Studies.

Hooker, M.B. (2003), *Indonesian Islam: Social Change through Contemporary Fatāwā*. Honolulu: University of Hawai'i Press.

Irianto, Sulistyowati (2009), 'Perlukah UU Pornografi dan Pornoaksi?' Presentation, Jakarta, June 2009, on file with the author.

Locher-Scholten, E. (ed.) (2000), *Women and the Colonial State: Essays on Gender and Modernity in the Netherlands Indies, 1900–1942*. Amsterdam: Amsterdam University Press.

Luhulima, Achie Sudiarti (2009), 'Pengujian Undang-Undang Republik Indonesia No 44 Tahun 2008 tentang Pornografi terhadap Undang-Undang Dasar Negara Republik Indonesia tahun 1945 dan Instrumen HAM Internasional'. Presentation, Jakarta, 1 June, on file with the author.

Lukens-Bull, Ronald (2005), *A Peaceful Jihad: Negotiating Identity and Modernity in Muslim Java*. London: Palgrave Macmillan.

Machrusah, Safira (2010), 'Islam and Women's Political Participation in Indonesia: Discourses and Practices' in Claudia Derichs and Andrea Fleschenberg (eds.), *Religious Fundamentalisms and Their Gendered Impacts in Asia*. Berlin: Friedrich-Ebert-Stiftung.

Martyn, Elizabeth (2005), *The Women's Movement in Post-Colonial Indonesia: Gender and Nation in a New Democracy*. New York: RoutledgeCurzon.

Mayer, Tamar (ed.) (2000), *Gender Ironies of Nationalism: Sexing the Nation*. London: Routledge.

Miller, Michelle Ann (2009), *Rebellion and Reform in Indonesia: Jakarta's Security and Autonomy Policies in Aceh*. New York: Routledge.

Nurmila, Nina (2009), *Women, Islam and Everyday Life: Renegotiating Polygamy in Indonesia*. London: Routledge.

O'Shaughnessy, Kate (2009), *Gender, State and Social Power in Contemporary Indonesia: Divorce and Marriage Law*. London: Routledge.

Ong, Aihwa and Michael G. Peletz (eds.) (1995), *Bewitching Women, Pious Men: Gender and Body Politics in Southeast Asia*. Berkeley: University of California Press.

Patung (2006), 'Gus Dur Rejects Anti Porn Bill', *Indonesia Matters*, 12 March, http://www.indonesiamatters.com/167/gus-dur-rejects-anti-porn-bill/

Patung (2009), 'Nikah Siri Marriages', *Indonesia Matters*, 17 April, http://www.indonesiamatters.com/3758/nikah-siri/

Perwita, Anak Agung Banyu (2007), *Indonesia and the Muslim World: Islam and Secularism in the Foreign Policy of Soeharto and Beyond*, Nordic Institute of Asian Studies (NIAS) Report no. 50. Copenhagen: NIAS Press.

Platzdasch, Bernhard (2009), 'In Indonesia: Aceh's Stoning By-law in Limbo', *OpinionAsia*, 13 October, http://opinionasia.com/AcehStoning

Poore, Grace (2010), 'LGBT Activism under Attack in Surabaya, Indonesia', *International Gay and Lesbian Human Rights Commission*, IGLHRC Blog, 2 April http://iglhrc.wordpress.com

Ricklefs, M.C. (2001) [1981, 1993], *A History of Modern Indonesia since c. 1200*, 3rd ed. London: Palgrave Macmillan.

Riddell, Peter G. (2002), 'The Diverse Voices of Political Islam in Post-Suharto Indonesia', *Islam and Christian–Muslim Relations* 13 (1): 65.

Rofiah, Nur (2010), *Memecah Kebisuan: Agama Mendengar Suara Perempuan Korban Kekerasan Demi Keadilan (Respon NU)*. Jakarta: Komnas Perempuan.

Sahetapy, J.E. (2009), [without title]. Presentation before the Indonesian Constitutional Court, Jakarta, 6 May, on file with the author.

Salim, Arskal (2007), 'Dynamic Legal Pluralism in Modern Indonesia: The State and the Sharia (Court) in the Changing Constellations of Aceh'. Paper presented at the First International Conference of Aceh and Indian Ocean Studies, Asia Research Institute, National University of Singapore & Rehabilitation and Construction Executing Agency for Aceh and Nias (BRR), Banda Aceh, Indonesia. Singapore, 24–27 February.

Salim, Arskal (2008), *Challenging the Secular State: The Islamization of Law in Modern Indonesia*. Honolulu: University of Hawai'i Press.

Siregar, Hasnil Basri (2008–9), 'Lessons Learned from the Implementation of Islamic Shari'ah Criminal Law in Aceh, Indonesia', *Journal of Law and Religion* 24: 143.

Sood, Neha (2010), *Transgender People's Access to Sexual Health and Rights: A Study of Law and Policy in 12 Asian Countries*. Kuala Lumpur: Asian-Pacific Resource and Research Centre for Women.

Stoler, A.L. (1997), 'Sexual Affronts and Racial Frontiers: European Identities and the Cultural Politics of Exclusion in Southeast Asia', in F. Cooper and A.L. Stoler (eds.), *Tensions of Empire: Colonial Cultures in a Bourgeois World*, 198–237. Berkeley: University of California Press.

Suardana, G. (2008), 'DPRD Bali Bakal ke Senayan Tolak RUU Pornografi', *detikNews*, 17 September, http://us.detiknews.com/read/2008/09/17/124034/1007774/10/dprd-bali-bakal-ke-senayan-tolak-ruu-pornografi

Tanuwidjaja, Sunny (2010), 'Political Islam and Islamic Parties in Indonesia: Critically Assessing the Evidence of Islam's Political Decline', *Contemporary Southeast Asia* 32 (1): 29.

Van Klinken, Gerry (2007), *Communal Violence and Democratization in Indonesia: Small Town Wars*. New York: Routledge.

Wieringa, Saskia (2003), 'The Birth of the New Order State in Indonesia: Sexual Politics and Nationalism', *Journal of Women's History* 15 (1): 70.

Wignjosoebroto, Soetandyo (2009), [without title]. Presentation, Jakarta, June, on file with the author.

***

―――― (2009), 'Atas Nama Otonomi Daerah: Pelembagaan Diskriminasi Dalam Tatanan Negara-Bangsa Indonesia', *Laporan Pemantauan tentang Kondisi Pemenuhan Hak-Hak Konstitusional Perempuan*, Komnas Perempuan.

―――― (2010), 'Court Decision Upholding "Defamation of Religions" Laws is Major Setback', Article 19/CIHRS/IFEX, *International Freedom of Expression eXchange: The Global Network for Free Expression*, 28 April, http://www.ifex.org/indonesia/2010/04/28/defamation_of_religions/

―――― (2009), *Report on Successful Campaign to Halt Sharia Laws in South Sulawesi*, Women's Empowerment in Muslim Contexts and Solidaritas Perempuan Anging Mammiri, http://www.wemc.com.hk/web/e-bulletin/09-2009/files/campaign_against_ discriminatory_regulations_bulukumba.pdf

***

Putusan No 10-17-23/PUU-VII/2009, Mahkamah Konstitusi Republik Indonesia.

Iran

> ## COUNTRY PROFILE[1]
>
> Iran is one of the largest countries in the Middle East, with a population of over 70 million. It is the only country whose official religion is Shi'a Islam (to which 10 per cent of all Muslims adhere); 89 per cent of the population are classified as Shi'a Muslims, 9 per cent Sunni Muslims and the remaining 1–2 per cent Christians, Jews, Zoroastrians, and Baha'is. More than half live in towns and cities; 80 per cent are literate; there are 22 million students, including three million enrolled in universities, well over 50 per cent of whom are female.
>
> A popular revolution in 1979 ended '2,500 years of monarchy' and gave birth to an Islamic Republic, a peculiar and unprecedented combination of theocracy and democracy. With the ascendancy of the Shi'a clerics, the state embarked on a process of 'Islamisation' of law and society, with some devastating consequences for women and civil society. Family and criminal laws became the main target of the 'Islamisation' of the legal system; the legal reforms introduced in the 1960s that gave women easier access to divorce and child custody were dismantled soon after the revolution, and in 1983, with the enactment of Islamic Criminal law, *zina* laws were revived.
>
> The uneasy marriage between theocracy and democracy continues to divide society and to animate politics. In 1997 the surprise election of Mohammad Khatami brought a shift towards a more democratic basis for the state, but efforts to foster a pluralistic and democratic politics have met with fierce resistance from theocratic forces and hardliners. The disputed results of the 2009 presidential elections gave a new dimension to the conflict between the theocratic and democratic elements, and led to massive protests and the emergence of a vibrant civil rights movement, in which gender equality and human rights are central demands.

In 1978–79 a popular revolution overthrew the modernising but autocratic and repressive Pahlavi monarchy and sought domestic justice and freedom and independence from foreign powers. However, the Islamic Republic that resulted was ruled by clergy, who sought to implement the '*shari'a*'; in practice this meant a return to outmoded laws derived from *fiqh* (Islamic jurisprudence), involving gender discrimination in family law (marriage, divorce, custody and inheritance) as well as in criminal laws, notably in relation to *zina* (sex outside marriage) and *hijab* (the dress code for women).

This chapter takes a critical feminist perspective, and analyses both the historical developments in the politics of religion, gender and law that led to this legal system, and the recent and current movements that are seeking to reform it in favour of a more just and

---

[1] This chapter builds on an earlier draft by Zara Saeidzadeh and her valuable research, for which the author is most grateful.

egalitarian system of laws. The wider context is that of the shifting political and cultural tensions in Iranian society, between despotism and democracy, and between authoritarian traditionalism and the modern liberal ideas spread by demographic pressures and the rapid expansion of education and new media. The main objectives of this study are to reveal the intimate links between patriarchy and despotism, and to show how *zina* laws are part of a complex system of norms and laws regulating sexuality in ways that serve patriarchy. The main argument is that to understand the revival of *zina* laws in the Islamic Republic of Iran we must transcend ideological dichotomies such as 'secular' versus 'religious' feminism, or 'Islam' versus 'human rights'. These dichotomies are both false and arbitrary, yet they have been invoked to obscure the real cleavage in Iranian society: the power struggle between despotic and democratic forces, to which women's struggle for equality and dignity have been held hostage for over a century.

The first section of this chapter relates the historical relationship, since mediaeval times, between religious and mundane power and authority, between the *ulama* and the monarchs. In the 20th century Iran experienced two revolutions: the Constitutional Revolution of 1905–11 and the Islamic Revolution of 1978–79. The former achieved an elected parliament and laid the foundations of modern judicial and educational systems. Subsequently, from 1925, Reza Shah Pahlavi instituted a programme of modernisation and secularisation of the state and country; a new Civil Code and educational system effectively marginalised the *ulama*. After a brief interlude of democracy under Mohammad Mossadeq, crushed by a US–UK-backed coup in 1953, Mohammad Reza Pahlavi's autocracy provoked the growth of leftist and religious opposition movements, severely repressed but eventually successful under Ayatollah Khomeini in the 1978–79 Revolution. The new regime brought a new constitution and new laws, but the ruling clerical elite was faction-ridden from the start – notably between those who favoured the theocratic or the democratic elements in the Islamic Republic.

The second section sketches the post-revolutionary legal system, focusing on family laws, criminal justice and *zina* regulations. This system was shaped in the context of the factional politics of the ruling elite, the structural tension between the theocratic and democratic elements and institutions in the post-revolutionary regime, and pressures from civil society. The state's policy of 'return to *shari'a*' brought a major restructuring of the legal system and reversed the process of secularisation begun under the Pahlavis.

The third section examines Iran's commitments under international human rights law, especially those relating to gender issues: the treaties and conventions Iran has signed; the major events and features of Iran's engagement and performance in relation to its obligations; and, again, how these are related to factional politics among the rulers.

The fourth section gives a detailed account of civil society activism since the 1979 Revolution, notably women's organisations and pressure groups. Important incidents and turning points are described, especially in the period since the first election of reformist president Khatami in 1997. Despite increasing repression by hardline elements in the ruling elite, women's activism for legal change has hugely expanded, and is a crucial element in the growth of the Green Movement since 2009. The tension between theocratic and democratic elements in the Islamic Republic is becoming a catalyst for change from within, as well as the emergence of indigenous forms of secularism and feminism.

The final section summarises the findings of the study, and suggests some lessons to be drawn from the Iranian case.

Historical Background

Islam came to Iran in the 7th century when the Umayyad Arabs brought an end to the Zoroastrian Persian Sasanid Empire. After centuries of foreign occupation and short-lived native dynasties, the country was unified in 1501 under the Shah Isma'il, founder of the Safavid dynasty, who declared the state religion to be Twelver Shi'ism.[2] Iran remains the only country where the official religion is Shi'a Islam (adherents number 10 per cent of Muslims worldwide). The Safavid dynasty was eventually replaced by the Qajars, who ruled from 1779 to 1925.

The birth of 'modern' Iran is often dated to the emergence, in the late 19th century, of the popular movement that culminated in the Constitutional Revolution of 1905–11. A wide range of different elements – merchants, clerics, Muslim reformist intellectuals, secular liberals and nationalists – came together with the common aim, if on differing grounds, of limiting the absolute power of the Shah through a constitution, an elected legislature and an independent judiciary. The clerics were ambivalent and took different positions. In August 1906, Mozaffar ad-din Shah was forced to establish a *majles* (parliament), and at the end of December, shortly before his death, he signed the 'Fundamental Law': the first constitution. This was a largely secular document; it emphasised popular sovereignty and codified several rights, such as freedom of expression and equality before the law. Following objections by the *ulama*, a Supplement to the Constitution was drafted to include more references to Islam and the necessity for the *ulama* to approve all laws. The new Shah, Mohammad 'Ali, signed the Supplement in October 1907; however, the following year, with Russian help, he staged a successful coup against the constitutionalists. In 1909, constitutionalist forces advanced on Tehran and deposed the Shah. Parliament was restored, along with the Constitution.

One of the main constitutionalist demands was the creation of a House of Justice, which they achieved in 1907. Nineteen articles (71–89) of the Supplement laid the basis for

---

2 For Shi'a Muslims, after the death of the Prophet, leadership of the Muslims passed not to elected caliphs but to his descendants, the Imams. The majority of Shi'as are Twelvers or Imamis, who believe in the line of 12 Imams, starting with 'Ali, the Prophet's cousin and son-in-law and ending with Mohammad Mehdi, the Imam of Time, who went into Occultation; his return will mark the end of time.

an independent judiciary and a unified legal system, and defined the power, nature and organisation of the courts (Amanat 1992). At the same time, the clergy were given a concession: Article 2 required Parliament's enactments to be in accord with the sacred precepts of Islam, and established a body of five clerics with veto power over bills deemed to be in contradiction to the *shari'a*. In 1911, Parliament set up a temporary committee to consider 'transitional laws', and the French jurist Pierny was charged with drafting criminal, trade and civil law. To contain the *ulama*'s opposition to these measures, their temporary and experimental nature was stressed (Banani 1961: 69). However, the process of law reform soon ground to a halt, as skirmishes erupted between Parliament and the clergy, who were adamant about retaining the *shari'a* as the only source of law and their power as its sole interpreters. The Qajars maintained a dual court structure: state courts supervised by a secular minister of justice, as well as religious (*shari'a*) courts. The *shari'a* courts, presided over by clerics, had jurisdiction over all matters relating to family, inheritance and civil law; the state courts had jurisdiction over matters involving the state. However, in practice the *shari'a* courts enjoyed almost all judicial power and dealt with cases in accordance with well-developed Shi'a rules of jurisprudence (*fiqh*) (Banani 1961: 68; Amin 1985: 52–60; Schneider 2005:85).

The early 1920s saw the rise to power of Reza Khan, a military officer, who founded the Pahlavi dynasty that ruled Iran from 1925 to 1979. A westernising secular nationalist, Reza Shah formed a strong military and a centralised bureaucracy. He also established both the secular judiciary and the greatly expanded secular educational system that the constitutionalists had wanted. In these and other ways, Reza Shah deprived the clerics of their former monopolies and resources, though he did not go as far as his model Kemal Atatürk in Turkey.[3] Though many of his reforms were popular, he ignored or manipulated the Constitution and ruthlessly suppressed dissent. The clerics, labelled fanatical reactionaries in this modernising milieu, were reduced to silence. Although the Shah retained Article 2 of the Supplement to the Constitution, regarding the primacy of the *shari'a*, his modernising zeal and the authoritarian nature of the Pahlavi monarchy rendered it irrelevant.

A number of measures between 1926 and 1936 led to the establishment of a predominantly secular legal system. Its conceptual and organisational inspiration was French, and its architect, 'Ali Akbar Davar, was a law graduate from the University of Geneva. As the new Minister of Justice, Davar dissolved the old judiciary with Parliament's approval in 1926. With the aid of French legal experts, he began a radical restructuring and reform of the system, which resulted in the complete exclusion of the clergy. Some 600 newly appointed judges, many with European education, replaced clerical officials in Tehran.

In most areas of law, Islamic jurisprudential concepts were put aside and European-inspired codes were enacted, including those of Commercial Law (1932), Civil Procedure (1939), Criminal Procedure (1932) and Criminal Law (1926, and 1940). Islamic concepts

---

3 See the chapter on Turkey in this volume.

were retained only in the new Civil Code; while it took the Belgian, French and Swiss codes as models, many of the Civil Code's 1,335 articles are in effect a simplification and codification of majority opinion within Shi'a jurisprudence.[4] Parliament approved the Civil Code in two phases, in 1928 and 1935. Volume 2, dealing with personal status and the family, retained classical Shi'a jurisprudence's patriarchal concept of the family. Meanwhile, in 1931, a separate marriage law required all marriages and divorces to be registered in civil bureaus set up in accordance with Ministry of Justice regulations. In the same year, Parliament passed a law defining *shari'a* courts as 'special courts', which not only reduced their jurisdiction to disputes involving the essential validity of marriage and divorce, but also placed *shari'a* courts under the authority of state courts (Banani 1961: 78–79). The secularisation of the judiciary culminated in 1936 when the employment of clerical judges was terminated, almost overnight, through a law that required serving judges to have a law degree from either the Tehran Faculty of Law or a foreign university. It was also in 1936 that Reza Shah's policy of 'unveiling', initiated a decade before, reached its zenith; a law was passed prohibiting women's appearance in public wearing either a headscarf or the traditional Iranian *chador*. This ultimate secularising measure sent the public a strong message about the emasculation of religious-based law and practice.

In 1941, during the Second World War, British and Soviet forces occupied Iran and forced Reza Shah, who favoured Germany, to abdicate in favour of his son Mohammad Reza. Over the next decade, renewed political debate and activity – dominated by the communist Tudeh party and the secular National Front – culminated in the nationalist government of Mohammad Mosaddeq (1951–53); it initiated grand economic and political reforms, notably the nationalisation of the oil industry, and led to the temporary exile of the Shah. Mosaddeq's secularism antagonised the clerical establishment; his nationalism, and the rise of the Tudeh, frightened Britain and the USA. In 1953, after a CIA-engineered coup, Mohammad Reza Shah resumed his reign. Throughout the following years, he alienated much of the country by allowing a massive increase in US influence, and by suppressing further dissent and parliamentary activity.

Under Mohammad Reza Shah there were very few adjustments made to the legal system, which was still based on the 1906 Constitution and the hierarchical French-model system implemented by his father. A major legal change of his era was the 1967 Family Protection Law (FPL), which curtailed men's rights to *talaq* (unilateral and extra-judicial divorce) and polygyny. The Civil Code was left intact, and reforms were achieved through procedural devices (Hinchcliffe 1968). New rules for the registration of marriage and divorce were introduced and new courts were set up to deal with familial disputes. All divorcing couples were required to appear in these courts, which had their own procedural rules and were presided over by civil judges, some of them women. In the absence of spouses' mutual

---

4 The three most authoritative Shi'a legal texts were used as sources: Najm ad-din Mohaqqeq Helli's *Sharaye' al-eslam*, Zein ad-din Shahed Sani's *Sharh-e lom'eh* and Mortaza Khorasani's *Makaseb* (see Mehrpoor 2001: 6).

consent to divorce, and upon the establishment of certain grounds, the court would issue a certificate referred to as 'Impossibility of Reconciliation'. Grounds available to men were parallel to those available to women; both could petition the court to appoint arbiters to try to bring about reconciliation, although the final decision on divorce and child custody arrangements rested with the court (Articles 6–13). It was illegal to register a divorce without a court certificate, the penalty being six months to a year's imprisonment for all parties involved, including the registrar (Articles 14, 16).[5]

The initiative for these reforms came from the nascent women's movement; however, by the time they became law, they had already been co-opted by the official Women's Organization of Iran under the patronage of Princess Ashraf, the Shah's twin sister. This compromised their legitimacy and significance. The left and the secular opposition identified the FPL with the despotic Pahlavi regime, which had already appropriated the women's movement. The *ulama*, for their part, were united and vocal in denouncing the reforms.[6]

The 1978–79 Revolution and the Creation of the Islamic Republic

In 1962, in an effort to gain popular support, the Shah instituted his 'White Revolution' or 'Revolution of the Shah and People', which included land reform and women's suffrage. Soon after, Ayatollah Ruhollah Khomeini came to prominence, publicly denouncing the Shah for his attacks on the clergy and his increasing dependence on foreigners. On 5 June 1963, Khomeini was arrested. The authorities violently put down large protest demonstrations in Tehran, Qom and other cities. Khomeini was released in April 1964, but was rearrested in October after giving a fiery sermon against the Shah. This time, he was exiled to Turkey. In October 1965, Khomeini was allowed to relocate to Najaf, Iraq, where he stayed until 1978.

In the 1970s, opposition to the Shah gained momentum and came from many directions. Among leftist groups, the Tudeh – discredited by their links to the USSR – lost support to the Marxist Fedayin-e Khalq and the Islamist-socialist Mojahedin-e Khalq, whose guerrilla activities against the regime escalated as the Shah's excesses further alienated the intellectuals and the people. The opposition forces soon united under the leadership of Ayatollah Khomeini from his exile in Iraq and later (in 1978) in Paris. They shared their main aim: to reject the autocratic, unjust and unaccountable Pahlavi monarchy, the inequalities in society, and the overwhelming influence of the USA. But the alternatives they sought were as multiple and varied (and often contradictory) as they were themselves: a popular democracy; a classless society; a socialist state; national autonomy; an Islamic government, with rulers guided by the *ulama* and the *shari'a*.

---

5 In 1975, the FPL was replaced by another law with the same title, which extended the reforms and formally repealed any prior laws conflicting with its mandate; see Mir-Hosseini (1999)

6 For analysis of the politics of the women's movement in pre-revolutionary Iran, see Paidar (1995) and Sanasarian (1982).

The success of the Revolution was assured on 16 January 1979, when the Shah left Iran for good, and on 1 February Ayatollah Khomeini returned in triumph. On 30 March, a referendum overwhelmingly endorsed the formation of an Islamic Republic; and a further referendum on 2 December approved a constitution produced by an assembly of experts, dominated by clerics. The unresolved tensions that brought about the Revolution were in effect written into the new Constitution, a compromise document with an uneven fusion of democratic and theocratic principles and institutions (Arjomand 1992; Schirazi 1997). On the one hand, it recognises the people's right to choose who will govern them, establishing democratic and legislative institutions such as the Parliament and the Presidency, both elected by direct popular vote. On the other hand, the Constitution subordinates the people's will to that of the clerical establishment through the institutions of *velayat-e faqih* (Guardianship of the Jurist) or *rahbari* (Leadership)[7] and the *shura-ye negahban* (Guardian Council), which is a 12-member council composed of six jurists appointed by the Leader and six laymen nominated by the head of the Judiciary and approved by the Parliament, with a tenure of six years.[8] The Constitution grants the Leader – the ruling jurist – a wide mandate and the final say in running the state; it charges the Guardian Council with deciding whether laws passed by Parliament conform to the *shari'a* and the Constitution. In effect, the Guardian Council is the official interpreter of both the Constitution and the *shari'a*.

The Constitution names Khomeini as Leader for life, and creates the *majles-e khebregan-e rahbari* (Assembly of Experts) whose responsibility is to choose his eventual successor and to supervise his activities, ensuring that he complies with his religious and constitutional duties. The 86 members of this Assembly are elected every eight years; only senior clerics are eligible, and conservative clerics have dominated the Assembly from the outset. In practice, to date the Assembly has merely endorsed the actions of the Leader. The Constitution allows the Guardian Council to oversee all elections, which they have interpreted as the right to vet candidates' eligibility. This means that, in effect, the Assembly of Experts and the Guardian Council form a closed system that allows the Leader unlimited power. Through his appointees to the Guardian Council, he can control both the legislative and executive branches of government (Schirazi 1997; Buchta 2000).

The Elected and Un-elected Institutions in the Islamic Republic

The first decade after the revolution was a period of establishment of the Islamic Republic, marked by the war with Iraq (1980–88) and by bitter struggles, first between the different elements that had contributed to the revolution, and then between the proponents of liberal-democratic and theocratic Islam.[9] Meanwhile, with the merging of religious and political authority in the persons of the Leader and his appointees, the politics of 'return to

---

7 Art. 110. *Rahbar*, or *rahbar-e enqelab* (Leader of the Revolution), is the term commonly used, both in the constitution and in everyday political discourse in Iran, for the leading jurist (*faqih*).

8 Articles 91–99 set out the role, composition, and scope of activity of this council.

9 For the early period see Bakhash (1985).

Control and Sexuality: The Revival of *Zina* Laws in Muslim Contexts

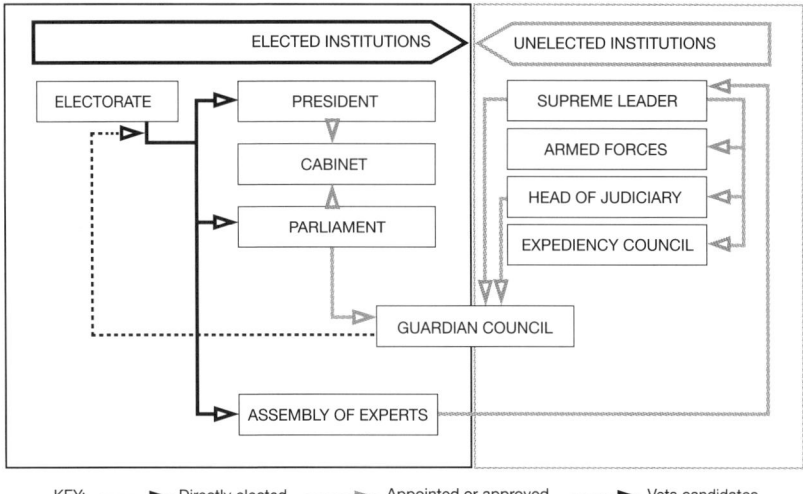

The elected and un-elected institutions in the Islamic Republic
[Source: BBC News (http://news.bbc.co.uk/1/shared/spl/hi/middle_east/03/iran_power/html)]

shari'a' unfolded. In measures mirroring those of Reza Shah, the courts were restructured and the civil judges were gradually purged and replaced by clerical judges. Laws and articles of the Civil Code were amended, and new laws based on Islamic legal concepts replaced those inspired by European laws. Islamic Revolutionary Courts entered the scene; local *komitehs* (supporters of the Islamic revolution in the 1980s) and *basij* (volunteer militia) acted as informal police and took the law into their own hands. A High Judicial School was created in order to train clerics to serve in the judiciary.[10] Places of recreation were closed; alcohol, prostitution and homosexuality were forbidden; the wearing of *hijab* became compulsory for women; and the education system was segregated. Although universities remained mixed, regulations were introduced to separate the sexes in class and on campus.

As the revolutionary fervour subsided, the tension between theocratic and democratic elements and institutions increased; cracks in the system began to appear. There were increasing signs of popular dissatisfaction with state policies. Either the notion of 'Islamic', as defined by the ruling clerics, had to adapt to the political exigencies of a modern democracy, or the people's choice must be restricted or bypassed, which would mean betraying the Revolution's democratic ideals and losing the popular support from which the Islamic Republic drew its legitimacy. Ayatollah Khomeini's death in 1989 forced a redefinition of the relationship between religious authority and the state. His successor as ruling jurist and Leader, Ali Khamene'i, lacked Khomeini's charisma and religious qualifications and sought to bolster his authority by increasing the power of the non-

---

10 For an analytical and critical account of these processes, see Mohammadi (2008).

elected bodies, which came to be identified with the theocratic side of the state, at the expense of the elected bodies, representing the democratic side, the republic. During the liberalising and 'pragmatic' presidency of 'Ali Akbar Hashemi-Rafsanjani (1989–97), factional politics within the ruling elite enabled Khamene'i to expand his own power base and to narrow the scope of democracy, by using the institutions at his disposal, and especially by introducing a more stringent vetting of candidates for elected office. This tactic misfired in the 1997 presidential elections, when people rejected the candidate endorsed and supported by the regime, and voted for en masse for Mohammad Khatami, the candidate who promised to promote civil society and the rule of law.

Khatami's election marked a turning point; pent-up demands for freedom and change were unleashed, and once again popular will began to assert itself. His government's relatively liberal policies allowed the voices of dissident intellectuals, both lay and clerical, to be aired in the press and to reach the public. A new public space emerged – comprising a vocal and dynamic press and virtual media (websites and weblogs), the universities, the seminaries and the Parliament – where the ambiguities and contradictions inherent in the original idea of the Islamic state, its translation into law and policy, the nature of the *shari'a* and its place in everyday life were all subject to debate.[11]

All this inaugurated a new round of factional struggles and a realignment of forces. Having lost the popular argument to the reformists, but buoyed by their success in frustrating the reformist programme of Khatami's government in both domestic policy and foreign relations, the theocratic forces used the Revolutionary Guards to ensure the consolidation of their control over all the institutions of state, culminating in the election of hardliner Mahmoud Ahmadinejad as president in 2005. But the demands, particularly by women and the youth, for legal and social reform, and the restoration of the freedoms they had tasted could not be suppressed; they erupted once more in the 2009 presidential election campaign. The Green Movement that emerged after the much-disputed re-election of Ahmadinejad, and the violent attempts by the 'Security Forces' to suppress it, showed clearly the extreme polarisation that has developed: it is no longer between Islamist conservatism and secularising reformism, but between despotism and democracy. Grand Ayatollah Hosein 'Ali Montazeri, one of the founders of the Islamic Republic, was now the Green Movement's spiritual leader. Before his death in December 2009, Montazeri denounced the state as a religious dictatorship and declared that it was now neither Islamic nor a republic (Torfeh 2009).

Domestic Legal System

After the Revolution, the Islamists' 'return to *shari'a*' policy focused on family and criminal laws, two areas where the *shari'a* courts' jurisdiction was terminated in the 1930s. However, they did not revive the classical *fiqh* notion of plural and uncodified laws; the Judiciary

---

11 Some of these debates are recorded and translated in Mir-Hosseini and Tapper (2006).

retained both a centralised and unified legal system and many of the laws and legal concepts of the Pahlavi era. The ultimate aim was to return both law-making and the administration of justice to the clerics, and to abolish what the authorities saw as the pernicious secularisation of the Pahlavi era. This section chronicles developments since 1979 in family law and criminal law, which became the arenas for defining and policing the state's 'Islamic' vision for society and gender relations. The section **'Existing Activism for Change'** will detail the political context of these developments and their entanglement with the core tensions – between the theocratic and republican elements and institutions – in the Islamic Republic.

Family Law

Post-revolutionary developments in family law have been marked by two parallel trends: validation of the patriarchal mandates of classical *fiqh*, and protection and compensation of women who conform to these rules. The latter was achieved just like the pre-revolutionary reforms; that is, by manipulating procedural rules and creating new courts while leaving the *fiqh* concept of marriage intact. In September 1979, the Revolutionary Council ratified the Special Civil Courts Legislation, which provided for the establishment of new courts by the same name to replace those created by the 1967 Family Protection Law (FPL). Clerical judges were to preside over these courts, free from the provisions of the Civil Procedure Code; hence, the term 'Special'.

The FPL courts were abolished but the law was not formally repealed; its procedural rules continued to govern the registration of marriages and divorces, though in an ad hoc and inconsistent manner. With respect to marriage, there is a double rule: registering a polygamous marriage without a court order is still, in theory, an offence, but the penalty was removed in August 1984 when the Guardian Council declared it not to be in conformity with *'shari'a'* (i.e. *fiqh*). Yet, in April 1986 a Ministry of Justice directive sent to all marriage registrars required them to comply with the 1931 Marriage Law regulation, according to which they must ascertain a man's marital status and write it into any marriage contract.[12]

Men's right to *talaq* (unilateral divorce) was partially restored, and they were no longer required to provide grounds; however, no divorce can be registered without a court order. Between 1979 and 1992, a man could register a divorce with his wife's consent or a court order. The 1992 Amendment to Divorce Regulations once again outlawed the registration of a divorce without a Certificate of Impossibility of Reconciliation – the same name as under the FPL. Since then, every divorcing couple must go to court. Men are still not required to provide grounds, but women can obtain a divorce only upon establishing one of the recognised grounds, which are basically the same as those available to them under the FPL and are similarly written into the marriage contracts. This Amendment also allows the appointment of female advisory judges to co-operate with the main judge.

---

12 Articles 6 and 7 of the Marriage Law only require a man to inform the woman whom he is marrying of his previous marriage, and only she can bring legal action for deception, not the first wife.

More importantly, it enables the court to place a monetary value on women's housework, and to force the husband to pay her *ujrat al-mithl* ('exemplary wages') for her work during marriage, provided that divorce is not initiated by her or caused by any fault of hers. Now,

---

CASES OF HUMAN RIGHTS VIOLATIONS

The Trial of Hajieh Esmailvand: Punished for not Understanding

Hajieh Esmailvand comes from Jolfa, a town in Azarbaijan, a mainly Turkish-speaking region in north-western Iran. She lived with her husband and her two children (a boy of 6 and a girl of 10) in a school where she and her husband were caretakers. She did not have a happy life; her husband was a gambler, an alcoholic, an irresponsible father and used to beat her. But she wanted to keep the marriage for the sake of her children, and she had nowhere to go. She had given her inheritance to her husband, who gambled it away. In 1999, a young neighbour, Ruhollah, started pestering her by phone and coming to the house. In a fight following a gambling dispute, Ruhollah killed Hajieh's husband; at the time, Hajieh had taken her daughter for treatment to the provincial capital Tabriz, where she was staying with her parents. On her return to Jolfa in January 2000, Hajieh was arrested and charged with *zina* and being an accessory to murder. In April 2000, Branch 3 of Jolfa Public Court convicted her on both counts and sentenced her to five years in prison for involvement in the murder, to be followed by hanging for *zina*. The Supreme Court upheld the death sentence, but changed the method of execution to stoning.

According to Asieh Amini, the journalist who investigated her case, Hajieh said in court that Ruhollah had tried unsuccessfully to rape her; however, later in the court proceedings she signed a confession to *zina* without knowing the meaning of *dokhul*, penetration. In jail she did not know she had been sentenced to stoning. She wrote several times to the Head of the Judiciary that she denied complicity in the murder, that she had only confessed under duress, and that she had not confessed to *zina*. She also stated that she could not speak Persian.

The stoning was scheduled for 1 September 2004 at Jolfa prison. The local judiciary reportedly distributed leaflets inviting the public to participate. However, the judge responsible found several flaws in the case and temporarily suspended the execution. Following pressure from international and local human rights groups, the Supreme Court overturned the stoning sentence. In November 2006, the case was retried in Jolfa Public Court, which acquitted Hajieh. A lawyer following her case also got her conviction for being an accomplice to murder overturned – though she had already served the sentence for it. Now she has her life back and later married a decent man.

[Source: The information is based on Amnesty International's 2008 report, supplemented by Zara Saeidzadeh's interview with the lawyer.]

every divorcing couple is required to go through a process of arbitration. If the arbiters, one chosen by each side, fail to reconcile them, the court allows the man to effect a divorce only after he has paid his wife all her dues: *mahr* (dower), *'idda* (waiting period) maintenance, and *ujrat al-mithl* (domestic wages).

Other legal measures enhanced women's bargaining position in marriage and provided them with better protection against men's unilateral rights to divorce and polygyny; notably, the creation of family courts, indexing the value of the dower to inflation, expanding the grounds on which women can obtain divorce, and raising the minimum age of marriage for girls from 9 to 13.

The election of Mahmoud Ahmadinejad as president (2005) brought hardliners into office and a shift of policy. In July 2007, his government presented a bill to Parliament that has caused a great deal of controversy. Entitled 'Protection of the Family', this bill aims to abolish not only the pre-revolutionary reforms that have been retained in practice, but also the protective measures introduced in the 1980s and 1990s. The judiciary originally prepared the bill to set up procedural rules for the Family Courts, but the government altered some of its articles. Four articles in particular alarmed women's groups and became the focus of protest; they facilitate polygyny and restrict women's ability to gain compensation; they relax the regulations for registering temporary marriages, allow a man to contract a second marriage without the consent of his first wife if the court decides that he can afford it, and require the Ministry of Finance to demand tax payments from women at the time of marriage if they stipulate a dower that exceeds a certain limit. Above all, Article 52, by repealing all previous laws and acts, in effect dismantles not only the reforms introduced under the FPL that have continued to ban the registration of plural marriages without a court order, but also the 1992 Amendment that requires a husband to pay 'domestic wages' before he can exercise his unilateral right to divorce. At the time of writing (August 2010), this bill is being debated in Parliament and has undergone some transformations. It has been fiercely opposed by a coalition of women and reformist personalities (see below) on the grounds that it will give men easier access to divorce and polygyny and make women even more vulnerable and insecure in marriage.

Criminal Law

Post-revolutionary developments in the criminal justice system have been more radical and far-reaching than in any other area of law. Reform of the criminal justice system was integral to the creation of a modern unified legal system, which was achieved when Reza Shah pacified the clerical opposition. Unlike family law, criminal law in pre-revolutionary Iran was modernised and secularised in terms of substantive and procedural law; the 1926 Criminal Code and the 1932 Criminal Procedure contained no elements of Shi'a jurisprudence, and were based on French and Belgian law.

The clerics who took power after the Revolution thus gave priority to reviving and implementing *fiqh* notions of crime and punishment – notions that had become obsolete in Iranian society.[13] In 1983, Parliament approved an experimental bill, prepared by the High Judicial Council, entitled 'Islamic Punishment: Fixed Punishments (*hudud*), Retaliation (*qisas*), Blood Money (*diyeh*) and Discretionary Punishments (*ta'zirat*)'. However, the Guardian Council rejected it on grounds of 'non-conformity with *shari'a*', since the section on discretionary punishments retained many elements of the 1926 Criminal law and 1932 Criminal Procedures Laws. The Council argued that the bill in effect limited the discretionary power that *fiqh* grants judges in defining *ta'zirat* crimes and punishments. Parliament, on the other hand, argued that both crimes and punishments in this area must be defined, since there are not yet enough religious judges qualified to do so. After Ayatollah Khomeini's intervention on the side of Parliament, the bill was ratified for an interim period of five years (Gholami 1999: 218; Rahami 2005: 593–4). It was also under *ta'zirat* that new offences were created in the category of 'Crimes Against Modesty, Public Morality and familial Obligations': these included appearing without *hijab* for women (Article 102) and non-payment of maintenance for men (Article 105), the punishment for each being 74 lashes.

In 1991, Parliament approved a new Criminal Code, which was once again rejected by the Guardian Council on the same grounds but eventually approved on an experimental basis for five years. The new code, entitled 'Islamic Criminal Punishments', was renewed in 1996 and 2001. It consists of five Books. Book One is on Generalities (Articles 1–62). Book Two (Articles 63–199) concerns *hudud*, crimes considered as violations of God's limits, with mandatory and fixed punishments derived from textual sources (Qur'an or Sunnah). Books Three and Four of the 1991 Code concern crimes against the person, such as bodily harm and homicide, for which the victim or the victim's family can demand either retaliation or blood money. Book Three, on Retaliation, contains two chapters: the first (Articles 204–268) deals with Retaliation for Life and the second (Articles 269–293) with Retaliation for Bodily Harm. Book Four is on Blood Money (Articles 269–497), defined as monetary compensation paid to the injured party or their relatives in case of murder, manslaughter or bodily harm. The sums of compensation are not equal for Muslim and non-Muslim victims.

Book Five, on Discretionary Punishments (first enacted in 1996), essentially reproduced the 1983 law on offences other than those named in Books Two to Four. These constitute the majority of all criminal offences, and include those named in the pre-revolutionary Criminal Code as well as creating a new class of offences (Rahami 2005). Of relevance here are: Article 637, which specifies up to 99 lashes for an 'illegitimate act' other than *zina*, such as kissing and sleeping together; and Article 638, which prescribes 10 days to two months in prison or up to 74 lashes for 'immoral acts' in public places. This article is followed by a note stating: "Women appearing in streets and public places without religious *hijab*

---

13 For accounts in English of the process of codification of *fiqh* criminal concepts and their consequences, see Gholami (1999), Mohammadi (2008) and Rahami (2005).

shall be sentenced to ten days to two months in prison and/or a fine of 50,000 tomans" (approximately US$50). However, there is no definition of 'religious' *hijab*.

In 2007, the government presented Parliament with a new Criminal Code, which soon became subject to a great deal of criticism inside and outside Iran for its non-adherence to human rights law. In 2008, Parliament debated the Code and modified several articles before ratifying it in September. In February 2009, the Guardian Council's spokesman told reporters that after studying the 470 Articles of the new Code, the Islamic jurists raised 90 objections and returned it to Parliament; he did not give any details (Islamic Republic News Agency, 10/11/1388). At the time of writing (August 2010) the 1991 Code is still in operation.

Revival of Zina *Laws*

This section outlines those aspects of the 1991 Criminal Code that define and regulate permissible expressions of sexuality and the boundaries of gender segregation. These are found in 101 articles of Book Two (*Hudud* or fixed punishments) that concern sexual offences, and in two articles of Section 18 of Book Five (*Ta'zirat* or discretionary punishments) that concern 'Crimes Against Chastity and Public Morals'. Together with family law, these articles function to uphold and police classical *fiqh*'s patriarchal conception of gender relations, as well as defining 'proper' norms and expressions of sexuality.[14]

Chapter One of Book Two (Articles 63–107) is on *zina*, any penetrative sex between a man and a woman outside legal marriage. Chapter Two (Articles 108–126) concerns *lawat*, penetrative and non-penetrative sex between men; the punishment for sodomy is death, and the judge determines the manner of execution (Article 110). Chapter Three is on *musahaqah*, sex between women, for which the punishment is 100 lashes (Article 130) or death if the offence is repeated after three convictions (131). Chapter Four deals with *qavadi* (pimping), defined as bringing two or more persons together for the purpose of *zina* or *lawat* and punishable by 75 lashes and (for a man) expulsion from his place of residence for three months to one year. Chapter Five is on *qazf* (slanderous accusation) of illicit sex, punishable by 80 lashes.

The chapter on *zina* is the most elaborate part of the penal code; it is written in the language and idiom of classical *fiqh*, containing technical terms that are obscure to the uninitiated. It comprises 45 Articles, grouped in four sections.[15] Section One (Articles 63–67) defines the crime: "any act of sexual intercourse, including anal intercourse, between a man and a

---

14 For laws regulating sexuality in Islamic legal tradition, see the chapter 'Criminalising Sexuality: *Zina* Laws as Violence Against Women in Muslim Contexts' in this book, also accessible at: http://www.stop-stoning.org/node/882.

15 English translations of this chapter are available online (Amnesty International Report www.amnestyusa.org/countries/iran/Stoning_report_FINAL.pdf and Women's Learning Partnership, http://www.learningpartnership.org/resources/legislation/nationallaw/iran). Ziba Mir-Hosseini finds both translations problematic, and in this chapter the translations are her own.

woman who are forbidden (*haram*) to each other, unless the act is committed unwittingly" (Article 63). The act is punishable (subject to *hadd*) when it is committed by a person who is sane, an adult of free will and aware of the illicit nature of the act (Articles 64–65); a party who claims to be unaware that the intercourse was illicit, or to have been forced into it, is exempt from punishment unless the claim is disproved (Articles 66–67).

Section Two (Articles 68–81) deals with 'ways to prove *zina* in court', elaborating the intricate rules of Shi'a *fiqh*, in which, as in other schools, *zina* can be established only by confession

---

CASES OF HUMAN RIGHTS VIOLATIONS

Jafar Kiani and Mokarrameh Ebrahimi: Punished for Daring to Love

Mokarrameh was 43 in March 2007 when she was sentenced to stoning for an 'illicit' relationship with Jafar. They had lived as a married couple for over 11 years and had a child together. They had been in prison for the past 10 years; she was pregnant at the time of her arrest and gave birth to their second child in prison near Takestan, a small town in central Iran. The stoning sentence issued by a court in Takestan was confirmed by the Supreme Court. Early one morning in July 2007, Jafar's sentence was carried out, which came as a shock to human rights activists. Mokarrameh's case was then taken up by the Stop Stoning Forever Campaign and received international attention.

Theirs was a love story: Jafar had helped Mokarrameh to leave an abusive and unhappy marriage that she no could longer endure. Two years later, the first husband accused Jafar of kidnapping his wife; the police arrested Jafar and Mokarrameh and brought them to court, but the judge released them. Four years after that, the first husband lodged a new complaint and the couple were arrested again, and this time charged with adultery. They were taken to court, found guilty and convicted to execution by stoning. Mokarrameh told the court that she had asked her husband for a divorce many times but he refused; each time she ran away, he came after her and brought her back. She told the court that she believed her relationship with Jafar was legal; they had entered a temporary marriage and had a certificate from a mullah. She believed that Jafar had managed to get her a divorce from her first husband. The judge, however, did not accept the legality of their marriage. The lawyer – Shadi Sadr – who took up the case argued that, as Mokarrameh believed that she was in a legal marriage, no *zina* had taken place and she should be acquitted. The judge was not convinced and relied on his 'own knowledge'.* The case eventually went to Tehran to the Committee for Pardon; Mokarrameh and her son were released on 18 March 2008, and are trying to rebuild their lives.

[*See the films by Mahboubeh Abbasgholizadeh at:
http://www.youtube.com/watch?v=aSHb1CVBfo8; http://www.wluml.org/node/5691]

or testimony. Articles 68–73 contain the rules for confession, and Articles 74–81 those for testimony; both allow a great deal of leeway. Only one who confesses four times in front of the judge is certain to incur punishment; fewer confessions leave the judge to decide (Article 68); confession is valid only when done by a person who is sane, adult, of free will, and with the intention to confess, and when the confession is clear and plausible (Articles 69 and 70); if the confession is retracted, punishment can be waived, but only if it concerns the type of *zina* that incurs the death penalty (Article 71); if the confession is followed by repentance, the judge may ask the Leader for a pardon (Articles 72); an unmarried woman's pregnancy by itself is not proof of *zina* (Article 73). The conditions for valid testimony are equally exigent: the act of *zina* must be witnessed by four just male witnesses or three male and two female ones (Article 75); the testimony must be without ambiguity; in the case of discrepancy among witnesses, not only is the *zina* charge dismissed but also the witnesses will be punished for *qazf* (slander) by 80 lashes; witnesses must testify one after another, without intermission (Articles 77–79).

Section Three (Articles 82–93) defines types of punishment for *zina*. Article 82 stipulates the death penalty for the man, regardless of age and marital status, in the following crimes: intercourse with close blood relatives;[16] intercourse with his step-mother; intercourse with a Muslim woman if he is a non-Muslim; and rape. Article 83 stipulates death by stoning (*rajm*) for: (1) *zina* by a *mohsen*, a man with a permanent wife with whom he has had intercourse and may have intercourse when he so desires; and (2) *zina* by a *mohseneh* with an adult man; a *mohseneh* is a woman in a permanent marriage who has had intercourse with her husband and is able to do so again.

Zina by married men and women not in the above condition (i.e. *ihsan*) is punishable by 100 lashes (Article 88).

Section Four, 'How to Administer the Punishment', comprises 10 articles (98–107). Articles 100–04 codify classical *fiqh* rulings and contain graphic details of executions that have been subject to criticism for their cruelty. To be lashed, a man must be standing and naked (only the genitals covered), and struck all over his body apart from face and the genitals; a woman must be sitting and covered (Article 100). A man to be stoned is buried in a pit up to his waist and a woman up to her breast (Article 102); the stones should not be so large that one or two kill the convict, nor too small to qualify as stones (Article 104). But the most significant article in this section is 105, which reads:

> The Shari'a judge can act upon **his own knowledge** in cases of [defending] God's Rights (i.e. crimes that come under *hadd*) and People's Rights (i.e. crimes that come under *qisas*) and administer the punishment constituted by God; it is necessary that he documents his knowledge. [emphasis added]

---

16 The code does not define this: the term used, *maharem-e nasabi*, usually covers first and second degree relatives, but there is reason to believe the penalty applies only to incest with first degree kin.

The notion of "his own knowledge" grants the judge a subjective power that amounts, in effect, to a negation of the intricate rules devised by classical jurists for establishing *zina*, which make conviction almost impossible. As we shall see, judges in Iran have used this article to issue judgments in cases where '*shari'a*-based' evidence is lacking.

The latest Criminal Code (ratified in 2008 but yet to be approved by the Guardian Council) retains the same notions of sexual crimes and punishments as the 1983 and 1991 versions, but departs from them in three ways. First, it groups all sexual offences together: in Chapter Two, '*Haddi* Crimes and Punishments', Subject One covers '*Zina* and related matters (*lawat, tafkhiz* and *musahaqah*)'. Articles 221.1–17 deal with *zina* (i.e. heterosexual penetrative sex outside marriage); Articles 221.18–25 with *lawat* (penetrative sex between men) and *tafkhiz* (non-penetrative sex between men); and Article 221.26 deals with *musahaqah* (sex between women). The second departure is that the Code devotes only three articles to how punishment for *zina* is to be administered (Articles 221.15–17), while the previous codes elaborated this in the separate section that led to international outcry.

The third and most significant departure is that the new code opens the way not only for containing 'judge's knowledge' but also for suspending execution by stoning. Article 210, in Book One on Generalities, Section Five, 'Establishing Proof in Criminal Matters', reads:

> Judge's knowledge denotes the certainty that the judge attains from clear evidence in a matter brought to him. In cases where the judgement is based on the judge's knowledge, the judge is required to document explicitly in the judgement the clear legal circumstantial evidence and proofs [that form the basis] of his knowledge.

Note 4 to Article 221.5 in Book Two on *hadd* crimes, reads:

> Whenever implementation of the punishment of stoning will, at the suggestion of the Public Prosecutor and with the approval of the Head of the Judiciary, entail weakening of the regime, then, if the cause of the hadd [i.e. zina] has been established through shar'i proofs, stoning will be replaced by [another form of] execution; otherwise it will be replaced by 100 lashes.

This note implicitly admits that stoning as a punishment is now abhorrent in the eyes of the people, as well as making it possible to replace stoning with lashes. This is because '*shar'i* proofs', as defined by classical jurists, make the establishment of *zina* possible only by confession (four times, free of compulsion, without retraction) or the testimony of four just male witnesses (all of whom must have witnessed the act of penetration at the same time).

These three departures, as we shall see, were due to both internal and external pressures, and show how the Iranian legislature will not question the *fiqh* precepts that define *zina* as a crime against religion with a prescribed punishment, yet they are undoubtedly sensitive both to contemporary notions of morality and to the image of Iran in the world. They have sought a compromise: to keep faithful to classical notions of crime and punishment but at the same time to make conviction difficult.

Implementation of Zina Laws: Court Practices, Statistics and Cases

There is little statistical or other data available on court practices in criminal cases and convictions relating to sexual offences. The government and judiciary have so far declined to disclose the relevant information: the number of cases brought to court, the number of convictions and details of trials. The criminal courts, in particular those dealing with *zina* and sexual offences, are carefully kept away from the public eye, and press coverage and reporting of cases are highly controlled. The available information comes from human rights activists, both inside and outside Iran, and international organisations. Amnesty International's 2008 report on execution by stoning remains the most comprehensive and reliable study.[17] While Iran has one of the highest rates of judicial executions (estimated at 10,000 since 1979), Amnesty notes that executions by stoning have been relatively few. In all known cases, sentences were issued in provincial courts outside Tehran and other large cities, and defendants did not have access to legal counsel. A large majority of those convicted and stoned were women; 9 out of 11 persons awaiting execution, whose cases were covered by the 2008 Amnesty report, were women.

Despite the small number of stoning cases, the criminalisation of consensual sex since 1979 has had a drastic impact on gender relations, in particular in the ways in which the regime has used it to impose patriarchy. It provides families, communities and the state with the means to keep individuals in line with the state's definition of 'correct' sexual behaviour, and to enforce the inequality and discrimination to which women are subjected in other areas of law and society.

In the absence of reliable statistics and first-hand data on judicial practices, it is impossible to ascertain the frequency of accusations of *zina* and other related sexual crimes that make their way to court, or the extent to which courts use their discretionary powers to pursue or dismiss these accusations. There are, however, a number of court cases that have become public knowledge through the efforts of journalists and human rights activists. The cases give us a glimpse into court practices, and allow us to make three observations. First, accusation and conviction of *zina* are always linked with other charges, such as the murder of a spouse. Secondly, the poor, the uneducated and those from minority communities are particularly vulnerable to accusations of *zina*, and since in most cases they do not have legal counsel, they are easily tricked into making confessions. Thirdly, in most cases,

---

17 Iran: End Executions by Stoning; for full report, see
 www.amnestyusa.org/countries/iran/Stoning_report_FINAL.pdf; and for the appeal see
 http://www.amnesty.org/en/appeals-for-action/end-execution-stoning-iran

convicted women have already attempted but failed to get a divorce, or have been in protracted conflict with their in-laws.

State Responsibility

According to Article 4 of the 1979 Constitution, the *shari'a* not only dominates positive law in Iran but also prevails over every form of customary law and international law, including matters of human rights. The Islamic Republic remained a party to the ICCPR, which Iran had joined in 1967; but like the previous regime, it did not sign the Optional Protocols 1 and 2 concerning the individual right of Iranian citizens to complain and the prohibition on the death penalty.

The *shari'a*, as interpreted by the Guardian Council and as reflected in the laws of the Islamic Republic of Iran, contains a number of provisions that contradict customary international human rights law. In addition, many of the numerous human rights provisions in the Constitution of the Islamic Republic have never been translated into law. For instance, 'due process' is regulated perfectly on paper: Articles 32 and 34–39 of the Constitution specify conditions by which the legal system in Iran must abide: the regulation of prosecution, appearing before the judge, the right to legal assistance, the right to cross-examination of witnesses, and the right of appeal. The Islamic Republic has systematically violated all these conditions from the outset, and violations have multiplied since the disputed 2009 election attracted further international attention.

Since 1979, the codification of Islamic criminal justice concepts – in particular stoning as punishment for adultery and the unequal legal treatment of women and non-Muslims – has been criticised and condemned by the international human rights community. In the 1980s, Iran took a rejectionist stance towards international human rights treaties; Iranian representatives adopted a confident tone, claiming that since *shari'a* is the essence of justice, its laws must take precedence over all others. For instance, in July 1982, the leader of the Iranian delegation to the United Nations Human Rights Committee in Geneva said: "Iran believes in the supremacy of Islamic laws, which are universal." He went on to clarify that "Iran would choose the divine laws" in cases where human rights treaties are irreconcilable with '*shari'a*' on some point (Amin 1985: 106).

In the 1990s, Iran adopted a more positive attitude towards international human rights law, and pursued a policy of engagement. It joined the Convention on the Rights of the Child (CRC), which went into effect in August 1994, but, like many other Muslim countries, with a general reservation: "The government of the Islamic Republic of Iran reserves the right not to apply any provisions or articles of the Convention that are incompatible with Islamic laws." In 1997, with the election of Khatami and the emergence of the reform movement, a lively debate emerged around the notion of Islamic human rights, and the government's policy of supporting civil society by allowing the creation of non-governmental organisations (NGOs) helped to improve the human rights situation (Mokhtari 2004). Nevertheless, there are some important human rights treaties that have still not been ratified, notably the Convention Against Torture (CAT) and the Convention on Elimination of all forms of Discrimination Against Women (CEDAW).[18] Efforts by Khatami's government and the reformist Parliament (2000–04) to ratify these conventions were frustrated by the Guardian Council.

After the 2005 presidential election brought Ahmadinejad into office, hardliners controlled the executive, the legislature and the judiciary. They began systematically to curb civil society and muzzle the press, closing down many NGOs and reformist publications.[19] Yet, debates over human rights have intensified; high-ranking clerics and reformists have published their views on Islam and human rights, and human rights activists have launched campaigns (see next section). At the same time, the government became more active on the international scene; Ahmadinejad took every opportunity to go to the United Nations and to attend other international meetings. He used these visits as a platform to challenge the justice and universality of international human rights laws and organisations, and to put forward what he called 'Just Islamic Governance'. Iranian delegations have also taken initiatives to build alliances with some Latin American and Muslim states, as well as conservative religious factions, and sought a presence in UN bodies. Thus, in 2010, Iran bid for a seat on the UN Human Rights Council, but then withdrew following increasing criticism of its human rights record, which had intensified after the disputed 2009 presidential election. Iran was then, despite massive external opposition, re-elected to the UN Commission on the Status of Women (CSW).[20] In July 2010, in response to the international outcry at news of an imminent case of stoning, Mohammed Larijani, Secretary-General of Iran's High Council for Human Rights, defended stoning as a legitimate punishment endorsed by the Iranian Constitution.[21]

Existing Activism for Change

Women and sexual rights were the first casualties of the policy of dismantling the pre-revolutionary legal codes and creating new ones based on Islamic legal concepts. Yet, the constant confrontations between the 'Islamic' and 'Republican' elements of the state proved a catalyst for change and for the emergence of new discourses and new forms of activism,

---

18 The only countries that have not signed CEDAW are: Iran, Somalia, Sudan, the Holy See (Vatican), and some Pacific states (Nauru, Tonga and Palau). The US has signed but not ratified.

19 On 15 February 2010, the Universal Periodic Review, to which all UN Members are subjected, severely criticised Iran's human rights record during the past four years; see http://www.hrw.org/en/news/2010/02/16/un-council-review-highlights-irans-poor-record; see Amnesty International's comments, http://www.amnesty.org/en/library/info/MDE13/021/2010/en.

20 See http://www.wluml.org/node/6229

21 http://planet-iran.com/index.php/news/18906; http://www.voanews.com/policy/editorials/Iran-Secures-Seat-On-CSW-93802899.html

which, despite severe repression, led to the emergence of a civil rights movement in the aftermath of the disputed 2009 presidential election. Four distinct phases of activism can be discerned in the history of what became known as the Green Movement, corresponding with wider political and socio-economic developments in the Islamic Republic.[22]

First Phase: Revolution and 'Islamisation'

This phase began with people's massive participation in demonstrations during the 1978 upheavals and ended with Ayatollah Khomeini's death in 1989. It remains ideologically charged, and subject to contested claims and representations.[23] As far as the politics of gender and law are concerned, there were two concurrent developments. First was the mushrooming of hundreds of women's groups all over the country, in mosques, government offices, factories, schools and so on. Ranging from small and spontaneous to large and organised, these groups represented the three main ideological tendencies – Islamic, Nationalist and Marxist – which together brought about the fall of the Pahlavi dynasty. Some had been affiliated to underground political organisations, while others were formed during the Revolution.[24] All these groups saw women's rights as secondary to wider anti-imperialist goals and interests. Women who were active in these groups shared this view: they were concerned to win the struggle for control of the Revolution, and women's rights were a minor issue on their agenda.

The second development was the dismantling of pre-revolutionary legal reforms and the imposition of patriarchal interpretations of the *shari'a*. On 26 February 1979, barely two weeks after the collapse of the Pahlavi monarchy, a directive from Ayatollah Khomeini's office declared the Family Protection Law to be 'non-Islamic' and announced its suspension and the reinstitution of the *shari'a*. Other announcements followed: women must appear in public in Islamic *hijab*; women cannot serve as judges; and women cannot study subjects such as mining and agriculture. These measures were promoted as 'protecting the Islamic dignity of women' – an argument that had popular appeal and resonated with the beliefs of some sections of society.

These developments soon led to a breakdown of the apparent unity among women, their division into two distinct but still diverse camps, the 'Islamists' and the 'secularists', and an open confrontation between the latter and the state. This happened on International Women's Day, 8 March 1979, when demonstrations planned by secular women's groups

---

22 For overviews of women and politics in Iran, see Paidar (1995), Sedghi (2007), Hoodfar and Sadr (2007); for sexual politics see Afary (2009); and for transnational feminism, see Tohidi (2009, 2010).

23 There are many different accounts and interpretations of this history. For significant events, see Foundation for Iranian Studies, 'Iranian Women and the Islamic Republic: A Chronology', http://www.fis-iran.org/en/women/milestones/post-revolution

24 For a partial list, see 'Part Three: Women's Organizations in Iran,' in Tabari and Yeganeh (1982: 203–230).

were held in Tehran and Shiraz to protest against the loss of their rights. Ayatollah Khomeini's statement on the eve of the demonstrations, requiring women working in government offices to observe the 'Islamic code' of dress, also made *hijab* an issue. Thousands of women gathered, but were attacked and harassed by groups of religious zealots and men drawn from the urban poor.[25] Leftist and nationalist political groups kept silent, and their forces – including the nationalists' armed militia – stood by watching and denied women any protection or support. The authorities ignored the demonstrations, and radical Islamist groups (including women's organisations) and radio and television (now dominated by Islamists) denounced them as agitation by promiscuous women and agents of the previous regime (Azari 1983; Nashat 1983).

After the onset of war with Iraq in September 1980, Islamist hardliners gained the upper hand; they suppressed leftists, nationalists and liberal Islamists and embarked on a fierce process of 'Islamising' law and society. As already indicated, this process began with the suspension of the Family Protection courts and the codification of *fiqh*-based criminal law. Women retained their suffrage rights, but political activity was only open to those who adhered to the state ideology and were affiliated to the ruling elite. Most active among them were female journalists who had taken over the pre-revolutionary women's magazines, and female deputies in the parliament.

Second Phase: Construction and Pragmatism

With the end of the war in 1988, and Ayatollah Khomeini's death in June 1989, the revolutionary fervour started to subside. The presidency of Ali Akbar Hashemi-Rafsanjani (1989–97) heralded a new era of 'Construction' and some modification to official discourses and policies. In this phase – marked by factional politics and the intensification of struggles between traditionalist and pragmatic interpretations of the *shari'a* – some aspects of the state's gender policies were questioned and debated in public.

Gender debates, harshly suppressed in the early 1980s, were resumed, but this time in an Islamic format and framework. Conducted publicly in the women's press, these debates revealed growing dissent and argued for the enactment of legislation to confront women's legal disadvantages. Meanwhile, the dismantling of pre-revolutionary legal reforms had negative effects that were becoming apparent; notably, the massively increased birth rate, and the plight of divorced women. Many women who had genuinely, although naively, believed that an Islamic state would automatically improve women's position, were now becoming disillusioned.

This all made a shift in policy and a modification of the legal rules inevitable. For instance, most of the earlier restrictions on the subjects women could study were removed (1986); family planning and contraceptives became freely available (1988); divorce laws were

---

25 For film footage of this demonstration, see http://www.wluml.org/fr/node/5845

amended so as to curtail men's right to divorce and to compensate women in the face of it (1992); and women were appointed as advisory judges (1992). By the mid-1990s, the revolutionary regime had modified many of its early decisions with regard to women, or were at least debating them – with the exception of aspects of penal law relating to *hijab* and *zina* (Ramazanian 1993, Mir-Hosseini 1996).

In some ways these modifications represented the official, establishment side of the debates, which was achieved by the activism of women of the establishment, in dialogue with the clerics. But there was another side, aligned with a new trend of thought in post-war and post-Khomeini Iran that sought a dialogue with secular thinkers and offered a radically different interpretation of Islam; this had the potential to change the terms of the Islamic Republic's discourses on women. It not only challenged patriarchal notions of gender in Islam, but also questioned the religious legitimacy of the laws enforced by the Islamic Republic.

These views were aired in *Zanan* (Women), a journal that first appeared in 1992 and soon became a forum for both Islamic and secular activists. Its founder and editor, Shahla Sherkat, had been one of the activists who played an important role in the Islamisation of the women's press in the early years of the Republic. Among early contributors were: Mehrangiz Kar, a female lawyer with a secular perspective, who was among the first to criticise the gendered biases in the 1991 Criminal Law; and Mohsen Sa'idzadeh, a male cleric whose articles on women's Islamic, legal and political rights featured regularly in the journal.[26]

By the mid-1990s, there were signs that the moderates were gaining ground and that the early revolutionary discourse was relaxing; there was some scope for debate and contestation; the media, in particular the periodicals, had become a forum for protest and for solidarity between secular and religious moderates. Youth and women were joining the debates and making their voices heard; their votes were among the decisive factors in the 1997 presidential elections, when Mohammad Khatami, the candidate of the moderates, gained an unexpected and overwhelming victory over the conservative candidate.

Third Phase: Reform, Division in the Ruling Elite and Women's Voices

Khatami's election brought a shift from the theocratic towards the democratic basis of the Islamic Republic. Rivalries in the ruling elite were realigned in a new power struggle. The major cleavage was now between 'Conservatives', who insisted on keeping the ideological construction of 'Islam' intact, and 'Reformists', who sought to reconcile Islam with the discourses of democracy and human rights. Conservatives continued to dominate the Fifth Parliament (1996–2000), but the massive victories of reformist candidates in the municipal and parliamentary elections of 1999 and 2000, and Khatami's re-election in June 2001 with

---

26 These articles appeared in *Zanan* between June 1993 and February 1994. See Mir-Hosseini (1996).

over 77 per cent of the votes, showed the strength of their mass support. However, even though the reformists now dominated government and parliament, they were unable to fulfill their election promises. Instead, they were locked in a fierce political battle with their opponents, who were now aligned with the theocratic side of the Islamic Republic. Using their power over the unelected institutions, conservatives managed to frustrate many of the reformists' initiatives and their legislative moves in the Sixth Parliament (2000–04). They also silenced key reformist personalities, first by assassinating, then by prosecuting and jailing them, and they closed down the vibrant free press that was one of the reformists' main early achievements and platforms.

Gender issues became a major arena of confrontation between reformists and conservatives. As regards the politics of gender and law, the reformist phase was marked by two developments. First, the working relationship forged in previous phases between women of opposing political tendencies in Parliament broke down. Women parliamentarians had lobbied strongly for the co-operation of eminent clerics and the seminaries in pushing for legislation; this had produced a fragile consensus on the need to reform laws related to women and the family, and led to the enactment of a number of measures redressing the gender discrimination introduced soon after the Revolution. But in the conservative-dominated Fifth Parliament (1996–2000), the newly created 'Women's Commission' proposed two bills that became infamous for their anti-women slant. The first, 'Adaptation of Medical Services to Religious Law', extended the imposition of gender segregation to medicine, a realm that had been left more or less unscathed since the Revolution. The second, 'Banning the Exploitation of Women's Images and the Creation of Conflicts between Men and Women by Propagating Women's Rights outside the Legal and Islamic Framework', sought to prohibit the lively press debate on women's rights as well as press coverage of the dynamic film industry. These bills were a prelude to invoking 'shari'a' and Islam once again to silence other voices in society (Mir-Hosseini 2002).

Reform of family law and women's rights were central issues in the reformists' successful campaign for the 2000 parliamentary elections, but the Guardian Council frustrated their subsequent legislative moves. Although they did not take any serious initiatives in the area of criminal law, reformists presented 41 bills that aimed to modify, in various ways, the inequalities that women face in law; the Guardian Council rejected almost all of them, including the proposal to join CEDAW. Eventually 21 of the bills were passed into law, albeit in some cases with their gender-egalitarian tone and intent weakened or nullified. A bill aimed at restoring the minimum age of marriage to 18 (as set by the 1975 FPL) was altered to 13 for girls and 15 for boys (as in the 1935 Civil Code). Another bill to make access to divorce equal for men and women was reduced to expanding women's grounds for divorce and custody rights. Most importantly, the Guardian Council rejected the proposal to join CEDAW.

The second development during the reformist phase was the emergence of a lively, if fragile, civil society and an independent press, nurtured by the liberal policies of Khatami's government. Despite the silencing of some human rights advocates, the Islamic Republic's gender codes began to be relaxed, and the press debated aspects of penal law – an issue that until then had been a red line that no one had dared to cross. In practice, many women had challenged the imposition of *hijab* from the outset, and constantly pushed back its frontiers, and the gender segregation codes had also been flouted, but in theory no debate had been tolerated. By the early 2000s, colourful and stylish outfits had made their way back onto the streets, and young people increasingly broke gender segregation rules with impunity. The death penalty, and in particular the *zina* laws, were debated in the press; activists regularly organised seminars, lectures and events in universities and cultural centres, to which reformists in Parliament or government ministries were sometimes invited. In 2002, following the internal debates and a 'constructive dialogue' with the European Union, the head of Judiciary issued a moratorium on stoning as punishment for *zina*, while keeping the laws on illicit sex unchanged. No case of stoning was reported during the period when the reformists were in office.

Activists started to direct their energies from 'cultural activities' – a euphemism for criticism of biases in law and society – to the newly created NGOs, which focused on issues such as the environment, defending the rights of political prisoners, legal services for disadvantaged women, and the protection of abused children. Notable among NGOs were the Committee for the Defense of Prisoners' Rights, founded in 1999 by Emad ad-ddin Baghi, a theologian and journalist,[27] and the Defenders of Human Rights Centre, founded in 2001 by five lawyers,[28] including Shirin Ebadi, whose Nobel Peace Prize in 2003 gave further confidence and hope to the activists. Celebrations of International Women's Day, 8 March, held during the second phase by some women activists in their private homes, now became public events. Some of these activists openly called themselves 'secular feminists' and started to distance themselves from the reformists in government. Others, exasperated by the conservatives' success in containing the reformists, became increasingly critical of reformists in government and their strategies, and turned to pursuing their activism independently of the state.

Fourth Phase: Return of the Radicals, Birth of the Women's Movement and Campaigns

Unable to deliver on their electoral promises and bring change in the structures of power, the reformists lost popular support. In February 2003 and 2004, theocratic and undemocratic forces won back the city councils and Parliament; with Ahmadinejad's election in 2005, they controlled all branches of the state. The new government set out to undo civil society's modest but steady gains during the reformist phase. Khatami had created a Centre for Women's

---

27 Baghi's theoretical work has focused on reconciling Islamic and human rights law; he has been imprisoned several times and his work has been internationally recognised; see http://www.youtube.com/watch?v=gpEfavHftco. For his work on stoning, see Terman and Fijabi (2010).

28 See http://www.humanrights-ir.org/php/view_en.php?objnr=233

Participation, which supported the formation of women's NGOs; Ahmadinejad changed its name to the Center for Women and Family Affairs, and many of its publications were pulped. Restrictions on celebrating 8 March were reinstated, and some women's meetings planned in universities were cancelled. In 2006, police and paramilitary forces broke up the 8 March meeting organised by women activists in a central Tehran park. Then in June, when women tried to stage a rally in a main square in Tehran to protest against discriminatory laws, they were beaten and over 70 arrests were made, including a number of men. Most detainees were released within a week, some on bail, to appear in a Revolutionary Court on charges of 'propaganda against the system' (i.e. the government), 'acting against national security' and 'participating in an illegal demonstration'; some were convicted and imprisoned, others still await charges (Mir-Hosseini 2006).

Despite increasing pressures (such as regular interrogation by security forces and detention after attending meetings abroad) and disagreements over what actions to take, women's rights activists remained undaunted and launched two major campaigns. Run by veteran activists and conducted through the Internet and on their websites, these two campaigns attracted a great deal of publicity and support inside and outside Iran. They became the focal point for opposition to discriminatory laws, raising consciousness, and opening a new forum for discussion and debate in the face of increasing press censorship and NGO closures. They also became the model for other campaigns and connected women activists inside Iran with those outside, particularly with Iranians living in the diaspora.

The first campaign, One Million Signatures Demanding Changes to Discriminatory Laws, was launched in August 2006. Inspired by the successful Moroccan women's campaign (1992) to change the family laws, activists aimed to take the message of gender equality into civil society through face-to-face meetings with women, and by organising workshops.[29] The second campaign, Stop Stoning Forever, was launched by a group of human rights defenders, lawyers and journalists.[30] They were spurred into action after the journalists revealed that in May 2006, near Mashhad, north-eastern Iran, a couple had been stoned in contravention of the 2002 moratorium. A coalition of veteran women activists inside and outside Iran mobilised support to prevent further stonings and raise public awareness. The lawyers took up cases of women condemned to stoning and defended them in court; the journalists wrote about their stories, highlighting that, in a large majority of cases, these women were victims of violence, came from marginal classes and had no access to lawyers or any understanding of law, and that the sentences had been issued by provincial judges who relied on 'judge's knowledge'.

The Stop Stoning Forever campaign has so far made two gains. First, it has helped to save a number of lives – Jafar Kiani, stoned to death in July 2007 (see above) was an exception

---

29 For the campaign site, see www.we-change.org; for an example of support for and explanations of the aims of the campaign in English, see www.iranian.com/BTW/2006/Agust/Women/Index.html

30 http://meydaan.info/; the website has not been updated since July 2009 but contains important campaign documents at http://meydaan.info/campaign.aspx?cid=46

– and in a few cases has obtained acquittals or commutations. Secondly, it has inserted human rights concerns into the very heart of the criminal justice system and engaged hardliners and members of the Judiciary in debate. Campaign members, such as Shadi Sadr and the Network of Volunteer Lawyers, took the Judiciary to task and played a central role in this debate, which has spilled over into the print media. Activists and journalists, such Asieh Amini and Mahboubeh Abbasgholizadeh, exposed the injustices that the imposition of classical Islamic legal punishments entail in practice. In so doing, they have opened up one of the fault lines in the Islamic Republic, putting the hardliners on the defensive and showing how such punishments are so offensive to contemporary sensibilities and notions of criminal justice that the old *fiqh* arguments and rationales have lost their power to convince.

The reformists – now ousted from the judiciary and Parliament – joined the debate and questioned the legitimacy of stoning on religious grounds. They have revealed that Ayatollah Khomeini issued a decree to the judiciary in 1982 advising that stoning as punishment should not be implemented (Terman 2007). In July 2007, *Zanan* magazine published a special dossier on stoning. These debates had an impact on the new Criminal Code that was being drafted at the time, as evident in the recurrent argument that is put forward to justify the reform of *fiqh* notions of crime and punishment: the notion that stoning might be a 'disgrace to Islam' is an admission that it is abhorrent to the public. As discussed earlier, the new version of the Criminal Code, approved by Parliament in 2008, not only plays down stoning but also in effect allows for its replacement by alternative punishments.

Having lost the public debate, Ahmadinejad's government resorted to intimidation and violence. On 4 March 2007, a group of women's rights activists gathered in front of the court where their colleagues were on trial for organising the June 2006 rally. The security forces harassed them and arrested 33, the leading women's rights activists in the country; all were released within days, apart from Abbasgholizadeh and Sadr, who were kept in solitary confinement for over two weeks and then released on heavy bail after their offices had been raided and closed down. In April 2007, the police launched an unprecedented aggressive drive to control women's presence in public space. The initiative – called Moral Security Plan – involved female police in full *chador*, and targeted young women sporting the new fashion of *hijab*, consisting of tight tunics, short trousers and narrow scarves, whom the authorities call 'mannequins'. Thousands of women were arrested in big cities, with many hundreds of thousands receiving verbal warnings. In January 2008 the government closed *Zanan* magazine for 'blackening the authorities' by reporting incidents of militia forces raping girls they had arrested on the pretext of 'bad *hijab*'.

Instead of silencing reformists and human rights and women's activists, Ahmadinejad's government has succeeded only in uniting them and radicalising their demands. Reformist and women's websites, now the only forums where activists could still interact, continued the debate and featured a number of well-documented and informative articles about the Ahmadinejad government's policy and agenda. As the 2009 presidential election approached, various reformist groups and individuals formed a coalition to mobilise people to vote. Former President Khatami was persuaded to run again. Mehdi Karroubi, who had lost the 2005 election to Ahmadinejad, also announced his candidacy on behalf of the party he had formed in 2005.[31] Then in March, Mir-Hosseini Mousavi, who had served as prime minister from 1980 to 1988, entered the presidential race after over 20 years of political silence; not long after, Khatami withdrew in Mousavi's favour. Having enjoyed the backing of Ayatollah Khomeini and a popular base due to his welfare polices, Mousavi now stood as an independent centrist candidate. His campaign, reminiscent in many ways of Khatami's in 1997, was run by a group of young activists, who, lacking access to state-controlled media – in particular television, which was heavily biased toward Ahmadinejad – skilfully used digital media to reach large numbers of people.

The pre-election polls were ambiguous – and notoriously unreliable – but it was widely expected that either Mousavi would win or the election would go to a second round. The hardliners were anxious that Ahmadinejad might not win a second term, and made preparations to ensure his victory. On election day, 12 June 2009, the turnout throughout the country was high, but the result was what many have interpreted as a military coup d'état. From the beginning, numerous serious irregularities were reported: the Revolutionary Guards and the Interior Ministry kept representatives of Ahmadinejad's opponents out of both polling booths and counting stations; they attacked Mousavi's campaign headquarters and arrested his aides and other prominent reformists and journalists. The official result was announced on TV only two hours after polling ended; Ahmadinejad was declared the winner with 63 per cent of the votes, Mousavi second with less than half that, and the other two candidates (Karroubi and Mohsen Reza'i, a former head of the Revolutionary Guards) with single figures. There were indications that the percentages, and even the actual numbers of votes, had been decided in advance of the polling. Mousavi and Karroubi refused to accept the results and asked for a recount. On 13 June, Ahmadinejad celebrated his victory, and in a provocative speech he referred to those objecting to the poll as "dirt and dust" that would soon be washed away. On 15 June, an estimated 2 million protesters marched through the streets of Tehran with a single slogan: 'Where is my vote?' This was the biggest protest march since the 1979 Revolution, and a direct challenge to the theocratic forces. It was followed by more protests, which the government met with violence. In a much-awaited Friday prayer speech on 19 June, Khamene'i, instead of finding a healing formula, threw oil on the fire. He blamed foreign media for "doubts over election results", dismissed the protesters and warned them of further government violence if they persisted. But the protests continued, leading to the formation of the popular movement for change that became known as the Green

---

31 Karroubi formed this party shortly after resigning from all his governmental posts in protest at what he described, in an open letter, as election-rigging by the Revolutionary Guards and one of Khamene'i's sons.

Movement, under the joint – but very diffuse – leadership of Mousavi, Karroubi and Khatami, with Rafsanjani attempting to mediate reconciliation with Khamene'i.

At the time of writing (August 2010), the movement is barely a year old, but it has grown well beyond the stage of 'Where is my vote?' into a pluralistic and dynamic civil rights movement with women and young people at the forefront. Despite the suppression of public demonstration and debate and the mass arrests and violent treatment of reformist politicians, women's and human rights activists, the current dominance of the theocratic forces cannot be taken as an indication of the defeat of their opponents. Despite the closure of all human rights and women's rights NGOs, and harsh measures that make activism extremely dangerous, activists in Iran have remained undaunted and have developed non-violent and innovative ways to resist repression. What makes the Green Movement inspiring is that its decentralised and pluralistic structure brings together all those Iranians, from different walks of life and ideological perspectives, who seek democratic change; it is laying the ground for the healing of old wounds and a much-needed national reconciliation.

Conclusion

Before considering the lessons that the Iranian case has to offer for the reform of discriminatory laws in Muslim contexts, let us first recap the main developments.

In Iran, the 20th-century quest for equality and the rule of law intensified two deep-rooted and cross-cutting tensions in politics and society: between despotism and democracy and between religiosity and secularism. Secular democrats gained the upper hand initially, in the 1905–11 Constitutional Revolution, yet democracy and the rule of law failed to take root for a combination of internal and external reasons; the resultant impasse was resolved by the modernising and secularising, but despotic, Pahlavi monarchy. A brief resurgence of democracy in the late 1940s was ended by foreign intervention in 1953. Over the next 25 years, both democratic and religious opposition to Pahlavi rule grew until they erupted in the 1978–79 Revolution.

The Revolution led to an Islamic Republic in which Shi'a clerics, as custodians and interpreters of the *shari'a*, took the reigns of power. With the merger of religion and politics in the state, it became clear that the tension between the 'Islamic' and 'Republican' elements was located in the institutions of the state – those deriving their legitimacy and power from theocratic or democratic sources. Three decades of an uneasy and unequal union of 'Islam' and 'Republic' changed the context and dynamics of the interactions between religion, state, law and gender. 'Islam', previously a rallying cry for justice, came to be used as a justification for holding onto power and preventing the 'Republican' institutions embodying the people's will from fulfilling their function. The systemic tension between theocratic and democratic elements and institutions became a catalyst for change from within, and opened a space where a critique of patriarchal interpretations of the *shari'a* could be sustained in ways that were previously impossible. With the emergence of the reformist movement in the aftermath of 1997 presidential election, the struggle for reform of discriminatory laws became part of a larger struggle between two notions of 'Islam': a pluralistic and tolerant Islam premised on the notion of 'rights' and an absolutist and legalistic Islam premised on the notion of 'duties'. Despite the failure of the reformist movement to bring the promised shift from theocracy towards democracy, the idea and the demand for reform have now gone deep into society and become part of a popular movement for democratic change. The Green Movement that emerged in the aftermath of the disputed 2009 presidential election, with women as its most vociferous and active supporters, holds the promise of an egalitarian shift in the politics of gender and sexuality. Its impact in Muslim contexts may prove to be as important as that of the 1979 Revolution.

There are three lessons to be drawn from the Iranian case that may help in devising strategies for action to reform *zina* laws. First, the revival of *zina* laws is part of the larger story of changing relations between religion, state and law in the course of the 20th century; and strategies for reform need to be pursued as part of a larger struggle for gender equality, democracy and rule of law in Muslim contexts. This means that activists must understand and expose the real cleavages in their own society, must be well versed in its power politics, and must develop working relations and alliances with other stakeholders.

Secondly, given the primacy of law in Islamic discourses, and the intimate links between religion, law and culture, it is important to be able to engage with religious and internal discourses within communities. This requires activists to go beyond the ideological dichotomies such as 'secular' versus 'religious' feminism, or Islamic law versus human rights, and develop a multi-pronged approach to bring about sustainable legal reform in Muslim contexts. Strategies for reform may involve negotiating within available spaces – no matter how narrow these spaces are – with that complex unified system of religion, legal jurisprudence and governance established by the modern but undemocratic Muslim states.

Finally, the real cleavage, the fundamental power struggle in Iran as in other Muslim contexts is between democracy and despotism, which is often obscured by religious politics and the instrumentalisation of religion. Thus, it is essential to demystify religious politics, to challenge those who attempt to invoke religious authority to justify autocratic rule, and to win power games by using religious language. It is only then that the intimate and intricate links between patriarchy and despotism can be revealed and challenged in sustainable ways.

Bibliography

Afary, Janet (2009), *Sexual Politics in Modern Iran*. Cambridge: Cambridge University Press.

Amanat, Abbas (1992), 'Constitutional revolution: Intellectual background', *Encyclopedia Iranica* 6: 163–176.

Amin, Seyyed Hossein (1985), *Middle East Legal Systems*. Glasgow: Royston.

Amnesty International (2008), 'Iran: women's rights defenders defy repression', http://www.amnesty.org/en/library/asset/MDE13/.../mde130182008eng.pdf

Arjomand, Said Amir (1988), *The Turban for the Crown: The Islamic Revolution in Iran*. Oxford: Oxford University Press.

Azari, Farah (1983), 'The post-revolutionary women's movement in Iran', in Farah Azari (ed.), *Women of Iran: Conflict with Fundamentalism*, 190–225. London: Ithaca Press.

Bakhash, Shaul (1985), *The Reign of the Ayatollahs: Iran and the Islamic Revolution*, London: I. B. Tauris.

Banani, Ali (1961), *The Modernization of Iran (1921–1941)*. Palo Alto, CA: Stanford University Press.

Buchta, Wilfried (2000), *Who Rules Iran? The Structure of Power in the Islamic Republic*. Washington DC: Washington Institute for Near East Policy and Berlin: Konrad Adenauer Stiftung.

Gholami, Hossain (1999), 'The Islamization of criminal justice and its development in Iran', *Tilburg Foreign International Review* 7: 213–220.

Hoodfar, Homa and Shadi Sadr (2007), 'Can women act as agents of the democratization of theocracy in Iran?' in *Religion, Politics and Gender Equality*, UNRISD, Heinrich Boll Stiftung, http://www.unrisd.org/research/gd/religionandgender.

Mehrpoor, Hossein (1995), *Didgah-haye jadid dar masa'el-e hoquqi* (New perspectives in legal issues). Tehran: Ettela'at (1374).

—— (2001), *The Civil Code of Iran*. Tehran: Daneshvar.

Mir-Hosseini, Ziba (1996), 'Divorce, veiling and feminism in post-Khomeini Iran', in H. Afshar (ed.), *Women and politics in the Third World*, 142–170. London: Routledge.

—— (1999), 'Family law iii. In modern Persia', *Encyclopedia Iranica* 9: 192–196.

—— (2002), 'The conservative-reformist conflict over women's rights in Iran', *International Journal of Politics, Culture and Society* 16 (1): 37–53.

—— (2006), 'Is time on Iranian women protestors' side?', *Middle East Report Online*, 16 June, http://www.merip.org/mero/mero061606.html

—— (2007), 'When a woman's hurt becomes an injury: "Hardship" as grounds for divorce in Iran', *Hawwa: Journal of Women in the Middle East and the Islamic World* 5 (1): 111–126.

―――― (2009), 'Broken taboos in post-election Iran', *Middle East Report Online*, 17 December, http://www.merip.org/mero/mero121709.html

―――― (2010), 'Sharia and national law in Iran', in Jan Michiel Otto (ed.) *Sharia Incorporated*, 178–217. Leiden University Press.

Mir-Hosseini, Ziba and Richard Tapper (2006), *Islam and Democracy in Iran: Eshkevari and the Quest for Reform*. London: I. B. Tauris.

Mohammadi, Majid (2008), *Judicial Reform and Reorganization in 20th Century Iran: State-building, Modernization and Islamicization*. London: Routledge.

Mokhtari, Shadi (2004), 'The search of human rights within an Islamic framework in Iran', *The Muslim World* 94: 469–479.

Nashat, Guity (1983), 'Women in the ideology of the Islamic Republic', in Guity Nashat (ed.), *Women and Revolution in Iran*, 318–371. Boulder, CO: Westview.

Paidar, Parvin (1995), *Women and the Political Process in Twentieth-Century Iran*. Cambridge: Cambridge University Press.

Rahami, Mohsen (2005), 'Development of criminal justice in the Iranian post revolutionary Penal Code', *European Journal of Criminal Justice* 13–14: 585–602.

Ramazani, Nesta (1993), 'Women in Iran: the revolutionary ebb and flow', *Middle East Journal* 47: 409–428.

Schirazi, Asghar (1997), *The Constitution of Iran: Politics and the State in the Islamic Republic*. London: I. B. Tauris.

Sanasarian, Eliz (1982), *The Women's Rights Movement in Iran: Mutiny, Appeasement and Repression from 1900 to Khomeini*. New York: Praeger.

Schneider, Irene (2005), 'Religious and state jurisdiction during Nasir Al-Din Shah's reign', in Robert Gleave (ed.), *Religion and Society in Qajar Iran*, 84–110. London, Routledge.

Sedghi, Hamideh (2007), *Women and Politics in Iran: Veiling, Unveiling, and Reveiling*, Cambridge: Cambridge University Press.

Shekarloo, Mahsa (2006), 'Iranian women take on the constitution', *Middle East Report Online*, 21 July, http://www.merip.org/mero/mero072105.html

Tabari, Azar and Nahid Yeganeh (eds.) (1982), *In the Shadow of Islam: The Women's Movement in Iran*. London, Zed Press.

Terman, Rochelle (2007), *Stop stoning forever campaign: A report*, http://www.stop-killing.org

Terman, Rochelle and Mufuliat Fijabi (2010), 'Stoning is not our culture: a comparative analysis of human rights and religious discourses in Iran and Nigeria', http://stop-stoning.org/node/883

Tohidi, Nayereh (1991), 'Gender and Islamic fundamentalism: feminist politics in Iran', in Chandra Mohanty (ed.) *Third World Women and the Politics of Feminism*, 251–267. Bloomington: Indiana University Press.

——— (2009), 'Iran', in Sanja Kelly and Julia Breslin (eds.), *Women's Rights in the Middle East and North Africa: Progress and Resistance*, 121–147. New York: Freedom House.

——— (2010), 'Women's movement and feminism in Iran: a global perspective', in Amrita Basu (ed.) *Women's Movement in the Global Ear: The Power of Feminisms*, 359–96. Boulder: Westview Press.

Torfeh, Masoumeh (2009), 'Neither Islamic nor a republic', *The Guardian*, 29 August, http://www.guardian.co.uk/commentisfree/belief/2009/aug/29/iran-clergy-infighting-ayatollah

Nigeria

COUNTRY PROFILE

The Federal Republic of Nigeria is the most populous African country, with approximately 155 million inhabitants; 50.5 per cent of the population are identified as Muslims, 48.2 per cent are Christian, and the remaining 1.3 per cent adhere to other belief systems. "[A] state steeped in pluralism" (Oba 2004: 859), Nigeria has over 250 ethnic groups, the largest being Hausa/Fulani, Igbo and Yoruba. The majority of Hausa/Fulani and about a half of Yoruba self-identify as Muslims, as well as a number of smaller ethnic groups, such as the Kanuri people. Muslims predominantly inhabit the northern provinces in Nigeria, where the first Muslim communities appeared as early as the 11th century, while Christians are the majority population in the south. The majority of Nigerian Muslims nominally subscribe to the mainstream Sunni elucidations of faith and legal traditions, of which the doctrines of the Maliki *madhhab* traditionally occupy the central place. A significant Shi'i minority is also present in the country. There are a variety of well-established Sufi orders – particularly the Qadiriyya and the Tijaniyya – that have traditionally enjoyed great respect among Nigerian Muslims despite the criticisms they face from the adherents of several Muslim right-wing factions, most notably the Yan Izala movement (Kane 2003).

Nigeria is a federal constitutional republic that consists of 36 states and one federal capital territory. It has a plural legally system comprising: English-style (statute and common) law rooted in its colonial history; customary laws derived from pre-colonial norms and practices; and Muslim laws based on the interpretations of classical *fiqh* (Islamic jurisprudence) and customary laws of Nigerian Muslim communities. Nigerian legal plurality owes much to its turbulent political and religious history. Under colonial administration, the jurisdiction of Muslim law was chiefly relegated to the ambits of personal status, inheritance and family law. In 1960, the year of Nigeria's independence from the United Kingdom, a new Penal Code was made applicable to the northern provinces (while a distinct Criminal Code was implemented in the south), which sought to include some elements of Muslim legal traditions in the criminal justice system. In May 1999, a new federal Constitution was introduced, reaffirming the state's principally secular character. A few months later, however, the governor of Zamfara (a northern Nigerian state) proclaimed that '*shari'a* law' was to become the principal legal system in that state, and that it would include criminal matters. Eleven other northern states quickly followed the Zamfara example. Under the new laws introduced in these states, adultery – which under the 1960 Penal Code (sections 387 and 388) is an offence punishable by two years imprisonment, a fine or both – and fornication are now jointly penalised as the *hadd* crime of *zina* for which the following punishments are prescribed: 100 cane lashes and one year imprisonment for unmarried Muslim offenders; or, stoning to death for Muslim offenders who are married. Rape, insulting the Prophet Muhammad, defiling the Qur'an, robbery, theft and the drinking of alcohol are also considered *hudud* or '*hudud*-related' crimes in these states; the punishments prescribed for them include various forms of execution, limb amputation and flogging.

The introduction of *hudud* laws came as a consequence of political crisis and opportunism (BAOBAB 2003a: 8), characterised by patriarchal oppression and the misuse of religion as a means of societal control. Other manifestations of this trend include renewed advocacy for child marriage and re-utterance of the custom of *ijbar*, which gives a father the 'right' to control the marriage of a never-married daughter. New gender discriminatory by-laws are also being introduced, such as the one in Gusau, Zamfara, which bans Muslim women from using motorcycle taxis, or a regulation in Kano state that prohibits Muslim women's sports and recreational activities (BAOBAB 2003a: 8–9). All these developments stand in stark contrast to the fundamental rights guaranteed in Chapter IV of the 1999 Constitution, as well as Nigeria's obligations under international human rights law.

The idea of Nigeria has its roots in various interconnected events of the early 20th century, most notably the 'amalgamation' of the British protectorates of Southern Nigeria and Northern Nigeria in 1914. This unification established the borders of the new state, which gained independence on 1 October 1960, and brought hundreds of ethnic groups with the distinct histories, customs and beliefs under the same roof. The north-eastern savannas hosted the Kanem-Borno Empire, which had been ruled by the Muslim dynasty of Saifawa for eight centuries (Kane 2003: 29). In the 19th century, the Saifawa dynasty was replaced by the Sokoto Caliphate, which collapsed in 1903. While Muslim-specific laws and *fiqh* were present throughout the long history of Nigeria's Muslim communities, they have been interpreted and applied in various ways, depending on changing circumstances within those historical polities. Therefore, the claim of 'reviving' *hudud* laws at the dawn of the 21st century in the Nigerian Muslim-majority northern provinces, orchestrated by their political elites, is not historically accurate. Instead, the origins of such laws can be seen in the distinctly gender-discriminatory and autocratic nature of executive, legislative and judiciary governance in Nigeria, caused by the long periods of rule by either military dictatorships or civilian elites – both profoundly corrupt. These laws are also founded in the deeply entrenched patriarchal ethos, justified by the references to culture and religion. Against this backdrop, Nigerian *hudud* laws are but a culmination of the decades of systemic political and legal opposition to gender justice.

This chapter offers a critical feminist analysis of the key historical, social, political and legal developments which lead to the emergence of *zina* laws and other discriminatory legislation and regulations in northern Nigeria. This chapter also assesses societal responses – in particular those spearheaded by Nigerian women's rights organisations – to these laws and the subsequent *zina* trials. The strategic resistance to *hudud* laws, primarily by the women's movement, which includes litigation on *hudud* cases and arduous national and international advocacy, has succeeded in saving many lives. Thanks to this valiant work, executions for *zina*-related crimes have never been carried out and, in most of cases, have been thrown out on appeal.[1]

The present chapter first discusses the historical conditions of the dominant societal discourses on sexuality and gender in Nigeria, in particular those founded on the experiences of its northern Muslim-majority provinces. The chapter goes on to interrogate the ways in which these discourses have been entrenched and reinforced in the state's pluralistic legal system, despite the rights guaranteed in the Constitution and Nigeria's obligations under international law, which are then analysed in some detail in the subsequent section of this chapter. Next, this study describes and assesses civil society's response to post-1999 northern Nigerian *hudud* laws. It is argued that *zina* laws and other gender-discriminatory regulations need to be repealed *gradually*, in line with the state's human rights duties and non-patriarchal interpretations of *shari'a*.

Historical Background

The territory of contemporary Nigeria comprises the homelands of numerous West African peoples, whose respective historical polities ranged from centralised kingdoms – such as the Yoruba and Benin states in the south-west or northern Muslim caliphates – to loosely organised eastern and middle-belt entities (Ostien & Dekker 2010: 555; Falola & Heaton 2008: 16). The continuous presence of Muslim rulers has, over time, ensured a profound cultural exchange amongst the northern provinces, which, in turn, resulted in the proliferation of distinctly heterogeneous Muslim communities. In those societies, faith, law and gender relations have been negotiated syncretically, with reference to both the customs of a particular group and the perceived tenets of Islam. For instance, in the Sokoto Caliphate, founded by the Fulani reformer and *'alim* Shehu Usman dan Fodio (1754–1817), *shari'a* was recognised as the principal basis of jurisprudence (Falola & Heaton 2008: 73; Ehrlemann 1986: 233–235). However, this provision neither resulted in a homogenous *fiqh*, nor prevented the Hausa majority and other ethnic groups from continued reliance on customary laws. In fact,

> [f]or Hausa Muslims[,] Shari'a did not exercise complete and monolithic control over litigation, but was one of several possibilities for finding legal relief. The choice was real, personal, and most likely weighed on the balance of personal experience and social identity as often as that of faith. (Wren Bivins 2007: 126)

In a similar vein, gender roles and regulations have not been made uniformly and universally applicable. Instead, they have largely depended on class and the overall familial standing.

---

1 In fact, the only case in which the sentence for adultery was not overturned on appeal was that of Fatima Usman and Ahmed Ibrahim. They were convicted of *zina* retroactively, in 2002, but were released on bail pending the hearing and determination of their appeal. The case, however, seems to have lapsed, as neither Fatima nor Ahmed have ever been called to court again. See BAOBAB 2003a: 15–17; Ostien & Dekker 2010: 604.

While it was possible, for example, for the daughter of Shehu Usman dan Fodio, Nana Asma'u (1793–1864), to become an excellent writer, poet, teacher and counsellor to the Caliph (her brother), the overwhelming majority of Nana's female contemporaries were not allowed education, despite her efforts and the exhortations of her father (Mack & Boyd 2000).

In addition, the negotiation of gender roles was always strongly related to prevailing political circumstances. The politics of veiling, for example, invariably depended on the type of religious 'outlook' desired by the ruling elite. In the 19th century, the majority of women of the Sokoto Caliphate did not wear *hijab*. Instead, hairdressing was a highly popular art form in both Hausa and Kanuri women's cultures (Mahdi 2009: 3). Under colonial oppression, however, women's headcoverings became a symbol of Muslim resistance and cultural diversity. Hence, Hausa women wore a variety of headscarves called *kallabi*, *gyale* and *mayafi*; the most popular Kanuri women's headcoverings were called *mandil* and *ləfaya*. In the 1970s and 1980s, by and large, "the *hijab* was a means for Muslim women to participate in the urban work place without men reducing women's contribution to their sexuality" (Mahdi 2009: 4). The *hijab* was mostly worn voluntarily, predominantly by a particular class of women. As of the late 1990s, however, along with the expansion of Muslim-specific laws and regulations, *hijab* became a compulsory segment of (non-legally) imposed dress codes, designed to subjugate women for the sake of the political gains of ruling patriarchal elites. It was no longer simply a question of choice or an expression of cultural and religious diversity.

Certain patriarchal customs, however, disguised as Muslim 'values', have been continuously practised and encouraged regardless of the given political circumstances. For instance, the old and oft-disputed Maliki concept of *ijbar* is still used to marry off young girls to much older men, regardless of their will (Ostien & Dekker 2010: 587). This practice, in particular when it comes to forced marriages (i.e. when a woman or girl is married against or without her consent), is becoming less common due to various factors.[2] *Purdah*, which amongst Nigerian Muslims came to mean the seclusion of women, is also practised and can take the form of 'complete' seclusion, 'partial' seclusion or the 'seclusion of the heart' (Abdullah-Olukoshi 1990). Polygyny is lawful and common throughout the country.[3] Family violence, in the form of wife battery, is blatantly protected under the law (Ostien & Dekker 2010: 587). Section 55(1)(d) of the Penal Code, and reinforced in the new Muslim penal codes of the 12

---

2 The author is grateful to Ayesha M Imam for pointing out, in her review of this chapter, three factors that have led to a decrease of forced marriages: the overall recognition in society that such marriages often result in divorce or girls running away; the sustained opposition over the last few decades of the *shari'a* courts to this practice; and the activism of women's non-governmental organisations.

3 It is legal in Muslim and customary laws. Federal law does not permit polygyny. However, even when men marry under the Marriage Act (which permits only monogamy), they can also marry under customary law with impunity; therefore, men can actually be polygynous. No man who has done this has ever been charged with bigamy. The author is grateful to Ayesha M Imam for highlighting this fact.

northern provinces, allows for the infliction of 'moderate' physical hurt "by a husband for the purpose of correcting his wife".

Despite the numerous disconcerting manifestations of patriarchal ethos throughout Nigerian history, it seems that there is no documentation of capital punishment – in any form – for *zina* crimes prior to 1999, when the Zamfara state introduced its *hudud* legislation (soon to be mirrored by other northern states) (Terman & Fijabi 2010: 27). Both the Kanem-Borno Empire and the Sokoto Caliphate had sought to attain some aspects of gender justice, which supposedly did not include stoning to death for *zina*, a charge that disproportionally affects more women than men. Since late colonial times, adultery was adjudicated exclusively under the British-style criminal and penal codes, which, although starkly patriarchal themselves, never treated it as a capital crime (Kane 2003: 93; Birai 1993: 193). Thus, the post-1999 Muslim penal codes not only infringe upon the state's legal system, but also the historical concepts of criminal and gender justice in Nigerian Muslim communities.

Domestic Legal System

Prior to British colonisation, Nigerian polities were ruled by a wide variety of customary laws. As already mentioned, much of the contemporary northern states, developed under continuous Muslim rule, had been strongly influenced by (classical) Islamic jurisprudence; even so, their own *fiqh* had been markedly pluralistic and intertwined with local customs. Although one of the primary goals of the Fulani reformers, who founded the Sokoto Caliphate in the early 1800s, was to eradicate or at least marginalise some customary laws deemed 'un-Islamic' (Schacht 1964; Ostien & Dekker 2010). This laborious task was never completed. Despite the fact that "the only existing tribunals [in the caliphate] were those of the *qadis* (Hausa: *alkalis*) who were competent in all matters, including penal law" (Schacht 1964: 86), custom remained an integral part of the justice system both within and outside these judicial institutions.

Under British colonial administration and its controversial 'indirect rule' policy, the northern Muslim-majority emirates, of which the former caliphates had consisted, remained the key administrative units; "the emirs [who did not resist colonisation] and those already holding office under them were confirmed in power" (Ostien & Dekker 2010: 558). Two distinct legal systems were founded: the 'native' system operated under customary laws and guided the 'native' courts staffed by local judges; the 'English' system operated under British colonial law, which was followed by the British judges in newly formed 'English' courts (Ostien & Dekker 2010: 559). In the emirates, which comprised a large part of the British Protectorate of Northern Nigeria, Muslim laws and courts, staffed by local *alkalis*, were an integral and predominant part of the 'native' legal system. The matters it covered were largely relegated to personal status, family and inheritance law, as well as criminal law for some time. In the later stages of colonial governance, however, Muslim penal laws were abolished and replaced by English-style codes; thereby, the jurisdiction over criminal matters was transferred to 'English' courts (Kane 2003: 93). Even prior to this, the colonisers enacted a clause stipulating that no 'native' law would be enforced that was deemed repugnant under English law; this was used extensively to curb the penalties and rules of the 'native' courts that the British disagreed with (Ostien & Dekker 2010: 560; Keay & Richardson 1966; Milner 1969). Other areas of public law, in particular constitutional and administrative law, were under the exclusive jurisdiction of the British colonisers. Hence, the 'indirect rule' of the colonial power was clearly direct in many ways.

Nigerian independence was achieved in 1960, but was followed from 1966 by decades of political instability, which by and large still persists today and greatly affects the country's legal system. Civilian and military establishments, interchangeably seizing control of the country and ruling it throughout its troublesome history, were too corrupt and incompetent to solve some of Nigeria's greatest problems – such as economic crises or often tumultuous inter-religious and inter-ethnic relations (Falola & Heaton 2008; Okafọ 2009).[4] The military regimes in particular, which illegally usurped state powers in the country through multiple coups d'état, significantly stalled post-independence Nigerian legal development: "Each military regime took steps to preserve and legitimize itself by enacting Decrees and Edicts mainly with the aim of removing or dampening official and unofficial oppositions" (Okafọ 2009: 60). Another goal of law-making under the military was, simply, subjugation of the populace (Onagoruwa 2009). The civilian governments, however, made little efforts to reverse and remedy such questionable legal conduct. In fact, some military-enacted laws caused positive developments, "while a lot of civilian-enacted laws violate the best interests of the majority of the citizens" (Okafọ 2009: 60). For instance, it was under the newly elected civilian government – which ended 16 years of military rule in 1999 – that the *hudud* by-laws were enacted in the northern states. In addition, militant religious movements, including armed factions thought to be linked with international terrorist networks, continue to wreak havoc, causing hundreds of deaths each year. It is plausible that some political 'moral campaigns', including those related to the introduction of *hudud* by-laws, were in fact partly mounted as a governmental response to 'public morality' and 'Islamisation' claims put forward by those paramilitary religious groups.

The Nigerian post-independence laws in this chapter are broken down into five subsections. First, the making of Nigeria's pluralistic legal system and the dynamics between its three constituent prongs are assessed. Second, an overview of the current hierarchical order of the state's courts is provided. Third, a brief analysis of the key gender-related legislative developments in Nigerian constitutional law is given. Fourth, Muslim personal status laws are elucidated. And finally, the impact of the Muslim criminal laws of the 12 northern Muslim-majority provinces, all enacted after 1999, on the Nigerian criminal justice system is assessed in some detail.

---

4 The complexity of inter-religious and inter-ethnic – including Muslim-Christian – relations were often caused (and frequently exacerbated) by the manipulation of identity politics for power and resource allocations – i.e. manipulated by both civilian and military elites vying for power. They were not inevitable.

Nigeria

'Settlement' and Dynamics of Nigerian Legal Pluralism

The outlook of the three-pronged legal system – setting the boundaries between English-style state law, customary laws and Muslim laws – was reached as a compromise in the so-called 'Settlement of 1960', just before independence (Ostien 2006; Ostien & Dekker 2010). Based on this agreement, the northern provinces of the newly sovereign state were to be governed by the new Penal Code, separate from the Criminal Code designed for the Christian-majority states. Although designed with a view to please the Muslim-majority

---

CASES OF HUMAN RIGHTS VIOLATIONS

Stoning to Death for *Zina* Charges Filed By the Police

Safiyyatu Husseini, a 38-year-old woman, was arrested by the police on 23 December 2000 and tried before the Gwadabawa Upper Shari'a Court, in the state of Sokoto, for adultery. The case was brought to this court under the new 2000 Sokoto Shari'a Penal Code by the Sokoto State Commissioner of Police. Safiyyatu's neighbor, Yakubu Abubakar, was also arrested, but then released for 'lack of evidence' after he denied all charges. The court opposed as 'contrary to Muslim law' the use of DNA testing to determine whether Yakubu was the father of Safiyyatu's child. A single judge, Mohammed Bello Sanyinawal, heard Safiyyatu's case and sentenced her to death by stoning. The reasons cited for such judgment were her pregnancy, statement of confession, and the fact that she was Muslim and had never been married; the consequences of 'confession' were not explained to her.

When BAOBAB and WRAPA offered their support, Safiyyatu agreed to appeal. The appeal was heard at the Sokoto Shari'a Court of Appeal, on 26 October 2001, before the three *alkalis*. The team of 11 experts, brought together by BAOBAB and WRAPA, appealed against the decision of the Gwadabawa Upper Shari'a Court on the following grounds: (1) lack of jurisdiction; (2) unlawful admission of the case, since the appellant was not given a chance to call witnesses or to defend herself; (3) failure to explain the charge of *zina* to Safiyyatu; (4) procedural errors, as no witnesses were called to testify that the appellant was a previously-married Muslim, or – even more importantly – that the act of *zina* was actually committed; (5) the appellant was not given an opportunity for a final address before the judgment was passed; and (6) the mere pregnancy cannot be considered conclusive proof of *zina*.

On 25 March 2002, the judgment was given on the basis of the above arguments of Safiyyatu's appellate team. She was immediately discharged and acquitted. This judgment effectively barred the police, at least within the Sokoto state, from the power to file *zina* charges.

[Source: BAOBAB 2003a: 13–14.]

populace and their leadership, at least symbolically, the new Penal Code practically made all criminal matters an intrinsic part of state law. In turn, as a concession to the Muslim judicial (and political) elite of the time, the Shari'a Court of Appeal was created; it was a permanent court equivalent in status to that of the Regional High Court (Ostien & Dekker 2010: 567). It was given final and non-appealable jurisdiction over matters pertaining to Muslim personal law, as well as other potential Muslim civil law disputes. In addition, the Shari'a Court of Appeal's judges were made members of the 'native' courts' appellate division in the High Court, which allowed them, for the first time, to adjudicate on the matters of *all* customary laws, Muslim and non-Muslim alike (Ostien & Dekker 2010: 567). This concession was controversially revoked nearly two decades later, after years of heated debate[5] between the southern and northern ruling elites, when the Shari'a Court of Appeal was abolished by the 1979 Constitution.

The 1979 Constitution provided a new script for the country's three-pronged legal system. Muslim judges were no longer able to make autonomous decisions on matters pertaining to 'Islamic personal law', as it was then termed. Instead of the abolished Shari'a Court of Appeal, the states were now allowed to establish their own *shari'a* courts of appeal, but their judgments were not final; instead, the state courts' decisions could be appealed in the Federal Court of Appeal, whose rulings were then subject to appeal before the Supreme Court (Ostien & Dekker 2010; Oba 2004). A few years later, the country once again came under military rule; numerous parts of the Constitution were suspended and autocratic martial law was imposed. Under the military regime, there were two unsuccessful constitution-making attempts (1989 and 1995). They were both characterised by rampant '*shari'a* debates' and certain concessions were promised, but never enforced, to the northern provinces pertaining to Muslim laws. Finally, at the end of yet another military era, the new Constitution was passed in 1999. Despite the previous constitutional debates on Muslim law under the military regime, the 1999 Constitution controversially reaffirmed the 1979 Constitution's provisions regarding the *shari'a* courts of appeal.[6] Article 277(1) of the 1999 Constitution provides:

> The Sharia Court of Appeal of a State shall, in addition to such other jurisdiction as may be conferred upon it by the law of the State exercise such appellate and supervisory jurisdiction in civil proceedings involving questions of Islamic personal law which the court is competent to decide in accordance with the provisions of subsection (2) of this section.

The following subsection (Article 277(2)(a–e)) goes on to determine that the competencies of such a court include the matters of marriage, divorce, inheritance, guardianship and, simply,

---

5 This is known as the '*shari'a* debate', 1976–78.

6 The only minor difference between the 1979 Constitution and the incumbent 1999 Constitution is that non-Muslims are no longer able to submit to the jurisdiction of the states' *shari'a* appellate courts (Article 260), and the former constitutional text establishes one such court in the Federal Capital Territory (Article 265). See Oba 2004: 866–867.

"any other question" within the ambit of 'Islamic personal law' brought forward by Muslim parties. Apart from explicating, in some detail, the specific questions of 'Islamic personal law' brought under the jurisdiction of the states' *shari'a* appellate courts, this constitutional article provides that the states can confer upon such courts other types of jurisdiction as well. Some authors argue that, perhaps, the northern states relied on this ambiguous provision when they started enacting, only a few months after the 1999 Constitution came into force, the laws that would expand the jurisdiction of these Muslim appellate courts to the matters of criminal law – i.e. *hudud* crimes (Ostien & Dekker 2010: 580).

The jurisdictions and institutions of the three prongs of the Nigerian state/customary/ Muslim legal system remain an acute, chronic source of political disputes, whereby the question of Muslim laws invariably triggers the fiercest debates (Oba 2004). They are, however, rarely fuelled by purely religious concerns of either Christian or Muslim parties, as the political 'value' of such quarrels, which resonate high and attract a lot of public attention,

---

CASES OF HUMAN RIGHTS VIOLATIONS

A Retroactive Punishment for *Zina*

In 2002, Fatima Usman, 32, and Ahmed Ibrahim, 35, were convicted of *zina* and sentenced to death by stoning by an upper *shari'a* court in Minna, the capital of the Nigerian state of Niger. The sentence was passed retroactively, as the alleged acts could have only been committed well before the time the state of Niger amended its Penal Code and thus introduced the offence of *zina* (sections 387 and 388). This sentence replaced the previous sentence of five years imprisonment; Fatima and Ahmed were already serving this sentence for adultery based on admission of guilt.

At that point, the accused persons asked BAOBAB to organise their defence. BAOBAB took up the case and filed a notice of appeal before the Niger Shari'a Court of Appeal, stating that the upper *shari'a* court in Minna erred in giving two conflicting judgments. The second conviction was made retroactively, on the basis of the appellants' previous confession, without giving them an opportunity to review it. Their confession was therefore heard only once, and no further witnesses were called to corroborate it.

In response, the Niger Shari'a Court of Appeal released Fatima and Ahmed on bail, pending the hearing and determination of their appeal. While the appeal was pending, the jurisdiction of the Niger Shari'a Court of Appeal was called into question by the state's High Court. For this reason, the appeal has never been decided by the state's *shari'a* appellate court; it has also never been transferred to the High Court. Fatima and Ahmed are, therefore, still out on bail, and it is highly unlikely that they will ever be called to court again.

[Source: BAOBAB 2003a: 15–17; Ostien & Dekker 2010: 604]

is often the primary goal. Furthermore, the debates and the resultant legislative changes have been markedly patriarchal, whereby the concerns for gender justice would be either completely neglected or politically misused in order to repudiate an opposing view. Muslim views, for instance, have been almost invariably represented by male-only establishments of *alkalis* and politicians. Even the so-called '*shari'a* implementation committees' – formed as of the early 2000s in each northern state in order to assist their respective governors in the implementation of the new Muslim penal codes – have only in one, Bauchi state, out of 12 states agreed to accept minimal women's membership. In Bauchi, there were only two women on a 29-person committee. Although they were clearly outnumbered in this committee, the inclusion of these two women has nevertheless been criticised (Nasir 2007: 94–95). Hence, despite their huge impact on women's lives, Muslim laws in Nigeria have been dealt with almost exclusively by patriarchal male elites. Their negotiation and "implementation has unquestionably been primarily a 'male thing', conceived and driven along by core groups of Muslim men, who tapped into deep reservoirs of emotion among the Muslim masses" (Nasir 2007: 93).[7]

The Present Hierarchy of Courts

The top-down hierarchy of Nigerian judicial institutions, as outlined in Chapter VII of the 1999 Constitution, is as follows: (1) Supreme Court; (2) Court of Appeal; (3) high courts (Federal High Court, High Court of the Federal Capital Territory (FCT) and high courts of states), *shari'a* courts of appeal (of FCT and the 18 northern Muslim-majority states) and customary courts of appeal (of FCT and the states); (4) magistrates and district courts; (5) area courts, *shari'a* courts and customary courts.

Shari'a appellate courts, established in each of the northern states, serve as the highest judicial instances dedicated exclusively to Muslim laws, which includes, as of the beginning of this century, matters pertaining to Muslim family law, personal status law and Muslim criminal law. These courts' judgments are appealable in the federal state's penultimate court – the Court of Appeal – whose decisions then can be reviewed by the highest court of the land – the Supreme Court. Apart from these official judicial institutions and their hierarchy, duly observed across the country, so-called 'Independent Shari'a Panels' have been established in some southern states. These panels are not part of the state's court structure as outlined in the Constitution; rather, they are a form of private arbitration board

---

7   Some women and women's groups, however, have been instrumentalised at the grass-roots level in order to bolster the post-1999 political 'Islamisation' agenda of the northern states. Women, for instance, were co-opted into newly established *hisbah* (moral supervision) and *da'awah* (preaching and teaching) organisations. Likewise, the Federation of Muslim Women's Associations in Nigeria (FOMWAN) produced an advertisement in 2000 in which "the courage of the Governor of Zamfara State and other States that have responded to the yearnings of their predominantly Muslim populations by enlarging the scope of Sharia in their States" was supported and saluted. This advertisement also declared that gender-based concerns of civil society organisations over the new hudud laws are "largely misplaced". See Nasir 2007: 94, 97–99.

set up by Muslims in the absence of institutions dealing specifically with Muslim laws in those particular states. Parties consenting to the jurisdiction of the 'Independent Shari'a Panels' typically submit private disputes relating to Muslim personal status and family law. Controversially, however, these panels sometimes deal with matters of Muslim criminal law as well (Ostien & Dekker 2010: 577). For instance, in October 2002 in Ọyọ state in southwestern Nigeria, Sulaiman Shittu, a 29-year-old unmarried Muslim man, was given 100 lashes inside a town mosque, accorded to him as a *hadd* punishment by one such panel after he voluntarily confessed to fornication (Olajide 2002; Ostien & Dekker 2010: 577).

Constitutional Law

All post-independence Nigerian constitutional texts, including the incumbent 1999 Constitution (in Article 10), provide that "[t]he Government of the Federation or of a State shall not adopt any religion as State Religion". When northern states started enacting measures that expand the jurisdiction of their *shari'a* courts to matters of criminal law, and when their *'shari'a* implementation' programmes commenced, numerous critics objected on the grounds of the above constitutional 'secularity clause'. Yet, in the absence of Supreme Court rulings involving, either explicitly or implicitly, this particular clause, it is difficult to speak to the envisaged constitutional limit to the states' right to accommodate the religious demands of their constituencies. Furthermore, there are other ambiguous constitutional provisions, such as the already mentioned Article 277(1), which permit the states to confer jurisdiction beyond matters pertaining to 'Islamic personal law' to their *shari'a* appellate courts and further complicate the matter. Finally, criminal law is not on the constitutional Exclusive Legislative List (set out in Part I of the Second Schedule to the 1999 Constitution), whereby 68 items are declared the responsibility of the National Assembly alone. Other relevant matters, however, are featured in this list, such as evidence (item 23) or the police and other governmental security services (item 45). Hence, the constitutionality of the northern Muslim evidentiary rules (which differ significantly from the federal ones) or of some police-like *hisbah* groups is certainly debatable.[8]

Legislative breaches of the human rights guarantees in the Constitution are, however, much more obvious. Since independence, all Nigerian constitutional texts have included a chapter on fundamental rights, safeguarding, for example, right to life (Article 33); freedom from torture or other inhuman or degrading treatment (Article 34(1)(a)); freedom from discrimination, including that on the basis of sex or religion (Article 42); and the right to freedom of expression (Article 39). Muslim penal codes, enacted after 1999 in

---

8 For one such discussion on the constitutionality of Muslim rules of evidence, *hisbah* groups and Muslim-specific taxation regulations in the Nigerian Muslim-majority northern states, see Ostien & Dekker 2010: 581–584. Regarding the evidentiary rules, Nigerian feminist human rights defenders have warned against the potential attempts to challenge the northern provinces' Muslim penal codes on this particular ground. The federal evidence requirements are broader than those set in Muslim penal codes and would make prosecutions more likely to succeed. See BAOBAB 2003a: 5.

many of the northern states, as well as some official measures adopted to facilitate their implementation, violate *all* of these constitutional rights. For example, the draconian *hudud* punishments, whether enforced or not, run against the prohibition of torture and other inhuman or degrading treatment; gender-biased evidentiary rules (demanding male-only witnesses or relegating women's evidence to a half that of men's) infringe on freedom from discrimination on the basis of one's sex. Freedom of expression and from religion-based discrimination is also violated by multiple provisions. For instance, the Muslim penal codes of several (but not all) northern states ban "acts of gross indecency by way of kissing in public, exposure of nakedness in public and other related acts of similar nature capable of corrupting public morals" (Ostien & Umaru 2007: 53). Other laws and by-laws across the northern states ban 'un-Islamic' dressing by female Muslims (thereby imposing *hijab*);[9] commuting female passengers by motorcycle;[10] gender-mixed seating on public or commercial transportation;[11] and praise-singing (*roko*).[12]

Non-Muslim-specific laws also violate rights guaranteed in the Constitution, in particular those relating to gender justice. In fact, the 1999 Constitution itself contains two gender-biased provisions: Article 26(2) limits the rights of Nigerian women to pass their nationality to foreign spouses; and Article 29(4) deems a woman to be 'of full age' (an adult) upon marriage, which is otherwise stated as "eighteen years and above". This provision effectively sanctions the marriage of young girls, which remains very common in Nigeria (Africa for Women's Rights – Nigeria: 2010). As previously mentioned, the 1960 Penal Code, applicable in the northern states along with their own Muslim penal codes, sanctions wife battery (section 55(1)(d)). The Criminal Code, implemented in the southern states, imposes (in section 358) remarkably strict evidentiary requirements to prove the offence of rape; thereby, rape convictions are nearly impossible. Similarly, some customary laws allow only men to own land, while widows are barred from inheriting marital property (Africa for Women's Rights – Nigeria: 2010).

Muslim Personal Status and Family Law

The 1999 Constitution states that the matters of Muslim 'personal law', including those of marriage, divorce, inheritance and guardianship, fall under the jurisdiction of the *shari'a*

---

9   See 2001 Yobe State Law to provide for the Prohibition of Un-Islamic Dressing in the State and to Make Provision for Proper Dressing to Be Used by Female Muslims throughout Yobe State, reproduced in Ostien 2007: Chapter 3, Part IV.

10 See 2000 Gusau Local Government (Zamfara State) By-law to Curb, Control and Eradicate Anti-Social Behaviours, Moral Decadence and Other Vices in the Society, reproduced in Ostien 2007: Chapter 3, Part IV.

11 See 2005 Kano State Law on Carrying Women in or on Commercial Vehicles, Including Motorcycles, reproduced in Ostien 2007: Chapter 3, Part IV.

12 See the Bauchi state's law on praise-singing (*roko*), begging, playing cards, etc, enacted by 2001 Bauchi State's Sharia Penal Code (Amendment) Law, reproduced in Ostien 2007: Chapter 3, Part IV. *Roko* is traditional Hausa eulogy or praise-singing, typically performed by musical artisans and bards called *maroka* (sing. *maroki*).

appellate court of "any [s]tate that requires it".[13] As the states are constitutionally allowed to establish "such other courts as may be authorised by law to exercise jurisdiction at first instance" below the higher-status courts, the 12 northern states that enacted their own Muslim penal codes replaced the ordinary area courts (which still exist in other provinces) with the new *shari'a* courts. Problematically, these new courts, staffed by the same former area court judges, are given first instance jurisdiction in *all* legal matters of Muslim (both criminal and 'personal'), customary or state law. Such an assortment requires judges to be versed in all these complex and varied areas of law; this is a near impossible task that paves the way for individual judges to issue rulings based on their own subjective selection of various legal traditions.

In matters of Muslim family and personal status law, judges of either first instance or appellate *shari'a* courts tend to follow the classical Maliki *fiqh*, which is markedly gender-biased. However, over the past several decades – i.e. well before the post-1999 criminal justice reforms that instated Muslim penal codes in some states – these judges have:

> increasingly recognised and upheld women's rights to inherit (especially to inherit land), to divorce on demand (often without, or with only token payments), to custody of their children, to being able to hold their children's property in trust, against forced marriages, and so on (BAOBAB 2003a: 4).

In doing so, they consciously depart from the old Maliki doctrines, perhaps in recognition that their work needs to meet the exigencies of contemporary Nigerian Muslim communities, including those relating to gender justice. Nevertheless, such progressive judgments have receded in the post-1999 social climate of fear and intimidation, cultivated by the rise of Muslim right-wing politics (BAOBAB 2003a: 5). That rise was particularly encouraged by the enactment of new Muslim penal codes in 12 northern Muslim-majority states. Hence, the *hudud* laws and other related penal regulations have had an indirect negative impact on the state of Nigerian Muslim 'personal law'. It remains to be seen whether the recently reached stalemate in politically motivated Muslim-specific legislation in the northern provinces (Ostien & Dekker 2010), as well as the relentless efforts of Nigerian women's human rights organisations to provide legal education and support for women affected by Muslim laws, will encourage *alkalis* to return to gender-sensitive *ijtihad* (independent legal reasoning).

In theory, in matters such as marriage and other aspects of 'personal law', Nigerians are free to choose either customary/Muslim law or relevant federal statutes. In practice, however, the choice is hardly there, given the overwhelming societal pressure to follow the 'traditional paths' to justice, epitomised in customary and Muslim laws (Okafọ 2009). For instance, under the federal Marriage Act, only monogamous matrimonial unions are allowed, while both customary and Muslim laws allow polygynous marriages. Yet, the

---

13 Currently, such courts exist in 18 out of 19 Nigerian northern states (the 19th state shares it with another state).

majority of Nigerians are married either under customary or Muslim laws and at least one-third of Nigerian women (of various religious affiliations) live in polygynous unions.[14] Moreover, even the federal Marriage Act and other state 'personal law' legislation contains gender-discriminatory provisions.[15]

Muslim Criminal Law

The ensuing analysis focuses on post-1999 Muslim-specific penal and criminal procedure codes of the 12 Nigerian northern provinces. Although, as previously noted, both the Penal Code, applicable in the north, and the Criminal Code, implementable in the south, are certainly not free from patriarchal bias; their negative impact on access to gender justice has been relatively low compared to the detrimental consequences of the new *hudud*, *qisas* (retaliatory) and other related provisions. The effects of Muslim penal codes are multifarious and not limited to the northern provinces; although, Muslim women within those constituencies, in particular, have suffered most directly. These codes left an unprecedented imprint not only on the Nigerian criminal justice system, but also on the country's social, cultural and political affairs, especially in relation to gender justice. As such, they warrant some closer examination.

The passage of the 1999 Constitution by a newly elected civilian government left many northern Muslims unsatisfied; the new constitutional text reiterated the provisions of the 1979 Constitution, which downgraded the jurisdiction and hierarchical position of Muslim judicial institutions compared to the previous arrangements. This momentum was seized by Ahmad Sani Yerima; he won the governorship of newly created Zamfara state in that same year, primarily on the promise that he would introduce religious reforms. Indeed, on 8 October 1999, a bill was passed in Zamfara that vests its inferior *shari'a* courts with the power to determine both civil and criminal matters in accordance with 'Islamic law'. The bill also established this state's Council of *Ulama*, who are empowered to "codify all the Islamic penal laws and their corresponding punishments, and the rules of criminal procedure and evidence".[16] On 27 January 2000, the Zamfara State Shari'a Penal Code[17] was enacted (Sada 2007: 22–24). The popularity of the reform of Zamfara's laws and institutions, pompously (and inaccurately) dubbed '*shari'a* implementation', was such

---

14 The statistical data on polygynous marriages in Nigeria is retrieved from an overview entitled 'Gender Equality and Social Institutions in Nigeria' in *Social Institutions & Gender Index* (OECD Development Centre, Paris 2008), http://genderindex.org/country/nigeria

15 For instance, in Article 18, the Marriage Act provides that if either party to an intended marriage is younger than 21 years, "the written consent of the father, or if he be dead or of unsound mind or absent from Nigeria, of the mother" is required. Obviously, the mother's consent is valid only if the father is unable to express his will.

16 1999 Zamfara State Shari'a Courts (Administration of Justice and Certain Consequential Changes) Law, Law No 5 of 1999, Zamfara State Gazette, Vol 1, No 1, 15 June 2000.

17 2000 Zamfara State Sharia Penal Code, Law No 10 of 2000, Zamfara State Gazette, Vol 3, No 1, 15 June 2000.

that the ruling elite of 11 other northern states – Bauchi, Borno, Gombe, Jigawa, Kaduna, Kano, Katsina, Kebbi, Niger, Sokoto and Yobe – rapidly followed suit. These orchestrated moves were, doubtless, primarily an expression of political opportunism (BAOBAB 2003a: 8), as the governors of the states embarking on 'shari'a implementation' were granted instant popularity amongst the northern Muslim populace. The then governor of Kano, for instance, was described as a *mujaddid* (reformer) of Muslim communities, whose appearance had been foretold by the Prophet Muhammad in a *hadith* in which he announces that one such person shall be raised up every 100 years (Sada 2007: 25).[18] Other state governors, including Zamfara's Ahmad Sani Yerima who initiated the reforms, have quickly become serious contenders for the highest political positions in Nigeria. Six governors – Mu'azu of Bauchi, Makarfi of Kaduna, Yar'adua of Katsina, Bafarawa of Sokoto, Ibrahim of Yobe, and Yerima of Zamfara – were either mentioned or contended for their political parties' nominations as candidates for the President of Nigeria in the 2007 elections. Two of them – Attahiru Dalhatu Bafarawa and Umaru Musa Yar'adua – were eventually on the ballot, and the latter (allegedly) won; thus being sworn in as the country's new President on 29 May 2007 (Ostien 2007: 203). The case of the then Zamfara governor Ahmad Sani Yerima is also quite telling: during his time in office, he was repeatedly accused of mismanagement and misappropriation of federal funds (Abubakar 2002), as well as bribery (Agbaje & Adesida 2006).[19] Apparently, religious zeal was hardly the main driving force beyond the introduced reforms.

The new Muslim penal codes and Muslim criminal procedure codes are substantially based on the 1960 Penal Code and the federal 1960 Criminal Procedure Code. For instance, the 1960 Penal Code – now applicable in parallel with the new Muslim penal codes in the 12 northern states that have legislatively pursued the 'shari'a implementation' trend – already stipulates that Muslim offenders, in addition to the punishments otherwise specified, are also made "liable to the punishment of Haddi [sic] lashing as prescribed by Muslim law" for adultery, consumption of alcohol, false accusations and so on (Article 68(2)). Such provisions were made as a concession to northern *alkalis*, despite their incongruence with the human rights guarantees enshrined in literally all Nigerian constitutions (Ostien 2007: Chapter IV, pp3–4). The new Muslim criminal procedure codes copy the 1960 Criminal Procedure Code almost verbatim, save for the omissions of certain provisions that make *zina* cases easy to prosecute. Specifically, under the federal Criminal Procedure Code, a woman can be charged with adultery only by her *wali*, husband or father, depending on her marital status. The Muslim criminal procedures have removed this safeguard, thus

---

18 Prior to such panegyrics, however, the governor of Kano was threatened with physical harm, as he was seen as an obstacle to the 'shari'a implementation' campaign, since he had set up a committee to review, rather than to just pass the new codes. Hence, it is debatable whether his subsequent pursuit of religious reforms came out of fear or opportunism, or perhaps both. The author is grateful to Ayesha M Imam for raising this point.

19 Ahmad Sani Yerima is also under investigation for his recent marriage to a 13-year-old child bride from Egypt. This came after a charge in 2006 that he then married a 15-year-old girl (BBC News 2010).

allowing *zina* charges to be lodged by practically any 'interested party', including the police (Ostien & Dekker 2010: 590).[20]

Despite reproducing some 89 per cent of the 1960 Penal Code's sections (Ostien & Dekker 2010: 589), the Muslim penal codes are organised and articulated in an unprecedented way; they take Muslim-specific criminal justice to an extreme, liminal realm, infused with both the neo-conservative interpretations of some classical Maliki *fiqh* and the 'innovative' compoundable injunctions that make the scope of 'Islamic' crimes and punishments even wider than in the old jurists' books. To be sure, the implementability of some of the new provisions was clearly not the drafters' main concern. Not a single offender has been crucified, beheaded or stoned to death, as prescribed for various *hudud* crimes. The states' governors, whose assent must be obtained before any death penalty is executed, and the benches of more superior courts have consistently ensured, albeit with a few notable exceptions,[21] that the alleged offenders under *hudud* and *qisas* sections be either acquitted or accorded some less harsh punishments. The question, therefore, remains: why have these draconian new provisions, in particular those pertinent to the so-called '*hudud* and *hudud*-related' crimes, been dealt with in such a way? Related to this query is the fact that, despite being acquitted on all charges or a commuted lesser punishments *at the end*, numerous women and children, typically of very poor background (BAOBAB 2003a: 26),[22] have been deliberately put through an ordeal of public humiliation, protracted intimidating trials and months or even years of prison. The answer, seemingly, is found in the patriarchal political power games, based on a purposefully skewed vision of 'public morality' and Muslim legal traditions, which needs not or cannot be fully 'implemented'. On the one hand, it suffices to say that this vision is asserted to a certain extent, deemed necessary to ensure social control and to mask the less-palatable vices of the ruling elite. Poor women and children have been chosen to stand *hudud* trials because they are expected to have the least political and social connections, and legal and religious education, necessary to understand their situation. On the other hand, an ardent resistance by civil society groups, in particular organisations for women's human rights, has undoubtedly made some of the more draconian '*shari'a* implementation' strategies obsolete. So, although the *hudud*

---

20 It should be noted, however, that in 2002, in the famous *zina* case against Safiyyatu Husseini, the Sokoto State Shari'a Court of Appeal interpreted this state's 2000 Shari'a Penal Code as implicitly inclusive of even higher safeguard than that existing in the federal 1960 Criminal Procedure Code, which essentially allows only the guilty persons themselves to file a *zina* case (Ostien & Dekker 2010: 590). The same court acquitted Safiyyatu, who was previously sentenced to death by stoning by a lower *shari'a* court judge, Mohammed Bello Sanyinawal (BAOBAB 2003a: 13–14).

21 For instance, Sani Yakubu Rodi, who fatally stabbed a woman and her two children in 2001, was sentenced under the new *qisas* provisions of the Katsina State Sharia Penal Code to be stabbed to death. Instead, on 3 January 2002, he was hanged. See, for example, Ostien & Dekker 2010: 592.

22 In 2003, BAOBAB for Women's Human Rights stated: "It is curious that the [*hudud*] cases involve mostly the hewers of wood and the drawers of water in the society. Our question is that why are the rich not also targets of this system?" (BAOBAB 2003a: 26). This trend is noted also in preceding and subsequent chapters of this book.

by-laws remain in force, *zina* trials no longer take place. It seems that the combination of judicial activism and the state leadership's embarrassment, caused primarily by civil society's litigation and advocacy around *zina* cases, has eventually halted these and some other '*shari'a* implementation' measures.

The northern states' Muslim penal codes are all very similar to each other, save for the case of Niger state, which did not enact a new penal code at all. Instead, it passed the brief 2000 Niger State Penal Code (Amendment) Law, which interpolates the new *hudud*, *qisas* and 'related' offences and punishments with other criminal provisions.[23] The other 11 states organised their new penal codes into three key chapters: "Hudud and Hudud-Related Offences"; "Qisas and Qisas-Related Offences"; and "Ta'azir Offences".

Under the "Hudud and Hudud-Related Offences" chapter, the following are lumped together:

(1) *zina*, defined as comprising both adultery and fornication;
(2) rape, whereby it is explicitly stated that "[s]exual intercourse by a man with his own wife is not rape";
(3) 'sodomy' (*liwat*), explained variably in different codes as either "anal coitus" between any two individuals or "carnal intercourse against the order of nature with any man or woman";
(4) incest, curiously omitted in the states of Kano and Katsina Muslim penal codes;
(5) 'lesbianism' (*sihaq*);
(6) bestiality (*wat al-bahimah*);
(7) 'gross indecency', which in some codes is left undefined and in other codes is outlined to include kissing in public and "exposure of nakedness" in public, as well as "other related acts of similar nature capable of corrupting public morals";
(8) false accusation of *zina* (*qadhf*);
(9) defamation;
(10) theft (*sariqah*);
(11) drinking alcoholic drink (*shurb al-khamr*);
(12) robbery (*hirabah*);
(13) extortion;
(14) criminal misappropriation;
(15) criminal breach of trust;
(16) receiving stolen property;
(17) cheating;
(18) criminal trespass.

---

23 For instance, section 2 of this law provides that "'adultery' includes sodomy". See 2000 Niger State Penal Code (Amendment) Law, *Niger State of Nigeria Gazette*, No 8, Vol 25, 9 March 2000.

The next chapter of these penal codes is entitled "Qisas and Qisas-Related Offences", and detail specific retaliatory offences, such as homicide, abortion, hurt, cruelty to children, criminal assault, abduction and forced labour. Perpetrators of these offences, depending on the circumstances, can either be pardoned by the victim or their heirs, or can be punished by retaliation, corporal or monetary penalties, imprisonment or *diyah* ('blood money'). The third key chapter, named "Ta'azir Offences", entails all the remaining criminal offences found in the 1960 Penal Code, which are 'enhanced' with 'fiqh-inspired' punishments, such as whipping, and are generally left to the discretion of the *alkalis* in charge.

Remarkably, in all Muslim penal codes, *zina* is featured as the first of the *hudud* crimes, and described as follows:

> Whoever, being a man or a woman fully responsible, has sexual intercourse through the genital [sic] of a person over whom he has no sexual rights and in circumstances in which no doubt exists as to the illegality of the act, is guilty of the offence of *zina*.[24]

Unmarried Muslim offenders are liable to a whipping of 100 lashes *and* imprisonment of up to one year. Some states limit liability to imprisonment for male offenders only, while others do not. Bauchi and Kebbi states specify that incarceration shall take place "in a location other than his [sic] domicile". Married Muslim offenders are to be stoned to death (*rajm*). As evident from the subsequent case law – in line with the majority opinion of Maliki *madhhab,* but refuted by all the other mainstream schools of classical *fiqh* as well as a notable minority of Maliki scholars – the lower courts' *alkalis* consider pregnancy as proof of *zina*.[25] Given this highly problematic doctrine, and the fact that the crime of rape is added to the list of '*hudud* and *hudud*-related offences', women who report being raped are at serious risk of their case being converted into a 'confession' of *zina*; if a victim lacks the evidence required to prove rape – four Muslim male witnesses of impeccable social repute – then they are instead taken to be confessing to adultery or fornication. Hence, the new Muslim criminal codes blatantly deny Muslim women protection from rape (BAOBAB 2003a: 9). In addition, they are made especially vulnerable to domestic violence, as marital rape and wife battery are not only free from any criminal liability, but, in fact, specifically protected by law. Finally, the case law under these provisions also invariably demonstrates that men involved in *zina* trials, either as the co-perpetrators of *zina* or as the rapists of women accused of *zina*, usually get off scot-free, supposedly due to 'lack of evidence'; women, on the other hand, get sentenced to stoning or whipping by the *shari'a* courts

---

24 The Bauchi State Shari'a Penal Code adds: "fully responsible and of Islamic faith". In the state of Kebbi, the relevant provision adds: "no doubt exists as to the committal of the act". The Kebbi code also adds: "PROVE: 1. Four male witnesses to the act of zina who shall be Muslims; 2. Self confession; 3. Pregnancy." See the draft '2002 Harmonised Shari'a Penal Code Law' (Article 125), compiled and annotated by the Centre for Islamic Legal Studies of Ahmadu Bello University, Zaria, reproduced in Ostien 2007: Chapter 4, Part III.

25 This is, however, explicitly stated only in the Kebbi State Sharia Penal Code. See supra note 22.

on first instance, and then end up in jail despite evidentiary insufficiencies (BAOBAB 2003; Nmehielle 2004; Ostien 2007; Adamu Bello 2009).

Patriarchal bias equally permeates all *'hudud* or *hudud*-related' sexual crimes. 'Sodomy' (*liwat*), incest and rape are lumped together as *zina* or *zina*-related offences, all of which are punishable by stoning to death if the offenders are married. If they are not, they could still face *rajm* for 'sodomy' – unless committed with their wife, in which case the punishment will be up to 50 lashes – and 100 lashes and imprisonment for rape or incest. Apparently, "mere penetration" is what matters in all of these cases, as it is sufficient to constitute those crimes. The act of penetration triggers the prescribed punishments; all other potential aspects of such an act are deemed irrelevant. This is obvious from the punishment accorded to 'lesbianism' (*sihaq*), which cannot exceed 50 lashes and six months imprisonment, regardless of marital status. Female-to-female sexual intercourse warrants, at its maximum, only half of the lesser punishment accorded to 'illicit' coituses involving men.[26] As this provision has no solid ground in the classical Maliki *fiqh*, one can only suspect that the legislators had followed the 'logic' of women's 'value' being half that of men's; this is epitomised in some of the traditional 'Islamic' evidentiary requirements and economic affairs.

Death penalties and lashes, in addition to more conventional prison and monetary fines, are also prescribed for other, non-sexual *'hudud* or *hudud*-related' offences. Theft (*sariqah*) is thus punished with amputations of hands and feet; the drinking of alcohol (*shurb al-khamr*) is punished with 80 lashes; while robbery (*hirabah*) is punished, maximally, with crucifixion (*salb*). Curiously enough, potentially due to constitutional guarantees of freedom of religion or to the lack of agreement amongst the classical jurists as to its criminal status, apostasy (*ridda*) is not criminalised in any code. Some of them, however, while describing offences to religion, provide that defiling the Qur'an or offending the Prophet Muhammad triggers the death penalty (Ostien & Dekker 2010: 589). All other criminal offences in this chapter, such as extortion or criminal misappropriation, which had been copied from the 1960 Penal Code, are also duly 'ornamented' with flogging punishments.

A decade after their enactment, the Muslim penal codes of the 12 northern states of Nigeria remain publicly criticised, yet legally (constitutionally) unchallenged. Their incongruence with the fundamental rights chapter of the 1999 Constitution, as well as with Nigerian international human rights obligations, is quite obvious to both legal experts and an increasing number of the general populace. Some authors have opined that the probability of such challenge is "quite high in the not too distant future" (Ostien & Dekker 2010: 604). Yet, with Muslim laws being always at the core of political debates and strategies in Nigeria, in the north and the south alike, it is unlikely these codes will simply be dispensed with in a purely legalistic process. Rather, the sustained civil society

---

26 One could suppose that there is an exception to this patriarchal logic in case of female-to-female incest. However, the offence of incest is defined in Muslim penal codes as if committable solely between different-sex parties.

pressure, coupled with rising awareness primarily within Muslim communities in the north that the enacted Muslim penal codes fail to reflect both their own legal traditions *and* their contemporary exigencies, in particular those related to gender justice, might slowly melt down the political ice around these oppressive pieces of legislation, thus causing their gradual disintegration. Some states have actually never even started implementing them, while others now quietly seek ways to remedy the damage these laws have caused, particularly in the first several years since their enactment (Ostien & Dekker 2010: 603). Nevertheless, the very presence of these codes, even if some of their provisions are no longer to be 'taken for granted', reproduces the mechanisms of patriarchal domination and threats of reprisals so skilfully used by the political, religious and judicial elites. As such, they severely impede the processes of both social and legislative reform that the Nigerian women's movement and other social justice groups so vehemently foster.

State Responsibility

The domestic responsibility of the Nigerian state to promote and protect human rights is primarily based on the fundamental rights chapter, contained in each of its Constitutions, including the incumbent 1999 Constitution. This study has already demonstrated how various pieces of Nigerian legislation, most notably the Muslim penal codes of the 12 northern states, outrightly encroach on a number of constitutional rights relevant to women and gender justice, such as: the right to life (Article 33); freedom from torture or other inhuman or degrading treatment (Article 34(1)(a)); freedom from sex- or religion-based discrimination (Article 42); and the right to freedom of expression (Article 39). However, impunity for human rights abuses, including those sanctioned or provided for by legislation, remains rampant. Despite some incremental steps made by the recent civilian governments to tackle gender-based discrimination, it is still obvious that social and gender justice are not high on the state's agenda (Iheduru 2010).

From the perspective of international law, the state's failure to adhere to its human rights obligations is equally obvious. The Federal Republic of Nigeria is party to a number of international human rights treaties, including: the African Charter on Human and Peoples' Rights (ratified by Nigeria on 22 July 1983); the International Covenant on Economic, Social and Cultural Rights and the International Covenant on Civil and Political Rights (Nigeria's accession to both treaties took place on 29 July 1993); the Convention on the Elimination of All Forms of Discrimination against Women (CEDAW) (Nigeria ratified it on 13 June 1985); and the Convention on the Rights of the Child (CRC) (ratified by Nigeria on 19 April 1991). All of these treaties require state parties to implement their human rights provisions in various ways, including the abrogation and/or reform of discriminatory national legislation. Nigerian governments, however, have been reluctant to pursue such steps. In fact, the domestic legal status of some of the above international human rights treaties has been left in 'legal limbo', ensuring their minimal (if any) enforceability.

Under the 1999 Constitution (Article 12), no international treaty has the force of law (despite being signed and ratified by the state) in Nigeria until it is 'domesticated' – i.e. enacted by the National Assembly, ratified by a majority of the houses of assembly of the states, and signed by the Nigerian President (Ostien & Dekker 2010: 598). Some international treaties that hold importance for regional politics, including the African Charter on Human and Peoples' Rights, have been promptly and expediently 'domesticated'. Other treaties, in particular those of relevance for women's and children's human rights, have not.

The Convention on the Rights of the Child (CRC) only made it to the first step of 'domestication' – becoming part of the national law, with the National Assembly's enactment of the 2003 Child Rights Act – more than a decade after it was ratified in 1991. Due to the CRC's stipulation that the minimum age of marriage be 18 years, as well as some other provisions, the northern Muslim-majority states have continuously resisted this treaty's implementation. Hence, no further steps towards its 'domestication' could be taken, as all northern states still steadily refuse to ratify it (Ostien & Dekker 2010: 601). In a similar vein, the vociferous resistance of Muslim and Christian male politicians to the Convention on the Elimination of All Forms of Discrimination against Women (CEDAW) has been a factor for keeping this treaty in 'legal limbo' since it was ratified in the mid-1980s. To date, no 'domestication' steps have been made; the northern male elite bloc's boycott – like that of the southern male elite – remains steady, despite the continuous pro-CEDAW advocacy by the national women's movement, including almost all Muslim-specific women's associations. However, the Nigerian Federal Ministry of Women Affairs and Social Development compiles and sends reports to the UN Committee on CEDAW, which supervises the implementation of the Convention's standards, while Nigerian women's rights organisations jointly submit shadow reports.[27] The political boycott is thus challenged to certain extent by both some state gender mechanisms and civil society organisations. These efforts are, unfortunately, still not enough to rescue CEDAW from the imposed 'legal limbo' and make it a stronghold of domestic gender justice claims, such as those relating to *zina* laws.

Even in the absence of full enforceability of CEDAW in Nigeria, there is a regional human rights treaty, duly 'domesticated' by the state, which clearly stipulates gender-related human rights standards; however, only a few have been attained nationally. That is the African Charter on Human and Peoples Rights, which prohibits sex-based discrimination (Article 2) and specifies that "[t]he [s]tate shall ensure the elimination of every discrimination against women and also ensure the protection of the rights of the woman and the child as stipulated in international declarations and conventions" (Article 18(3)). As the African Charter is, without a doubt, part and parcel of the Nigerian legal system – it is now Chapter

---

27 See, for example, *CEDAW and Accountability to Gender Equality in Nigeria: A Shadow Report*, prepared by the Nigeria NGO Coalition on CEDAW Report for the 41st session of the Committee on the Elimination of All Forms of Discrimination against Women (Women Aid Collective, Lagos 2008), http://www.iwraw-ap.org/resources/pdf/41_shadow_reports/Nigeria_SR_by_WACOL_NGO_Coalition.pdf

A9 of the 2004 Laws of the Federation – the state is fully responsible to protect and promote gender-related human rights. In this sense, the northern states' legal justifications for their legislative and social abuses of women's human rights are doubly untenable; not only are these deplorable acts unconstitutional, they also violate the 'domesticated' regional treaty safeguarding women's human rights. This is, of course, only the clearest level on which the state and its federal units violate international law. It is arguable, for instance, that some international human rights instruments, like the UN Convention against Torture and Other Cruel, Inhuman or Degrading Treatment or Punishment (which Nigeria signed in 1988 and ratified in 2001, but never 'domesticated'), contain some norms for which no derogation is permitted (*jus cogens*); they have attained the status of customary international law, and as such are applicable globally, regardless of a particular state's stage of 'domestication'. Although Nigerian governments have often managed to circumvent their international human rights duties, they are binding nevertheless. The more the state engages in democratic processes and moves away from autocratic rule, the harder it will be for the ruling elites to ignore both domestic and international embarrassment with its poor human rights record. Gender justice has long been forfeited for the sake of Nigerian patriarchal political power games. This needs to be changed and remedied at the executive, legislative and judicial levels.

Existing Activism for Change

Nigerian women's self-organising and socio-political activism is not at all a recent phenomenon. In fact, well before British colonialism and the idea of the Nigerian state, the Tiv people and other ethnic groups had formed women's age grade associations; the Igbo women had had some specific judicial powers, which were enforceable on their fellow villagers regardless of gender (Imam 1997: 290). In the northern caliphates, there had emerged some Muslim female rulers and famed warriors, such as the 16th century princess (*gimbiya*) Amina Sukhera of Zazzau (now Zaria) (Adamu 1978; Davidson 1998), though their rule had not always ushered in reforms for women of the general populace. Under colonial rule, Nigerian women's activism had been suspiciously looked upon and often suppressed; nevertheless it produced some remarkable examples of civilian resistance to an oppressive and exploitative (male-dominated) foreign administration. Perhaps the instance most recounted was the 1929 'Women's War', organised at a grass-roots level by Igbo women's associations against the threat of the colonial imposition of the poll tax on women[28]. In these riots, 55 women activists lost their lives (Falola & Heaton 2008: 133); but, following the violence, women were appointed to native courts and continued their collective organising. Another important resistance movement was born in Abeokuta, the capital of the Ogun state in south-west Nigeria, under the charismatic leadership of Olufunmilayo Ransome-Kuti, who organised the Abeokuta Ladies' Club in 1944 (Johnson-Odim & Mba 1997). Initially founded as a charity group, this club eventually became a strong political

---

28 This tax had already been imposed on men

organisation fighting for women's rights against both the colonial administration and the local (male) elites. Renamed the Abeokuta Women's Union in 1946, this organisation won many concessions for local women, such as the elimination of the flat rate tax and women's participation in the Abeokuta administration. In 1949, its leader went on to found the Nigerian Women's Union, one of the most important civil society groups in the pre-independence nation-building movement (Falola & Heaton 2008: 140; Johnson-Odim & Mba 1997). In sum, over the centuries, women of various Nigerian territories have used multiple strategies to assert their interests, including "access to political power, religious authority, autonomous institutions, etc" (Adeleye-Fayemi 2000: 6).

Following independence, in 1960, the Nigerian Women's Union and other well-established organisations – such as the Federation of Nigerian Women's Societies – were gradually join by a large number of women's charities, workers' unions, political, cultural and religious organisations, and many other kinds of associations. The National Council of Women's Societies (NCWS) was founded in 1958, purporting, not without a great deal of controversy,[29] to represent all Nigerian women's organisations (Imam 1997: 291).

In 1985, the Federation of Muslim Women's Associations of Nigeria (FOMWAN) was formed, "as a result of dissatisfaction with the liberal academic feminist philosophy of the Nigerian National Council of Women's Societies" (Jones-Pauly 2005: 280). Instead, FOWMAN pursues a distinctly conservative take on women's rights, and it "seems to be operating cautiously within traditional gender boundaries and seeking to maintain legitimacy with existing religious and state authorities" (Salime 2008: 206). It has sister faith-based federations in Gambia, Ghana, Liberia and Sierra Leone (Jones-Pauly 2005: 280).

As aptly illustrated by FOMWAN's case, in Nigeria "[v]ery few women leaders accept that the [national women's] movement is feminist in orientation" (Abdullah 1995: 212). On the one hand, their repudiation of feminism is often associated with the rejection of global northern (neo)liberal misreading and misappropriation of the distinct African women's histories and their (undoubtedly feminist, yet culturally specific) resistance to patriarchies. On the other hand, by resisting the 'feminist' label some women's groups try not to 'disturb too much' the dominant state and religious patriarchal authorities, which are the main providers of financial means and political power in the state.[30]

---

29 The National Council repeatedly tried to assert its hegemony by ensuring the membership of the newly founded women's groups, by means of deception and coercion. Those groups would be given the false impression that their membership in the National Council was a legal requirement, or the confirmation of their independent legal status would indeed be barred before they would agree to join the Council (Imam 1997: 291–292). The National Council still exists and is recognised by the state as an 'umbrella' women's forum. Its first international chapter was formed in 2010 in the US.

30 For example, a Nigerian women's rights activist apologetically remarks: "When African women demand equality, we are only asking for our rights not to be tampered with, and the removal of laws that oppress and dehumanize women. We are not asking for equality with our husbands. We accept them as the bosses and heads of the family" (Antrobus 2004: 10; Basu 1995: 212).

In a stark contrast to such tendencies, a secular socialist feminist organisation named Women in Nigeria (WIN) was formed in 1983; it was conceived after an academic seminar in 1982 (Imam 1997: 281). Endowed with a clearly articulated political programme, while maintaining the necessary distance from the state's insidious apparatus (unlike both NCWS and FOWMAN), WIN soon became the leading civil society organisation fighting for gender justice in its manifold economic, political, cultural and other aspects (Imam 1997: 292). Its well thought of, holistic approach to research, documentation, awareness-raising, policy formulation and advocacy has contributed exceptionally to further the development and capacity-building of the Nigerian women's movement, as well as civil society as a whole (Awe & Mba 1991: 860; Salime 2008: 206).

In the wake of the post-1999 Muslim penal codes and 'shari'a implementation' policies, spanning the 12 northern states, women's human rights organisations from across Nigeria and beyond warned against the inherent gender bias of these measures. When the first *zina* trial commenced in September 2000 in Zamfara and subsequently sentenced Bariya Ibrahim Magazu, a 13-year-old girl pregnant due to a gang rape, to 100 lashes for *zina* and 80 lashes for *qadhf* (false accusation), while the three perpetrators were acquitted due to 'lack of evidence', BAOBAB for Women's Human Rights was first to react (BAOBAB 2003a: 10–11). This organisation – co-founded by the late Hajara Usman and Ayesha M Imam, one of Nigeria's most prominent feminist scholars and human rights defenders – quickly realised that Bariya was not given appropriate legal defence and that an appellate procedure against the wrongful sentence was necessary. Thus, BAOBAB persuaded Bariya and her family to appeal, and requested experts and activists from diverse international Muslim contexts to provide arguments from relevant Muslim legal traditions for the defence of a *zina* case. With information collected this way, as well as via its activists' independent research, BAOBAB formed a team of seven lawyers to organise and carry out Bariya's appeal. The subsequent judicial review decided that the lashes for *qadhf* should be revoked, but her *zina* sentence was carried out only 22 days after her child was born (BAOBAB 2003a: 10–12). BAOBAB secured legal representation and spearheaded both national and international advocacy for all subsequent *zina* cases,[31] as well as for some cases of theft (*sariqah*) involving minors[32] (BAOBAB 2003a). In these efforts, it was soon joined by several women's and human rights organisations; most notably, the Women's Rights Advancement and Protection Alternative (WRAPA), which took the lead in the defence of Amina Lawal, whose *zina* case received unprecedented international publicity.

---

31 The following women have been subsequently helped by BAOBAB and other prominent national human rights groups in *zina* proceedings: Hafsatu Abubakar Gwiwa (of Sokoto state), Aisatu Musa (Sokoto), Hauwa Garuba (Sokoto), Maryam Abubakar Bodinga (Sokoto), Safiyyatu Husseini Tungar-Tudu (Sokoto), Amina Lawal (Katsina) and Fatima Usman (Niger; together with her lover, Ahmed Ibrahim). For more information, see BAOBAB 2003a: 12–17.

32 Until mid-2003, BAOBAB has taken up the cases of the following minors (boys) prosecuted under the charges of theft: Lawal Garba, Bashir Alkali, Aminu Bello, Mohammed Sulaiman, Bawa Magaji, Umaru Guda, Sirajo Idris, Bello Garba, Malami Aliyu and Altine Hassan. For details of these cases, see BAOBAB 2003a: 17–20.

As a result of these litigations and widespread public outcry against *zina* trials, none of the women sentenced to either death by stoning or whipping received such punishments. Most of them were discharged and acquitted on appeal.

According to Ayesha M Imam, the strategic approach to '*shari'a* implementation' that BAOBAB has developed, in co-operation with other women's and human rights non-governmental organisations (NGOs), has three prongs: legal defence of those convicted for '*hudud* or *hudud*-related' offences, in particular *zina* and *sariqah*; demystification of the new Muslim penal codes, which their legislators defended as 'God-given'; and collaborative work amongst civil society organisations toward the improvement of women's rights, both across Nigeria and specifically within Muslim communities (Imam 2005: 77–78).

The defence of those convicted under Muslim penal codes was decidedly centred on the appellate procedures before the states' *shari'a* courts of appeal. Imam recounts the following reasons for choosing this strategy: (1) an immediate action was necessary in order to delay the execution of *hudud* sentences, including those of death by stoning; (2) the common view among the activists, based on previous experience, was that the higher courts would be fairer to women than lower courts; (3) advocacy directed at the states' governors to pardon the accused would be ineffective, given the political climate; and (4) challenging the constitutionality of the new Muslim penal codes at that particular time, even if successful, would have alienated the majority of Nigerian Muslims, who initially supported '*shari'a* implementation' as a way to reclaim their religious and national identity in the politically troubled Nigerian Federation (Imam 2005: 78). The appeals, built concomitantly on the arguments of classical *fiqh* and national constitutional law, revealed numerous deficiencies and patriarchal biases inherent in these new laws and their application. They also significantly helped to demystify the Muslim penal codes as 'man-made' law – fallible and appealable (Imam 2005: 78). Following BAOBAB's initial example, the Coalition for the Protection of Women's Rights in Secular, Customary and Religious Laws was formed of 60 NGOs, as well as the Shari'a Stakeholders Group, involving 18 civil society groups (Imam 2005: 79).

The task of demystification of the new Muslim penal codes and other detrimental '*shari'a* implementation' measures – such as the gender-discriminatory dress code, seclusion and transport-related policies and by-laws – was taken up by various national civil society groups working in the northern Nigerian states. They strove to expose all maladies of the *hudud* proceedings, such as the obvious class and gender bias, given that all defendants in these trials hailed from poor backgrounds and women were given distinctly less fair trials and invariably accorded harsher punishments than men. For instance, women's allegations of rape were ignored or dismissed, while out-of-wedlock pregnancy was accepted as evidence of *zina* (Imam 2005: 79). The activists also tried to demonstrate how, for example, gender-based discrimination in access to public transport, the imposition of *hijab* and the ban on women's sports and recreational activities have no substantial grounding in Muslim legal and cultural traditions. Rather, a form of political misuse of religion was taking place (dubbed imprecisely as 'political *shari'a*')³³ for the purposes of control and subjugation of women's sexuality and sociality. Critiquing and opposing this patriarchal project, far from being an obstruction of 'God-given law', was thus not only possible, but necessary.

Finally, collaborative efforts to improve women's rights in Nigeria were also instigated and intensified via an organised resistance to the discriminatory '*shari'a* implementation' measures. These were characterised by the formation of non-governmental networks, most notably the Coalition for the Protection of Women's Rights in Secular, Customary and Religious Laws, the Shari'a Stakeholders Group, the Network for Police Reform in Nigeria and the Legislative Coalition against Violence against Women. The Legislative Coalition, for instance, has prepared and submitted a draft federal law against gender-based violence (Imam 2005: 80–81).

The most prominent Nigerian *zina* case, with international coverage far exceeding all others, was that of Amina Lawal, of Katsina state, who was charged with adultery on 15 January 2002 and subsequently sentenced to death by stoning. Her new-born baby girl, Wosilat, was taken as a proof of *zina*, while the male person with whom Amina allegedly conceived Wosilat was set free; he pleaded not guilty. The first appeal, which appeared before the Funtua Upper Shari'a Court, failed on all grounds; the second one, which appeared before the Katsina Shari'a Court of Appeal, was successful. On 25 September 2003, Amina was finally discharged and acquitted. Procedural mistakes and the Maliki doctrine of the 'sleeping embryo'³⁴ were cited as the main reasons for this judgment (BAOBAB 2003a: 14–15). Importantly, the judgment of the Katsina Shari'a Court of Appeal effectively discouraged any potential subsequent attempts to bring *zina* charges against women, as it restored the burden of proof to the prosecution and ruled that an out-of-wedlock pregnancy or child is not in itself sufficient grounds to file a *zina* charge. Indeed, after this judgment on Amina's case, although it set a legal precedent only for the state of Katsina, no other *zina* proceedings were instigated anywhere in Nigeria (Imam 2005: 82).

Two years elapsed between Amina's death sentence and acquittal. During that period, Nigerian women's and human rights activists, in particular the Women's Rights Advancement and Protection Alternative (WRAPA) and BAOBAB for Women's Human Rights, fought hard on Amina's behalf on separate two fronts. The first one was in the *shari'a* courts, where the defence lawyers worked hard to reverse the failure of the first appeal. The second was, however, set against (neo)liberalist 'cosmopolites' from across the world, who took up Amina's case to lament on Muslim and, indeed, African 'backwardness' (Adamu Bello 2009: 18). Thus, in May 2003, BAOBAB activists urged the international public:

---

33 See Human Rights Watch (2004).

34 The concept of the 'sleeping embryo' pertains to divorcees, such as Amina, who are said to be able to carry a pregnancy for a period of five or even seven years after her divorce. Therefore, Amina's child was attributed to her former husband.

> Dominant colonialist discourses and the mainstream international media have presented Islam (and Africa) as the barbaric and savage Other. Please do not buy into this. Accepting stereotypes that present Islam as incompatible with human rights not only perpetuates racism but also confirms the claims of right-wing politico-religious extremists in all of our contexts (Imam & Medar-Gould 2003).

In addition, international petitions and open letters demanding, for example, that the then President Obasanjo, a 'born-again' Christian, pardon Amina Lawal – although he had no legal powers to do so – and repeal Muslim criminal laws were both misinformed and insensitive. As such, they might have provoked a serious backlash from the Muslim religious right in the country, burdened with such a negative international portrayal, which potentially could have endangered the lives of Amina and her domestic defenders (Imam 2005: 85–86).

As Amina Lawal was eventually acquitted, and no *zina* cases emerged thereafter, international attention quickly moved away from Nigeria. The women's movement and other social justice groups, which gained considerable public respect in the northern provinces for their strategic approach that operationalised rather than outright refuted the instruments of Muslim legal traditions, continue to raise awareness of the political and discriminatory nature of '*shari'a* implementation' reforms. Muslim women now publicly oppose some of the imposed measures, and politicians are generally less keen to promote them. Thus, the myth of 'God-given' legislation slowly withers away.

Conclusion

This chapter has offered an analysis of certain historical, political and cultural catalysts of Nigerian *zina* laws, as well as their consequences, epitomised in *hudud* trials and other discriminatory measures. It has emphasised the continuity and dominance of patriarchal discourses on law, religion, politics and gender, which facilitated a markedly gender-biased application of those laws. The present study, however, has also sought to reveal a significant discrepancy between the ways on which Nigerian Muslim communities had traditionally relied to ensure social justice – whereby gender and criminal justice had not necessarily collided with one another – and the course taken with the novel Muslim penal codes. Unlike the ways of the past, the new codes and measures have been primarily predicated on political, rather than religious, ambitions. Hence, their intolerance to interpretative pluralism, expressed in the attempt to codify Muslim laws, or their attempts to amalgamate Victorian with conservatively explicated classical Maliki jurisprudence. This chapter has also demonstrated that these codes and other gender-discriminatory Nigerian legislation stand in a stark contrast to the state's human rights obligations, enshrined both in its constitutional law as well as in numerous international human rights treaties. The latter laws, Nigeria has duly ratified, but still largely fails to 'domesticate' and implement. Finally, this study has offered a brief insight into the Nigerian women's movement and its strategies of resistance to the 'shari'a implementation' measures, particularly in relation to zina trials. The sustained efforts of this movement, as well as other Nigerian social justice groups, managed to expose what has been the underpinning argument of this study: at the heart of Nigeria's gender-oppressive legislation, in particular the Muslim penal codes and the related regulations, lay political deals and aspirations, coupled with an inherent patriarchal bigotry. Hence, their gradual removal, attuned to socio-political developments in the country, remains an ultimate necessity.

Now that 'shari'a implementation' slowly descends into its political and social nadir, NGOs should revisit their strategic decision not (yet) to constitutionally challenge the Muslim penal codes. Even though zina and some other 'hudud or hudud-related' offences are no longer so easily prosecutable, these laws still greatly impede women's rights; for instance, in relation to domestic violence. In a similar vein, and perhaps simultaneously, federal and customary gender-discriminatory laws, such as both 1960 Penal Code and 1960 Criminal Code, should also be challenged. The lessons learnt and networks built from the collaborative work around past zina trials should be extensively used towards a new strategic approach to the necessary legal reform.[35]

A great deal of the Nigerian troubles with these forms of oppressive legislation stem from decades of political instability and dilettantism within an inherently patriarchal society. In that sense, the introduction of hudud laws was but another phase of chronic malady in the state's political system. As Nigeria currently enjoys the longest period of civilian rule in its history, and an increasingly democratic outlook, it is hoped that the climate for comprehensive societal reforms, including those relating to gender justice, is finally materialising.

---

35 In fact, this 'forward thinking' has been repeatedly advanced within the national public space, most notably by the Nigerian women's movement. Its reiteration here is an attempt to summarise and help the further dissemination of an important strategic orientation of Nigerian human rights defenders in relation to gender-discriminatory laws and regulations.

Bibliography

Abdullah, Hussaina J (1995), 'Wifeism and Activism: The Nigerian Women's Movement' in Amrita Basu (ed.), *The Challenge of Local Feminisms: Women's Movements in Global Perspective*, 209–225. Boulder, CO: Westview Press.

Abdullah-Olukoshi, H (1990), 'Women in Islamic Societies in the Kano Setting', mimeo. Hull: University of Hull.

Abubakar, Mohammed (2002), 'Groups Petition Anti-Graft Panel over Alleged Fraud in Zamfara', *The Guardian*, 15 June, http://news.biafranigeriaworld.com/archive/ngguardian/2002/jun/15/article09.html

Adamu Bello, Aminu (2009), 'Zina (Adultery) under Islamic Law in Nigeria: The Gender Issues in Amina Lawal's Case', *Social Science Research Network*, http://ssrn.com/abstract=1119684

Adamu, Mahdi (1978), *The Hausa Factor in West African History*. Zaria: Ahmadu Bello University Press.

Adeleye-Fayemi, Bisi (2000), 'Creating and Sustaining Feminist Space in Africa: Local-Global Challenges in the 21st Century', Fourth Annual Dame Nita Barrow Lecture, Centre for Women's Studies in Education, Ontario Institute for Studies in Education. Toronto: University of Toronto.

Africa for Women's Rights (2010), 'Africa for Women's Rights: Nigeria', http://wikigender.org/w/index.php/Africa_for_Women's_Rights:_Nigeria

Agbaje, Ola and Seun Adesida (2006), 'Ribadu Blasts Zamfara Gov, *Daily Sun*, 11 August, http://www.sunnewsonline.com/webpages/news/national-/2006/aug/11/national-11-08-2006-01.htm

Agbalajobi, Damilola Taiye (2010), 'Women's Participation and the Political Process in Nigeria: Problems and Prospects', *African Journal of Political Science and International Relations* 4 (2): 75.

Akpan, Eno-Obong (2003), 'Early Marriage in Eastern Nigeria and the Health Consequences of Vesico-Vaginal Fistulae (VVF) among Young Mothers' in Caroline Sweetman (ed.), *Gender, Development, and Marriage,* 70–76. Oxford: Oxfam Focus on Gender.

Amrita, Basu (ed.) (1995), *The Challenge of Local Feminisms: Women's Movements in Global Perspective*. Boulder, CO: Westview Press.

Antrobus, Peggy (2004), *The Global Women's Movement: Origins, Issues and Strategies.* New York: Zed Books.

Awe, Bolanle and Mba, Nina (1991), 'Women's Research and Documentation Center (Nigeria)' *Signs* 16: 859.

BAOBAB for Women's Human Rights (2003a), *Sharia Implementation in Nigeria: The Journey So Far*. Lagos: BAOBAB for Women's Human Rights, http://www.baobabwomen.org

BAOBAB for Women's Human Rights (2003b), *Women's Human Rights Violation in Nigeria*. Lagos: BAOBAB for Women's Human Rights, http://www.baobabwomen.org

Bilal Philips, Abu Ameenah (1995), *The Evolution of Fiqh: Islamic Law and the Madh-habs*. New York: Islamic Book Service.

Birai, Umaru (1993), 'Islamic Tajdid and the Political Process in Nigeria' in Martin Marty and R Scott Appleby (eds.), *Fundamentalisms and the State: Remaking Polities, Economies and Militance,* 185–203. Chicago: University of Chicago Press.

Center for Reproductive Law and Policy (1997), *Women of the World: Laws and Policies Affecting Their Reproductive Rights – Anglophone Africa*. New York: Center for Reproductive Law and Policy.

Davidson, Basil (1998), *West Africa before the Colonial Era: A History to 1850*. London: Longman.

Ehrlemann, Veit (1986), *Music and the Islamic Reform in the Early Sokoto Empire*. Stuttgart: Deutsche Morgenländische Gesellschaft.

Falola, Toyin and Matthew M. Heaton (2008), *A History of Nigeria*. Cambridge: Cambridge University Press.

Gaudio, Rudolf Pell (2009), *Allah Made Us: Sexual Outlaws in an Islamic African City*. Chichester: Wiley-Blackwell.

Human Rights Watch (2004), 'Political Shari'a': Human Rights and Islamic Law in Northern Nigeria', *Human Rights Watch* 16 (9): 1.

Iheduru, Okey C. (2010), 'Gender Quota and Positive Change in Nigeria', *BusinessDay*, 1 April, http://www.businessdayonline.com/-index.php?option=com_content&view=article&id=9705:gender-quota-and-positive-change-in-nigeria&catid=96:columnists&Itemid=350

Imam, Ayesha M. (2008), 'Strategies for Successfully Ensuring Legal Coverage for Women's Human Rights in Nigeria', funded by the UK Department for International Development (DFID) Security, Justice and Growth Programme, on file with author.

——— (1997), 'The Dynamics of WINning: An Analysis of Women in Nigeria (WIN)' in M Jacqui Alexander & Chandra Talpade Mohandry (eds.), *Feminist Genealogies, Colonial Legacies, Democratic Futures,* 280–307. New York: Routledge.

——— (2005), 'Women's Reproductive and Sexual Rights and the Offense of Zina in Muslim Laws in Nigeria' in Wendi Chavkin & Ellen Chesler (eds.), *Where Human Rights Begin: Health, Sexuality, and Women in the New Millennium,* 65–94. Piscataway, NJ: Rutgers University Press.

Imam, Ayesha M., Mufuliat Fijabi, and Hurera Akilu-Atta (2005), *Women's Rights in Muslim Laws: A Resource Document*. Lagos: BAOBAB for Women's Human Rights, http://www.baobabwomen.org

Imam, Ayesha M. and Sindi Medar-Gould (2003), 'How Not to Help Amina Lawal: The Hidden Dangers of Letter Campaigns', *Counterpunch*, 15 May, http://www.counterpunch.org/iman05152003.html

Johnson-Odim, Cheryl and Nina Emma Mba (1997), *For Women and the Nation: Funmilayo Ransome-Kuti of Nigeria*. Campaign, IL: University of Illinois Press.

Jones-Pauly, Christina (2005), 'Sub-Saharan Africa' in Suad Joseph and Afsaneh Najmabadi (eds.), *Encyclopedia of Women & Islamic Cultures: Family, Law, and Politics*, 279–281. Leiden: Brill.

Kane, Ousmane (2003), *Muslim Modernity in Postcolonial Nigeria: A Study of the Society for the Removal of Innovation and Reinstatement of Tradition*. Leiden: Brill.

Keay, Elliot Alexander and Sam S. Richardson (1966), *The Native and Customary Courts of Nigeria*. Lagos: African University Press.

Mack, Beverly B. and Jean Boyd (2000), *One Woman's Jihad: Nana Asma'u, Scholar and Scribe*. Bloomington, IN: Indiana University Press.

Mahdi, Hauwa (2009), 'The *Hijab* in Nigeria, the Woman's Body and the Feminist Private/Public Discourse', Institute for the Study of Islamic Thought in Africa Working Paper Series. Evanston, IL: The Roberta Buffett Center for International and Comparative Studies, Northwestern University.

Milner, Alan (1969), 'Sentencing Patterns in Nigeria' in Alan Milner (ed.), *African Penal Systems*. London: Routledge.

Nasir, Jamila M. (2007), 'Sharia Implementation and Female Muslims in Nigeria's Sharia States' in Philip Ostien (ed.), *Sharia Implementation in Northern Nigeria 1999–2006: A Sourcebook*. Ibadan: Spectrum Books Ltd. Full text at http://www.sharia-in-africa.net/pages/publications/sharia-implementation-in-northern-nigeria.php.

Nigeria NGO Coalition on CEDAW Report (2008), *CEDAW and Accountability to Gender Equality in Nigeria: A Shadow Report*, prepared for the 41st session of the Committee on the Elimination of All Forms of Discrimination against Women. Lagos: Women Aid Collective, http://www.iwraw-ap.org/resources/pdf/41_shadow_reports/Nigeria_SR_by_WACOL_NGO_Coalition.pdf.

Nigerian NGO Coalition for a Shadow Report on the Implementation in Nigeria of the Convention on the Elimination of All Forms of Discrimination against Women (1998), 'NGO Report on the Implementation in Nigeria of the Convention on the Elimination of All Forms of Discrimination against Women', submitted to the United Nations Committee on the Convention for the Elimination of All Forms of Discrimination against Women, 17th Session, July 1998, on file with author.

'Nigerian Senator Sani Denies Marrying Girl of 13', *BBC News*, 30 April 2010, http://news.bbc.co.uk/1/hi/world/africa/8651043.stm.

Nmehielle, Vincent O. (2004), 'Sharia Law in the Northern States of Nigeria: To Implement or Not to Implement, the Constitutionality Is the Question', *Human Rights Quarterly* 26: 730.

Oba, Abdulmumini Adebayo (2004), 'The Sharia Court of Appeal in Northern Nigeria: The Continuing Crises of Jurisdiction', *American Journal of Comparative Law* 52: 859.

Odinkalu, Chidi Anselm (2008), 'Domesticating CEDAW in Nigeria: A Stakeholder Analysis and Report', prepared for UNIFEM, on file with author.

OECD Development Centre (2008), 'Gender Equality and Social Institutions in Nigeria' in *Social Institutions & Gender Index*. Paris: OECD Development Centre, http://genderindex.org/country/nigeria

Okafọ, Nọnso (2009), *Reconstructing Law and Justice in a Postcolony*. Surrey: Ashgate.

Olajide, Abdulfattah (2002), 'Shariah Gains More Ground in Yorubaland', *Weekly Trust*, 15 November, http://www.corpun.com/ngj00211.htm.

Onagoruwa, Olu (2009), 'Law-Making Process in Nigeria', parts 1 and 2, *The Guardian*, 17–18 March.

Ostien, Philip and Albert Dekker (2010), 'Sharia and National Law in Nigeria' in Jan Michiel Otto (ed.), *Sharia Incorporated: A Comparative Overview of the Legal Systems of Twelve Muslim Countries in Past and Present*, 553–612. Leiden: Leiden University Press.

Ostien, Philip and MJ Umaru (2007), 'Changes in the Law in the Sharia States Aimed at Suppressing Social Vices' in Philip Ostien (ed.), *Sharia Implementation in Northern Nigeria 1999–2006: A Sourcebook*. Ibadan: Spectrum Books Ltd. Full text at http://www.sharia-in-africa.net/pages/publications/sharia-implementation-in-northern-nigeria.php.

Ostien, Philip (ed.)(2007), *Sharia Implementation in Northern Nigeria 1999–2006: A Sourcebook*. Ibadan: Spectrum Books Ltd. Full text at http://www.sharia-in-africa.net/pages/publications/sharia-implementation-in-northern-nigeria.php

Sada, Ibrahim Na'iya (2007), 'The Making of the Zamfara and Kano State Sharia Penal Codes' in Philip Ostien (ed), *Sharia Implementation in Northern Nigeria 1999–2006: A Sourcebook*. Ibadan: Spectrum Books Ltd. Full text at http://www.sharia-in-africa.net/pages/publications/sharia-implementation-in-northern-nigeria.php

Salime, Zakia (2008), 'Mobilizing Muslim Women: Multiple Voices, the Sharia, and the State', *Comparative Studies of South Asia, Africa and the Middle East* 28: 200.

Schacht, Joseph (1964), *An Introduction to Islamic Law*. Oxford: Clarendon Press.

—— (1957), 'Islam in Northern Nigeria', *Studia Islamica* 8: 123.

Sowell, Thomas (2004), *Affirmative Action around the World: An Empirical Study*. New Haven: Yale University Press.

Tar, Usman A. (2009), *The Politics of Neoliberal Democracy in Africa: State and Civil Society in Nigeria*. London: Tauris Academic Studies.

Terman, Rochelle and Mufuliat Fijabi (2010), 'Stoning is Not Our Culture: A Comparative Analysis of Human Rights and Religious Discourses in Iran and Nigeria', Global Campaign to Stop Killing and Stoning Women and Women Living under Muslim Laws, http://www.stop-stoning.org/node/883

Wren Bivins, Mary (2007), *Telling Stories, Making Histories: Women, Words, and Islam in Nineteenth-century Hausaland and the Sokoto Caliphate*. Portsmouth, NH: Heinemann.

Yawuri, Aliyu Musa (2007), 'On Defending Safiyatu Hussaini and Amina Lawal' in Philip Ostien (ed.), *Sharia Implementation in Northern Nigeria 1999–2006: A Sourcebook*. Ibadan: Spectrum Books Ltd. Full text at http://www.sharia-in-africa.net/pages/publications/sharia-implementation-in-northern-nigeria.php

Pakistan

COUNTRY PROFILE

The Islamic Republic of Pakistan is home to some 170 million people, 96 per cent of which are from Muslim communities. As such, it is the world's sixth most populous country with the second largest Muslim population (after Indonesia). Muslim communities in Pakistan are markedly heterogeneous: the majority of them nominally subscribe to mainline Sunni interpretations of their faith and legal traditions, in particular that of the Hanafi *madhhab*; a substantial minority, some 10–30 per cent, consider themselves Shi'a and some 2.3 per cent are self-defined Ahmadis (and, as such, declared non-Muslim by the state). In addition to these formalistic delineations, Pakistani Muslim diversity is founded upon distinct socio-religious trends permeating the country's religious ethos; such as those of the so-called Deobandi and Barelvi schools of thought, named after two seminaries established in colonial India. The former has pursued an exoteric purist scripturalism, while the latter has preferred an esoteric path, which is associated with the subcontinent's numerous Sufi orders and often accused of syncretism (Malik 2008: 16).

Nominally, Pakistan is a parliamentary federal democratic republic, wherein Islam is considered the state religion. Successive constitutions in Pakistan have tried, albeit without a great deal of precision, to define the role and the scope of 'Injunctions of Islam' in the domestic legal system (Mullally 2006: 167). The 1956 Constitution, for instance, simply declares (in Article 198) that all state laws ought to be brought into conformity with those 'injunctions', and that no law or regulation can be enacted that is 'repugnant to Islam'. The incumbent, 1973 Constitution, maintains this provision (in Article 227). This was found insufficient by the Muslim right-wing political instances in the country. Thus, fuelled by the then military regime of General Muhammad Zia-ul-Haq and its need for legitimisation before the general populace, the process of legal 'Islamisation' was instigated in the late 1970s, which resulted in many unprecedented forms of state-sanctioned injustices, including many related to gender.

In 1979, as an attempt to 'Islamise' the country's criminal justice system, General Zia promulgated the five Hudood Ordinances, thereby reinstating the classical Muslim judicial concept of *hudood* (*hudud*) crimes and punishments. One of these ordinances, namely the Offence of Zina (Enforcement of Hudood) Ordinance, 1979, stipulated that married Muslims who have committed *zina* be punished by stoning to death, while unmarried Muslim offenders or non-Muslims in general should receive 100 cane lashes. In the same ordinance, the offences of *zina* and so-called *zina-bil-jabr* (rape) were lumped together, with the effect that a woman alleging rape could end up being charged with the offence of *zina*. According to the Pakistani National Commission on the Status of Women, in March 2003, some 80 per cent – around 1,500 – of the women in jail were there because "they had failed to prove rape charges and were consequently convicted of adultery" (NCSW Report 2003). Finally, in 2006, after decades of advocacy by women's and other civil society organisations, the Criminal Law Amendment (Protection of Women) Act revised, amongst other things, the Zina Ordinance by removing *zina-bil-jabr* – now prosecutable under the 1860 Penal Code – and by making the offence of *zina* inconvertible to *zina-bil-jabr*, and vice versa. The problematic Hudood Ordinances, however, still remain in force, along with other discriminatory provisions from the 'Islamisation' era; for instance, the 1984 Qanun-e-Shahadat Order, a revision of the 1872 Evidence Act, which (in Article 17(2)(a)) restricted the evidence of women in financial matters simply due to their gender. This is despite Pakistan's obligations under international human rights law and the constitutional guarantees (Article 25) that there "shall be no discrimination on the basis of sex" and that "all citizens are equal before law".

Pakistan emerged on the world map as an independent Muslim-majority state on 14 August 1947 (Shah 2006: 91). Its founder, Muhammad Ali Jinnah, proclaimed in 1943 that, although the aim of nation-building is "to bring about Islamic renaissance", the new state is envisioned as "modern [and] democratic [...], with the sovereignty resting in the people and the members of the new nation having equal rights" (Iqbal 1986: 33). Both Jinnah and Muhammad Iqbal, another key figure in the struggle for Pakistan's independence, have sought to see *shari'a* in the emergent national legal system interpreted in such ways as to "meet the exigencies of modern times" (Shah 2006: 92; Ghazali 1996), including that of gender justice. Indeed, over the 30 years following independence, the country's ruling political establishments managed to consciously allocate an almost entirely symbolic role to religion in the constitutions of 1956, 1962 and 1973, while retaining the British colonial legacy of Muslim family law (Lau 2010: 373). Although this legacy was clearly founded on patriarchal interpretations of Muslim legal traditions, societal control of women's sexuality could not easily be managed by the criminal justice system. In the late 1970s, however, in the wake of the politically motivated 'Islamisation' of Pakistani laws, the regulation and definition of women's legal status was found to be central to the objectives of this process (Mullally 2006: 177), and criminal law seemed best placed to ensure the desired social and political control. The blatant manifold injustice that 'Islamisation' has caused was opposed, albeit in vain, by numerous Pakistani institutional and civil society stakeholders, even including the highest judicial religious instances. In its famous 1981 judgment in the Bakhsh case,[1] the Federal Shariat Court demanded that the government review the Zina Ordinance so that stoning to death (*rajm*) for *zina* was removed, as it was 'repugnant to the Injunctions of Islam'. In response, the then military president, General Zia-ul-Haq, issued Order V of 1981 (Constitution (Amendment) Order) that empowered this court to review its own prior decisions. In addition, he replaced all but one – the one dissenting

---

1 *Hazoor Bakhsh* v *Federation of Pakistan*, PLD 1981 FSC 145; see also *Federation of Pakistan* v *Hazoor Bakhsh* PLD 1983 FSC 255.

vote in the Bakhsh case – of the Court's judges. Unsurprisingly, the new court judges 'decided' that stoning to death, as stipulated by General Zia's Zina Ordinance, did not run contrary to the 'Injunctions of Islam' (Jones-Pauly 2000: 545). Thus, sheer military power and political calculations were the decisive factors in the institutionalisation of gender injustice with an 'Islamic' label. Although opposed throughout by the various stakeholders, particularly the national women's movement, the patriarchal normative system remains deeply entrenched in the Pakistani social and legal systems, thereby causing continuous and systemic gender discrimination.

This chapter is an attempt to critically interrogate the catalysts and consequences of Muslim adultery laws in Pakistan, especially in relation to their socio-legal impact on access to gender justice. The rise of *zina* criminal cases, in particular those stemming from women's 'unfounded' rape charges, was instrumental in shaping the national women's movement (Rouse 1988: 12), whose strategies of resistance are also briefly assessed in this study.

The proceeding analysis first captures the momentous developments in Pakistani political, cultural and religious history that have shaped the dominant societal discourses on sexuality and gender. It then looks at how those discourses have been represented and manipulated by the country's relevant legislation, i.e. constitutional, criminal and family law. It is argued that, to varying degrees, the identified discriminatory laws and ordinances, while securing considerable political gains for the ruling elites responsible for their promulgation, betray the constitutional promise of gender justice as well as Pakistan's obligations under international human rights law, which are also discussed. The chapter then turns to interrogate civil society's response to the criminalisation of *zina* and the resultant influx of cases predominantly against women, many of whom have been languishing for years in Pakistani jails awaiting criminal trials. It also briefly investigates the revision of relevant criminal legislation in 2006; it was an important 'success' for national civil society organisations' advocacy. The concluding remarks, once again, underline the markedly political nature of Pakistan's venture into the criminalisation of *zina*, which has little (if anything) to do with the state's constitutional commitment to the 'Injunctions of Islam'.

Historical Background

The dramatic events surrounding India's independence from British colonial rule in 1947, followed by its partition along imagined religious lines, forming separate Muslim and Hindu entities, resulted in the formation of a Muslim-majority state named Pakistan (Lau 2010: 376). The name itself is a portmanteau,[2] arguably coined in the 1930s by a group of then Indian Muslim students at the University of Cambridge (Cohen 2004: 26; Malik 2008:

---

2 The portmanteau (a blend of several words and their meanings into one new word) 'Pakistan' represented the population of "thirty million Muslims […] who live in the five Northern Units of British Raj", namely: **P**unjab, **A**fghania (now known as Khyber Pakhtunkhwa), **K**ashmir, **S**indh and Baloch**istan** (Wolpert 1984: 131). Also, *pak* in Urdu means 'pure', so the state is often colloquially referred to as 'Land of the Pure'.

16). The new state was curiously composed of two territorial units – East Pakistan (now Bangladesh) and West Pakistan (now Pakistan) – physically separated by over 1,000 miles, with distinct cultural and linguistic differences. Pakistan was envisaged by its founders as a Muslim democracy, wherein religion was the key 'cohesive factor' among culturally and politically variant Muslim groups. A liberal bourgeois ideology (Rouse 1988), with largely symbolic Muslim elements, was thus developed to galvanise the support of various elements within Muslim communities, as well as to appeal, to some extent, to both Indian and British political establishments. Facing continuous and grave challenges – first, an open-ended and seemingly insolvable armed conflict with India over the Kashmir border; and then, a civil war that led to the partition of its eastern wing, which became, in 1971, a new independent state called Bangladesh – Pakistani ruling elites, both civilian and military, relied on the power of a strong centralised state. Hence, social and religious discourses, including those of sexuality and gender, were predominantly shaped in an effort to condone the particular visions of those in charge of an increasingly autocratic and militarised polity.

Muslim communities that were brought together with the advent of Pakistan have retained a strong bias in their construction and utterance of both class and gender. While upper class women have at least had a limited space in which to challenge the overall patriarchal system, which had relegated them to largely inferior social and familial roles, no such opportunity could materialise within the lower classes' milieux. Hence, "Pakistan may have had female prime ministers, ministers, ambassadors, and governors, but most Pakistani women […] are preoccupied with issues of family survival" (Malik 2008: 14). Political instability, economic crises, inter-ethnic divisions and class oppression, combined with an inherited patriarchal bias, made the Pakistani populace particularly vulnerable to the indoctrination of right-wing religious and political groups, such as Jamaat-e-Islami. The head of this radical faction until his death in 1979, Sayyid Abul A'la Maudoodi, realised very early that he could secure popularity and support for his political aspirations through the discourse of Muslim patriarchal morality, grounded on control over female bodies and sexualities. In 1939, he published a book called *Purdah*, which has since gone through numerous reprints and minor revisions (Pal 1990: 450, 462–463; Maudoodi 1967). *Purdah*, literally meaning a veil or a curtain, has come to mean an entire code of conduct for Muslim women, and in South Asia is usually a by-word for seclusion in general. In sum, Maudoodi advanced four key positions as to the roles and responsibilities of the woman: (1) she is solely responsible to make domestic life 'a paradise of peace and joy'; (2) she is inferior to men; (3) she is unable to perform most outdoor work, including any economic, political or administrative duties; and (4) "[s]he is a tragic being, with all those bodily and reproductive functions to perform; the domestic role is ordained for her by nature" (Pal 1990: 453; Maudoodi 1967: 193, 199).

When General Muhammad Zia-ul-Haq assumed power through a military coup d'état, in 1977, and imposed martial law, Maudoodi's vision of *purdah* in Pakistani society was quickly adopted by the state. In alliance with Jamaat-e-Islami and other right-wing factions, General Zia began the process of 'Islamisation' through martial law ordinances and discriminatory policies, which effectively (if not always overtly) followed the maxim of *chador aur char diwari* (literally "veil and four walls"; i.e. women veiled and within the confines of the home) (Mullally 2006: 170). For instance, in 1980, one state policy required all female government employees to wear *chador* over their other clothes (Pal 1990: 452). Similar requirements were also imposed on women in certain public offices – such as news broadcasters and airline stewardesses. However, under these imposed reforms, the women's movement managed to overcome some of its internal ideological and class-based differences and organise a widespread resistance. In 1981, a grassroots-based popular front called the Women's Action Forum (WAF) was born, which brought together seven strong women's groups and individual supporters under the initial leadership of professional, middle-class women (Rouse 1988: 12). It still serves as a catalyst for other women's groups of various political and religious convictions to publicly and collectively stand up against gender injustice (Rouse 1988: 12), as well as for mounting international solidarity.

Although General Zia's dictatorship ended in 1988 with his death in a plane crash, the problematic legacy of his 'Islamisation' policies is still deeply felt in Pakistani society. It took another military leader's demand for public legitimacy, General Pervez Musharraf, after his own coup d'état in 1999, before some of the most detrimental instances of Zia's reforms could be reversed. Musharraf termed his policy orientation 'enlightened moderation', whereby extremist stances on any issue – including the role and interpretation of religion in the state of Pakistan – were to be 'rationally opposed'. In 2000, after years of lobbying by women's groups, the National Commission on the Status of Women was finally formed. In 2004 and 2006, important amendments to domestic criminal law were introduced. The 2004 Criminal Law (Amendment) Bill (referred to as Act I of 2005) introduced section 156B into the 1898 Code of Criminal Procedure, which barred the arrest of women accused of *zina* without a court's permission. This section also required that the investigation of a *zina* case be conducted by an officer with the rank of Superintendent of Police. The 2006 Code of Criminal Procedure (Second Amendment) Ordinance (Act XXXV of 2006) made the offences under General Zia's 1979 Zina Ordinance bailable, resulting in the release of hundreds of women accused of *zina* from jails all over the country. Another set of amendments, known as the 2006 Protection of Women Act, removed rape from the Zina Ordinance and, in procedural law, barred the conversion of any complaint of rape into a charge of adultery or fornication against the complainant. The legislative changes, however, remain partial and insufficient to significantly challenge the patriarchal ethos permeating much of Pakistan's tumultuous inter-Muslim and gender-based relations. The Eighteenth Amendment to the Constitution of Pakistan, passed in April 2010 by Parliament, turned Pakistan from a 'semi-presidential' into a parliamentary republic. The Amendment reversed a number of the infringements on the Constitution made over several decades by its military rulers, in particular by transferring many of the presidential powers to Parliament and the prime minister's office. If Pakistan is indeed to embark on reforms towards a decentralised parliamentary democracy, perhaps its vital institutions in the judicial and executive sectors, along with civil society organisations, will finally have a chance to address gender injustice in a more substantive way.

Domestic Legal System

Muslim laws and a variety of Islamic legal traditions are present in the territories of today's Pakistan, and have been for an exceptionally long time. Some 80 years after the death of the Prophet Muhammad (c. 570/571–632), Muhammad bin Qasim Al-Thaqafi began the conquest of the Sindh and Punjab regions on behalf of the Umayyad Caliphate. Three centuries later, Punjab was made part of the Ghaznavid Empire, while the Delhi Sultanate was formed in the 12th century. A strong and culturally magnificent Mughal Empire emerged in the 16th century, asserting its rule over almost the entire northern half of the Indian subcontinent. Its administrative and, to some extent, legal systems were upheld by the East India Company and, later on, the British colonial administration, whose gradual takeover was initiated in the 17th century and completed in 1857, when the Mughal rulers were fully removed from power (Lau 2010: 377).

Prior to colonisation, the laws of Mughal Northern India were not rigidly imposed by the central administration. Instead, they had consisted of elements of both the classical *fiqh* and a variety of local customary laws, the latter often being adjudicated upon by a council of elders known as *jirga* (Lau 2010; Menski 1997). The colonial encounter, however, brought a stark division between family law and all other legal matters, which is still clearly visible in the contemporary Pakistani legal system. The Warren Hastings Plan of 1772 in India stipulated that Muslims and Hindus were to rely on their own laws in matters of marriage, divorce, inheritance, caste and the related religious concerns, while other, 'public' and 'general' matters were to be governed by British laws and courts. This had two major far-reaching consequences. First, the division between the so-called 'private' and 'public' spheres, whereby religion was invariably relegated to the former (Mullally 2006: 171), angered and gradually marginalised local Muslim communities. Although the concept of private space has a distinctive place in Muslim laws and cultures, it is certainly not the only realm to which Islamic legal traditions pertain. Second, the arrival of colonial laws and courts deeply transformed all legal spheres, *including* that of supposedly indigenous family law. Judges of the new courts have not possessed substantial knowledge in either *fiqh* or Hindu jurisprudence; hence, they have had to appoint local 'experts' to help them deal with family law matters. This has meant that "elements of local, customary law were gradually replaced with [...] text-based interpretation of Hindu and Islamic law" (Lau 2010: 380). By and large, the emerging establishment of family law 'experts' has endeavoured to assert and retain control over women's sexuality and sociality, thus entrenching the patriarchal legacy even deeper into the social fabric. As 'the last post' of the lost judicial and political independence, Muslim family law has become an important means for the purported remake of an injured and contested communitarian self. Thus, a legalistic and puritanical discourse on family and gender has made it possible for Muslim men to (re)construct and manage familial hierarchies, in exchange for any considerable 'public' power.

In the closing years of British colonial rule, the *political* importance of Muslim family law – understood within the, arguably, broader ambit of 'personal law' – became even more apparent. In 1937, Muslim delegates of the Imperial Legislative Assembly adopted the Muslim Personal Law (Shariat) Application Act. This act, together with other similar legislative measures passed around that time, effectively and symbolically ensured the existence of a unified Muslim legal identity, governed by a central political system. Such manoeuvres were of exceptional importance for the formation of the state of Pakistan, even though, ironically enough, they received little support from the conservative *'ulama'*. In fact, the nationalist movement was spearheaded by the All India Muslim League, a populist political organisation with a distinctly 'modernist' orientation.

Throughout colonial times, all criminal law matters on the Indian subcontinent were governed by British secular laws. For instance, fornication – sexual relations between unmarried individuals – was not considered a crime. In contrast, adultery was an offence punishable by imprisonment for five years, a fine or both. Interestingly, only the husband of an alleged adulteress could make a complaint and only her male 'partner in crime' could be prosecuted. A woman could not file a compliant, nor could she stand a trial. This distinctly 'male' crime was both bailable and compoundable. All this was regulated by the 1860 Penal Code, which is, importantly, still in force in Pakistan as the Pakistan Penal Code (Act XLV of 1860). The section on adultery (s 497) was repealed by General Zia's notorious 1979 Zina Ordinance. In sum, in Pakistani legislation until 1979, there was no explicit reference to *zina*. Instead, a Victorian 'male only' concept of crime and punishment for adultery was upheld, while fornication was not considered an offence at all.

Having surveyed the pre-independence social and legal conditions that set the stage for many later legislative developments, this chapter now turns to an examination of the Pakistani legal system after the state was born. First, in an introductory assessment, two acute maladies of the system under scrutiny are identified. Subsequently, an overview of the domestic judicial system and its key institutions is offered, followed by a concise analysis of one of these institutions' momentous episodes in the dramatic political saga which befell the country, which had enormous legal and social impacts on gender justice, in general, and the *zina*-based criminalisation of women (and some men), in particular. It is then demonstrated how gender-relevant legislative changes, arguably with an 'Islamic' grounding, have been negotiated and introduced; first within constitutional and family law, and finally and most problematically in the domain of criminal law.

The Laws of Pakistan:
Between Ubiquitous Colonial Legacy and Un-Islamic 'Islamisation'

Interestingly enough, more than 60 years after independence, a significant part of the Pakistani legal system is still dominated by British colonial laws, more than a century old. Over the course of time, they were 'ornamented' with the general references to 'Islamic

Injunctions' and, in some instances, the terminology and topics from the classical Sunni *fiqh*. During, at least, the first three decades since the independence, the majority of those 'ornamentations' were either symbolic general provisos in constitutional law or specific developments in Muslim family law; the latter owed significantly to Muslim-specific acts that were promulgated in the colonial time. Extraordinarily, however, Zia-ul-Haq's process of 'Islamisation', largely by means of autocratic martial law ordinances, made an unprecedented impact on the domestic criminal justice system. In consultations with Saudi 'experts', Zia, too, tried to formulate his ordinances as if they were a resurrected classical *fiqh*, although they were supplemented with inexplicable (from the classical point of view) additions, such as that of *zina-bil-jabr*. It is, therefore, submitted that Pakistan's legislation is doubly impaired and, consequently, disharmonic and clearly open to political abuse. On the one hand, it relies on an outmoded colonial legal legacy, which does not meet the demands of contemporary Pakistani society. On the other hand, it was infused with quasi-*hudood* laws which, even if bereft of any real applicability (and that is, at the moment, only partially so), are but an oppressive, dilettante and politically motivated encroachment on the rights to Muslim pluralism and gender justice. In such circumstances, the judicial system remains in constant checkmate, even though, as will be demonstrated, it made some significant steps forward, despite the real risk of political retaliation. The most salient piece of legislation, numerous shortages notwithstanding, is the much-amended 1973 Constitution, particularly its human rights chapter. It is, therefore, not surprising that it remains the bedrock of Pakistan's social justice movements, including women's human rights groups.[3]

Judicial System and the Role of Federal Shariat Court

The pyramid of Pakistan's judicial system is as follows (top-down): (1) Supreme Court of Pakistan; (2) High Courts (one for each province and one in the federal capital); (3) district and sessions courts (one in each district); and (4) judicial and executive magistrate courts and courts of civil judge. In parallel with this structure, the Federal Shariat Court operates as a special court. Its decisions on matters within its jurisdiction are *binding* on the High Courts. Similarly, the Supreme Court's interpretation on any question of law is binding on the Federal Shariat Court. There is, however, no direct link between the Federal Shariat Court and the High Courts.

The judicial system is derived from English common law and is formally based on the 1973 Constitution and the official interpretations of *shari'a*, which are arguably substantiated on

---

3 Another important source of legislative support against oppressive domestic laws and practices are international human rights conventions, either those that Pakistan has ratified or those that are considered part of customary international law, even though the state has made significant efforts to limit and condition their implementation. They are discussed in some detail later on in this study.

predominantly Hanafi classical *fiqh*. In practice, however, the courts have demonstrated a great deal of *ijtihad* (independent judicial reasoning). The subsequent discussion focuses on the Federal Shariat Court as an exemplary model of the ongoing judicial crisis in Pakistan's legal system, instigated and perpetuated, in the first place, by past military regimes and their political allies. This Court has, also, played an important role in relation to the 1979 Hudood Ordinances and the subsequent criminal cases, predominantly based on the charges of *zina*.

The Federal Shariat Court was founded by the 1980 Constitution (Amendment) Order of General Zia-ul-Haq, as an important instrument of his 'Islamisation' programme. A year later, Zia removed the judges who had refused to endorse his coup d'état from the benches of the higher courts, thereby ending the tradition of a relatively independent judiciary. The new Shariat Court was given a mandate to review the validity of Pakistani laws in accordance with the 'Injunctions of Islam', either *suo motu* (on its own motion) or in response to a citizens' petition. It was to exercise appellate provisional jurisdiction over the criminal courts, deciding on *hudood* cases under the Hudood Ordinances. Importantly, however, the 1973 Constitution, procedural laws and 'Muslim personal law' were excluded from its jurisdiction (Lau 2010: 400). In addition, it was established that any appeal against the decisions of the Federal Shariat Court went to the Shariat Appellate Bench of the Supreme Court, which consisted of three Muslim judges from the Supreme Court and two *'ulama'* appointed by the President. This way, Zia was hoping to

---

CASES OF HUMAN RIGHTS VIOLATIONS

The Victim of Rape Found Guilty of *Zina*

Zafran Bibi, a 28-year-old woman, was at the time of conviction married to Naimat Khan, who had been jailed for life for murder. She lived in a village Keri Sheikhan in Pakistan's Khyber Pakhtunkhwa Province. Zafran was sentenced to stoning to death by a session court in Kohat under the Zina Ordinance for alleged adultery in 2002. Zafran reported rape to the police station and then became the victim of sexual abuse by her brother-in-law. She was sentenced on the basis of her statement before the court, as well as due to the fact that she became pregnant and gave birth as the result of being raped by her husband's brother, while the former was in jail. The judge ruled that the medical evidence showed no signs of force and that her pregnancy was evidence of adultery. The male person accused was acquitted. The law offered her no protection, as she was unable to prove rape by producing the required four male witnesses. Instead, she was found guilty of adultery. She was in prison for a while with her newborn baby and was then released on the appeal.

[Source: Research conducted by Zara Saeidzadeh for this study. The author is grateful for her valuable contribution.]

ensure that control over the official interpretations of the 'Injunctions of Islam' and their supremacy above almost all other legal regulations in the country would be entirely in his hands.

Only one year after its formation, however, the Federal Shariat Court challenged the prime token of the President's rule, his 1979 Zina Ordinance, by declaring that stoning to death for *zina* runs contrary to the 'Injunctions of Islam'.[4] While upholding cane lashing as a legitimate form of punishment for *zina*, with the reference to Qur'anic verse 24:2, the court established that stoning to death (*rajm*) is nowhere to be found in the Qur'an and that the *ahadith* on this matter are mutually incongruent. This was concluded by four out of the five judges who heard the case, while the one dissenting judge, Karimullah Durrani, maintained that the Sunna, which he personally found congruent enough on the matter, is a source of law equally important to the Qur'an. Hence, by the majority of four judges' opinions, stoning to death was declared a non-*hadd* punishment; therefore, the Zina Ordinance was deemed repugnant to the correct interpretations of *shari'a* (Jones-Pauly 2000: 542–544).

Outraged by this open disobedience, Zia promulgated another presidential order under the imposed martial law, which allowed the Federal Shariat Court to review its own decisions.[5] In addition, he replaced the four judges who refused to recognise *rajm* as a form of *hadd* with new 'experts'; Justice Durrani remained on the Court. Zia's message was crystal-clear: whoever opposed his supreme authority in any matter would be removed. The new Court quickly reversed its judgment on *rajm* and declared the Zina Ordinance fully in line with the 'Injunctions of Islam'.[6]

Constitutional Law

The Islamic Republic of Pakistan is still governed by its 1973 Constitution, even though it has since been heavily amended, time and again (Mehdi 1994; Lau 2010: 407). It establishes Pakistan as an 'Islamic' republic, and makes the lofty declaration that all the existing laws should be brought into conformity with the 'Injunctions of Islam' and no new law should depart from such course either (Shah 2006: 100). It, however, also contains a whole chapter on fundamental rights, whereby almost all the human rights enshrined in the 1948 Universal Declaration of Human Rights are solemnly guaranteed (Shah 2006: 109). Against this backdrop, there have been many attempts, especially in the time of Zia's 'Islamisation' agenda, to amend or re-interpret the Constitution so that patriarchal and gender-discriminatory views gain prominence in the political and legal configurations of the state. All those attempts were justified by reference to Islam. After Zia's abrupt demise, however, the subsequent regimes have sought, to varying degrees, to restore the 'balance'

---

4 *Hazoor Bakhsh* v *Federation of Pakistan*, PLD 1981 FSC 145.
5 Presidential Order V of 1981 (Constitution (Amendment) Order).
6 *Federation of Pakistan* v *Hazoor Bakhsh*, PLD 1983 FSC 255.

between an ideological Muslim apparatus and the increasing demands for social justice. It seems, however, that the gradual abandonment of Zia's 'Islamisation' route, as well as the strategic adoption of human rights language and base-line institutional reform, is still significantly conditioned by the political and military elite's power games. For example, the most recent Eighteenth Amendment to the 1973 Constitution, promulgated in April 2010 by the Parliament, remedied an important part of the dictatorial legacy of Zia's (and, later on, Musharraf's) regime by returning a number of the excessive presidential powers to Parliament. Parliament is, however, still reluctant to review the Hudood Ordinances, as they are, supposedly, too contentious an issue for the time being. Seemingly, the interest behind the new reforms is in regaining sizeable political power, rather than in ameliorating the state's revolting human rights record.

The constitutional provisions of particular significance to gender justice and women's human rights are the equality clause, right to employment, right to political participation, right to access to public space and the forbidding of human trafficking (Shah 2006: 109). In particular, Article 25 of the current Constitution is regularly cited by the women's rights groups in their advocacy and litigation efforts. It consists of the famed equality clause "All citizens are equal before law and are entitled to equal protection of law"; an explicit assurance that "no discrimination on the basis of sex" shall be permitted; and a statement that encourages the state to make "special provision[s] for the protection of women and children". The case law of the Supreme Court, for instance, confirms that the same article was also regularly interpreted and applied by the top domestic judicial bodies in defence of women's fundamental human rights.[7] Finally, for the specific cases of *zina*, Article 14 may also be relevant, as it stipulates that the "dignity of man and, subject to law, the privacy of home, shall be inviolable". It goes on to proclaim that "[n]o person shall be subjected to torture for the purpose of extracting evidence". These fundamental guarantees are, however, already predicated on the oscillating, politically motivated interpretations of the ostensibly 'Islamic' character of the Constitution. So far, whenever the constitutionally stipulated human rights have been neglected for the purposes of the ruling elite, its military or political opponents, women have invariably suffered worse consequences than men.[8] An inherently gendered face of such derogations underlines the need for an astute feminist interrogation of Pakistan's constitutional law and its inability to meet the exigencies of *all* of its constituencies, *irrespective* of their gender. For instance, only if the equality clause is interpreted and implemented beyond the superficial and formalistic space it currently occupies (Khan 2004) can one hope that the women of Pakistan will be constitutionally safeguarded against state and non-state patriarchy disguised in Muslim outfits.

---

7 See, for example, the cases of *Shirin Munir*, PLD 1990 SC 295; *Azizullah Memon*, PLD 1993 SC 341; and *Ghulam Mustafa Ansari*, PLD 2004 SC 1903. For an analysis of these and other relevant cases, see Shah 2006: 110–114.

8 For a good example, see Amnesty International, *'As if Hell Fell on Me': The Human Rights Crisis in Northwest Pakistan* (Amnesty International Publications, London 2010).

Family Law

As previously noted, Muslim family law in Pakistan was commonly regulated within the realm of so-called 'Muslim personal law'. This expression is, however, understood to encompass both the areas of Muslim family law and "all statutory laws applying only to Muslims" (Mullally 2006: 174). Excluded from the general colonial law (that is, English common law), 'Muslim personal law' has long been seen as central to ensuring formal unity among various Indian Muslim communities, whose customary laws it had replaced.[9] It has, however, served to perpetuate gender injustice as well, as a number of its longstanding provisions have been unfavourable to women.

A notable reform of the status of women in Muslim family law occurred with the promulgation of the 1961 Muslim Family Laws Ordinance (MFLO). Most importantly, the Ordinance imposed procedural restrictions on polygyny and the power of *talaq*. It, however, left the discrimination inherent to both practices intact (Mullally 2006: 176). Numerous shortcomings aside, it was an important step forward in the struggle for gender justice. This was immediately recognised by women's human rights groups, and the Ordinance quickly became one of the most valuable instruments for their advocacy efforts. Furthermore, in both the 1962 and 1973 Constitutions, the MFLO was granted a protected status, which excluded it from any constitutional challenge with reference to fundamental rights (Mullally 2006: 176–177). The Ordinance was also instrumental in attaining some recent case law, which has further improved the conditions for Muslim women to seek a judicial dissolution of their marriage (Lau 2010: 416) and confirmed that a *sui juris* Muslim female could enter into valid marriage of her own free will (Mullally 2006: 182).[10] Finally, it has been used as a springboard for further legislative adjustments designed to protect women's rights, such as the 1976 Dowry and Bridal Gifts (Restrictions) Act (Pal 1990: 458).

Criminal Law

A positive trend set by the modest changes introduced by the 1961 Muslim Family Laws Ordinance was abruptly halted in 1977, when General Zia-ul-Haq rose to power. Under the ideological banner of 'Islamisation' of Pakistan's law and society, Zia imposed significant changes to the domestic criminal justice system, which had particularly detrimental effects on women. These include: the 1979 Hudood Ordinances, in particular the one relating to *zina*; amending and renaming the 1872 Evidence Act; and the draft ordinance on criminal punishments that include *diyat* (blood money) and *qisas* (retaliation). All of these are briefly discussed below. Problematically, long after Zia's death, this oppressive legislation remains in force in its entirety, save for the significant amendments made to the Zina Ordinance in 2006.

---

9   See, for example, the 1962 West Pakistan Muslim Personal Law (Shariat) Application Act.
10 See also *Abdul Waheed* v *Asma Jehangir*, PLD 2004 SC 219, 237.

The 1979 Hudood Ordinances were prepared by an *ad hoc* committee[11] selected by Zia-ul-Haq, which has also sought the assistance of the jurist Ma'aroof al-Dawalibi.[12] They consist of five separate presidential ordinances, namely: the Offence against Property (Enforcement of Hudood) Ordinance; the Offence of Qazf (Enforcement of Hadd) Ordinance; the Offence of Zina (Enforcement of Hudood) Ordinance; the Prohibition (Enforcement of Hadd) Order; and the Execution and Punishment of Whipping Ordinance (IX of 1979). The last ordinance was deemed necessary, as all the above ordinances stipulate flogging as a legitimate form of punishment. Other prescribed punishments for the four *hudood* offences (*zina*, *qadf* (*qazf*) or false accusation of *zina*, theft and the drinking of alcohol) include the amputation of limbs and stoning to death. On the one hand, the superior judicial authorities, most notably the Federal Shariat Court, have consistently prevented death by stoning and, in most cases, amputations from occurring in practice. On the other hand, public or prison-based floggings were executed in the 1980s across Pakistan, on a regular basis (Lau 2010: 418). Interestingly enough, the ordinances stipulate that all *hadd* sentences must be 'confirmed' by the Federal Shariat Court. This Court would, however, usually either reduce on appeal the punishments awarded by trial courts, or simply acquit the accused. Given that, as was shown earlier, the judiciary was forcibly made loyal to Zia's regime, one cannot help but wonder why the punishments introduced by the Hudood Ordinances were so selectively carried out. It seems that the fear and an overall control of the Pakistani populace were at the heart of the Hudood Ordinances' *raison d'être*, not least the concern for the supposedly 'Islamised' legal order (Khan 2007). Furthermore, a public outcry against the ordinances, spearheaded by the women's movement, which was going on throughout the 1980s, must have made the ruling elite wary of societal reactions to the execution of some of those punishments (Shaheed 2010). Nevertheless, although the state has not implemented many punishments under the Hudood Ordinances, it in effect legitimated the countless forms of 'community justice' around alleged 'honour' crimes, which continue to this day.

Half of the cases based on the Hudood Ordinances were actually concerned with the 1979 Offence of Zina (Enforcement of Hudood) Ordinance (Lau 2010: 418; Chadbourne 1999: 3). This ordinance notoriously lumped together wilful sexual intercourse between persons who were not validly married to each other (termed *zina*) and rape (termed *zina-bil-jabr*; literally: *zina* by force). Both *zina* and *zina-bil-jabr* were made offences liable to either a *hadd* or *ta'zir* punishment. The evidentiary requirements for a *hadd* punishment were either the confession of the accused or the testimony of four male Muslim witnesses of good standing. On the other hand, a discretionary punishment could be accorded on the basis of other types of available evidence. If the perpetrator was *muhsan* (defined in Pakistani

---

11 The committee's membership was as follows: four '*ulama*' (Mufti Muhammad Taqi Usmani, Maulana Zafar Ahmed Ansari, Pir Karam Shah Al-Azhari, Mehmood Ahmed Ghazi); three legal experts (Khalid M Ishaque, Sharif-ud-din Pir Zada, K Burohi); and three retired judges (K Samdani, Muhammad Afzal Cheema, Salahuddin Ahmed).

12 A former Prime Minister of Syria, President of the World Muslim League and an advisor to the King of Saudi Arabia.

law as either a married or previously married Muslim), the punishment for both *zina* and *zina-bil-jabr* liable to *hadd* was public stoning to death (*rajm*). If the perpetrator was non-*muhsan* (unmarried Muslim or non-Muslim of any marital status), the punishment for *zina* liable to *hadd* was 100 lashes, while the punishment for *zina-bil-jabr* liable to *hadd* was 100 lashes *with* any other punishment, including death. In cases liable to *ta'zir*, whereby the evidentiary requirements for a *hadd* punishment could not be satisfied, the punishment for *zina* was 10 years of rigorous imprisonment, 30 lashes and a fine, or both. Outrageously, the punishment for rape liable to *ta'zir* was lesser than that for *zina* liable to *ta'zir*; it was not less than four years and not more than 25 years imprisonment and 30 lashes (Shah 2006: 129). In a similar vein, marital rape was not considered an offence. However, for *zina-bil-jabr* committed by two or more offenders, the ordinance (through an amendment in May 1997) prescribes mandatory capital punishment for all. Both *zina* and *zina-bil-jabr* were made non-bailable and non-compoundable offences, and the complainant was not given an option to drop the charge. Anyone, whether personally aggrieved or not, including the police, could make the charge (Shah 2006: 129).

Perhaps the most controversial feature of the Zina Ordinance was the possibility of the conversion of a rape charge into one of *zina*. If a complainant of *zina-bil-jabr* failed to prove the charge, the police would occasionally take circumstantial evidence into consideration to interpret the complainant's accusation of rape as a cover for *zina*. This was done, for instance, when the victims of rape initially chose not to complain, fearing the social stigma of such a complaint for themselves and their families, but were later forced to prosecute upon the realisation that the rape had resulted in pregnancy. In such cases, relying on

---

CASES OF HUMAN RIGHTS VIOLATIONS

A Blind Girl Raped and then Accused of *Zina*

Safia Bibi, a 20-year-old girl, almost blind, was raped by her employee and ended up in jail on the charge of *zina*. She was working as a domestic servant in Magsood Khan's house. Her father filed a report with police claiming his daughter has been raped and had, consequently, given birth to a child. Both Safia and Magsood Khan were arrested. The accused was released on a benefit of doubt, but Safia was convicted of adultery on the basis of her pregnancy and punished with three years in prison, whipping and a monetary fine. After the pressure from women's rights groups and the appeal of her case in the appellate Federal Shariat Court, she was released.

Although there was no evidence of Safia's consent to sexual intercourse, she was convicted of having extramarital sexual relationship. This is one of the numerous cases in which the victim of rape, instead of getting redress, has been criminalised.

[Source: Research conducted by Zara Saeidzadeh for this study. The author is grateful for her valuable contribution.]

the absence of medical evidence of resistance, the police would often convert charges of *zina-bil-jabr* into those of *zina* (Cheema 2006). Moreover, if a complainant of *zina-bil-jabr* was a never-married woman or girl, and if the mandatory medical examination of her hymen resulted in it being labelled as 'habitual', it would not only be taken as proof of her immoral character generally, but it would also, in many cases, lead to a presumption that she must have consented to the alleged rape as well (Cheema & Mustafa 2008–2009: 16–18). Finally, while, purportedly, the 1979 Offence of Qazf (Enforcement of Hadd) Ordinance was promulgated in order to check malicious (*mala fide*) accusations of *zina* and rape, in practice it was rarely invoked, even if the appellate court clearly established such misconduct. These and other gaps and misconceptions made the Zina Ordinance the prime legal instrument of oppression and discrimination against Pakistani women. As admitted by the legislators of a 2006 amendment, "[t]he Zina Ordinance has been abused to persecute women, to settle vendettas and to deny basic human rights and fundamental freedoms" (2006 Criminal Law Amendment (Protection of Women) Act, Statement of Objects and Reasons, para 19).

Another serious problem created by the introduction of the Zina Ordinance was its effect on other laws related to women's rights. *Zina* cases came in direct conflict with various provisions of the 1961 Muslim Family Laws Ordinance (MFLO), which safeguarded women's rights to a certain extent. This led to many judgments of the Federal Shariat Court and other courts[13], which negatively affected the MFLO provisions, particularly those relating to divorce rights (Warraich & Balchin 1998). One of the effects of the Zina Ordinance was that charges of *zina* could – and did, in many cases[14] – befall a woman because she remarried without having registered her divorce in accordance with the MFLO stipulations. She (and her new spouse) would be accused of *zina*, usually by her ex-husband, and then sentenced to death by a lower court. Hence, "[i]n numerous instances, the courts have sought to provide relief to individual women who have remarried following an unregistered divorce, but have achieved this through interpretations which have further eroded the regulatory effect of the MFLO" (Warraich & Balchin 1998: 215). This, on the whole, jeopardised women's personal status.[15]

An overwhelming majority of the Zina Ordinance's victims were poor, lower-class women (Khan 2003; Rouse 1988). Although they were usually acquitted at the appellate proceedings, a large number of these women languished in jail for years, simply waiting for such proceedings to occur (Khan 2003: 77). Many of them, although incarcerated under the charge of *zina*, were actually there "because their families or former husbands used the *zina* laws to jail the women when they went against their families' wishes" (Khan 2003: 77). The long and undeserved incarceration, during which some of these women were

---

13 See, for example, the landmark case *Alladad* v *Mukhtar*, 1992 SCMR 1273.
14 See, for instance, *Malik Javed* v *Abdul Kadir*, 1987 SCMR 518.
15 The author is grateful to Sohail Akbar Warraich for pointing out this aspect of the introduction of the Zina Ordinance in his review of this chapter.

victims of custodial rape and other forms of violence and discrimination, would almost invariably bring devastating consequences for their lives outside the prison. Some of them, afraid or unable to return to their families, would 'disappear' and "make their lives anew in whatever way they can"; while others would be shuttered from public life by their families immediately upon their release from jail (Khan 2003: 81). The state condoned this utter abuse of its criminal justice system for years, for the sake of inherently patriarchal political power games.

Unfortunately, the Hudood Ordinances were not the only drastic legislative change introduced via Zia's 'Islamisation' programme. In 1984, the old 1872 Evidence Act was revised and renamed the 1984 Qanun-e-Shahadat Order. Article 17(2)(a) of this Order restricted the evidence of a woman "[i]n matters pertaining to financial or future obligation" simply because of her gender. This bias was, once again, instituted with reference to the 'Injunctions of Islam'. The changes in other provisions of the Order were minimal compared to its colonial common law precedent. In fact, one can certainly conclude that the whole point of revising and renaming the old 1872 Evidence Act was to infuse a noticeable reference to the Qur'an (i.e. the gender-discriminatory interpretations of Qur'anic verse 2:282), despite (or, perhaps, precisely because) the possible detrimental consequences to women's access to justice.

The law on *qisas* (retaliation) and *diyat* (blood money), which originated from an earlier draft ordinance, came into force in October 1990 as the Criminal Law (Amendment) Act. Following the principles of classical *fiqh*, the act allowed the murder victim's heirs to decide the degree of punishment accorded to the perpetrator of that crime. According to this regulation, the available options are: retribution, including death penalty; financial compensation (blood money); and pardon. According to the new legislation, blood money is to "be disbursed among the heirs of the victim according to their respective shares in inheritance" (1860 Pakistan Penal Code, the amended section 330). This provision is, however, clearly gender-discriminatory, since a man's share of inheritance is twice that of a woman. Another biased provision of this act relates to a situation in which the victim has a *wali* (guardian) who is a minor or mentally ill. In such case, the *qisas* is devolved to the father or grandfather; if both men are deceased, the *qisas* goes to the state. Apparently, female family members are not considered capable of being a *wali*. The inherently patriarchal nature of this Act is further visible in its treatment of the customary compensation (*badal-i-sulh*) for compounding of the cases related to *qisas* and *diyat*. The traditional *badal-i-sulh* almost invariably used to be a woman given in marriage to a member of the victim's family (Shah 2006: 146). The new Act declared this custom invalid, but did not expressly forbid it. Hence, handling a woman as *badal-i-sulh* was allowed to continue in an informal manner. This was the case until 2004, when an amendment (discussed below) was introduced that clearly prohibits *badal-i-sulh* and subjects this practice to rigorous punishment.

The legislation discussed above wreaked havoc on Pakistani society for decades. It was understood by many a patriarchal male as official encouragement for numerous deplorable acts, ranging from the subjugation and commoditisation of female family members' sexuality and sociality to the most extreme forms of violence against women, including 'honour' killings. Women and other concerned groups demanded that these harmful laws be abrogated. The political (and military) elite, however, responded unfavourably, save for a few instances in which the societal pressure seemingly reached too high a degree. Those were the enactments of the 2004 Criminal Law (Amendment) Bill against 'honour' killings and the 2006 Criminal Law Amendment (Protection of Women) Act.

By the powers of the 2004 Criminal Law (Amendment) Bill, crimes of 'honour' (*ghairat*), as such a murder was mildly dubbed, was finally made an offence punishable by imprisonment for between 10 and 25 years. This set of amendments also made the custom of giving a woman in marriage as *badal-i-sulh* a criminal offence. The major flaw of the bill is, however, that it did not abrogate the *qisas* and *diyat* laws in any significant way. Therefore, in practice, the heirs of a victim of an 'honour' killing are to be directly involved in the decision regarding the degree of punishment accorded to the murderer. Given that, in the great majority of cases, 'honour' killings are perpetrated and condoned by the immediate family members, it is hard to imagine that their 'right' to *qisas* and *diyat* shall be exercised without prejudice.

The 2006 Criminal Law Amendment (Protection of Women) Act significantly revised the 1979 Zina Ordinance. It removed *zina-bil-jabr* from the Ordinance altogether, while reinstalling the offence of rape into the 1860 Penal Code. *Zina* was made an offence inconvertible to other criminal charges, including that of rape. Rape was also made inconvertible to *zina* or the newly inserted offence of fornication.[16] In both *zina* and *qadf* proceedings, the police no longer have any role, as far as the investigation or registration of a case are concerned. Complaints are now to be filed solely before the competent courts, and the high evidentiary requirements are upheld (four male adults of good reputation as eyewitnesses for *zina*, or two such witnesses for fornication). The failure to fulfil these strict evidentiary requirements triggers a *qadf* punishment of 80 lashes for the accusation of *zina* and imprisonment and a monetary fine for the charge of fornication. *Ta'zir* punishments for *zina* are removed. With such high evidentiary and procedural requirements, it is unlikely that there will be many, if any, proceedings under this Ordinance (Lau 2010: 419). Its problematic, symbolic social 'value' was, however, left intact. While women can no longer be easily harassed and persecuted under the Zina Ordinance, its very existence continues to bolster the politics of gender injustice.

---

16 As a concession to conservative '*ulama*', who were not pleased with the proposed Protection of Women Act, after long negotiations, the new offence of fornication was added as section 496(B) to the 1860 Penal Code. It reads: "A man and a woman not married to each other are said to commit fornication if they willfully have sexual intercourse with one another". A complaint of fornication can be launched with a magistrate if the act has been seen by two male eye-witnesses (section 203(B)). The author is grateful to Sohail Akbar Warraich for a detailed account of how the offence of fornication was inserted into the Pakistani Penal Code.

Since independence, there have been two major streams in Pakistan's legislative reforms of significance for gender justice. The first stream – particularly detectable in the realms of constitutional and family law, as well as within specific case law of the state's supreme courts – sought to protect and promote some women's human rights within Muslim communities. The second stream – underpinning the dictator Zia's 'Islamisation' project – went starkly against the elementary constitutional tenets of gender justice, and reformed, in particular, the country's criminal justice system. Despite continuous public outrage against the latter stream, the recent legislative changes that sought to remedy some of its worst outputs – most notably the infamous *zina* laws – were weak and insufficient. This renders Pakistan's legal system incongruent and largely based on patriarchal bias. As such, it betrays its own constitutional promise of equity and equality before law. It also warrants the question of state responsibility before international human rights law. The constitutionality and international liability of Pakistan's gender-discriminatory legislative affairs is, therefore, examined in the subsequent section of this study.

State Responsibility

Although the constitutional framework for the protection and promotion of human rights, including those relating to gender justice, seems to be exceptionally broad, the clauses demanding all laws to be in congruence with the 'Injunctions of Islam' can and have been read in ways that restrict the guaranteed fundamental rights and freedoms. The ambiguity of the constitutional text was, of course, intentional; the legislators continuously sought to 'balance' demands for social justice with those requiring a more explicit role for the conservative and often gender-discriminatory interpretations of classical *fiqh* in the state legal system. Nevertheless, the fundamental rights chapter, in particular its equality clause, remains the constitutional stronghold of the state's human rights obligations to its citizens of either gender. In this sense, it is possible to conclude that the Hudood Ordinances and other previously discussed gender-discriminatory legislations are both unconstitutional and *un-Islamic*, as they rely on the conservative and by large dubious interpretations of *fiqh* and its principal sources – the Qur'an and the Sunna. This assertion, however, is not in itself enough to legally challenge the laws in questions. As demonstrated throughout this chapter, Pakistan's legislative changes were, more often than not, a result of political or even military interventions, with the role of key domestic judiciaries and legislators reduced to a mere (and usually coerced) confirmation of the will of the rulers of the day. In such circumstances, the Constitution itself usually could not stop the autocratic rulers' abuse of legislative powers. Instead, the Constitution was often and heavily amended, so as to allow for whatever legal changes were deemed necessary in a given time. Zia-ul-Haq, for instance, held the 1973 Constitution (with its fundamental rights chapter) in abeyance for a certain period of time, just to make sure that no domestic legal mechanism could invoke it against his 'Islamisation' plans. Despite such extreme abuses, however, the fundamental rights guaranteed in the Constitution have survived and, seemingly, gained greater prominence in the course of the latest political changes towards a more parliamentary democratic system of governance. Should this positive trend continue, it is hoped that the power of human rights provisions within the Constitution will prevail over the political need to uphold discriminatory interpretations of the 'Injunctions of Islam' in the country's complex legal system.

On the international plane, the state of Pakistan has been extremely reluctant to accede to human rights treaties which would trigger its supranational legal responsibility to attain certain human rights standards. Nevertheless, during the two democratic mandates of the government of Benazir Bhutto, Pakistan became, in 1990, a member party to the Convention on the Rights of the Child (CRC), and then, in 1996, to the Convention on the Elimination of All Forms of Discrimination against Women (CEDAW). However, in a special declaration, the state outlined that its ratification of CEDAW was "subject to the provisions of the Constitution of the Islamic Republic of Pakistan". The provisions in question were, no doubt, those allowing for gender-discriminatory interpretations of classical *fiqh* as it relates to the 'Injunctions of Islam'. But, gender-based discrimination, on whatever grounds, runs contrary to the object and purpose of the Convention, which, according to Article 28(2), cannot be abrogated by any state reservation or declaration. Still, the vague language of Pakistan's declaration allows for multiple readings and, thus, saves it from repudiation. Besides CRC and CEDAW, the state signed, in 2008, the International Covenant on Civil and Political Rights (ICCPR) and the UN Convention against Torture and Other Cruel, Inhuman or Degrading Treatment or Punishment (CAT). It also ratified, in the same year, the International Covenant on Economic, Social and Cultural Rights (ICESCR).

Under the abovementioned international human rights instruments, which Pakistan is now fully obliged to respect, gender-discriminatory laws are expressly forbidden. It is particularly true for the promulgated *hudood* punishments, such as amputations, stoning to death and whipping, which amount to torture and other cruel, inhuman and degrading treatment. Upholding the *hudood* laws therefore constitutes an international offence most seriously repudiated by CAT, which arguably has attained the status of customary international law. Furthermore, CEDAW clearly stipulates that Pakistan and other states parties to the Convention ought to "take all appropriate measures, including legislation, to modify or abolish existing laws, regulations, customs and practices which constitute discrimination against women" (Article 2(f)); and must, without delay, "repeal all national penal provisions which constitute discrimination against women" (Article 2(g)).

Repealing discriminatory legislation is, indeed, an essential step in the domestication and implementation of the international human rights standards that Pakistan has agreed to abide by. State responsibility to do so, under international law, is clearly pronounced. Yet the political calculations, which are at the heart of Pakistan's reluctance to act upon its international human rights obligations and exist in state, quasi-state and non-state decision-making circles, remain a very challenging obstacle on the country's road to gender justice. The emerging national 'gender mainstreaming' mechanisms, together with numerous human rights civil society organisations, have repeatedly urged the changing governments of Pakistan to repeal the Hudood Ordinances and other discriminatory laws. This plea is yet to be answered. Until then, Pakistan's gender-discriminatory legislation is not only in conflict with the 1973 Constitution, but it also clearly constitutes a grave breach of the country's international human rights obligations.

Existing Activism for Change

The emergence of Pakistan's women's movement can be traced well before the country's independence. Women played a considerable role in the nationalist movement, whose leader, Muhammad Ali Jinnah, publicly demanded that the new state's female citizens be accorded full equality and human rights (Rouse 1988: 11). Indeed, some important victories, such as the attainment of the right to vote, were soon won; and the Muslim family law reform was instigated, resulting in women's rights to inherit agricultural property, to at least partially curb polygyny, to file for divorce, to register their marriages, and so on. A handful of women's organisations existed in this early period. They were generally either upper-class charitable organisations (e.g. All Pakistan Women's Association) or political associations (e.g. Democratic Women's Association (Anjuman-e-Jamhooriat Pasand Khawateen), linked with a pro-Moscow communist party) (Rouse 1988: 11). In the late 1950s, however, the overall crisis of the political system and the military takeover took gender justice issues off the official agendas. During the almost two decades that followed, the movement was no longer visible, save for the occasional cameo appearance of a few individual activists (Shaheed 2010).

From the late 1970s throughout the 1980s, however, the promulgation and continuous implementation of gender-discriminatory legislation, particularly related to violence against women, triggered a strong and sustained resistance from within Pakistan's civil society; a reinvigorated and seemingly reunited national women's movement being at the forefront. This was a period of "intense publicly visible activism inwardly focused on national issues", quite distinct from "a more diffused movement since the 1990s" (Shaheed 2010) that was more directly engaged with the international human rights system. The 1980s' movement was chiefly preoccupied with organising street demonstrations and other forms of civic resistance to the dramatic domestic affairs, most notably those related to the Hudood Ordinances and Zia's other deplorable legislative inventions. The movement's activism in the 1990s, however, "shifted from the streets to the courts and other institutions" (Shaheed 2010), whereby it sought partnerships with other social movements, both domestically and internationally. By the mid 1990s, it was instrumental in shaping the National Plan of Action for Women. Numerous legislative and political changes occurring at the beginning of the new millennium were, by and large, the result of the sustained and skilful lobbing of the women's movement.

In 1975, a small voluntary collective called Shirkat Gah – Women's Resource Centre was formed, aiming at raising awareness on issues related to women's human rights. In

September 1981, while working on press clippings to collect information on women's rights issues, a member of the collective spotted a short news item on the first reported *zina* case. Fehmida, a 15-year-old college student, had married the driver of her school bus. Unsatisfied with her choice of partner, her parents filed an abduction case, unaware that, under the new Zina Ordinance, the absence of evidence on abduction and the failure to provide proof of marriage gave the police the right to register a *zina* case. A lower court sentenced the already married bus driver, Allah Bux, to stoning to death and Fehmida to 100 cane lashes (Shaheed 2010; Rouse 1988: 12). Horrified with these sentences, the collective tried to mobilise opposition to this particular judgment and sought co-operation with other likeminded women's groups in order to counter Zia's 'Islamisation' programme. This is how the Khawateen-Mahaz-e-Amal or Women's Action Forum (WAF) was formed, as an umbrella platform for women's rights defenders of various socio-political orientations.

Seven leading women's groups spearheaded the activities of the Women's Action Forum, which gradually grew into a mass-based popular front (Rouse 1988: 12). The WAF's street protests, campaigns, symposiums, workshops and lobbying actions – in which concerned citizens of diverse backgrounds participated – managed to cut across the country's geographical, political and class divide. This in itself was an unprecedented success, which would transform the composition of Pakistani civil society. Throughout the 1980s and 1990s, WAF "continued to be the main vehicle for articulating a collective demand", although particular women's organisations – such as the Aurat Foundation (est. 1986) – provided the workforce and structural basis for a number of important projects (Shaheed 2010).[17]

Right from the outset, from its revival in early 1980s, the women's movement in Pakistan had to face the challenge of its two-pronged relationship with the state. On the one hand, it was the centre of an organised civic resistance to the state's gender-oppressive policies and legislation, which in the 1980s was generally 'street-based' and media-based and in the later years more geared towards institutional reform and the strengthening and education of civil society. On the other hand, the movement had to seek ways of co-operation with the ruling elite, with a view to prevent further retrogressive measures and secure political support for their cause. After the demise of Zia's regime, the second prong, which was determined to establish bridges between the movement and the state, gained greater prominence, particularly during Prime Minister Benazir Bhutto's two incomplete terms in office (1988–90 and 1993–96). Although Bhutto, the first woman elected to lead a Muslim-majority state, made considerable efforts to support the movement's activities, she could not mount sufficient political and military backing to challenge the legislative stronghold of Zia's oppressive legacy. Hence, despite her promises, the Hudood Ordinances remained in force. Faced with such a political reality, the women's movement throughout the 1990s

---

17 Shirkat Gah, the WAF and the Aurat Foundation still remain very active members of Pakistani civil society.

and early 2000s largely focused on (1) lobbying for new laws protecting women; and (2) international co-operation and national advocacy targeted at compelling Pakistan to accede to various international human rights treaties, CEDAW in particular, that would then trigger domestic legislative reform.

Although a Pakistan's *ad hoc* commission on the status of women had recommended ratification of CEDAW without reservation as early as 1985 (Mullally 2006: 184), it took 11 years (and a change of government) before the state acceded to the Convention. Even then, Pakistan made its implementation of CEDAW subject to a general declaration, invoking the precedence of the 1973 Constitution. This vague and problematic declaration was the result of a compromise reached between the Ministry for Religious Affairs and other hard-line governmental agencies on the one side and the Ministry for Women's Development and the women's movement on the other, following long and bitter negotiations. Soon after ratification, CEDAW became an invaluable advocacy tool and source of legitimacy in the struggle for gender justice. It was repeatedly invoked in progressive case law on women's rights; in the new quota for women's participation in local, provincial and national systems of governance, introduced in 2000 and 2002; and in the subsequent laws targeting gender-based discrimination and violence within the domain of the criminal justice system.

Today, the Human Rights Commission of Pakistan, an independent countrywide non-governmental organisation founded in 1987, is generally seen to lead the women's movement (Shaheed 2010). Certain governmental 'gender mainstreaming' instruments also play important roles; most notably, the National Commission on the Status of Women, which was established in 2000. This governmental body was given the bold mandate to 'examine and review' all national laws and policies effecting the status of women. In 2002/2003, it conducted a comprehensive review of the Hudood Ordinances in which it strongly recommended their repeal. It also engaged in an arduous lobbying, together with women's rights civil society organisations, which finally made the government enact certain criminal laws amendments. Firstly, the women jailed under the Zina Ordinance were released on bail in 2004, and then, in 2006, this ordinance was significantly reformed.

The experience of the women's movement from the 2000s onwards demonstrates that the strategic partnerships established with certain governmental bodies, whose mandates include the protection of women's human rights, is bringing significant results. Such co-operation seems an even more plausible and salient choice in the future, given the recent moves towards a more independent judiciary and parliamentary democracy. Yet, the very fact that, despite those concentrated efforts, the Hudood Ordinances and other discriminatory legislation have not yet been repealed shows the strength of the patriarchal grip on Pakistan's law and politics.

Conclusion

The present chapter has sought to capture the dynamics of historical, cultural, legal and political fluctuations between the idea of Pakistan governed by the principles of equity and social justice, enshrined in its constitutional law, and the conservative and gender-discriminatory interpretations of *fiqh* purported to govern the state's adherence to the 'Injunctions of Islam'. Both of these currents have been vividly present throughout the state's existence, thus compelling its military and democratic leadership to seek legitimacy in either trend. One such manoeuvre in the late 1970s, designed to shore up support for the dictatorial regime of General Zia-ul-Haq, gave birth to the Hudood Ordinances, which remain the greatest obstacle to the state's increasing orientation towards more gender-just laws and policies. Ever since the introduction of *zina* laws and other *hadd* crimes into the criminal justice system, the women's movement has been leading a concerted and multifaceted resistance. Started as a 'street-style' civic opposition movement, in the 1990s the women's movement began penetrating state institutions and succeeded in making Pakistan accede to some of the most important international human rights treaties. The new laws have thus been enacted, and the infamous Zina Ordinance amended, to ensure greater protection of women's human rights. Still, the legislative relics of Zia's gender-oppressive regime, including the Hudood Ordinances, remain in force. The harbingers of further political and legislative reforms seem to have left those laws *ad acta*, as if the revision of the Zina Ordinance was good enough. In reality, however, the very existence of gender-discriminatory laws supports the survival of patriarchal ethos in law and society, resulting in perpetual gender-based violence and discrimination.

The cultural, religious and political diversity of Pakistan's society has always required the existence and state-based furtherance of certain 'cohesive factors'. Those were, predominantly, an ideological take on Islam as the state religion and the official discourse on fundamental (human) rights. Thanks to sustained civil society efforts, the ambiguous relationship between these concepts is currently negotiated with an increased focus on gender justice. It is within this ambit that one can hope that the *hudood* laws and other discriminatory legislation will soon be repealed, and that crimes against the alleged 'transgressions' of the populace are not subject to violent and discriminatory retributions by community members.

Bibliography

Amnesty International (2010), *'As If Hell Fell On Me': The Human Rights Crisis in Northwest Pakistan*. London: Amnesty International Publications.

Cheema, Moeen H. and Abdul-Rahman Mustafa (2008–9), 'From the Hudood Ordinances to the Protection of Women Act: Islamic Critiques of the Hudood Laws of Pakistan', *UCLA Journal of Islamic and Near Eastern Law* 1(1).

Cheema, Moeen H. (2006), 'Cases and Controversies: Pregnancy as Proof of Guilt Under Pakistan's Hudood Laws', *Brooklyn Journal of International Law* 32: 121.

Cohen, Stephen P. (2004), *The Idea of Pakistan*. Washington DC: Brookings Institution.

Cook, Nancy (2007), *Gender, Identity, and Imperialism: Women Development Workers in Pakistan*. New York: Palgrave Macmillan.

Ghazali, Abdus Sattar (1996), *Islamic Pakistan: Illusions and Reality*. Islamabad: National Book Club.

Iqbal, Afzal (1986), *Islamisation of Pakistan*. Lahore: Vanguard Books.

Jones-Pauly, Chris (2000), 'Use of the Qur'ān in Key Pakistani Court Decisions on zinā' and qadf', *Arabica* 47 (3): 539.

Khan, Shahnaz (2003), '"Zina" and the Moral Regulation of Pakistani Women', *Feminist Review* 75: 75.

——— (2004), 'Locating the Feminist Voice: The Debate on the Zina Ordinance', *Feminist Studies* 30 (3): 660.

——— (2007), *Zina, Transnational Feminism, and the Moral Regulation of Pakistani Women*. Vancouver: University of British Columbia Press.

Lau, Martin (2010), 'Sharia and National Law in Pakistan' in Jan Michiel Otto (ed.), *Sharia Incorporated: A Comparative Overview of the Legal Systems of Twelve Muslim Countries in Past and Present*, 373–432. Leiden: Leiden University Press.

Malik, Iftikhar H. (2008), *The History of Pakistan*. Westport, CT: Greenwood Press.

Maudoodi, Sayyid Abul A'la (1967), *Purdah and the Status of Women in Islam*. Lahore: Islamic Publications Ltd.

Menski, Werner F. (1997), 'South Asian Muslim Law Today: An Overview', *Sharqiyyat* 9 (1): 16.

Mullally, Siobhán (2006), *Gender, Culture and Human Rights: Reclaiming Universalism*. Oxford: Hart Publishing.

National Commission on the Status of Women (2003), *Report and Recommendations on 1979 Hudood Ordinances*. Islamabad: National Commission on the Status of Women.

Pal, Izzud-Din (1990), 'Women and Islam in Pakistan', *Middle Eastern Studies* 26 (4): 449.

Rouse, Shahnaz (1988), 'Women's Movement in Pakistan: State, Class, Gender', Women Living Under Muslim Laws Dossier 3, http://www.wluml.org/node/241

Saigol, Rubina (2010), 'Decades of Disaster: Islamization and the Women of Pakistan' in *The Islamization of Pakistan, 1979–2009* (*Viewpoints* Special Edition): 71. Washington DC: The Middle East Institute.

——— (2008), 'Militarization, Nation and Gender: Women's Bodies as Arenas of Violent Conflict' in Pinar İlkkaracan (ed.), *Deconstructing Sexuality in the Middle East: Challenges and Discourses*, 165–175. Surrey: Ashgate.

Shah, Niaz A. (2006), *Women, the Koran and International Human Rights Law: The Experience of Pakistan*. Leiden: Martinus Nijhoff Publishers.

Shaheed, Farida (2010), 'The Women's Movement in Pakistan: Challenges and Achievements' in Amrita Basu (ed.), *Women's Movements in the Global Era: The Power of Local Feminisms*, Chapter 4. Boulder, CO: Westview Press.

Warraich, Sohail Akbar and Cassandra Balchin (1998), 'Confusion Worse Confounded: A Critique of Divorce Law and Legal Practice in Pakistan' in Farida Shaheed, Sohail Akbar Warraich, Cassandra Balchin and Aisha Gazdar (eds.), *Shaping Women's Lives: Laws, Practices and Strategies in Pakistan*, 181–226. Lahore: Shirkat Gah – Women's Resource Centre.

Wolpert, Stanley (1984), *Jinnah of Pakistan*. Oxford: Oxford University Press.

Zaman, Muhammad Qasim (2005), 'Pluralism, Democracy, and the 'Ulama' in Robert W Hefner (ed.), *Remaking Muslim Politics: Pluralism, Contestation, Democratization*, 60–86. Princeton, NJ: Princeton University Press.

Cited National Case Law

Abdul Waheed v *Asma Jehangir*, PLD 2004 SC 219

Alladad v *Mukhtar*, 1992 SCMR 1273

Federation of Pakistan v *Hazoor Bakhsh*, PLD 1983 FSC 255

Ghulam Mustafa Ansari v *Government of Punjab*, PLD 2004 SC 1903

Government of Baluchistan v *Azizullah Memon*, PLD 1993 SC 341

Hazoor Bakhsh v *Federation of Pakistan,* PLD 1981 FSC 145

Malik Javed v *Abdul Kadir*, 1987 SCMR 518

Shirin Munir v *Government of Punjab*, PLD 1990 SC 295

Turkey

COUNTRY PROFILE

The Republic of Turkey is a European and Asian country with 72.5 million inhabitants (TurkStat 2010), some 99 per cent of which are officially registered as Muslims. Out of these, up to 15 million citizens are considered Alevi (Zürcher & van der Linden 2004: 123), while others mainly self-identify as Sunni Muslims, predominantly of the Hanafi *madhhab*. The Bahá'í minority (some 10,000–20,000 citizens) are also curiously considered Muslim by the state, and are consequently not allowed to claim a separate religious identity on official documents. In addition, at least 3 per cent of the Turkish population is declared as having no religious convictions (KONDA 2007). Religious affairs are mainly co-ordinated by the Presidency of Religious Affairs (Diyanet İşleri Başkanlığı), a public institution within the organisation of the state. Sufi orders are officially banned since 1925, yet their religious and political activism, via semi-underground networks, is widespread, particularly that of the Nakşibendi groups (in Arabic: an-Naqshbandiyya) and their various offshoots (Zürcher & van der Linden 2004: 116–122). Continuous attempts at state systematisation, organisation and control of the *ulema* ('*ulama*') and religious groups date back to the Ottoman Empire (1299–1923), the historical predecessor of the Turkish Republic, most notably through the institution of the highest-ranking religious legal advisor to the sultan, the *şeyhülislam* (*Shaikh ul-Islam*). This is in spite of another important Ottoman legacy, the *millet* system, which used to accord a great deal of legal independence, mainly in family law and taxation matters, to Muslim, Jewish and various Christian communities in the then distinctly multi-religious empire (Kanra 2009: 39).

Out of the remains of the Ottoman Empire, Turkey was established as a unitary constitutional republic in 1923. Its founder and first President, Mustafa Kemal Paşa, and his ideological compatriots – the Kemalists – declared that the following 'Six Arrows' were to direct the new state's socio-political orientation: populism, republicanism, statism, laicism, reformism and nationalism (Kanra 2009: 72). The reforms pursued thereupon, although presented as a clear-cut break from the previous regime, have in fact largely benefited from earlier Ottoman modernisation and reconstitution attempts, most notably the 1839–79 Tanzimat ('Reorganisation') era (Meeker 2001). The Turkish Republic officially ended the Ottoman dualistic legal system, based on the Hanafi interpretations of *şeriat* (*shari'a*) and *örf* (Arabic: *'urf*; customary law). All references to *shari'a* were removed from the legislation, thereby asserting Turkey's peculiar secular character (*laiklik*), which henceforth tends to fully control rather than only separate religion from the state (Koçak 2010). The position of *şeyhülislam* ceased to exist. *Fez*, an imam's headgear and various religious garments were prohibited by law, while the misuse of religion for political purposes was made an offence against state security. Both the Civil and Penal Code were now based on Western European models (Koçak 2010). Simultaneously, the government pursued what was dubbed as 'state feminism' (White 2003: 154; Kadıoğlu 1994: 651) – an ideological project that, while granting or expanding numerous important human rights to women (to vote, to work, to be *formally* equal to men, to education, etc.), primarily aimed at exploiting them as the key nation-building symbol of 'modern republicanism' (White 2003; İlkkaracan 2008). The state, hence, remained little if at all interested in gender justice, aside from its 'cosmetic effects', and the new legislation, civil and criminal alike, continued to carry strong patriarchal bias, implicitly based on the Ottoman *fiqh* (Yıldırım 2005; İlkkaracan 2008). This was significantly altered only recently, when the sustained advocacy of numerous women's human rights organisations led to the new 2001 Civil Code and 2004 Criminal Code (İlkkaracan 2008).

Stoning to death or *rejm* (*rajm*) for *zina* offences apparently occurred just once in the Ottoman Empire in the 17th century (Koçak 2010; Zürcher & van der Linden 2004), when it was effectively replaced with much lesser punishments, which were also rarely enforced (Shalakany 2008). All other *hudud* crimes were abolished by the 1858 Penal Code, except capital punishment for apostasy (Koçak 2010: 236). Adultery remained a minor offence in the Turkish Republic for a long time, until Articles 441 (criminalising men) and 440 (criminalising women) of the 1926 Penal Code were abolished by the Turkish Constitutional Court, in 1996 and 1998 respectively. However, the 1858 Ottoman Penal Code pardoned (Article 188) and the 1926 Penal Code reduced (Article 462) the punishment for 'honour' killing one's allegedly adulterous spouse. The latter provision was in force until 2004. Thus, the concept of *zina* as an offence, which in local patriarchal traditions translates to crimes against the 'honour' of one's family, survived in the Turkish social and legal milieux. While official prosecutions are no longer possible, *zina* and other 'honour-related' acts are still regularly punished by death by the victims' closest family members. Every year, hundreds of women are brutally murdered in Turkey in the name of honour (Kaser 2008: 207; Turkish Daily News 2008; Kardam 2005). Increasing instances of suicide, including self-immolation, have also been linked to so-called 'honour' crimes. This reveals, in the most dramatic way, the state's overall incapability to translate its formal legislative human rights commitments into effective policies against the patriarchal ethos, which permeates all spheres of Turkish society.

In the year 1680, a woman convicted of *zina* was being stoned to death on Sultan Ahmet Square (Sultanahmet Meydanı) in İstanbul, in front of Sultan Mehmet IV. Deeply disturbed by the cruelty of the deed, the Sultan reportedly proclaimed: "From now on, I do not want such disgrace in the Ottoman lands" (Koçak 2010: 234; Toprak 2003: 118). Henceforth, indeed, *rajm* was no more in the mighty caliphate. That this particular *hadd* was so easily abrogated by an Ottoman ruler comes as no surprise. Based on their customary powers as caliphs (i.e. leaders/representatives of the Muslim *umma*), the Ottoman sultans significantly reformed the domain of classical *fiqh* by introducing a new way to deal with all legal matters deemed 'unclarified' through 'direct' revelations of the Qur'an and the Sunna.

In theory, under this system, each new law, called *kanun* (Turkish: *kanun*; Arabic: *qanun*; from Byzantine Greek *kanon*) was promulgated by the sultan 'in accordance with the *shari'a*' – i.e. its mainstream interpretations as furthered by largely pre-Ottoman *fiqh*. However, the *kanun* soon provided for new jurisprudence and unambiguous, codified rules on matters previously understood an the exclusive domain of the classical *fiqh*, such as that of the *hudud* offences (Shalakany 2008). In fact, the very first *kanun*, introduced by Sultan Mehmet II in the mid-15th century, "presupposes that *hadd* punishments are obsolete and replaces them by *ta'zir*, i.e. beating, and/or monetary fines which are graded according to the economic position of the culprit" (Schacht 1964: 91). Several decades later, Süleyman I (1494–1566), known as the Lawmaker (*Kanuni*; *al-Qanuni*) for his comprehensive reconstruction of the Ottoman legal system, made sure that *zina* was thereafter punished primarily with monetary fines (Shalakany 2008: 20). This was achieved in two phases. First, the *hudud* as constructed by the classical *fiqh* were not necessarily openly dispensed with; rather, their next-to-unattainable evidentiary requirements were emphasised to the effect of full unimplementability of the majority of *hadd* punishments. Second, the codified provisions, based on the concept of *ta'zir* (judicial discretion), which for the offence of *zina* amounted to a monetary fine, were introduced in lieu of the impracticable *hudud*. Thus, this Empire, spanning at its historical peak three continents and an overwhelming majority of Muslim communities, stood free from *rajm* and other excessive *hadd* punishments for half a millennium.

This fact is either ignored (Schacht 1964: 208) or unknown in contemporary discussions around *shari'a* and Muslim laws, as if the Muslim legal traditions mysteriously disappeared a great many centuries ago, only to be 'rediscovered' and 'reclaimed' by eager Muslims of today. The continuity and a transformative nature of Muslim legal thought, espoused in the Ottoman *kanun*, is thus readily concealed in favour of the myth of 'an immutable law'.

This chapter discusses how the patriarchal concept of *zina* lives on in the Republic of Turkey, despite the Ottoman legal mastery and the succeeding laicist state's largely superficial commitment to gender justice. It is, by and large, the story of unfulfilled promises and failed expectations against the backdrop of complex Turkish political tampering with both religion and gender. It is, however, also an appraisal of the national women's movement's legislative and social achievements, despite political setbacks and an outburst of *zina*-related murders, predominantly of women, throughout Turkey (and its diaspora), committed on the pretext of a man's or family 'honour'. It is argued that the societal survival of *zina* is predicated upon the perseverance of gender biases in the state's executive and legislative political elites, almost irrespectively of their varying ideological leanings. Their inability to dislocate the concept of 'honour' from women's bodily and sexual sociality (İlkkaracan 2008) abets the recurrence of the most severe cases of violence against Turkish women, based on the very same patriarchal notion. The idea of *zina* is, therefore, re-ushered in through crime (deemed 'custom') and effectively condoned by the state's puny justice system.

The chapter first offers an analytical overview of the historical conditions of gender and religious dynamics in Turkish society relating to the notion(s) of *zina*. These dynamics are then contextualised in a survey of the state's legal system, particularly its constitutional, family and criminal laws. Subsequently, Turkey's manifold constitutional, regional (European) and international legal responsibility to promote and protect human rights is scrutinised, revealing a considerable gap between the state's *formal* commitments and its implementation policies. Finally, this study assesses the development of Turkey's feminist movement and its laudable strategies to address the concept of *zina* and related phenomena in law and society.

Historical Background

The Ottoman Empire rose at the turn of the 14th century in Turkish Anatolia, from a hotchpotch of smaller emirates, under the leadership of Osman I. By that time, the Turkish dynasties, all formally Sunni and of the Hanafi *madhhab*, dominated much of the 'abode of Islam' (*Dar al-Islam*) (Zürcher & van der Linden 2004: 96). The Ottomans' military, administrative and socio-political skills ensured that, by the late 17th century, the Empire controlled a vast territory, including much of central and south-eastern Europe, northern Africa, the Middle East, and western and central Asia. Throughout its history, the Empire remained an essentially centralist state (Köker 1995: 54), which was governed by the sultan and his ruling class (*askeri*) via a highly advanced administrative system. It was primarily composed of provinces (*vilayet*) and vassal states with varying degrees of autonomy.[1] The ruling class comprised the military and court officials, the nobility and the *ulema* ('*ulama*'). Apart from the *askeri*, there were the *reaya* (tax-paying lower class) and the *kul* (slaves).

Not only had the Ottoman zest for governance made the *ulema* part of an elite class; numerous incentives and, with them, a hierarchical system were provided to ensure their allegiance to the state. Hence,

> [b]y the sixteenth century, virtually all legal scholars who presided over a *medrese* [(public school)] classroom or a religious *şeriat* court in the Turkish-speaking areas of the empire, along with imperial appointees everywhere, were ranked, graded and pensioned under central state auspices (Zilfi 2006a: 210).

Accordingly, they were also given specific duties in the state apparatus. For example, the role of a *kadi* (Arabic: *qadi*; judge), apart from courtroom tasks, included reporting on the conduct of the sultan's administrators and supervision of market transactions (Zilfi 2006a: 213). The *ulema* as a whole was organised into an institution – the *ilmiye* – the head of which was made the *müftü* (*mufti*) of İstanbul as the *şeyhülislam*. This way, the *şeyhülislam*'s

---

1 Besides the provinces and vassal states, the Empire also exercised a temporary authority over certain distant overseas lands. For instance, in 1565, the Sultan of Aceh declared allegiance to the Ottoman Sultan (Azra 2006).

authority in religious knowledge (*'ilm*) was 'complemented' with an administrative responsibility. Moreover, like all other key dignitaries of the state, the *şeyhülislam* was directly appointed (and dismissed) by the sultan. The ruler's supremacy in all matters of governance, including religious law, was thus carefully ensured.

In the first quarter of the 20th century, struck by a series of military defeats and political upheavals, the Ottoman Empire shrunk much in its territorial size and ethnic diversity. Mustafa Kemal, a military officer belonging to a faction of the Young Turks, an intellectual nationalist movement driven by 'scientific' materialism and liberalism, emerged as the leader of the new republican movement. Eventually, their ideas prevailed over those in favour of a monarchic system. In 1922, the Türkiye Büyük Millet Meclisi (Turkish Grand National Assembly) abolished the sultanate, and two years later the caliphate (Koçak 2010: 241–242). In 1923, the Ottoman state ceased to exist and the Turkish Republic was born, with Mustafa Kemal – soon to be also known as Atatürk[2] – as its first President.

The ideological conception of the new republic rested primarily on a peculiar combination of nationalism[3] and liberalism,[4] which resulted in a centralist state with powerful military and judiciary sectors. Another salient feature of this system was laicism (*laiklik*) of the state, supposedly modelled after the French *laïcité*, although in Turkey it meant – and still means – the governmental control over religious affairs instead of the 'mere' absence of religious involvement in government matters, and vice versa. *Laiklik* was zealously asserted in all public spheres deemed relevant for the production and corroboration of state authority, such as the education, civil and military bureaucracy, and, of course, law. This was radical, even for the state already 'tendered' by previous Ottoman reforms, given the society's profoundly religious foundations. The new system established a rather unique relationship between the state and religion, which has since (arguably) evolved through five stages (Kanra 2009: 46). These are briefly summarised below.

The first phase (1923–45) was characterised by a series of measures designed to relegate the religious elements deep into the so-called 'private sphere' and to divorce them from any political power (Koçak 2010: 244; Lapidus 2002: 502). Hence, for example, all Sufi orders were banned and their possessions impounded; religious courts and titles were abolished;

---

2   Atatürk means 'the Father of the Turks' and it was exclusively added to Mustafa Kemal's name via a legal act (Law No 2622), passed by the National Assembly in 1934 (Cagaptay 2006: 62).

3   Thus wrote, in 1923, Ziya Gökalp, one of the leading ideologues of the nationalist movement: "When a nation experiences a great disaster or when it is confronted with grave danger [...] in such times it is only the national personality who lives in the soul of the individual" (quoted in Cagaptay 2006: 4).

4   Liberalist political thought 'inspired' by sociological positivism produced in the nascent Turkey an accentuated, state-imbued fascination with science, modernisation and capitalism, all of which were thought to be the tenets of a 'civilised' and 'rational' society. The idea was hardly new, since it has been entertained, to various degrees, in the Ottoman state as well, through many decades prior to the birth of the Republic. For the first time, however, it was able to thrive as an official ideology of the state.

the educational system was reformed; and the state constitutionally declared secular (Kanra 2009: 47). The second stage (1946–69) commenced with the first multi-party elections. The new conservative government, consisting of persons close to now underground religious circles, relaxed some regulations concerning religious practice and education. However, in 1960, it was ousted by a military coup d'état, and its prominent members either executed or imprisoned. The Kemalists were, thus, back in power; however, they were defeated in elections only a short while later by another party with quite distinctly religious overtones, which, once in office, continued to relax the overall grip of the *laiklik* ideology (Kanra 2009: 47–48). The third phase (1970–79) was marked by coalitions between nationalist and conservative parties (Kanra 2009: 48), some of which were abolished by the Constitutional Court because of their purported use of religion for political purposes. This was, in fact, an ordinary practice of this court, which is still occasionally exercised to address any perceived 'constitutional threat'. Similarly, military interventions and 'warnings' have been regularly used throughout Turkey's republican history to guard Atatürk's ideological legacy; hence, the military forces are colloquially referred to as *laikliğin bekçileri* – the guardians of *laiklik*. The fourth stage (1980–97) began with one such military coup. Intensive clashes were sparked between left- and right-wing groups in which references to and systematic political usage of religion became, perhaps for the first time, open and plenteous (Kanra 2009: 48). For instance, Atatürk was now reinterpreted as "a reformer of Islam" and *laiklik* as "a necessary step in purifying Islam" (Zürcher & van der Linden 2004: 109; Yavuz 2003). The 'women's headscarf controversy' also originates from this period, including their ban in the state institutions of higher education (Koçak 2010: 248). The fifth phase started in the late 1990s and persists to the present. It saw the rise and a swift electoral victory of the Adalet ve Kalkınma Partisi (AKP or Justice and Development Party), a liberal conservative party that remains in power due to an unprecedented ability to appeal to the religious populace and underground power centres; AKP embraces the *laiklik* ideology to the extent deemed necessary to avoid judicial or military dethronement (Kanra 2009: 52).

As evident from the above timeline, after the initial Kemalist 'de-politicisation' of religion, it took the religious political ideologues a relatively long time before they were able to devise a successful 'comeback strategy'. The singlemost important element of this struggle was their eventual discovery of the 'secret device', so skilfully employed by their Kemalist opposition, just like the generations of Ottoman patriarchs before them. The device is called 'womankind', and the following analysis attempts to contextualise its Machiavellian usage in the historical and contemporary dominant discourses on gender.

Gender relations in the Ottoman Empire were as complex as its multicultural and multi-religious make-up. Feminist researchers of Ottoman history emphasise an intrinsically patriarchal *collective* representation of women – the 'womankind' – that dominated much of the societal discourses (moral, literary, legal, etc.) of the time; this mostly failed to account for the cultural, religious and – perhaps most importantly – class-based diversity in Ottoman women's narratives (Zilfi 2006b). What the totalising chauvinistic discourse on what 'women are like' and the male guides to an expected female etiquette have been unable or unwilling to convey is, therefore, an ample multiplicity of gender and sexual experience in the Ottoman state, curiously intertwined with the access to power. "Sexuality was not a fit topic for polite Ottoman conversation, but it was a salient feature of Ottoman political and social governance" (Zilfi 2006b: 232). As such, it has been used both pro and contra the dominant androcentric matrix. Despite the ubiquity of "the ideology of women's limited proper sphere" (Newton *et al* 1983: 10; Zilfi 2006b: 227), which the 16th century Ottoman moralist, Mehmed Birgivi, describes as "within the home, [wherein they are expected] to bake bread, clean up the dishes, do the laundry, prepare the meals and the like",[5] numerous Ottoman women have managed to challenge or circumvent it. Some 130 years, spanning the late 16th and the early 17th century, are even known as 'the Sultanate of Women' (*Kadınlar Saltanatı*); in that time the mothers of the sultans (*valide*) exercised almost all imperial prerogatives on behalf of their sons, many of whom were still minors (Akşit 2005). Similar examples are found from across the class divide. For instance, the 14th century Moroccan Muslim scholar and traveller, Ibn Battuta, who roamed throughout the young Ottoman state, observed that "among the Turks and the Tatars their wives enjoy a very high position" (Peirce 1993).

Many centuries later, in the construction of the new Turkish republican identity, such early accounts were vigorously sought after in order to support the emergent republican myth of pre-Ottoman 'gender equality' amongst the Turkic tribes. Ironically, however, those narratives of resistance were used to construct yet another type of 'womankind': the idealised, 'modern republican' woman (White 2003). This prototype of the 'Kemalist woman' – working, politically active and clothed in accordance with the European fashion of the time (such attire was 'encouraged' by law) – was, however, premised upon the same old patriarchal bias; she was also expected to be modest, chaste and "devoid of [her] essential femaleness" (Kandiyoti 1998; İlkkaracan 2008: 44), save for her *primary* role as the mother of her children and of the state. The latter was expressly iterated by the first President and chief ideologue of the republic, Mustafa Kemal:

> I will not cease to repeat it, woman's most important duty, apart from her social responsibilities, is to be a good mother. As one progresses in time, as civilization advances with giant steps, it is imperative that mothers be enabled to raise their children according to the needs of the century (quoted in Jayawardena 1986: 36).

The new 'Kemalist woman' – much like the rest of this ideological project – was imposed from the top (Köker 1995: 58) of the state apparatus, sternly yet superficially. Schools

---

5   Madeline C Zilfi (2006b: 227) provides this quote from Mehmed Birgivi's *al-Tariqah al-Muhammadiyyah*, as translated in 1981 into Turkish by Celâl Yıldırım (*Tarikat-i Muhammediyye Tercümesi*, İstanbul, p 478). The new English 'translation/interpretation' of the same book, however, uses much 'softer' language, perhaps in an attempt to 'dilute' its patriarchal overtone. See Imam Birgivi, *The Path of Muhammad: A Book on Islamic Morals and Ethics* (interpreted by Shaykh Tosun Bayrak al-Jerrahi al-Halveti, World Wisdom, Bloomington IN 2005), p318.

were ordered to teach women household techniques, child rearing, fashion and hygiene in accordance with the new Fordist 'science' of home economics (White 2003: 154).[6] Yet the gender roles they furthered were 'traditionally' patriarchal and the state was obviously disinterested in women's rights in the privacy of the 'modern' family setting (Kaya 2004). Education of women and their participation in civil service was highly encouraged, but conditioned on their 'proper' appearance – i.e. the discarding of headscarves. This particular measure – ridding the public 'sites of modernity' of women's headscarves – gradually took more radical proportions; it culminated in acrimonious legal and political battles, and polarisation in the late 1980s (Kadıoğlu 1994: 645). These are analysed later in this chapter.

The 'headscarf controversy' provided an excellent springboard for the political parties relying on strong religious agendas and symbolism, which are commonly yet problematically branded as 'Islamists'.[7] These parties "hijacked the headscarf from the women wearing it and declared it the symbol of their political ideology" (Çinar 2005: 85). It helped them immensely to win a considerable electoral constituency and to, eventually, rise to power.

Both Kemalist and Muslim conservative political camps, though ideologically opposed, "have seen women as key actors for the achievement of their ambitions" (Kaya 2004: 14). This is, however, hardly paradoxical, since both sides have simply followed the well-trodden path of Ottoman patriarchy in the politically motivated construction of 'womankind'. After all, the three resulting versions of women's desired collective identity are not that different from each other, despite being draped in seemingly clashing ideological garments, because of their *common* origin, motivation and superficiality. Even the language, employed by each of these camps alike to morally corroborate their constructs, is invariably centred around notions such as *namus* (honour), *iffet* (chastity) and *ırz* (purity, honour) (İlkkaracan 2008: 44). This, in particular, is an important reason for the continuous presence, albeit in varying legal and societal forms, of the concept of *zina* as a 'transgression against honour'.

Having briefly discussed the historical and contemporary socio-political milieu in which the Turks have conceived and negotiated their religious and gender affairs, this chapter

---

6 'Fordism' was named after Henry Ford, a prominent American industrialist, and it refers to certain social theories on mass production, standardisation and labour discipline (Burrows *et al* 1992). The Kemalist use of these theories was largely simplistic and ideologically, rather than economically, driven.

7 'Islamism' was coined by 18th century French academia as a synonym for 'Islam' (much like 'Mohammedanism'), only to be gradually abandoned, in favour of the other, generic term (Islam). It was, however, rediscovered in the 1980s, once again by French academics, yet its meaning was changed. Islamism, as understood nowadays, is employed "to distinguish Islam as modern ideology from Islam as a faith" (Kramer 2003). This is highly problematic, since it confuses an entire faith system with the political ideologies of the day. In addition, the very absence of such constructs in the articulation of similar phenomena, associable with other religions (e.g. 'Christianism'), suggests a peculiar Orientalist reminiscence in today's scholarship on Muslim political movements. Therefore, in this study, the term 'Islamism' is not used.

now turns to investigate how such dynamics, in particular in relation to *zina*, have been reflected and reinforced legally. Adultery in Turkey is no longer a crime. Even when it used to entail criminal liability, it was but a minor offence, devoid of any religious reference. The subsequent analysis, however, shows how legislative and societal misconceptions of this act have allowed for its extrajudicial 'punishment', within a broader misogynous concept of 'honour' crimes, to thrive.

Domestic Legal System

The discourse of 'reformism', as one of six mainstays of the Kemalist ideology,[8] remains a salient feature of Turkish legal politics, which produces an impression – by and large fallacious – of an audacious national legal system, perpetually striving to respond to the exigencies of the 'modern' Turkish nation. Mustafa Kemal's legal reforms were carefully designed to provide a solid script for "a project of state that is cut free from a past of degeneracy and corruption" (Meeker 2001: xviii) and that would ultimately 'liberate' all those under the yoke of the dying empire, including women. This purported 'liberation', however, was mainly imposed from the top of the centralist state apparatus and, hence, often resisted or only formally accepted at the grass-roots level, particularly in the rural areas. The reforms that ensued after the proclamation of the republic seemed radical and far-reaching, indeed. The new republican legal façade resembled very much the Western European liberalist coulisses of the time: all laws were quite straightforwardly copied from the Swiss, Italian, French and other 'modern' legislation, including that allowing for female suffrage, an equitable access to workforce, marriage and divorce 'free' from past inequalities, even a Romanised instead of an Arabic script. Women and men were to get rid of their traditional clothes and to embrace 'European' fashion; religious titles (*hacı*, *hafiz*, *hoca* and the alike) were forbidden; even the Muslim call to prayer (*ezan*; *adhan*) was heard, until 1947, in Turkish (Zürcher & van der Linden 2004: 106; Koçak 2010: 244). All this was regulated by law, which was gradually expurgated from all direct references to Islam.[9] The two fields of reformers' intervention were particularly accentuated: a laicist character of the new state and women's equal rights to those of men. While the first construct (laicity) was largely achieved through legal reforms, although by means of an autocratic system that still preferred to control rather than simply 'de-politicise' the religious spheres, the second promise (women's rights) was from the very start hypocritical and largely "based on premises of male privilege and women's sexual subordination" (İlkkaracan 2008: 52). They are both further scrutinised below.

---

8 It is one of the so called 'Six Arrows', declared by the Kemalist ideologues to be the foundational principles of the new Turkish Republic. The 'Six Arrows' are: populism, republicanism, statism, laicism, reformism and nationalism (Kanra 2009: 72).

9 For instance, in 1928, Sections 2 and 16 of the 1924 Constitution, providing that the "religion of the Turkish State is Islam" and that the National assembly is "to apply the Shari'a Law", were deleted (Koçak 2010: 243). Obviously, the reforms like those were introduced gradually, making sure that the societal shock they were causing was controllable.

The first 'quasi-Kemalist' reforms on the territory of today's Turkey – to the extent that they were constructed around the demand for a radical break from a corrupted previous system – took place no less than a half a millennium before, under the visionary rules of the Ottoman sultans Mehmet II 'the Conqueror' (1432–81) (Meeker 2001: xviii) and Süleyman I 'the Lawmaker' and 'the Magnificent' (1494–1566). These sultans developed what was later termed the Ottoman *millet* system (Najarian 2008), whereby Muslim, Christian and Jewish communities – organised as 'nations'/'peoples' (*millet*) – enjoyed a semi-autonomous status within the empire and were to be guided, predominantly in family law and internal administrative matters, by their own religious laws. This system has been praised as the most advanced group-rights form of ethno-religious coexistence and tolerance (Kymlica 1996). The two sultans also managed to entrench the *kanun* system, which implicitly rendered the *hudud* concept of the pre-Ottoman *fiqh* obsolete and made other previously 'untouchable' subjects of the classical Sunni jurisprudence open to debate and multiple interpretations (Shalakany 2008).

Another far-reaching reformist era, this time a century apart from Atatürk's breakthrough, was the 1839–79 Tanzimat ('Reorganisation') period (Yıldırım 2005), under the 'Noble

---

CASES OF HUMAN RIGHTS VIOLATIONS

Six Years in Prison for Killing a Raped Girl

In early March 2010, a court sentenced a man from Diyarbakır, eastern Turkey, to six years in prison for killing his daughter six years prior, but released the woman's brother, who also participated in the 'honour' killing.

The incidents leading up to the murder started when 18-year-old Gülseren Tanrıkut was raped by her stepbrother. When other members of the family found out about the rape, they decided to marry her off to another man. Upon learning that his wife was not a virgin, the husband began to beat Gülseren, who then returned to her family's house. Following her return, people in their neighbourhood began spreading rumours, implying she was 'unchaste'. To restore the family's honour, her family decided to kill her.

Hasan Tanrıkut, Gülseren's father, strangled her with a cable while his son Mehmet held her legs to prevent her from fighting back; his other son, 12-year-old İdris, witnessed the incident unfold. The father then poured molten nylon on her face to make her unrecognisable, and put her body in a sack before ordering his sons to throw the body away.

The murder came to light after Gülseren's mother discovered the body and recognised her daughter. İdris's testimony revealed what had happened, but the statement was not officially recorded because he was a minor at the time. Mehmet, 15, tried to take responsibility for the crime, claiming that he had warned his sister to be careful and

Rescript' – a programme of comprehensive legal and societal reconstitution developed by Mustafa Reşit Paşa (1800–58), a high-ranking Ottoman politician (Koçak 2010: 235). The *millet* system was abolished, in favour of the new general principle that everyone is equal before the law, regardless of religion (Yıldırım 2005: 352). A parliamentary system was created and the empire passed its first Constitution (1876) in which both the role of religious authorities and the sultan's powers were restricted. Several penal codes were promulgated, most notably the 1858 Ottoman Penal Code, an almost verbatim translation of the 1810 French Penal Code, which – apart from the apostasy offence – officially abolished all *hudud* penalties, including that for *zina* (Koçak 2010: 236), which had already been made inapplicable several centuries before due to the legal reforms of Süleyman I. This code also decriminalised homosexuality. A new civil code, the Mecelle (Majalla), was promulgated in 1868 and fully completed in 1876 (Koçak 2010: 237). Despite the attempts to model it on its French counterpart, the Mecelle was eventually drafted with the reference to the classical Hanafi jurisprudence (Yıldırım 2005: 353) and its subsequent Ottoman (re)interpretations. It covered contracts, torts and some principles of civil procedure, while family law was left outside its domain. It is significant as the first ever attempt to codify

> not disgrace the family; but, she did not heed his warnings and, instead, harshly rebuked him. İdris later recanted his testimony.
>
> A Diyarbakır penal court sentenced both father and son to life imprisonment, as stipulated in the former 1926 Penal Code, for murder. The father's sentence was later reduced to 30 years for good behaviour and Mehmet's sentence reduced to 15 years due to his age; the mother and İdris were released. The Supreme Court of Appeals reversed the ruling in accordance with the new 2004 Penal Code, which carries a life sentence for 'honour' killings and changes provisions that address 'unjust provocation' in an attempt to prevent its use as a defence in cases of 'honour' killings. Hearing the case for the second time in recent months, the court sentenced the father and son to aggravated life imprisonment; however, the punishment was later decreased to 24 years in prison each. With further reductions for good behaviour, the father's punishment was decreased to 20 years, while the son's dropped to six years and eight months. As Mehmet has already been in prison for more than six years, he has been released. The father will serve six more years in prison.
>
> The court ruled that Gülseren's 'lifestyle', considered to have 'dishonoured' her family, and her dismissal of her brother's warnings and speaking harshly with him, amounted to 'unjust provocation'; thus, leading to a reduction in the sentences. The Supreme Court of Appeals upheld this court ruling.
>
> [Source: *Today's Zaman*, İstanbul, 03 February 2010, http://www.todayszaman.com/tz-web/news-200437-100-father-gets-six-years-brother-released-in-honor-killing.html]

certain (classical or otherwise) jurisprudential interpretations of *shari'a*, and as such was in use in different countries well after the dissolution of the Ottoman Empire.[10] The Tanzimat also reformed the army, financial and administrative systems. Railroads and factories were introduced, along with other 'modernisation' wonders. The concept of new laws carried a strong reference to individual rights and liberties. Most importantly, however, it thoroughly reformed the educational system and established universities and academies, within which the new young intelligentsia would be raised, including the future reformist Mustafa Kemal.

While the Ottoman reforms allowed for an easier (albeit still largely inequitable) access to gender justice, it was certainly not their priority concern. Muslim family laws, for example, with their inherent gender-discriminatory provisions, were only reformed as late as 1917, when the new Law of Family Rights was promulgated and made part of the Mecelle (Yıldırım 2005: 355). This law restricted the husband's unlimited right to divorce and gave the wife a right to apply for separation if her husband took another wife (Knaus 2007; Yıldırım 2005: 355). This way, polygyny was curtailed without being explicitly outlawed. The husband was, however, still considered the 'head' of the family and viewed preferably in a variety of legal matters, which was justified in reference to the Hanafi and other Sunni classical *fiqh* (Welchman 2007: 12). This law generally applied to non-Muslims as well, although for two years only due to strong objections (Yıldırım 2005: 355).

Even the 1858 Ottoman Penal Code, which abrogated the *hudud* punishments and relied heavily on its French counterpart, contained numerous gender-biased provisions distilled from the prevailing patriarchal ethos. Perhaps the most notorious of them read (Article 188):

> He who has seen his wife or any of his female *mahrams* [close relatives] with another in a state of disgraceful adultery and has beaten, injured, or killed one or both of them will be exempted [from liability] (*ma'fu*). He who has seen his wife or one of his female *mahrams* with another in an unlawful bed and has beaten, injured or killed one or both of them will benefit from an excuse (*ma'dhur*) (Welchman 2009).

This provision scandalously provided a legal incentive *par excellence* to 'honour' crimes, including brutal murders, within the familial circles, the victims of which have been – and still are – primarily women suspected of committing *zina* or other sexuality and marriage related 'transgressions' against the 'honour of the man and the family'. The "disgraceful adultery", although decriminalised as a form of *hadd* by the very same legal act, was left to the full discretion of the husband and the family. Most importantly, according to this code, only a male individual (either husband or family member) is given the right to punish 'adulterers'; the one belonging to his family being necessarily female. Hence, it is, by definition, a provision that explicitly gives the Ottoman men the 'right' to do as they

---

10 The Mecelle was used in Albania, Lebanon, Syria, Iraq, Cyprus, Palestine and Israel, Jordan and Kuwait. It is still used today in the Israeli-occupied territories of Palestine.

please with 'their' women in cases of suspicion of *zina*. It remained in force throughout the remaining decades of the Ottoman Empire.

The laws of the Republic of Turkey, although presented as a radical break from the previous legal system, in fact retained a deeply patriarchal 'logic', much to the detriment of Turkish women. The following pages first outline the Turkish court system and then briefly analyse the patriarchal discourse and the role of religion within the state's constitutional, family and criminal law.

Hierarchy and Role of Courts

Pursuant to Chapter III of the 1982 Constitution and the subsequent constitutional and judicial reforms, the Turkish court system consists of general law courts (both criminal and civil); specialised heavy penal courts (grown from the former 'security courts'; entrusted with the cases of organised crime, terrorism and state security); military courts (all military justice cases); and the courts responsible for administrative justice. The system is fairly complex and designed to establish a strong judicial presence – and influence – in all aspects of public life.

The Constitutional Court (Anayasa Mahkemesi) is the state's highest court and it is known for regulating the Turkish political sphere by closing down parties and – consequently – overturning governments perceived to be on either extreme of the left/right divide, in particular those appealing to the religious right-wing establishments. If need be, the Constitutional Court may also function as the Supreme Criminal Court (Yüce Divan) to hear cases concerning the state's top executive or judicial representatives. Other supreme courts are the Court of Cassation (Yargıtay), the Council of State (Danıştay), the Military Court of Cassation (Askeri Yargıtay), the Supreme Military Administrative Court (Askeri Yüksek İdare Mahkemesi) and the Court of Jurisdictional Conflicts (Uyuşmazlık Mahkemesi). The Yargıtay is divided into civil law and penal law chambers; it hears the appeals on the decisions of the vast number of lower courts, save for the cases concerning administrative justice (the appellate domain of the Danıştay), military justice and administration (the domains of the Askeri Yargıtay and the Askeri Yüksek İdare Mahkemesi respectively), state security (the responsibility of the heavy penal courts) and jurisdictional conflicts (processed by the Uyuşmazlık Mahkemesi). Since 2004, the supreme courts can have regional appellate instances, which allow them to work more efficiently across the country.

Judicial independence and separation of civilian and military justice, both enshrined in the 1982 Constitution, remain the most prominent characteristics of this system. It provides concomitantly for a strong and fairly independent national army and a judiciary vested in regulating the public space, although both sectors are ideologically faithful to Atatürk's legacy. Another important feature of the national judicial system is its acceptance of the jurisdiction of the European Court of Human Rights (ECtHR) as compulsory and its fairly consistent adherence to these judgments. As the supranational body, the ECtHR has adjudicated upon diverse matters concerning the implementation of the 1950 European Convention on Human Rights (ECHR) in the Republic of Turkey. In some highly publicised cases – such as that concerning the court-ordered dissolution of a political party (*Refah Partisi and others* v *Turkey* [2003]) or the ban of women's headscarves in the Turkish educational institutions (*Leyla Şahin* v *Turkey* [2005]) – the ECtHR corroborated the Constitutional Court's controversial 'secularist' rulings, which made the national judiciary even more resolute in safeguarding the Kemalist ideological purviews.

Constitutional Law

Much like all Turkish constitutional texts since the establishment of the Republic, the incumbent 1982 Constitution provides that the state is committed to democracy, laicism, human rights and – of course – Atatürk's national ideology (Article 2). The principle of equality before the law is particularly emphasised, and it includes the forbiddance of "any discrimination [...], irrespective of [...] sex" (Article 10). The Constitution dedicates four chapters, containing 62 articles (Articles 12–74), to "fundamental rights and duties", such as the protection of physical integrity and freedom from torture (Article 17); the right to freedom of conscience, religious belief and conviction (Article 24); freedom of expression (Article 26); and the right to 'protection of the family', in particular of the mother and the children (Article 41). Other interesting provisions include the abolition of the death penalty, "excluding the cases in time of war, imminent threat of war and terrorist crimes" (Article 38), and the exemption from the right to vote for all army personnel and students in military schools (Article 67). Article 24 puts "[e]ducation and instruction in religion and ethic" under firm "state supervision and control" and further enjoins:

> No one shall be allowed to exploit or abuse religion or religious feelings, or things held sacred by religion, in any manner whatsoever, for the purpose of personal or political influence, or for even partially basing the fundamental, social, economic, political, and legal order of the state on religious tenets.

In order to facilitate such a peculiar vision of *laïcité*, the 1982 Constitution vests the Constitutional Court with the powers to supervise and dissolve the political parties (Article 69) and the Presidency of Religious Affairs (Diyanet İşleri Başkanlığı, or Diyanet for short). It is a specialised governmental body, with the task of controlling and organising all religious affairs in the state "in accordance with the principles of laicism, removed from all political views and ideas, and aiming at national solidarity and integrity" (Article 136).

In reality, the Diyanet deals almost exclusively with the religious affairs of Muslims, and it curiously resembles the Ottoman phenomenon of state-controlled 'official *'ulama*' (*resmi ulema*) (Zilfi 2006a: 211). On 1 July 2010, the Turkish National Assembly passed the Diyanet Organisation Act (Diyanet İşleri Başkanlığı Teşkilat Kanunu Yasası), which placed all of the country's approximately 80,000 mosques under the administration and direct control of the Presidency of Religious Affairs (Diyanet 2010; Koçak 2010: 254). Prior to this, only some 4,000 Turkish mosques belonged to this state agency (Koçak 2010: 254).

By far the most publicised and hotly debated expression of the state *laiklik* is, however, the ban of women's headscarves (*türban*)[11] at state universities, as well as in the civil service and political institutions. The prohibition was not uniformly applied, even though it was reiterated by the state on several occasions. For instance, in 1982, the Turkish Higher Education Council prohibited the *türban* specifically on all higher education premises. Two years later, the Council of State upheld this ban, stating that women's headscarves were "no longer an innocent tradition" (Koçak 2010: 248). The issue was subsequently picked up by the conservative parties and turned into the major source of political mobilisation, whereby the media-branded 'turbaned feminists' (Kadıoğlu 1994: 657) suddenly proliferated. In the late 1990s, the protests of veiled women increased as a reaction to yet another reiteration of the *türban* ban by the Higher Education Council (Koçak 2010: 251). In 1998, this prohibition was challenged before the European Court of Human Rights (ECtHR), in the *Leyla Şahin v Turkey* [2005] case. Several years later, the ECtHR upheld the ban, saying that it is within Turkey's 'margin of appreciation' to resort to such measures for the sake of its constitutional values (i.e. laicism and 'public order'). In 2008, the conservative majority in the national parliament even managed to pass a bill allowing female students to attend university wearing *türban*. It was quickly annulled by the Constitutional Court, which retorted that such a law might "cause conflict in society" (Koçak 2010: 257).

Meanwhile, women who oppose the ban are regularly discriminated against. Many of them have moved abroad to complete their education, while some others wear a wig or a hat covering their headscarves (IRBC 2008). The situation has reached a bizarre turn, since the conservative politicians seemingly lost their interest in the matter – as there can be no appeal against a decision of the Constitutional Court – while some leftist discourses finally began to see the ban as a gender-biased restriction on women's individual choice as to how they express themselves (religiously or otherwise) in public (Toprak & Uslu 2008). In fact, an individual's choice is precisely what has been lost in the grand political battle between the Kemalist and the Muslim conservative patriarchs, through the regulation of women's bodies. For, although the women have been critical agents in the 'headscarf controversy', their manipulated polarisation into 'typical groups' – either for or against the ban – obscured the diversity found in their expression of faith for the sake of two politically salient 'womankinds'. This polarisation is socially unjustifiable (Toprak & Uslu 2008) and utterly chauvinistic (Saktanber & Çorbacıoğlu 2008; Vojdik 2010).

---

11 *Türban* is a Turkish equivalent for *hijab* and it is usually worn (together with a long coat regardless of the season) by female students in higher educational institutions. In contrast, the traditional Turkish head cover for women is called *başörtü* and it is still worn by elderly women in rural areas; those with a very limited access to education (Kadıoğlu 1994: 647–648). *Türban* is, therefore, but another token of 'modernity', although its political usage indicates an opposition to Kemalist 'modernism'.

The constitutional prohibition of discrimination on the basis of one's sex is also systematically neglected in relation to the rights of persons outside the hetero-normative patriarchal matrix, such as the Turkish lesbian, gay, bisexual, trans, intersex and queer (LGBTIQ) communities. The Court of Cassation (Yargıtay) ruled against a lower court's order to close an İstanbul-based LGBTIQ organisation on the condition that its future activities do not "encourage lesbian, gay, bisexual, transvestite and transsexual behaviour [sic] with the aim of spreading [sic] such sexual orientations [sic]" (Commission of the European Communities 2009: 19). Representatives of the state's legislative and executive branches have demonstrated a similar bias during a large-scale, three-year feminist campaign that led to the new 2004 Turkish Penal Code; such representatives rejected the campaign's demand to expressly prohibit discrimination on the basis of one's sexual orientation in that code (İlkkaracan 2008: 56–60). In fact, this particular issue united the (male) Kemalists and the (male) Muslim conservatives in vehement patriarchal opposition to sexual and gender diversity, which is perceived as an imminent threat to their own 'masculinity' and 'Turkish values' (İlkkaracan 2008: 59).

Family Law

In 1926, the young Turkish Republic abrogated the 1868 Ottoman Mecelle, including the 1917 Ottoman Law of Family Rights that was integrated into it. Instead, the 1889 Swiss Civil Code was modified and then promulgated as the new 1926 Turkish Civil Code (van Os 2007: 179). This code would remain in force until 2001 (İlkkaracan 2002), with 15 different amendments introduced over the course of 77 years (Yıldırım 2005: 363). At the time of its enactment, the 1926 Civil Code (Türk Kanunu Medenisi) was described by the republican regime as the latest product of its 'modernisation' (*çağdaşlaşma*) scheme (van Os 2007); the fact that the Civil Code was derived from the Swiss Code – "the best among the existing ones" – was greatly emphasised (Hirsch 1968: 186; Oguz 2005: 381). Unlike its Ottoman predecessor, the new Civil Code contained no reference to religious law and it brought some rather significant changes to inter-gender familial relations. However, much of the old patriarchal reasoning was left intact and given an undue second life in the new Republic for many decades to come. Of course, this is *also* due to patriarchal concepts inherent to the Swiss code, much like the rest of the model European laws that Turkey then used. Gender-discriminatory provisions within the 1926 Civil Code, which are analysed below, were only abrogated in 2001, thanks to an unprecedented campaign of women's civil society organisations (WWHR 2005; İlkkaracan 2008). Until then, the 1926 Civil Code provided a legislative script for the societal preservation of many pre-republican gender-biased concepts, rooted in the 'silenced' and 'invisibilised' yet still largely present legacy of the classical *fiqh* (Yıldırım 2005).

On the one hand, the 1926 Civil Code, indeed, introduced some changes in the domain of family law which seemed to suggest the reformers' break with the Turkish/Ottoman (religious and cultural) tradition: polygyny was finally outlawed (Article 93); the right to and the grounds for divorce were made gender-neutral (Articles 129–150); and the marriageable age for both girls and boys was increased, but still left unequal (Yıldırım 2005: 357–358). On the other hand, the husband was still considered the head of the marriage union (Article 152), "thus granting him the final say over the choice of domicile and children" (WWHR 2005: 5). His surname was to become the family name (Article 153); his permission (or a court certificate) was necessary should the wife decide to work outside the household

---

CASES OF HUMAN RIGHTS VIOLATIONS

Wife Killed for Alleged Adultery, Despite the Family's Will

Satı Korkmak was the wife of filling station attendant Hasan Korkmak, and mother of two sons aged 9 and 14. After some rumours had emerged about Satı, suggesting that she had a relationship with her brother-in-law, her husband got the family together to discuss the matter. The family did not want to harm Satı's reputation and decided that "there was no such relationship". Upon this family verdict, Hasan Korkmak chose to act on his own behalf and strangled his wife with a television cable on 14 February 2009.

Satı's brother, Ahmet Karatay, addressed Mor Çatı Kadın Sığınağı (Purple Roof Women's Shelter) in a letter, urging them not to leave them alone. The Karatay family expressed that their grief about the possibility of mitigation due to 'provocation' was even larger than their grief about the defamation of their daughter.

In the first hearing of the case on 10 August 2009, witnesses from the family of Hasan Korkmak stated that nobody actually said that Satı had a relationship with her brother-in-law. The husband said that his wife had mentioned this only to him. Allegedly, he lost control after the family meeting when his wife supposedly insulted him, and strangled her with the television cable. He claimed to regret what he had done. However, the fact that he brought his children out of the house on the day of the murder can account as evidence that he planned the killing.

In the latest hearing, Hasan's lawyers repeated allegations of adultery resulting from the rumours about Satı. Referring to the "Turkish family structure" and "traditional values", the joint attorneys asked: "if we do not apply unjust provocation to a case like this, where else are we going to apply it?" The prosecutor, however, did not mention mitigation of punishment because of 'unjust provocation' in his final speech. The judge decreed for applying mitigation for 'good conduct' and 'regret' only, so he converted the sentence of 'aggravated life imprisonment' into 'lifelong imprisonment'. Feminist groups monitored this case.

[Source: Y Cingöz, "'Unjust Provocation' no Excuse for Honour Killing', *BİA News Center*, İstanbul, 19 November 2009, http://bianet.org/english/women/118374-unjust-provocation-no-excuse-for-honour-killing]

(Article 159); and he was considered generally 'responsible' for his wife (Articles 155–160) (Yıldırım 2005: 359). This also meant that, although both spouses were entitled to keep whatever they have brought into the marriage, the husband was to manage and control all property within the marriage union (Articles 196, 212) (Yıldırım 2005: 360). Adultery – termed *zina* in this code – was still considered a valid ground for divorce (Article 129), while any children born within 300 days after the divorce were considered fathered by the ex-husband (Article 241). Along the same lines, in the event of spousal death or divorce, the wife was expected to wait for at least 300 days to re-marry, while the husband had no such requirement (Article 95). All these provisions significantly undermined the Kemalist claim that the new Civil Code was a 'radical break' from Muslim family law as practised in the Ottoman state; on the contrary, the Civil Code was but their *outright* yet 'silent' continuation. Moreover, the Code clearly followed the same old patriarchal 'logic' (Yıldırım 2005), which treated the wife less favourably and gave the husband an overall control of the family unit.

Although the first attempts at reforming the 1926 Civil Code occurred as early as the 1950s, it remained in force, by and large, in its original, gender-discriminatory form for 77 years (WWHR 2005; İlkkaracan 2002; İlkkaracan 2008).[12] In 2001, 126 women's groups, representing different sectors of society and coming from all around the country, united to launch a comprehensive campaign to reform the Code. They were confronted with a strong opposition, orchestrated by both Kemalist and Muslim conservative political establishments, which insisted particularly on retaining a separate property regime, instead of allowing for an equal sharing of the matrimonial property, as demanded by the campaign. As usual, the patriarchal opposition insisted that this and other proposed changes were against 'Turkish tradition' and that they would "destroy love", "increase the rate of divorce" and ultimately "ruin Turkish society" (WWHR 2005: 8). Nevertheless, the campaign successfully led to the enactment of a new and far more gender-just Civil Code.

The new Civil Code was passed by the National Assembly on 22 November 2001, and came into effect on the first day of the following year (İlkkaracan 2002). Patriarchal language is mostly dispensed with in the new Code – i.e. the husband is no longer considered the head of the family and the custody of a child born out of wedlock, which is no longer termed 'illegitimate', belongs to the mother. Such a child is given full inheritance rights and equal distribution between the spouses of the property acquired during marriage is now also stipulated by this Code (İlkkaracan 2002). The minimum marriageable age is now 18 for both girls and boys (17 with parental consent). However, the Code also provides that a child born up to 300 days after the divorce is still considered to be fathered by the ex-husband, unless he can prove otherwise (Article 287). Thus, this proviso implicitly perpetuates the old Hanafi doctrine of a 'waiting period' for female divorcees (up to 300 days), despite

---

12 Although, some gender-discriminatory provisions (e.g. the wife's obligation not to retain her maiden name and the requirement to seek her husband's permission before deciding to work outside the household) were abrogated in the 1990s (Yıldırım 2005: 363–364).

the technological advances which allow for an easy medical determination of paternity (Yıldırım 2005: 366). In addition, much like in other fault-based divorce systems, adultery is still considered a major ground for divorce (Article 161). Unsurprisingly, the new Code does not accord matrimonial rights to same-sex unions; it also renders the legal change of one's sex even more difficult than under the 1926 law (WWHR 2005).

In addition to the Civil Code, owing to nearly two decades of women's activism, the 1998 Law on the Protection of the Family (Law No 4320) is also in force (WWHR 2005: 54). This act specifically prohibits family violence and provides a range of protection measures for its victims. In 2001, Article 41 of the 1982 Constitution was amended; it now proclaims that "[t]he family is the foundation of Turkish society and is based on equality between spouses" (İlkkaracan 2002).

Criminal Law

The first Turkish Penal Code was an adapted version of the 1889 Italian Criminal Code (Yıldırım 2005: 356). It was promulgated in 1926, the same year in which the young Republic passed its Civil Code. Much like its civil counterpart, the Penal Code was in force for a very long time; it was replaced in 2004, following a three-year campaign by Turkish women's rights organisations, with a new, more gender-just Penal Code (İlkkaracan 2007; İlkkaracan 2008). The 1926 Turkish Penal Code (Türk Ceza Kanunu) made redundant the notorious 1858 Ottoman Penal Code, which had pardoned 'honour' crimes against women. The new republican code, however, despite the official Kemalist laudations about its 'modernity', made relatively modest efforts to remedy the grave mistakes of its imperial predecessor. In fact, despite some undeniably progressive measures, it effectively made sure that an oppressive patriarchal concept of women's sexuality, as a potential threat to 'public order' and 'honour' of the family, was preserved in its numerous provisions (İlkkaracan 2008: 45). The 1926 Code lumped all sexual crimes, including adultery, under the section entitled "Crimes against Society" and its subsection "Crimes against Traditions of Morality and Family Order" (*Adab-ı Umumiye ve Nizam-ı Aile*), instead of referring to them as crimes against persons (İlkkaracan 2008: 45; İlkkaracan 2007: 8). This was a paradigmatic decision, revealing a deep-rooted gender bias and the inherently conservative face of the Kemalist 'modernisation' project:

> The determination of crimes such as rape, abduction or sexual abuse against women as crimes against society [...] was not only a manifestation of the Code's foundational premise that women's bodies and sexuality are the property of men, family or society; it was also a reflection of the social anxiety about a perceived need for stricter state control of sexuality in the context of the liberalizing impact of the Kemalist revolution. (İlkkaracan 2008: 45)

The 1926 Penal Code defined all sexual crimes in reference to the notion of *ırz* (honour, purity). Hence, rape was described as 'penetrating one's honour' (*ırza geçmek*), instead as an 'attack' or 'violation' (*tecavüz*). In a similar vein, marital rape was not made an offence, as "sexual acts within the context of marriage – even if forced or brutal – could not be considered an assault against one's honor" (İlkkaracan 2007: 8). The code also stipulated (Article 434) a suspension of the sentence, if a male offender, who raped or abducted a woman, decided to marry his victim. Even in the case of gang rape or group abduction of a woman, should one of the offenders marry the victim, all perpetrators would be acquitted (Articles 415–416) (İlkkaracan 2007: 8). Finally, similar to its Ottoman predecessor, this Code provided (Article 462) for a significant reduction of sentence in the case of an 'honour' crime, including homicide, committed against the family member caught *in flagrante delicto* – i.e. while committing adultery, fornication or other 'dishonourable' deeds (WWHR 2005: 38; İlkkaracan 2007: 8–9). This particular provision was subsequently "activated when perpetrators were seen as protecting their family honour, especially in cases of rape, impregnation, adultery or elopement" (Sev'er 2005). Reductions were applied sequentially, to the effect that "a life sentence may be reduced to a six-year sentence for an adult (three with good behaviour), or to just community service for a teenager" (Sev'er 2005). Although Article 462 was repealed in 2003, other similar provisions granting reductions for the crimes committed due to an 'unjust provocation' or to 'save honour' remained in use, protecting the 'honour' killers (İlkkaracan 2007: 9).

In addition to *ırz*, sexual crimes in the 1926 Penal Code were also constructed around the notion of *haya* (shame). For example, a 'shameless' sexual behaviour constituted an offence termed 'shameless behaviour' (*hayasızca hareketler*), liable to imprisonment (Articles 426–428). It was frequently used to justify police brutality against members of the Turkish LGBTIQ communities (İlkkaracan 2007: 9). Of course, as a term complementary to *ırz*, *haya* was also employed in this Code to provide for its strict moralist overtone, entirely based on a skewed, patriarchal concept of honour.

While adultery was a relatively minor criminal offence, punishable by up to three years in prison until the mid-1990s, when it was fully decriminalised, its qualification as a 'crime against honour' remained a salient feature of the 1926 Penal Code. This provided for an alarming rate of 'honour' killings in Turkey, which does not seem to have decreased even after such legal incentives were abrogated in the 2004 reform. Each year, hundreds of women – and to a lesser extent men – are cruelly murdered on the pretext of *zina* and other presumably 'honour-related' 'transgressions' (Kaser 2008: 207; Turkish Daily News 2008; Kardam 2005). The decades, even centuries, of legal protection unduly accorded to 'honour' killers, conceptualised within a state 'justice' system obsessed with 'honour', provided for such murders and other related crimes to remain an intrinsic part of the societal patriarchal ethos. Their eradication, even with the new 2004 Penal Code in place, will therefore require a long and sustained commitment. Until then, the concept of *zina* – transformed, over time, by patriarchal law and society into a transgression even more broad and gender-biased than that imagined by the classical *fiqh* – will continue to take its deadly toll.

In September 2004, the National Assembly enacted the new Penal Code; this was after nearly three years of a nationwide campaign, co-ordinated by the Platform for the Reform of the Turkish Penal Code, on behalf of a broad coalition of women's organisations and two Turkish LGBTIQ groups (İlkkaracan 2008: 62; İlkkaracan 2007: 3). The 2004 Penal Code terminated any legal distinction and categorisation of women in relation to their marital status or 'virginity'. Sexual crimes are no longer perceived as transgressions against society, public morality or 'honour'. Marital rape is explicitly outlawed, while the offence of rape is now described as a "sexual act violating a person's bodily inviolability" (Article 102). However, some of the coalition's demands were rejected, including: "designation of honor crimes as aggravated homicide; criminalization of virginity tests; [...] and the penalization of discrimination based on sexual orientation" (İlkkaracan 2008: 48).

In August 2004, just a few weeks before the Parliament's expected approval of the new Code, the ruling Muslim conservative party announced that a clause might be added that would re-criminalise adultery. The Prime Minister and Women's Minister both supported this proposal. A heated debate ensued "that split the nation in two, irrespective of traditional, political or ideological positions" (İlkkaracan 2008: 61). Eventually, the idea was dropped due to the pressure from the European Union (EU). This episode, nevertheless, revealed the significance of the concept of adultery in perseverance of the Turkish patriarchal matrix. It endures in spite of the state's human rights commitments, which are briefly discussed in the subsequent section of this study.

State Responsibility

In 2004, Article 10 of the 1982 Constitution was revised to clearly enjoin that "[w]omen and men have equal rights" and – even more importantly – that "[t]he State is under an obligation to ensure that this right operates in everyday life". The Constitution, in the same article, guarantees freedom from discrimination, including on the basis of one's sex. A further 62 articles list a number of protected human rights, many of which are directly relevant for gender justice – e.g. the right to freedom of expression (Article 26) or the right to 'protection of the family', which specifically mentions the mother and the children (Article 41). In addition, both criminal and civil law now contain provisions relating to gender rights in the public *and* private spheres; for example, the 1998 Law on the Protection of the Family (Law No 4320), which targets domestic violence and provides remedies and protection measures for its victims. While there is certainly room for further improvement – e.g. in terms of the rights of Turkish LGBTIQ individuals, or in relation to the legal treatment of 'honour' crimes – the overall situation suggests that the legislative protection against gender-based discrimination is quite clearly articulated, but poorly implemented in practice (WWHR 2005). Hence, the state's responsibility not only to criminalise but also to systematically tackle and gradually eliminate gender injustice remains largely unfulfilled.

This failure does not only concern the state's domestic human rights obligations; it even more clearly infringes upon the Turkish regional (European) and international responsibility to guarantee and ensure a wide range of sexual and gender rights, as articulated in the 1950 European Convention on Human Rights; 1966 International Covenant on Economic, Social and Cultural Rights; 1966 International Covenant on Civil and Political Rights; 1989 United Nations Convention on the Rights of the Child; and – most explicitly – the 1979 United Nations Convention on the Elimination of All Forms of Discrimination against Women (CEDAW). Turkey has duly signed and ratified all these treaties, thus making them – according to the domestic law – an intrinsic part of the national legal order. Article 90 of the 1982 Constitution stipulates that "international agreements duly put into effect bear the force of law" and that, "[i]n the case of a conflict between international agreements in the area of fundamental rights and freedoms duly put into effect and the domestic laws due to differences in provisions on the same matter, the provisions of international agreements shall prevail". This proviso clearly puts international human rights conventions ratified by Turkey into a privileged legal position, which trumps all potentially conflicting domestic laws and obliges the state to bring all legislation in full conformity with these supranational treaties.

The legislative reforms, including the previously described revisions of the Turkish Penal Code and Civil Code and gender-relevant amendments to the Constitution, significantly rose on the state's priority list since Turkey was given, in 1999, the status of a candidate member for future accession to the EU. The comprehensive accession negotiations commenced in 2005, and it is unclear how long they might take before the Turkish candidature is finally approved (or rejected). The state has fully embraced the *acquis communautaire*, that is, the 'accumulated' legislation, legal acts and case law which constitute the body of EU law (Koçak 2010: 231, 267); this will most certainly necessitate further legal reforms.

Apparently, one of the most difficult yet inevitable steps that all governance sectors of the Turkish state will have to face is the bridging of an enormous gap between the reformed legislation and its comprehensive implementation and societal acceptance. So far, mere legislative changes, bereft of the related policy and social awareness measures, proved insufficient to curb the acute maladies of Turkish society – such as violence against women, including that on the pretext of the dangerous concept of *zina* as a 'crime against honour'. The failure to *systematically* address such atrocities makes the Turkish state inept to accomplish its most serious legal and political duties on the domestic, as well as the international and regional, planes. This inadequacy stems, primarily, from the deeply patriarchal condition of the domestic *body politic* and its dominant socio-cultural matrices. Tackling such a compound phenomenon obviously necessitates measures other than purely legislative, that the state, as the principal guarantor of its citizens' wellbeing, is fully responsible to conceptualise and implement.

Existing Activism for Change

The women's movement on the territory of today's Turkish Republic dates back well into the first years of the Tanzimat era (1839–79); hence, it is estimated to be less than half a century younger than its European counterparts, which presumably originates with the French Revolution (1789–99). It has since gone through three historical stages: the Ottoman, republican and post-1980 phase (Yeşilyurt Gündüz 2004: 115). In its latest, still incumbent, stage of development, sometimes called the 'new feminist movement' (İlkkaracan 2008: 45; WWHR 2005: 5), women's activist groups have become "one of the most influential players within civil society on the Turkish political scene" (Knaus 2007: 2). The movement has also become exceptionally diverse: there are conservative, Kemalist and Kurdish women's human rights activists; there are also Muslim, liberal and radical feminists (Knaus 2007). Their interactions, although not always harmonious, have had an enormous impact on the state of women's human rights in Turkey, and their access to social, political, legal and religious aspects of gender justice.

The Ottoman phase of the (Turkish) women's movement was marked, predominantly, by elite women's efforts to counter rampant societal and legal patriarchy. The profound reforms initiated in the Tanzimat period provided an extraordinary opportunity for those women to organise themselves in pursuit of specifically women's interests. One of the ways to discuss such interests, as well as to appeal to the general populace, was through a variety of women's journals, the first of which was published in 1869 under the name *Terakki-i Muhadderat* (Progress of Muslim Women). Education for girls and women's political and religious rights were the favoured topics of these magazines (Knaus 2007: 3–4). However, their impact was limited, given that they reached out only to the urban and educated part of the citizenry. A notable activist of the time was Fatma Aliye Topuz (1862–1936), the daughter of one of the Tanzimat's most prominent co-initiators, Ahmet Cevdet Paşa. She was a prolific writer. One of her books from 1892, entitled *Namdaran-ı Zenan-i İslamyan* (Famous Muslim Women), was a valuable scholarly account of women's contribution to the long Ottoman history (Knaus 2007: 4). A number of similar examples suggest that the movement, despite the education and class-based setbacks, gained considerable ground in the society (Erol 1992).

With the birth of Atatürk's Republic in 1923, a new era of the Turkish women's movement commenced. As an initially elitist project, whose idea of social change relied on imposing rather than negotiating reforms (in line with its famous maxim: *halka rağmen halk için* ('despite the people, for the people')), the Kemalist regime preferred to realise its own, shallow and largely patriarchal vision of the ideal 'republican woman' rather than allow the genuine women's movement to articulate the visions and needs of Turkish women. Hence, women gained the right to vote, but female candidates for any higher political office were hand-picked by the new (male) leadership. Certain women's political and cultural associations were banned, as "the state claimed that 'gender equality being a reality in Turkey' [sic], women did not need an organization of their own" (Tekeli 1995: 12). In 1923, women sought permission to form a Republican Women's Party; it was denied on the pretext that such a party would be an 'unnecessary distraction' in the state-building process (White 2003: 155). The Women's Union, a non-governmental association led by Nezihe Muhiddin (1889–1958), was founded instead; only to be forced into 'voluntary' self-disbandment in 1935, after it hosted an international congress on feminism and women's issues (Knaus 2007: 6). This congress issued a declaration against the rising perils of Nazism, which displeased the 'neutral' Kemalist state (White 2003: 155). Muhiddin, one of the leading republican feminist activists, was already politically marginalised by the state in the late 1920s, as she was trying to push for a feminist voice in the Parliament. She died forgotten in an İstanbul-based mental institution, while her feminist and political legacy was erased in its entirety from Kemalist history books (Knaus 2007: 5–6).[13] After the end of the Second World War and Turkey's transformation into a multi-party state, the women's movement was finally given some 'breathing space' in the state's social and political life. This space was, however, seldom used; the movement's unsettled, internal ideological differences considerably hampered its public impetus. Thus, a strong rivalry between right and left-wing political movements, throughout the 1960s and 1970s, subsumed gender issues under various ideological discourses; most notably, those inspired by Marxism, since many leading female intellectuals and human rights activists belonged to the country's Marxist movement (İlkkaracan 2008: 45).

The military intervention in 1980 put an end to the political polarisations that had ravaged the public arena over the two preceding decades. Yet, this 'de-politicisation', however beneficial, was but an expression of sheer military power. This was particularly evident in relation to the so-called 'Kurdish question' – i.e. the protracted crisis between the central government and the Kurdish-majority areas of Turkey. Following the 1980 coup, the Kurdish language was officially prohibited in government institutions. This and numerous other measures of forceful assimilation, including violent repression of any Kurdish resistance, resulted in decades of conflict, and overall social and political instability, which disproportionally affects Kurdish women. The gendered face of the crisis is especially visible in both the Turkish and Kurdish political leaderships' reluctance to protect and promote the human rights of Kurdish women, particularly in relation to a very high number of 'honour' killings in the Kurdish-majority regions of the country.

The 'new feminist movement' emerged in the 1980s as the first democratic opposition to both the military hegemony and the politics of the past (Yeşilyurt Gündüz 2004: 117), including the discriminatory measures against Kurds. This marked the beginning of the third, present phase in the development of the Turkish women's movement. Some of the leading feminist activists of the time describe this period as significantly different

---

13 In one such book, written by Ayşe Afet İnan, one of Mustafa Kemal's adoptive daughters, entitled *Atatürk ve Türk Kadın Haklarının Kazanılması* (Atatürk and the Attainment of Women's Rights), a reference to Nezihe Muhiddin and her activist legacy is nowhere to be found (Knaus 2007: 6).

from the previous ones, as the movement's activities made an unprecedented impact on the society's perceptions of gender, finally crossing the urban/rural and educational divide (WLUML 1994). In the 1980s, socialist and radical feminists parted ways, yet they continued to co-operate. Women's marginalisation in socio-political life, 'gendered' division of labour and domestic violence became the primary targets of the movement's actions. For instance, in 1989, the First Women's Congress took place, hosting over 800 delegates who issued a 'Manifesto for the Rescue of Women', where they particularly criticised the unjust division of the labour (Arat 1994: 245; Yeşilyurt Gündüz 2004: 119). Public demonstrations and petitions urging the government to implement CEDAW were also regularly organised (Sirman 1989).

The 1990s witnessed a proliferation of women's organisations and their mutual collaboration. In response to numerous cases of family violence and 'honour' crimes, which were now being documented by human rights defenders, Mor Çatı Kadın Sığınağı (Purple Roof Women's Shelter) was co-founded by Şirin Tekeli, the country's prominent feminist academic and activist (Knaus 2007: 10). Pınar İlkkaracan, another leading researcher and activist, co-founded Kadının İnsan Hakları – Yeni Çözümler (Women for Women's Human Rights (WWHR) – New Ways), which became an omnipresent voice of the women's movement in Turkey and spearheaded civil society coalitions for the reform of the state's gender-discriminatory Criminal and Civil Codes. Advocacy for the reform of the Civil Code had already commenced in the 1990s, along with relentless efforts to keep the state more accountable to the provisions of CEDAW and other international human rights instruments relevant to gender justice.

The most notable achievement of the Turkish women's movement in the new millennium is the thorough reform of Civil and Criminal Codes, which resulted from two large-scale campaigns involving over 100 women's human rights organisations and other concerned groups (İlkkaracan 2008). The holistic view and furtherance of sexual rights and bodily integrity; co-operation across the governance sectors and political camps; and skilful use of legal norms to formulate concrete and comprehensive requests were among the most efficient strategic solutions that these campaigns employed (İlkkaracan 2008). Women's rights were advocated as an integral part of the state's domestic and international human rights obligations, whose fulfilment remained in Turkey's immediate best interest, given, in particular, its hopes to join the EU. Advocacy efforts included feminist groups and individuals of all ideological and political orientations, as the single common goal – to improve the position of Turkish women before the law – was repeatedly and unambiguously articulated. Finally, all the campaigns' activities were highly publicised, in particular those approaching the final, parliamentary deliberations. All of these aspects contributed to the success of the campaigns, despite the generally unfavourable political climate and deeply patriarchal condition of the Turkish political and legislative milieux.

Conclusion

This chapter has analysed the historical, socio-political and legal circumstances that enabled an aberrant concept of *zina*, as a 'crime against honour', to survive in Turkish society, despite the seemingly 'gender-sensitive' laws of the state. It has shown that stark patriarchal discourses in law remained throughout Turkish history, despite the Ottoman and later republican legal and social reforms. The reformers – whether Ottoman, Kemalist or religious conservative – had all strived to impose their own version of an idealised, de-individuated 'womankind' – a collective and highly emblematic identity of Turkish women, designed to suit the reformists' political ends. The irony of these 'role model' exercises is that they had all been strikingly similar, despite being presented as mutually opposite projects; the main purpose of each of the three 'womankinds' had been the same – to preserve patriarchy and androcentric purviews, regardless of formally accepted 'equality' between the genders. In line with this 'logic', the reformers designed – and managed to keep in force for a very long time – the laws and policies bursting with references to human rights, freedom from sex-based discrimination, gender equality and the like, while – at the same time – promoting the same old patriarchal vision of honour, chastity, virginity and shame – all connected to the woman's body and contrasted with the male power to regulate and control it. In asserting this 'right' over 'his' women's sexuality and sociality, the Ottoman and the Turkish man was *legally* vested with an unjustifiable freedom of choice, including, in essence, a 'licence to kill'. The same 'logic' had elevated *zina* and other 'transgressions of honour' to the status of crimes against the Turkish state. This process completes a vicious circle, in which male dominance is reproduced, no matter how hard the legal and social reformers of the day are trying to prove otherwise.

Some women of Turkey quickly came to question the true nature of this charade. The 'new feminist movement', in particular, since the early 1980s, arduously works to expose and revise gender-biased legislation, social policies and 'cultural' habits, whether they are promoted and perpetuated under the banner of 'Turkishness', 'modernity', religion or any other excuse. The sustained efforts of this movement have been tremendously successful in the domains of civil and criminal law, which are now largely expurgated of patriarchal language and provisions, while simultaneously working to change societal attitudes through grassroots initiatives. With further legislative reforms planned or underway, the movement has obviously seized the momentum and developed strategies that will eventually sever the patriarchal project from Turkish law. The social consequences of its long subsistence are, however, such that the successes of Turkish feminist actions will take a long time to germinate. Nevertheless, with the eradication of *zina* and similar concepts from the state's legislation and courtrooms, surely societal change will also ensue. This process, no matter how slow, will further assist the state of Turkey to conceive, promote and defend gender justice – not merely formally, but substantially.

The history of Turkey, including its imperial past and most recent republican stages, is curiously pierced with reforms. Moreover, these orchestrated ruptures have been claimed as an intrinsic part of 'Turkishness' itself. Reformism (*inkılapçılık*) – as it is known – supposedly compels the Turkish citizen to attain prosperity by breaking away from the malpractices of the past. Yet a single tradition, that of patriarchy, cunningly survives and asserts itself as an intrinsic element of each 'new' system in place. The time has certainly come to reform such a failed 'reformism' – not only in law, but in Turkish society as a whole.

Bibliography

Akşit, İlhan (2007), *The Mystery of the Ottoman Harem*. İstanbul: Akşit Kültür Turizm Yayınları.

Altınay, Ayşe Gül and Yeşim Arat (2009), *Violence against Women in Turkey: A Nationwide Survey*. İstanbul: Punto.

Arat, Yeşim (1998), 'Feminists, Islamists, and Political Change in Turkey', *Political Psychology* 19 (1): 117.

Arat, Yeşim (1996), 'On Gender and Citizenship in Turkey', *Middle East Report* 198: 28.

——— (1994), 'Toward a Democratic Society: The Women's Movement in Turkey in the 1980s', *Women's Studies International Forum* 17 (2–3): 244.

——— (2005), *Rethinking Islam and Liberal Democracy: Islamist Women in Turkish Politics*. New York: State University of New York Press.

Atabaki, Touraj (ed.) (2007), *The State and the Subaltern: Modernization, Society and the State in Turkey and Iran*. London: IB Tauris.

Atasoy, Yildiz (2005), *Turkey, Islamists and Democracy: Transition and Globalization in a Muslim State*. London: IB Tauris.

Azra, Azyumardi (2006), *Islam in the Indonesian World: An Account of Institutional Formation*. Bandung: Mizan Pustaka.

Birgivi, Mehmet (2005), *The Path of Muhammad: A Book on Islamic Morals and Ethics*, interpreted by Shaykh Tosun Bayrak al-Jerrahi al-Halveti. Bloomington, IN: World Wisdom.

——— (1981), *Tarikat-i Muhammediyye Tercümesi*, translated by Celâl Yıldırım. İstanbul.

Burrows, Roger, Nigel Gilbert, and Anna Pollert (eds.) (1992), *Fordism and Flexibility: Divisions and Change*. New York: St. Martin's Press.

Cagaptay, Soner (2006), *Islam, Secularism, and Nationalism in Modern Turkey: Who Is a Turk?* London: Routledge.

Çınar, Alev (2005), *Modernity, Islam, and Secularism in Turkey: Bodies, Places, and Time*. Minneapolis: University of Minnesota Press.

Delaney, Carol (1991), *The Seed and the Soil: Gender and Cosmology in Turkish Village Society*. Berkeley: University of California Press.

Diyanet İşleri Başkanlığı (Diyanet) (2010), '"Diyanet İşleri Başkanlığı Teşkilat Kanunu Tasarısı" 01 Temmuz 2010 Tarihinde TBMM Genel Kurulu›nda Kabul Edilerek Yasalaştı', *Diyanet İşleri Başkanlığı*, 2 July, http://www.diyanet.gov.tr/turkish-/dy/Diyanet-Isleri-Baskanligi-Duyuru-6681.aspx.

Erol, Sibel (1992), 'Feminism in Turkey', *New Perspectives on Turkey* 8: 110.

Göle, Nilüfer (1997), 'Secularism and Islamism in Turkey: the Making of Elites and Counter-Elites', *Middle East Journal* 51 (1): 46.

Hirsch, Ernst (1968), 'Vier Phasen im Ablauf eines zeitgenössischen Rezeptionsprozesses: Ein Beitrag zur Rechtsvergleichung zwischen Mutter- und Tochterrecht', *Zeitschrift für Vergleichende Rechtswissenschaft* 69: 182.

'Honor Killings Claim 1,000 Lives in Five Years', *Turkish Daily News*, 21 June 2008, http://www.hurriyetdailynews.com/h.php?news=turkish-press-scanner-2008-06-21

İlkkaracan, Pınar and Ayşe Berktay (2002), 'Women in Turkey Finally Gain Full Equality in the Family: The New Civil Code in Turkey', *The Middle East Women's Studies Review* 7: 19.

İlkkaracan, Pınar (2008), 'How Adultery Almost Derailed Turkey's Aspirations to Join the European Union' in Pınar İlkkaracan (ed.), *Deconstructing Sexuality in the Middle East: Challenges and Discourses*, 41–64. Surrey: Ashgate.

——— (2007), 'Reforming the Penal Code in Turkey: The Campaign for the Reform of the Turkish Penal Code from a Gender Perspective'. Research Paper. Brighton: Institute of Development Studies, http://www.wwhr.org/files/-reformingPenalCode.pdf.

Jacoby, Tim (2004), *Social Power and the Turkish State*. London: Frank Cass.

Jayawardena, Kumari (1986), *Feminism and Nationalism in the Third World*. London: Zed Books.

Kadıoğlu, Ayşe (1994), 'Women's Subordination in Turkey: Is Islam Really the Villain?', *Middle East Journal* 48 (4): 645.

Kandiyoti, Deniz (1998), 'Slave Girls, Temptresses and Comrades: Images of Women in the Turkish Novel', *Feminist Issues* 8 (1): 35.

Kanra, Bora (2009), *Islam, Democracy and Dialogue in Turkey: Deliberating in Divided Societies*. Surrey: Ashgate.

Karasipahi, Sena (2009), *Muslims in Modern Turkey: Kemalism, Modernism and the Revolt of the Islamic Intellectuals*. London: IB Tauris.

Kardam, Filiz (2005), *The Dynamics of Honor Killings in Turkey: Prospects for Action*. Ankara: UNDP.

Kasapoğlu, M Aytül and Mehmet C. Ecevit (2004), 'Culture and Social Structure: Identity in Turkey', *Human Studies* 27 (2): 137.

Kaser, Karl (2008), *Patriarchy after Patriarchy: Gender Relations in Turkey and in the Balkans, 1500–2000*. Vienna: Lit Verlag.

Kaya, Ibrahim (2004), *Social Theory and Later Modernities: The Turkish Experience*. Liverpool: Liverpool University Press.

Knaus, Katharina (2007), 'Turkish Women: A Century of Change'. Report of the European Stability Initiative, İstanbul, http://www.esiweb.org/pdf/esi_turkey_-tpq_id_90.pdf

Koçak, Mustafa (2010), 'Islam and National Law in Turkey' in Jan Michiel Otto (ed.), *Sharia Incorporated: A Comparative Overview of the Legal Systems of Twelve Muslim Countries in Past and Present,* 231–272. Leiden: Leiden University Press.

Köker, Levent (1995), 'Local Politics and Democracy in Turkey: An Appraisal', *Annals of the American Academy of Political and Social Science* 540: 51.

KONDA (2007), *Religion, Secularism and the Veil in Daily Life*, Survey, September 2007, http://www.konda.com.tr/html/dosyalar/ghdl&t_en.pdf

Kramer, Martin (2003), 'Coming to Terms: Fundamentalists or Islamists?' *Middle East Quarterly* 10 (2): 65.

Kymlica, Will (1996), 'Two Models of Pluralism and Tolerance' in David Heyd (ed.), *Toleration: An Elusive Virtue*, 81–105. Princeton, NJ: Princeton University Press.

Lapidus, Ira M. (2002), *A History of Islamic Societies*. Cambridge: Cambridge University Press.

Meeker, Michael E. (2001), *A Nation of Empire: The Ottoman Legacy of Turkish Modernity*. Berkeley: University of California Press.

Najarian, Ari S. (2008), 'The *Millet* System and Ottoman Decline', *Pangæa* : 40.

Netherlands Scientific Council for Government Policy (2004), *The European Union, Turkey and Islam*. Amsterdam: Amsterdam University Press.

Oguz, Arzu (2005), 'The Role of Comparative Law in the Development of Turkish Civil Law', *Pace International Law Review* 17: 373.

Peirce, Leslie P. (1993), *The Imperial Harem: Women and Sovereignty in the Ottoman Empire*. Oxford: Oxford University Press.

Rebouché, Rachel (2009), 'The Substance of Substantive Equality: Gender Equality and Turkey's Headscarf Debate', *American University International Law Review* 24: 711.

Saktanber, Ayşe and Gül Çorbacioğlu (2008), 'Veiling and Headscarf-Skepticism in Turkey', *Social Politics* 15 (4): 514.

Schacht, Joseph (1964), *An Introduction to Islamic Law*. Oxford: Clarendon Press.

Shalakany, Amr A. (2008), 'Islamic Legal Histories', *Berkeley Journal of Middle Eastern and Islamic Law* 1: 2.

Sirman, Nükhet (1989), 'Feminism in Turkey: A Short History', *New Perspectives on Turkey* 3: 1.

Tapper, Nancy and Richard Tapper (1987), 'The Birth of the Prophet: Ritual and Gender in Turkish Islam', *Man* 22 (1): 69.

Tapper, Richard (ed.) (1991), *Islam in Modern Turkey: Religion, Politics and Literature in a Secular State*. London: IB Tauris.

Tekeli, Şirin (ed.) (1995), *Women in Modern Turkish Society: A Reader*. London: Zed Books.

Tekeli, Şirin (1995), 'Women in Turkey in the 1980s' in Şirin Tekeli (ed.), *Women in Modern Turkish Society: A Reader*. London: Zed Books.

Toprak, Binnaz (2003), 'Türk Modeli Laikliğin 21. Yüzyılda Geleceği' in *Devlet ve Din* İlişkileri: *Farklı Modeller, Konseptler ve Tecrübeler*. Ankara: Konrad Adenauer Vakfı Yay.

Toprak, Metin and Nasuh Uslu (2008), 'The Headscarf Controversy in Turkey', *Munich Personal RePEc Archive*, Paper No. 16052, 22 November, http://mpra.ub.uni-muenchen.de/16052/1/MPRA_paper_16052.pdf

Turam, Berna (2007), *Between Islam and the State: the Politics of Engagement*. Palo Alto, CA: Stanford University Press.

TurkStat – Turkish Statistical Institute (2010), 'Address Based Population Registration System Population Census Results, 2009', Press Release, 25 January 2010, http://www.turkstat.gov.tr/PreHaberBultenleri.do?id=6178.

van Os, Nicole A.N.M. (2007), 'Polygamy Before and After the Introduction of the Swiss Civil Code in Turkey' in Touraj Atabaki (ed.), *The State and the Subaltern: Modernization, Society and the State in Turkey and Iran,* 179-192. London: IB Tauris.

Vojdik, Valorie K (2010), 'Politics of the Headscarf in Turkey: Masculinities, Feminism, and the Construction of Collective Identities', *Harvard Journal of Law & Gender* 33: 661.

Welchman, Lynn (2009), 'Extracted Provisions from the Penal Codes of Arab States Relevant to "Crimes of Honour"', Resource Paper, CIMEL/INTERIGHTS Project on Strategies to Address 'Crimes of Honour', London: School of Oriental and African Studies, University of London, http://www.soas.ac.uk/honourcrimes/-resources/file55421.pdf

Welchman, Lynn (2007), *Women and Muslim Family Laws in Arab States: A Comparative Overview of Textual Development and Advocacy*. Amsterdam: Amsterdam University Press.

White, Jenny B. (2003), 'State Feminism, Modernization, and the Turkish Republican Woman', *NWSA Journal* 15 (3): 145.

White, Jenny B. (2006), 'The End of Islamism? Turkey's Muslimhood Model' in Robert W Hefner (ed.), *Remaking Muslim Politics: Pluralism, Contestation, Democratization*. Princeton, NJ: Princeton University Press.

Women for Women's Human Rights – New Ways (WWHR) (2005), *Turkish Civil and Penal Code Reforms from a Gender Perspective: The Success of Two Nationwide Campaigns*. İstanbul: WWHR.

Women Living under Muslim Laws (WLUML)(1994), 'Feminism in Turkey in the 1980s: An Interview with Ayfle Düzkan and Meltem Ahiska', WLUML Occasional Paper No. 6. Grabels: WLUML, http://www.wluml.org/node/351

Yavuz, M. Hakan (2003), *Islamic Political Identity in Turkey*. Oxford: Oxford University Press.

Yeşilyurt Gündüz, Zuhal (2004), 'The Women's Movement in Turkey: From Tanzimat towards European Union Membership', *Perceptions*: 115.

Yıldırım, Seval (2005), 'Aftermath of a Revolution: A Case Study of Turkish Family Law', *Pace International Law Review* 17: 347.

Zilfi, Madeline C. (2006b), 'Muslim Women in the Early Modern Era' in Suraiya N Faroqhi (ed.), *The Cambridge History of Turkey: The Latter Ottoman Empire 1603-1893*, Vol. 3, 226–254. Cambridge: Cambridge University Press.

Zilfi, Madeline C. (2006a), 'The Ottoman *ulema*' in Suraiya N Faroqhi (ed.), *The Cambridge History of Turkey: The Latter Ottoman Empire 1603–1893*, Vol. 3, 209–225. Cambridge: Cambridge University Press.

Zürcher, Erik-Jan and Heleen van der Linden (2004), 'Searching for the Fault-Line: A Survey of the Role of Turkish Islam in the Accession of Turkey to the European Union in the Light of the "Clash of Civilisations"' in Netherlands Scientific Council for Government Policy, *The European Union, Turkey and Islam*, 83–173. Amsterdam: Amsterdam University Press.

Conclusion

This book opened with a brief sketch of the first *zina* trial in Nigeria, which took place in 2000. The defendant was a 13-year-old Muslim girl called Bariya, who eventually received 100 cane lashes for 'fornicating', despite the fact that she was legally too young to consent to the act. At first, she had no legal representative and was supposed to receive an additional 80 lashes. Then, BAOBAB for Women's Human Rights came on board and started working on Bariya's appeal.[1] The commitment of BAOBAB's activists and their allies to save this and many later victims of the *zina* by-laws in Nigeria made a tremendous difference. The true, embarrassing face of *zina* trials – with all their patriarchal, political and legally doubtful connotations – quickly emerged. Within a few years, such trials – although still theoretically possible – were made, by and large, obsolete in Nigeria.

Bariya's and other similar narratives – found across the studied countries and briefly reported throughout this book – demonstrate the incredible power of, primarily, women's human rights organisations to resist and transform the situations created by the revival of *zina* laws. They also show the ways in which often defenceless victims of political processes and patriarchal ethos in Muslim contexts can eventually benefit from sustained and concerted civil society actions. In each of the five countries analysed in this book, the right actions were chosen – and are still being refined – through analytical processes that engaged both local knowledge and trans-national strategies of resistance. Local knowledge is largely based on the assessments of historical and present-day factors specific to each country which, when combined, enable the (re)emergence of *zina* laws and customs. Trans-national resistance strategies are born of domestic non-governmental organisations' studying and co-operating with like-minded international partners, which are, in most cases, sister organisations or activists/experts dealing with similar Muslim and non-Muslim contexts. This book has researched both of these processes in order to bring to light what seem to be the key aspects of the revivals of *zina* laws and the subsequent resistance to them. Those aspects are generally historical, cultural and political. Legal frameworks – whether secular, religious or both – are often used as mere tools to achieve or maintain certain historical, cultural and political agendas. In other words, law is always a means, not an end. When a new *zina*-related regulation emerges, one must go beyond the official rhetoric that usually portrays it as the product of the legislator's sincere wish to instate or uphold a '*shari'a*-based' moral and legal system. For *shari'a* has little – if anything at all – to do with contemporary *zina* laws. They are not about religious piety and a Muslim obligation to strive towards greater comprehension and adherence to God's will. Rather, *zina* laws and customs are about the usurpation of legal power and religious discourses for the sake of social control.

Historical Aspects

The ways in which Muslim communities in Indonesia, Iran, Nigeria, Pakistan and Turkey deal with their common and specific pasts are of direct relevance to the revivals of *zina* laws and customs in each of these states. In Indonesia, for example, historical anxieties between

---

1 For a detailed account on this case, see BAOBAB 2003.

the central government and the Acehnese political and religious elites have resulted in an exceptionally large political and legal autonomy in this province. The provincial authorities, again drawing on historically constructed appeals amongst their constituencies of the idea of Aceh as an 'Islamic state', have thus seized the opportunity to assert even greater 'moral' and societal control by enacting *zina*-related by-laws and regulations. In Turkey, however, where the Ottoman legacy is still widely present, despite or – in some instances – precisely because of the subsequent nation-building secularist regime of Mustafa Kemal Atatürk, *zina* could not re-emerge as a legal offence. It has survived, rather, as an 'honour-related' social transgression. Historical reasons – such as the decision of Ottoman sultans to implicitly do away with most of the classical *hudud* punishments, including that for *zina*, and the Kemalist obsession with separation of religion and state (whereby the former is still 'duly' controlled by the latter) – barred Turkish patriarchs from criminalising *zina* as an offence against 'the (purported) right of God'. Yet, another historical trajectory – that in which 'crimes of passion' associated with adultery and fornication were legally condoned in the late Ottoman Empire as well as in the succeeding Turkish Republic – allowed for the most extreme extrajudicial regulation of *zina* by which the alleged 'offenders' are murdered, mutilated or otherwise seriously assaulted by the (male) member(s) of their closest familial circle. In Iran, the revival of *zina* laws, in the aftermath of the 1979 Revolution that brought clerics to power, is part of a larger story of changing relations between religion, state and law in the course of the 20th century. The 'Islamisation' of the criminal justice system in post-revolutionary Iran, in so many ways, has been a reaction to the modernising and secularising but despotic Pahlavi monarchy.

Different historical circumstances have resulted in the re-emergence of *zina*-related laws and customs in each of the studied countries. But, in each of the five societies this book explores, regulating *zina* has meant, to a great extent, attempting to 'revive' or 'remake' the country's imagined historical 'moral fabric'. The patriarchal reliance on discourses of history and tradition is, of course, an old recipe. When wedded with religion and religious laws – as in the case of *zina* laws – it becomes a weapon of control: not only does the subject think that regulating one's sexuality is a 'moral necessity'; it also becomes an opportunity to relive a 'glorious' past or to right wrongs of 'decadent' eras. Naturally, in doing so, the subject will fully surrender to the will of charismatic leaders. Thus, for example, the introduction of *zina* by-laws in some Muslim-majority states of Nigeria has been popularly promoted as the fulfilment of the historical right of Nigerian Muslims to a certain amount of legal autonomy (Ostien & Dekker 2010).

Resistance to *zina* laws can hardly be effective without a thorough re-examination of Muslim collective and community/country-specific pasts. This obviously includes the historiographies of Islamic legal traditions (Shalakany 2008). In re-assessments of classical *fiqh* and later developments in Muslim legal systems, the dynamics of power, patriarchy and changing social mores becomes apparent. They confirm, beyond any doubt, the evolutionary rather than static nature of laws associated with the Muslim faith, including those related to *zina*. This is an important departure point for countering the oppression and injustice justified with reference to 'immutable' and 'sacred' 'laws of Islam'. This perspective is widely shared by the national women's movements in each studied country, as well as by numerous Muslim scholars across the globe (e.g. Kamali 2008; Baderin 2003; Hallaq 2009; An-Na'im 1990; An-Na'im 2008; El-Fadl 2001; Mir-Hosseini 2009). Particular historical circumstances shape legal traditions in Muslim communities, which must be contextualised within each region or state. One of the key issues emerging from such examinations is the question of who today has the authority to codify, interpret and apply Muslim laws (El-Fadl 2001). Another, perhaps, equally important issue is how such regulations can be harmonised with international human rights system (An-Na'im 1990; An-Na'im 2008; Baderin 2003). Feminist insights into the role of history in an ongoing creation and recreation of Muslim laws (e.g. Mir-Hosseini 1993; Mir-Hosseini 2009; Wadud 2006; Ali 2006) are particularly valuable, since they reclaim the Muslim woman's agency and, indeed, her right to be in control of her own sexuality and sociality, as well as to independently interpret God's will. This is particularly relevant in combating gender-based violence (Rofiah 2010), including that caused or encouraged by *zina* laws.

Cultural Aspects

Even the most extreme *zina*-related patriarchal customs – such as 'honour' killings in Turkey or Pakistan – are often justified as legitimate expressions of certain cultures (Greiff 2010). In a similar vein, state ideologies designed to control women's sexuality, including the Indonesian *ibuisme* ('motherism') from the Suharto era and the Turkish Kemalist 'state feminism', rely on an idealised image of woman as an imagined 'cultural mirror' that reflects the 'true' (i.e. ideologically correct) outlook of the nation. Both in the case of 'honour' killings and in the case of the nation's 'model woman', *zina* is construed as a transgression against the dominant culture. Resisting *zina* laws and regulations is, thus, scorned as an act against cultural norms, encroaching upon the collective 'right' of the society in question to maintain its distinct 'way of life'. Moreover, Islam is often taken as equivalent to a particular 'Muslim culture', which in effect 'consecrates' an entire set of patriarchal customs, including those related to regulation of *zina*.

The women's movements in each of the countries discussed have deeply engaged with cultural justifications of the various patriarchal systems in place. They have demonstrated that "[t]raditions, cultures [and] community interests are usually defined by the dominant voices within a group, often at the expense of women" (Mullally 2006: 53). Then, they have highlighted how such discrimination results in systemic violence against women. Their research (e.g. Rofiah 2010; Greiff 2010) and activities have further endeavoured to separate patriarchal and other oppressive elements from the common understanding of their specific cultures, traditions and beliefs. This process can involve the reclaiming of cultures, instead of rejecting them, or emphasising the individual's right to adopt new cultural identities.

The process of gender-just reclamation of communal cultural experiences and customs is, however, far from complete in any of the researched countries. The complexities it encounters are many, including an intrinsically problematic relationship between human rights and 'traditional values' – both of which have been used to justify oppressive politics and ideologies. Re-examining and, indeed, *revolutionising* these terms is, therefore, an important task that national women's movements now increasingly take on. In this process, concepts such as dignity, justice and recovery are being analysed from a gender perspective (e.g. Rofiah 2010: 5–6) and then, also, from an Islamic viewpoint (e.g. Rofiah 2010: 187). This provides for new ways of understanding, demanding and creating cultures divorced from patriarchies and gender-based violence.

Political Aspects

Politics play the crucial role in the relatively recent revivals of laws and customs related to *zina* in Indonesia, Iran, Nigeria, Pakistan and Turkey. The rise of the political misuse of religion, whether orchestrated by state political elites or non-state actors, has been, in all of these societies, marked by attempts to take actions that would further criminalise social behaviour, including human sexuality, for clearly political gains. *Zina* laws and other 'moral restoration measures' have been seen as particularly effective ways of controlling women and Muslim constituencies in general, as they have empowered their legislators and enforcers with a seemingly 'prophetic' outlook and an almost instant general popularity, towards the objective of securing political support. During an election campaign in the late 1990s, Ahmad Sani Yerima, the governor of the Nigerian Zamfara state, which first introduced *zina* by-laws in the country, presented himself *primarily* as a moral/religious reformer: "I am in the race not to make money, but to improve on our religious way of worship, and introduce religious reforms that will make us get Allah's favour. And then we will have abundant resources for development" (quoted in Ostien & Dekker 2010: 575). Once he rose to power, the governor introduced *zina* laws and other similar measures to cover up his bribery, mismanagement and misappropriation of federal funds.

Another political catalyst of the revival and persistence of *zina* laws and customs are ongoing armed conflicts and political instability of post-war zones. The riots of Nigerian religious militias, the question of Kurdish autonomy in Turkey and the post-conflict sensitivities in Aceh have all empowered politically hopeful elites to employ a distinctly simplistic discourse on religion in which the restoration of *hudud* punishments is seen as a 'shortcut' towards an 'Islamic society'. Conversely, the rhetoric of opponents of such reforms is often equally fallacious, since it perpetuates the language of global northern imperialisms without being able to comprehend and resolve the social, political and religious complexities that cause such 'radical' movements to thrive. In other words, branding, for instance, an insurgent political movement as 'terrorist' or 'Islamist' makes its often purely political motives and causes much less visible. Moreover, it unjustly portrays violence and political extremism as *intrinsic* to Muslim communities, as if such are stipulated by their faith. *Zina* trials, for example, have often been misused by the international media to further entrench the myth of 'barbaric Islam'. The women's movements and individual scholars in each of the studied countries have been careful not to fall into this trap. In fact, they have been at the forefront of the resistance to these discourses, as well as to the movements that have pursued the restoration of *zina* laws and *zina*-related customs.

In such efforts, international solidarity networks – such as Women Living Under Muslim Laws (WLUML) – have played an important role. Their ability to disseminate important local standpoints, to create action alerts and to bring together activists and scholars from different regions has proven an extremely valuable asset to numerous local struggles around laws and customs that criminalise consensual personal choices. Consequently, the very existence of and the internal dialogues within these trans-national fora has challenged the domineering discourses at both sides of 'ideological extremes' – be they 'pro-*hudud*' or neo-liberalist and Islamophobic. In addition, they have immensely contributed to ongoing intra-feminist debates on how to approach the question of women's human rights in certain Muslim communities. Finally and, perhaps, most importantly, they have greatly influenced the way Muslim women and women who live in Muslim contexts imagine themselves and frame their social and gender justice claims.

The Role of Law and Rights

Legislative changes, whether country-wide or on the provincial/local level, through which *zina* laws have been introduced in some of the studied countries, suggest an acute fragility and openness to political abuse of the respective national legal systems. The presence of constitutional human rights frameworks, for example, has been severely undermined by multiple/parallel legal systems (often divided into state, religious and customary laws), which enabled politically motivated legislative reforms to be couched in religious terms and presented as within the ambit of religious rights. In other instances, either lower or supreme courts have been misused to legitimise injustice brought by the (re)introduction of *zina* laws or by *zina*-related customs. Political regimes have even succeeded in creating special courts to administer their 'religious reforms', often resulting in various forms of *legal* gender-based violence, including unfair *zina* trials, the unlawful and protracted detention of victims of *zina* laws, impunity for even the most severe cases of '*zina*-related' violence against women and, of course, draconian *hudud* sentences regularly amounting to torture or cruel and inhumane treatment. In turn, both domestic (constitutional) and international human rights mechanisms have been invoked by oppositional movements, including women's civil society organisations. State responsibility to protect and promote gender-related human rights has thus emerged as an indispensable element of the resistance to *zina* laws.

The results of these efforts vary from country to country. In some cases, states have endeavoured to ameliorate their human rights records by striking down or at least amending some gender-oppressive laws, including those related to *zina*. In other situations, discriminatory laws have been made redundant by progressive case law of the high courts. Civil society's advocacy towards states' (unreserved) ratification and implementation of gender-relevant international human rights treaties – in particular the Convention on the Elimination of All Forms of Discrimination against Women (CEDAW) – has succeeded in creating national platforms, campaigns, institutions and joint cross-sector teams committed specifically to gender justice, working arduously towards remedying the consequences of the legislative and societal revival of *zina* laws. This way, national legal systems, whether pluralistic or not, have somewhat regained or further developed their deeply challenged human rights frameworks. The retention of (even dysfunctional) *zina* laws and by-laws in some of the studied countries, however, continues to pose a serious question as to what extent the states are willing to abandon the political misuse of religion in favour of gender justice. Ultimately, although identified as an all-important political and social tool by both sides in this struggle, law once again comes across as quite inept at addressing the complexities surrounding both the revival of and resistance to *zina* laws. Here, the question of how to comprehensively and effectively frame and claim gender justice is, indeed, crucial. Going beyond (yet certainly not abandoning) legal battles and exploring other communal (religious, social, political, cultural...) aspects of gender relations becomes inevitable. Yet, to what extent it will reform and revolutionise still widely predominant (legalistic) human rights discourse remains to be seen.

Reflection on Ways Forward

Confronting oppressive laws and practices promoted as inseparable and fundamental to religion necessitates an ability to devise and implement multi-level, strategic approaches addressing a variety of their causes. In other words, because the catalysts of the revival of *zina* laws and similar phenomena are complex and many, the resistance strategies must be able to confront them all in some way, within a broader social justice framework. They have to be 'owned' and, indeed, driven primarily by the groups representing the voices of victims of such laws and practices. Violence embedded in regulations of human sexuality, particularly that which disproportionally affects women, is of such a nature and urgency that it calls for sustained civil society action, overcoming the existent ideological and class divisions. It requires individuals, groups and movements to remain in constant search for common grounds, instead of those that divide them. What follows are some summary thoughts based on the insights gained from studying the movements resisting the revival of *zina* laws and customs in Indonesia, Iran, Nigeria, Pakistan and Turkey. They reflect the successful strategies employed by those movements and, as such, are potentially salient for those and other societies affected by *zina* regulations.

Promoting and Supporting Gender-Just Religious Research and Legal Frameworks
In each of the studied societies, the emergent non-patriarchal interpretations of religious legal traditions, including those related to gender and sexuality, have made a positive impact. They have underscored the importance of gender justice within both religious

and secular legal systems, and reinforced the possibility to challenge discriminatory regulations on multiple grounds, including those related to moral values derived from the Muslim faith. Therefore, they need to be further explored and exchanged through a variety of national and cross-national initiatives and networks.

Holding the State Accountable for Breaches of International Human Rights Law

One way to reform and revolutionise the dominant human rights discourse is to find more effective and viable ways to convince states to fulfil their international human rights obligations. The civil society movements researched in this book have been very active – both domestically and internationally – in attempting to make their governments accede to, ratify and implement key international human rights treaties. These efforts have highlighted the need to reform laws on social and familial life that have enabled systemic gender-based discrimination and violence. By exposing the atrocities condoned or encouraged by discriminatory legislation, they have publicly 'blamed and shamed' their political elites for their reluctance to take responsibility for providing and defending gender and social justice. In each of our case studies, this worked, at least, to a limited extent. It is, however, obvious that this approach, while indispensable, needs further refinement and cross-border co-operation. Taking into account local concepts of justice and getting the grassroots communities more engaged in negotiation and reclamation of their rights is just one of many possible avenues towards this goal. What is ultimately needed is a sort of 'critical mass' – i.e. a well-developed and thought-out social movement – which is represented both in civil society and the governmental bodies. Overall, getting the widely negotiated and explored common principles of justice and social prosperity heard and adhered to by elites in power necessitates a stable and equitable legal framework. Therefore, the role of judiciaries in this process should not be underestimated.

Rejecting Cultural Justifications of Gender-Based Violence

Further improvements to the resistance of civil society groups against culturally justified discrimination and violence should focus on the hierarchical dimensions of such claims and practices. Internal diversity and power contestations within groups thought to belong to a certain common culture must be highlighted, and those who claim to speak on behalf of supposedly homogeneous entities must be challenged. This includes exposing the self-serving interests of non-state actors, such as local and patriarchal elites who seek political control by using 'culture' (including religion) to legitimise themselves, as well as analysing and refuting state-sponsored discriminatory 'cultural' projects and identity politics.

Strengthening Women's Voices in the Face of Attempts to Silence Them

Attempts to silence women and women's rights advocates occur at multiple levels. At the local level, individual women, especially victims of violence, are silenced by the members of their familial and community circles through threats or acts of violence, ostracism and accusations of betrayal of family, community, religion or nation. Those who work for women's rights are also silenced, and those who refuse to be silenced often risk reprisals, which may take various forms, ranging from murder to ostracism. It is, therefore, always necessary to support women's initiatives and struggles to assert their right to fully participate in the (re)shaping of their culture, society and religious community. Without this, the 'cultural' or 'religious' legitimisation, and hence perpetuation, of violence against women cannot be eliminated. As long as women are forced into a position of being passive subjects manipulated by realities imposed by men, they will continue to be vulnerable to violence. This approach particularly locates women's resistance to patriarchal violence within their entitlement to citizenship rights. It requires women and their allies to view gender-based violence in the larger context of state structures, instead of reducing it to a problem of social dysfunction that can be dealt with – for example – through counselling and shelters.

Resisting the Oppressive Interpretations of the Right to Freedom of Religion
The 'cultural' and 'political' dimensions of the right to freedom of religion, which is often used against women's rights, needs further examination and more concentrated resistance. It necessitates the sustained civil society opposition to mentalities and embedded patriarchal norms that regard women as second-class members of their family, society and polity. Campaigns of education and consciousness-raising have proven their worth and are needed to target religious leaders, governments, media and other key actors in systemic patriarchal oppression, including that related to the implementation of *zina* laws. Further strategising should, however, particularly focus on the misuse of human rights concepts – such as the right to freedom of religion – for a variety of chauvinistic purposes. This focus could significantly strengthen the efforts to revolutionise the idea of human rights.

Developing an Integrative Discourse on Gender Justice in Muslim Contexts
Overcoming the ruptures created by the (re)emergence of *zina* regulations depends heavily on the ability of the national women's movements, human rights activists, Islamic feminists and Muslim activists and scholars in general to instigate a comprehensive dialogue and co-operation, resulting in a new common understanding of the role and plurality of Islamic jurisprudence, education and moral norms, including those pertinent to sexuality and gender relations. Dialogues and co-operation of this kind already exist on the ground, yet they need to be further developed and more interconnected. Moreover, it is necessary to address both specific and common experiences and approaches encountered and employed across societies struggling with *zina* laws and other similar gender-discriminatory regulations. In these examinations, class, poverty and access to information and education are some of the relevant dimensions of a problem that should not be overlooked. Such analyses are crucial for building up a holistic discourse on gender justice in Muslim communities.

This study has endeavoured to showcase the extraordinary agency of grass-roots movements, groups and individuals in resisting and challenging systemic oppression. No matter how hard the situation may seem, clearly, there is always a way to gradually counter the encroachments on one's sexuality and sociality through *zina*-related legislative and social regulations. The first step in this process is to understand that the existence and revival of *zina* laws have no sound grounding in any fundamental aspect of Muslims' faith, and are informed by a history of opportunism that uses control as a means to a political end.

Bibliography

Abou El Fadl, Khaled (2009), 'The Human Rights Commitment in Modern Islam' in Zainah Anwar (ed), *Wanted: Equality and Justice in the Muslim Family*. Kuala Lumpur: Musawah.

—— (2001), *Speaking in God's Name: Islamic Law, Authority and Women*. Oxford: Oneworld.

—— (2005), *The Great Theft: Wrestling Islam from the Extremists*. New York: HarperCollins.

Ali, Kecia (2006), *Sexual Ethics and Islam: Feminist Reflections on Qur'an, Hadith, and Jurisprudence*. Oxford: Oneworld.

An-Na'im, Abdullahi Ahmed (2008), *Islam and Secular State: Negotiating the Future of Shari'a*. Cambridge, MA: Harvard University Press.

—— (1990), *Toward an Islamic Reformation: Civil Liberties, Human Rights, and International Law*. Syracuse, NY: Syracuse University Press.

Baderin, Mashood A. (2003), *International Human Rights and Islamic Law*. Oxford: Oxford University Press.

BAOBAB for Women's Human Rights (2003), *Sharia Implementation in Nigeria: The Journey So Far*. Lagos: BAOBAB for Women's Human Rights, http://www.baobabwomen.org

Chandrakirana, Kamala (2009), 'Women's Place and Displament in the Muslim Family: Realities from the Twenty-First Century' in Zainah Anwar (ed.), *Wanted: Equality and Justice in the Muslim Family*. Kuala Lumpur: Musawah.

Greiff, Shaina (2010), 'No Justice in Justifications: Violence against Women in the Name of Culture, Religion, and Tradition', Resource Paper, *Global Campaign to Stop Killing and Stoning Women*, March 2010, http://www.stop-stoning.org/node/881

Hallaq, Wael B. (2009), *Sharī'a: Theory, Practice, Transformations*. Cambridge: Cambridge University Press.

International Council on Human Rights Policy (2009), *When Legal Worlds Overlap: Human Rights, State and Non-State Law*. Geneva: International Council on Human Rights Policy.

Kamali, Mohammad Hashim (2008), *Shari'ah Law: An Introduction*. Oxford: Oneworld.

Mir-Hosseini, Ziba (2009), 'Classical *Fiqh*, Contemporary Ethics and Gender Justice' in Karl Vogt, Lena Larsen, and Christian Moe (eds.), *New Directions in Islamic Thought: Exploring Reform and Muslim Tradition*, 77–88. London: IB Tauris.

—— (1993), *Marriage on Trial: A Study of Family Law in Iran and Morocco*. London: IB Tauris.

Mullally, Siobhán (2006), *Gender, Culture and Human Rights: Reclaiming Universalism*. Oxford: Hart Publishing.

Ostien, Philip and Albert Dekker (2010), 'Sharia and National Law in Nigeria' in Jan Michiel Otto (ed.), *Sharia Incorporated: A Comparative Overview of the Legal Systems of Twelve Muslim Countries in Past and Present*, 553–612. Leiden: Leiden University Press.

Quraishi, Asifa (1996–7), 'Her Honor: An Islamic Critique of the Rape Laws of Pakistan from a Woman-Sensitive Perspective', *Michigan Journal of International Law* 18: 287.

——— (2008), 'Who Says Shari'a Demands the Stoning of Women? A Description of Islamic Law and Constitutionalism', *Berkeley Journal of Middle Eastern & Islamic Law* 1: 163, http://ssrn.com/abstract=1140204

Rofiah, Nur (2010), *Memecah Kebisuan: Agama Mendengar Suara Perempuan Korban Kekerasan Demi Keadilan (Respon NU)*. Jakarta: Komnas Perempuan.

Shalakany, Amr A. (2008), 'Islamic Legal Histories', *Berkeley Journal of Middle Eastern and Islamic Law* 1: 2.

Wadud, Amina (2006), *Inside the Gender Jihad: Women's Reform in Islam*. Oxford: Oneworld.

About the Authors

Ziba Mir-Hosseini is an independent consultant, researcher and writer on Middle Eastern issues, based at the London Middle East Institute and the Centre for Middle Eastern and Islamic Law, both at the School of Oriental and African Studies (SOAS), University of London. She specialises in gender, family relations, Islamic law and development. She has a BA in Sociology from Tehran University and a PhD in Social Anthropology from the University of Cambridge, and has held numerous research fellowships and visiting professorships, including Girton College, Cambridge (1990–93), Wissenschaftskolleg zu Berlin (2004–05), and Hauser Global Law Visiting Professor at New York University (2002–08). She is a founding member of Musawah Global Movement for Equality and Justice in the Muslim Family (www.musawah.org). Her publications include *Marriage on Trial: A Study of Islamic Family Law in Iran and Morocco* (I. B. Tauris, 1993, 2002); *Islam and Gender: The Religious Debate in Contemporary Iran* (Princeton University Press, 1999); and *Islam and Democracy in Iran: Eshkevari and the Quest for Reform* (I. B. Tauris, 2006), co-authored with Richard Tapper. She has also directed two award-winning feature-length documentary films, with Kim Longinotto, on contemporary issues in Iran: *Divorce Iranian Style* (1998) and *Runaway* (2001).

Vanja Hamzić is a doctoral candidate and visiting lecturer at the School of Law, King's College London. He holds First Class Honours undergraduate degrees from the University of Sarajevo and an LLM with Distinction degree in Human Rights Law from the University of Nottingham. He has worked as an activist and researcher with various international and civil society organisations in Europe, the Middle East, South Africa and South East Asia. In Bosnia and Herzegovina, where he was born, he co-founded and served as the President of Non-Patriarchal Inter-Faith Organisation Logos. At an international level, he co-founded and co-headed the Initiative for the Advocacy of Gender, Sexuality and Human Rights in Muslim Communities. His academic research focuses on gender and sexuality in Muslim contexts and legal traditions, while his broader interests span social and legal theory, human rights, mental health law, and non-patriarchal approaches to social and gender justice. His publications include *Reforming Mental Disability Law in Africa: Practical Tips and Suggestions* (University of Nottingham, August 2010), co-authored with Peter Bartlett; and *Base-Line Study on Faith-Based Development in Bosnia and Herzegovina: Challenges of Non-Patriarchal Communities and Approach* (Logos, June 2007).

Index

A

Abbasgholizadeh, Mahboubeh 97, 109
abduction 59, 136, 175, 201, 202
Abeokuta 140, 141
Abeokuta Ladies' Club 140
Abeokuta Women's Union 141
abortion 136
Abubakar, Yakubu 125
Aceh v, xiv, xv, xix, 9, 27, 52, 53, 54, 57, 58, 59, 64, 65, 66, 67, 69, 70, 73, 74, 75, 186, 218, 220
Aceh Party 67
adultery ix, 3, 4, 7, 10, 12, 21, 30, 31, 38, 52, 64, 65, 97, 101, 119, 121, 123, 125, 127, 133, 135, 136, 144, 156, 157, 159, 161, 163, 168, 184, 191, 194, 199, 200, 201, 202, 203, 218
African Charter on Human and People's Rights 138, 139
Ahmadinejad, Mahmoud 91, 94, 102, 107, 108, 109, 110
alkalis see judicial system
All Pakistan Women's Association 174
Amini, Asieh 93, 109
Amnesty International 93, 96, 100, 102, 165
amputation 28, 120, 137, 167, 173
apostasy xvi, 27, 28, 72, 137, 184, 193
Asma'u, Nana 122
Assembly of Experts (Iran) xiii, 89
Atatürk *see* Kemal (Paşa), Mustafa
Aurat Foundation 175

B

Bafarawa, Attahiru Dalhatu 133
Baghi, Emad ad-ddin 107
BAOBAB for Women's Human Rights 125, 127, 134, 142, 143, 144, 217
bestiality xix, 135
Bhutto, Benazir 173, 175
Bibi, Safia 168
Bibi, Zafran 163
Birgivi, Mehmed 189

blood money, *diyeh/diyat* ix, 28, 95, 136, 166, 170, 171
Bux, Allah 175

C

cane lashing/caning *see* lashing
Center for Women and Family Affairs 108
Centre for Women's Participation 107
Cevdet (Paşa), Ahmet 205
Civil Code
    Iran 84, 87, 90, 106
    Turkey xviii, 184, 198, 200, 201, 204, 207
Civil Procedure Code (Iran) 92
civil society 3, 8, 9, 14, 53, 58, 66, 67, 70, 71, 72, 73, 74, 75, 83, 84, 91, 101, 102, 106, 107, 108, 121, 128, 134, 135, 137, 139, 141, 142, 143, 156, 157, 159, 173, 174, 175, 176, 177, 198, 205, 207, 217, 221, 222, 223, 224, 227
Coalition for the Protection of Women's Rights in Secular, Customary and Religious Laws (Nigeria) 143, 144
Committee for Pardon (Iran) 97
Committee for the Defense of Prisoners' Rights (Iran) 107
confession 11, 12, 29, 30, 31, 59, 67, 93, 97, 98, 99, 100, 125, 127, 129, 136, 167
Constitution
    Indonesia 51, 52, 56, 58, 62, 64, 67, 68, 69, 70, 71, 75
    Iran 85, 86, 87, 89, 101, 102
    Nigeria 119, 120, 121, 126, 127, 128, 129, 130, 132, 137, 138, 139
    Pakistan 155, 156, 159, 162, 163, 164, 165, 172–174, 176
    Turkey 191, 193, 195, 196, 201, 203, 204
Consultative Council of 'Ulama' (Indonesia) xiii, 67
Convention on the Elimination of All Forms of Discrimination against Women (CEDAW) 25, 26, 51, 69, 70, 102, 106, 138, 139, 173, 176, 204, 207, 222
Convention on the Rights of the Child (CRC) 101, 138, 139, 173, 204

courts *see* judicial system
Criminal Code
    Iran 94, 95, 96, 99, 109
    Muslim (Indonesia) xv, 9, 52, 58, 67
    Nigeria 119, 125, 130, 132, 146
    Turkey 184, 201, 207
Criminal Procedure Code (Nigeria) 133, 134
custody rights *see* family law

D

dan Fodio, Usman 121, 122
Darul Islam *see* Indonesian Islamic State
Davar, 'Ali Akbar 86
al-Dawalibi, Ma'aroof 167
death penalty/sentence 9, 10, 11, 12, 21, 27, 29, 30, 35, 37, 52, 58, 66, 67, 93, 96, 98, 101, 107, 108, 119, 123, 125, 127, 134, 136, 137, 143, 144, 155, 156, 157, 163, 164, 167, 168, 169, 170, 173, 175, 184, 196
Defenders of Human Rights Centre (Iran) 107
diyat/diyeh see blood money
divorce *see* family law
dress code 15, 22, 26, 28, 33, 52, 53, 64, 83, 122, 143
Durrani, Karimullah 164

E

Ebadi, Shirin 107
Ebrahimi, Mokarrameh 97
Esmailvand, Hajieh 93
European Convention on Human Rights (ECHR) 196, 204
European Court of Human Righ (ECtHR) 195, 196, 197

F

family law *see also* marriage 12, 31, 36, 40, 53, 58, 83, 84, 92, 94, 96, 106, 108, 119, 128, 129, 130, 156, 157, 160, 161, 162, 166, 169, 172, 174, 183, 192, 193, 194, 198, 200, 227
    custody rights 83, 88, 106, 131, 200
    divorce vii, x, xi, xii, xiii, xvii, xviii, 3, 10, 30, 31, 33, 35, 38, 55, 56, 57, 58, 60, 69, 72, 83, 87, 88, 92, 93, 94, 97, 101, 104, 105, 106, 122, 126, 130, 131, 144, 160, 166, 169, 174, 191, 194, 199, 200, 201, 227
    guardianship, *wilaya* xix, 3, 31, 72, 126, 130, 133, 170
fatwa, fatawa ix, 56
Federation of Muslim Women's Associations of Nigeria (FOMWAN) 128, 141
feminism/feminist 16, 22, 36, 84, 85, 103, 112, 141, 184, 206, 219
    analyses/critique v, 3, 8, 13, 21, 22, 23, 37, 83, 120, 165, 188, 219, 221
    groups/organisations *see* women's groups
    movement/activists *see* women's movement
fiqh 7, 8, 9, 10, 11, 12, 23, 24, 26, 27, 28, 30, 31, 33, 34, 35, 36, 37, 38, 39, 51, 53, 54, 56, 58, 60, 63, 65, 66, 68, 83, 86, 91, 92, 95, 96, 97, 98, 99, 104, 109, 119, 120, 121, 123, 131, 134, 136, 137, 143, 160, 162, 163, 170, 172, 173, 177, 184, 185, 192, 194, 198, 202, 218
First Women's Congress 207
flogging *see* lashing
fornication vii, ix, 3, 4, 7, 10, 30, 31, 119, 129, 135, 136, 159, 161, 171, 202, 217, 218

G

guardianship *see* family law
Geertz, Clifford 53
gender xii, xv, 3, 4, 8, 15, 22, 25, 34, 35, 37, 39, 53, 64, 66, 72, 74, 83, 84, 92, 96, 100, 103, 106, 111, 112, 121, 139, 140, 145, 155, 156, 157, 158, 159, 160, 165, 170, 172, 185, 186, 188, 189, 190, 198, 199, 203, 204, 206, 207, 208, 221, 222, 223, 224
    analysis/consciousness vii, 22, 36, 71
    -based discrimination 26, 51, 83, 138, 143, 173, 176, 203, 223
    -based violence 3, 7, 13, 26, 39, 144, 177, 220, 221, 223, 224
    -biased policies/legislation 12, 14, 26, 51, 53, 70, 72, 75, 104, 105, 107, 120, 124, 130, 132, 143, 146, 161, 172, 174, 175, 177, 194, 197, 200, 202, 207, 208, 221, 224
    discourse 37, 52, 104, 121, 188
    interpretations 61, 74, 131, 172, 177,

Index

equality 3, 25, 36, 37, 51, 83, 108, 112, 132, 139, 189, 205, 208

ideologies/stereotypes 35, 36, 51, 53, 60, 71, 105, 141

justice/injustice 7, 8, 13, 14, 16, 51, 53, 58, 63, 70, 71, 73, 75, 120, 123, 128, 130, 131, 132, 138, 139, 140, 142, 146, 156, 157, 159, 161, 162, 165, 166, 171, 172, 173, 174, 176, 177, 184, 185, 194, 203, 205, 207, 208, 221, 222, 224, 227

mainstreaming xi, xviii, 71, 72, 173, 176

perspective 4, 131, 220

relations 36, 92, 96, 100, 121, 159, 188, 222, 224

roles 22, 55, 121, 122, 190

segregation viii, 26, 96, 106, 107, 130

Green Movement 85, 91, 103, 110, 111, 112

Guardian Council xvii, 89, 92, 95, 96, 99, 101, 102, 106

H

hadd, *hudud/hudood* ix, x, 11, 12, 26, 27, 28, 29, 30, 35, 38, 39, 52, 66, 95, 96, 97, 98, 99, 119, 120, 121, 123, 124, 127, 128, 129, 130, 131, 132, 133, 134, 135, 136, 137, 143, 145, 146, 155, 156, 162, 163, 164, 165, 166, 167, 168, 169, 170, 172, 173, 174, 175, 176, 177, 184, 185, 192, 193, 194, 218, 220, 221

hadith vii, ix, 10, 23, 35, 37, 38, 133, 164

Hashemi-Rafsanjani, 'Ali Akbar 91, 104

Hatta, Mohammad 56

headscarf *see also hijab* 87, 190

'headscarf controversy' 188, 190, 197

High Council for Human Rights (Iran) 102

hijab see also headscarf x, xviii, 22, 27, 31, 33, 34, 83, 90, 95, 96, 103, 104, 105, 107, 109, 122, 130, 143, 197

hisbah 128, 129

homosexuality 62, 90, 193

honour ix, xi, xiv, 9, 29, 34, 185, 190, 202, 203, 204, 208, 218

'honour' crime/killing 9, 12, 15, 28, 167, 171, 184, 191, 192, 193, 194, 201, 202, 203, 206, 207, 219

hudud/hudood see hadd

human rights

activists/advocates/defenders v, 22, 26, 37, 39, 53, 55, 57, 64, 73, 74, 75, 97, 100, 102, 107, 108, 109, 111, 129, 142, 144, 146, 205, 206, 207, 224

groups/institutions/organisations 13, 15, 61, 62, 71, 73, 93, 102, 111, 131, 134, 142, 143, 162, 166, 173, 184, 207, 217

law 3, 16, 22, 23, 25, 28, 37, 39, 40, 69, 70, 84, 96, 101, 102, 107, 120, 156, 157, 172, 223, 227

violations/abuse 10, 15, 25, 26, 27, 57, 59, 61, 64, 67, 73, 74, 93, 95, 97, 125, 127, 138, 163, 168, 192, 199

Human Rights Commission of Pakistan 176

Husseini, Safiyyatu 125, 134, 142

I

Ibrahim, Ahmed 121, 127, 142

Ibrahim, Muslim 67

Idrati, Maria Farida 62

ijtihad xi, 131, 163

İlkkaracan, Pınar 207

Imam, Ayesha M v, 122, 133, 142, 143

incest 98, 135, 137

Indonesian Holy Warrior Assembly xiii, 72

Indonesian Islamic State xiv, 54

'Injunctions of Islam' 155, 156, 157, 163, 164, 170, 172, 173, 177

International Covenant on Civil and Political Rights (ICCPR) 69, 101, 138, 173, 204

International Covenant on Economic, Social and Cultural Rights (ICESCR) 69, 138, 173, 204

International Women's Day (8 March) 103, 107, 108

Iqbal, Muhammad 156

Islam vii, xiii, xv, xvi, xvii, 4, 10, 16, 21, 22, 23, 24, 25, 26, 34, 35, 36, 37, 39, 54, 56, 57, 58, 83, 84, 85, 86, 89, 102, 105, 106, 109, 111, 112, 121, 145, 155, 164, 177, 188, 190, 191, 219, 221

'Islamisation' 9, 15, 21, 26, 39, 73, 83, 103, 105, 124, 128, 155, 156, 158, 159, 161, 162, 163, 164, 165, 166, 170, 172, 175, 218

Islamists xiv, 25, 26, 27, 28, 35, 36, 39, 40, 88, 91, 103, 104, 190, 220

231

Isma'il, Shah 85

J

Jamaat-e-Islami 158

Jinnah, Muhammad Ali 156, 174

judicial system, judiciary

   alkalis, judges, *kadi/qadi* vii, ix, xi, xv, xvii, 24, 28, 31, 33, 86, 87, 90, 92, 93, 95, 96, 97, 98, 99, 101, 103, 105, 108, 123, 125, 126, 128, 131, 133, 134, 136, 157, 160, 162, 163, 164, 167, 186, 199

   constitutional courts vii, xiii, 57, 62, 72, 74, 75, 184, 188, 195, 196, 197

   independence of 56, 60, 85, 86, 128, 129, 163, 176, 183, 195

   Indonesia 9, 51, 52, 53, 56, 68, 69, 70

   Iran 84, 85, 86, 87, 89, 90, 91, 93, 94, 95, 99, 100, 102, 107, 109

   Nigeria 120, 123, 126, 128, 132, 135, 138, 140, 142

   Pakistan 155, 156, 159, 160, 161, 162, 163, 164, 165, 167, 172, 176

   shari'a courts xiii, 86, 87, 122, 125, 126, 127, 128, 129, 131, 132, 134, 136, 143, 144

   Turkey 187, 195, 196, 223

Justice and Development Party (AKP) vii, 188

K

kadi see judicial system

Karatay, Ahmet 199

Kar, Mehrangiz 105

Karroubi, Mehdi 110, 111

Kartosuwirjo, SM 54

Kemal (Paşa), Mustafa (Atatürk) viii, 86, 183, 187, 188, 192, 194, 195, 196, 205, 218

Kemalists x, 183, 188, 189, 190, 191, 192, 196, 197, 198, 200, 201, 205, 206, 208, 218, 219

khalwat xii, 52, 53, 58, 59, 64, 65, 66, 67, 69, 74

Khamene'i, Ali 90, 91, 110

Khan, Magsood 168

Khan, Naimat 163

Khatami, Mohammad 83, 85, 91, 101, 102, 105, 106, 107, 110, 111

Khomeini, Ruhollah (Ayatollah) 84, 88, 89, 90, 95, 103, 104, 105, 109, 110

Kiani, Jafar 97, 108

kissing xv, 61, 95, 130, 135

Korkmak, Hasan 199

Korkmak, Satı 199

L

Larijani, Mohammed 102

lashing, caning, flogging, stripes, whipping xv, 7, 9, 10, 11, 12, 21, 27, 28, 29, 30, 31, 52, 58, 61, 65, 66, 67, 95, 96, 98, 99, 119, 120, 129, 133, 136, 137, 142, 143, 155, 164, 167, 168, 171, 173, 175, 217

Lawal, Amina 142, 144, 145

lawat/liwat see sodomy

Legislative Coalition against Violence against Women (Nigeria) 144

lesbianism xvii, 15, 62, 72, 135, 137, 198

LGBTIQ (lesbian, gay, bisexual, trans, intersex and queer) communities 15, 72, 198, 202, 203

M

Magazu, Bariya Ibrahim 7, 142, 217

Malik ibn Anas, Imam 11, 29

marriage vii, xiii, xiv, xvi, xvii, xviii, 3, 21, 22, 27, 28, 29, 30, 31–38, 51, 55, 56, 57, 58, 60, 63, 66, 69, 72, 83, 87, 92, 93, 94, 96, 97, 98, 99, 122, 126, 130, 131, 160, 166, 191, 194, 199, 200, 202

   contract vii, x, xi, xiii, xix, 31–35, 63, 92, 94

   elopement 202

   forced/child xi, 66, 67, 120, 122, 130, 131, 133, 170, 171

   minimum age of 60, 94, 106, 139, 199, 200

   polygyny/plural marriage 31, 33, 60, 87, 92, 94, 122, 131, 132, 166, 174, 194, 198

   registration of 60, 87, 92, 94, 174, 175

   temporary 30, 33, 94, 97

   women's rights in 32, 36, 93, 94, 200

Maudoodi, Sayyid Abul A'la 13, 158

Ministry for Religious Affairs (Pakistan) 176

Ministry for Women's Development (Pakistan) 176

Ministry of Justice (Iran) 87, 92
Ministry of Women Affairs and Social Development (Nigeria) 139
Montazeri, Grand Ayatollah Hosein 'Ali 91
Mossadeq, Mohammad 84
'motherism' x, 52, 219
Mousavi, Mir-Hosseini 110, 111
Muhiddin, Nezihe 206
Mulia, Siti Musdah 72
Musharraf, Pervez 159, 165

N

Nahdlatul Ulama (NU) ix, xiv, 54, 55, 62, 72
National Awakening Party (PKB) xiv, 54
National Commission on the Status of Women (Pakistan) 155, 159, 176
National Commission on Violence against Women (Indonesia) xii, 57, 63, 64
National Council of Women's Societies (Nigeria) 141
National Plan of Action for Women (Pakistan) 174
Network for Police Reform in Nigeria 144
Network of Volunteer Lawyers (Iran) 109
Nigerian Women's Union 141

O

Obasanjo, Olusegun 145
One Million Signatures Demanding Changes to Discriminatory Laws campaign (Iran) 108

P

Pahlavi, Ashraf (Princess) 88
Pahlavi, Mohammad Reza 84, 87
Pahlavi, Reza Shah 84, 86, 87, 90, 94
Pancasila (Five Principles) (Indonesia) xiv, 56, 67, 70, 75
patriarchy, patriarchal 4, 7, 9, 10, 12, 13, 14, 15, 21, 22, 26, 31, 34, 35, 36, 37, 39, 51, 52, 53, 54, 55, 60, 63, 70, 71, 75, 84, 87, 92, 96, 100, 103, 105, 112, 120, 121, 122, 123, 128, 132, 134, 137, 138, 140, 141, 143, 144, 145, 146, 156, 157, 158, 159, 160, 164, 165, 170, 172, 176, 177, 184, 185, 188, 189, 190, 194, 195, 197, 198, 200, 201, 202, 203, 204, 205, 207, 208, 209, 217, 218, 219, 220, 222, 223, 224, 227
Penal Code
  France 193
  Iran 96
  Muslim ix, 122, 123, 128, 129, 130, 131, 132, 133, 134, 135, 136, 137, 138, 142, 143, 145, 146
  Nigeria 119, 122, 125, 126, 130–135, 136, 137, 146
  Ottoman 183, 184, 193, 194, 201
  Pakistan 156, 161, 170, 171
  Turkey xi, xviii, 184, 193, 198, 201–204
People's Consultative Assembly (Indonesia) xiii, 58
polygyny *see* marriage
'pornoaction' xv, xvi, 61
pregnancy x, 7, 29, 97, 98, 125, 136, 142, 143, 144, 163, 168
Presidency of Religious Affairs (Turkey) ix, 183, 196, 197
Purple Roof Women's Shelter 199, 207

Q

qadhf/qazf xv, 11, 27, 29, 96, 98, 135, 142, 167, 169
qadi *see* judicial system
Qur'an ix, x, xv, xvi, 7, 10, 11, 16, 23, 24, 27, 29, 30, 31, 35, 37, 38, 40, 52, 95, 119, 137, 164, 170, 172, 184

R

rajm/rejm *see* stoning
Ransome-Kuti, Olufunmilayo 140
rape *see also zina-bil-jabr* xi, xix, 3, 15, 29, 67, 93, 98, 119, 130, 135, 136, 137, 142, 143, 155, 157, 159, 163, 167, 168, 169, 170, 171, 192, 201, 202, 203
Republican Women's Party 206
Reşit (Paşa), Mustafa 193
Revolutionary Council 92
Revolutionary Court 90, 108

Revolutionary Guards 91, 110
Reza'i, Mohsen 110
right to vote 174, 196, 205

S
Sadr, Shadi 97, 109
Sa'idzadeh, Mohsen 105
Sanyinawal, Mohammed Bello 125, 134
Shah, Mozaffar ad-din 85
shari'a/şeriat x, xvi, 7, 10, 11, 12, 23, 24, 26, 27, 35, 36, 37, 39, 52, 53, 56, 57, 58, 63, 67, 88, 103, 104, 106, 111, 112, 119, 121, 125, 126, 128, 130, 131, 144, 156, 162, 164, 183, 185, 186, 191, 194, 217
shari'a courts *see* judicial system
'shari'a implementation' 128, 129, 132, 133, 134, 135, 142, 143, 144, 145, 146
Shari'a Stakeholders Group 143, 144
Sherkat, Shahla 105
Shirkat Gah – Women's Resource Centre 174, 175
Shittu, Sulaiman 129
Stop Killing and Stoning Women (SKSW) Campaign *see* Violence is Not Our Culture (VNC) Campaign
sodomy, *lawat/liwat, tafkhiz* xiii, 21, 96, 99, 135, 137
'state feminism' 184, 219
stoning, *rajm/rejm* xvi, 9, 10, 11, 12, 21, 26, 27, 29, 37, 38, 40, 52, 58, 66, 67, 93, 97, 98, 99, 100, 101, 102, 107, 108, 109, 119, 123, 125, 127, 134, 136, 137, 143, 144, 155, 156, 157, 163, 164, 167, 168, 173, 175, 184, 185
Stop Stoning Forever campaign 97, 108
stripes *see* lashing
suffrage 88, 104, 191
Suharto (former President of Indonesia) 51, 52, 53, 54, 55, 63, 70, 219
Sukarno (former President of Indonesia) 51, 56
Sukarnoputri, Megawati 55
Sukhera, Amina (Princess of Zazzau) 140
Sultanate of Women, the xii, 189
Sunna/Sunnah xvi, xvii, 7, 11, 23, 27, 29, 37, 38, 52, 95, 164, 172, 184

T
Tanrıkut, Gülseren 192
Tanrıkut, Hasan 192
tafkhiz see sodomy
ta'zir, ta'zirat xvii, 66, 167, 168, 171, 185
Tekeli, Şirin 207
Terakki-i Muhaddarat (journal) 205
testimony 11, 29, 98, 99, 167, 192, 193
Al-Thaqafi, Muhammad bin Qasim 160
Topuz, Fatma Aliye 205

U
ulama/ulema vii, xi, xiii, xviii, 15, 61, 63, 65, 71, 73, 74, 84, 85, 86, 88, 132, 161, 163, 167, 171, 183, 186, 196
UN Commission on the Status of Women (CSW) 102
UN Committee on the Elimination of All Forms of Discrimination against Women 60, 69, 139
UN Convention against Torture and Other Cruel, Inhuman or Degrading Treatment or Punishment (CAT) 69, 102, 140, 173
UN Human Rights Committee 101
UN Human Rights Council 102
United Nations (UN) 1, 15, 23, 25, 68, 74, 102
Universal Declaration of Human Rights 23, 69, 164
Usman, Fatima 121, 127, 142
Usman, Hajara 142

V
Violence is Not Our Culture (VNC) Campaign – formerly Stop Killing and Stoning Women (SKSW) Campaign v, 3, 4, 8, 21, 38

W
Wahid, Abdurrahman 55, 62, 71, 72
whipping *see* lashing
widows x, 3, 10, 59, 130
wilaya, wali see family law
Wilayatul Hisbah (Indonesia) xix, 59, 66
Women for Women's Human Rights (WWHR) – New Ways 207

Women in Nigeria (WIN) 142

Women Living Under Muslim Laws (WLUML) v, 3, 4, 8, 221

women's

    groups/organisations 4, 13, 60, 61, 62, 71, 84, 94, 103, 104, 120, 122, 128, 129, 131, 134, 139, 141, 142, 143, 159, 162, 165, 166, 168, 171, 174, 175, 176, 184, 198, 199, 200, 201, 203, 205, 207, 217, 221, 222,

    movement/activists 8, 9, 13, 15, 25, 26, 53, 65, 70–73, 75, 83, 88, 107–111, 120, 138, 139, 140–145, 146, 157, 159, 167, 174–177, 185, 186, 197, 198, 205–208, 219, 220, 221, 222, 223, 224, 227

    rights 3, 4, 21, 22, 25, 26, 39, 64, 69, 70, 73, 103, 106, 131, 141, 143, 144, 146, 166, 169, 174, 175, 176, 190, 191, 206, 207, 223, 224

Women's Action Forum (WAF) 159, 175

Women's Commission (Iran) 106

Women's Organization of Iran 88, 103

Women's Rights Advancement and Protection Alternative (WRAPA) 125, 142, 144

Women's Union (Turkey) 206

Women's War 140

Y

Yaqub, KH Ali Mustafa 72

Yar'adua, Umaru Musa 133

Yerima, Ahmad Sani 132, 133, 220

Yusuf, Irwandi 73

Z

Zanan (journal) 105, 109

Zia-ul-Haq, Muhammad 9, 15, 155, 156, 157, 158, 159, 161, 162, 163, 164, 165, 166, 167, 170, 172, 174, 175, 177

zina-bil-jabr *see also* rape xix, 155, 156, 162, 167, 168, 169, 171

Zina Ordinance (Pakistan) 156, 157, 159, 161, 163, 164, 166, 168, 169, 171, 175, 176, 177